Protestantism
in the
United States

MARTIN E. MARTY
University of Chicago

Protestantism in the United States

Righteous Empire

SECOND EDITION

Charles Scribner's Sons
New York
Collier Macmillan Publishers
London

Copyright © 1986, Scribner Book Companies, Inc., an affiliate of Macmillan, Inc.
Printed in the United States of America

Earlier edition, entitled *Righteous Empire: The Protestant
Experience in America,* copyright © 1970 by Martin E. Marty;
published by Harper & Row, Publishers, Inc.; first Harper Torchbook
edition published 1977.

Macmillan Publishing Company
866 Third Avenue, New York, New York 10022

Collier Macmillan Canada, Inc.

Library of Congress Cataloging in Publication Data
Marty, Martin E.
  Protestantism in the United States

  Rev. ed. of: Righteous empire. 1970.
  Includes index.
  1. Protestant churches—United States. 2. United
States—Church history. I. Title.
BR515.M328 1986   280'.4'0973   85-10475
ISBN 0-02-376500-3

Printing: 1 2 3 4 5 6 7 8   Year: 6 7 8 9 0 1 2 3 4 5

ISBN 0-02-376500-3

PREFACE

Protestantism was the dominating spiritual force in the American past, and today seven out of ten citizens identify themselves as Protestants. Yet their story has been slighted by historians.

During the past two centuries a score of histories of American religion or Christianity and hundreds of denominational chronicles have appeared. Only two or three histories isolating Protestantism have been published, and this is the first to concentrate on those two hundred years of national life.

The attempt to retrace the history of several hundred denominations would be distracting and futile in a book of this type. I have chosen to concentrate in partly chronological, partly topical fashion—always asking how best to communicate the main themes to the general reader—on the whole Protestant complex, particularly insofar as it had public and extra-ecclesiastical impact.

In the first period and the first half of the book the Protestant *experience* is treated in properly active form (= the fact of being consciously the subject of a state or condition). The actors styled themselves *evangelical* (= since the Reformation, adopted as the designation of certain theological parties, who have claimed that the doctrines on which they lay especial stress constitute "the Gospel"). They set out consciously to create an *empire* (= realm; domain) and, despite their great diversities, knew considerable success. They set out to attract the allegiance of all the people, to develop a spiritual kingdom, and to shape the nation's ethos, mores, manners, and often its laws.

In the second, more recent, period and thus in the second half of the book, *experience* takes on a slightly more passive character (= what has been experienced; the events that have taken place within the knowledge of . . . a community). The old empire was threatened from without by non-Protestant people and forces, and was divided within into an informal "two-party system."

With the plot given away and the terms defined, five things remain to be said.

The reader will note that concerns of the present generation, such as race and conflict, receive a prominence that had been obscured in many recent accountings of American religious history. In this expanded version, Chapter 11 includes separate attention to the role of women. At the same time, attention given to these motifs has not been permitted to obscure elements of spiritual concord and political consensus achieved by the dominant, ordinarily white male characters in the Protestant past.

Second, wherever possible I have tried to let people of the past speak for themselves, by introducing numerous quotations; since these are illustrative more than demonstrative and because the format of books in this series discourages footnoting, references have not been provided, but some suggestions for further reading have been appended.

In a book of broad scope one builds on the efforts of others, with dependencies that cannot always be specifically acknowledged. At the same time, one risks one's credentials in those circles which believe that all history should be highly specialized and monographic. Given the infrequency of attempts to style the whole Protestant story in general terms in the past, and thus the public's unfamiliarity with its story, I willingly take that risk.

Most important is this final cautionary word about the main theme of the book. I am not saying that only mainline, white Anglo-Saxon Protestant denominations—the people lately suffering under the acronym "WASP" and accused of representing the most self-serving kinds of establishment—make up *the* Protestant experience in America. I make no apologies for concentrating on people of that provenance in this first half of the book, for during the first century of United States history they were statistically the overpowering force. During the ensuing century nonwhites and non-Anglo-Saxons (especially from the Continent) have become vastly more numerous and articulate. They are just as much a part of *the* Protestant experience in America. "The" Protestant experience, then, refers to all the people somehow called Protestant and includes their internal struggles (mainliners versus outsiders, fringe-group members, latecomers, and so on) as well as their attempts to define themselves over against and to relate to non-Protestants in America and in the larger world.

This expanded version indicates an awareness that the original charter for this book was not sufficiently encompassing for its present purposes. The first edition appeared in a series in which it was to have been accompanied by books written by other authors on evangelicalism, women, and blacks, books that never were published. The new Chapter 11 and Chapter 26 help make the work more comprehensive. I have chosen not to extend the scope of this work and the Protestant concept to those religions which grew up on Protestant soil but were not regarded by their founders or by the established Protestants as parts of the movement: the Mormons, Christian Scientists, Jehovah's Witnesses, and other groups that, in the terms of Professor Jan Shipps make up "new religious traditions."

In the first half of the book, "evangelical" could apply to most of the members of the groups that are usually seen to be in the Protestant mainstream, and I use evangelical = Protestant virtually interchangeably most of the time except in Chapter 13. In recent decades one conservative party in almost all the most notable denominations has taken the adjective "evangelical" to apply to itself, so the historian finds the word gradually restricted to that element and relinquished it as a term simply to be equated with the word Protestant. Rather than play word games, I would prefer to get on with the story and to let nuances of definition become clear in various contexts.

I thank Rehova Arthur and Judith Lawrence for typing and reproducing the manuscript and its expansion in various stages of editing.

A number of graduate students in the Divinity School, the History Department, and the Committee on the History of Culture at the University of Chicago have made witting and unwitting contributions to my work on these themes through the past years. In classes or seminars, but most of all while directing their dissertations, I have profited from their work, even as I hope they benefited from my research on these subjects. Since many of the motifs of this purely American study were developed first in intercultural contexts, even those students who have worked British and European themes should be recognized, so this is my "card of thanks" to them.

Section II: Barbara Akin, Stephen Carleton, Samuel Pearson, and George Smith; Section III: Margaret Clarke, Clifford Crummey, Vincent Harding, Richard Kern, James Overbeck, and the late Isaac Strain; Section IV: Melvin Buxbaum, Jay Dolan, Marvin Hill, Trygve Skarsten, and Gerrit 'ten Zythoff; Section VI: Richard Gowan, John Groh, Channing Jeschke, Bernard Markwell, Jean Miller, and Roland Nelson; Section VII: Suzanne Gwiazda, Elizabeth King, and Dale Pattison. I believe that only Jean Miller can legitimately complain that I plagiarized (in Chapter 19) but almost all will find occasional plundered ideas on these my pages. They have stimulated my thought and inquiry more than they could have known during classroom and blue-pencil sessions in Swift Hall. Kent Druyvesteyn is to be thanked for preparing the index. My wife, Harriet Julia Marty helped prepare this revised version; my debt to her grows.

Professor Jerald C. Brauer, himself an author of a book on American Protestantism, and the man to whom this book is dedicated, also made many contributions as teacher, Dean, and friend.

Martin E. Marty
The University of Chicago

CONTENTS

PART ONE

The Evangelical Empire, 1776–1877

I · THE PEOPLE

    1 · The People Called Protestant   3
    The European Stock

    2 · Clearing Space: The Removal of the Native American   13
    The American Indian

    3 · The Builders of Empire   21
    The White Anglo-Saxon

    4 · The Overlooked Protestants   30
    The Black American

II · THE LAND

    5 · A Charter for Empire   39
    The Civil and Religous Settlement

    6 · Enlarging the Territory   48
    From East to West

    7 · Dividing the Territory   58
    North and South

III · THE EMPIRE

    8 · The Invention of Forms   67
    Denomination, Parish, Education

ix

9 · The Command of Christ, Interpreted   76
Theological Interpretation

10 · Forays for Reform   86
Means of Reforming and Serving

IV · TESTS OF EMPIRE
   11 · The Protestant Majority   97
The Struggles of Women

   12 · The Great Tranformation   107
The Present City, The Industrial Beginnings

   13 · The Fire from the Fringes   116
Protestants Beyond the Evangelical Churches

   14 · The Beginning of the End   126
Stresses and Strains Before the Civil War

PART TWO

From Evangelical Empire to Protestant Experience, 1877—

V · A COMPLACENT ERA
   15 · The Failure to Bind   137
Reconstruction and After

   16 · A Decorous Worldliness   147
Popular Protestant Accommodation

   17 · Perils—The City   157
A Bewildering Urban-Immigrant Environment

   18 · A Private Place for Religion   167
Life in the Churches

VI · FROM EMPIRE TO EXPERIENCE

   19 · The Two-Party System   177
     A Division Within Protestantism

   20 · From Providence to Progress   187
     A New Theology

   21 · Protestants for Protest   197
     Progressives, Reformers, the Social Gospel

   22 · Conflicting Experiences   207
     Controversies Through the Twenties

VII · THE EXPERIENCE TRANSLATED, TRANSFORMED

   23 · Two Styles of Complacency   217
     Southern and Urban Ways of Life

   24 · The Church Against the World   227
     The Recovery of Protest and Realism

   25 · Any Number Can Play   237
     The Rise of Ecumenism and Pluralism

   26 · Everything Can Become Almost Anything Else   247
     The Revival and the Revolution

   27 · Can You Go Home Again?   257
     Power Shifts and Protestant Prospects

NOTES   267

INDEX   271

PART ONE

The Evangelical Empire
1776–1877

I · THE PEOPLE

1 · The People Called Protestant

The European Stock

Over 100 million of the world's 370 million Protestants live in North America, and most of that 100 million reside in the United States. Taken together, they are the largest of the religious groups in the United States, where they outnumber Roman Catholics almost two to one and Jews by twenty to one. Yet Protestants are ordinarily not "taken together," since the most visible fact about them is their division into denominations. The yearbooks on American religion list about 200 such separate groups. This makes them difficult to describe, however visible and numerous they are almost everywhere in the United States. Any attempt to trace their career through more than two centuries of national history should begin with some effort to describe them.

First, they are *religious.* The point seems so obvious that, at first glance, it hardly bears noting. One would never bring up the subject of Protestants in America at all except in connection with something broadly religious. Yet it happens that in some contexts a name has to cover both race or ethnicity and religion. Some people are listed with a group that bears a religious name whether they are personally religious or not. Thus it is difficult to sort out the specifically religious element when one mentions Jews. To be born of a Jewish mother makes one a Jew; religion, in a sense, is passed on genetically, whether one practices it or not.

While more people are named Protestant by census takers than practice their faith, for the most part Protestantism has been a religious movement.

Born in the sixteenth century during a breakup of homogeneous Catholic Europe, Protestantism came to represent a key element, choice, in modern understandings of religion. At first people followed and often had to follow their civil leaders in making a move from Catholicism to, say, Anglicanism in England, Lutheranism in Scandinavia, or Reformed faith in Scotland or the Lowlands. Then, in the course of time, these versions of Protestantism became matters of personal choice. Someone could be born of a Protestant mother yet not be considered Protestant unless he or she chose to be a member of a Protestant church. Protestant, in America, does not simply mean "other than Catholic, Jewish, Buddhist, or Mormon," although sometimes observers have spoken of America as a Protestant nation simply because so many people identified with that adjective make it up.

Protestants, moreover, are members of *western* religious traditions. While Asians in America can be and often are Protestants, by becoming so they also leave behind the Oriental modes of being religious. Western religions, influenced by Greece and Rome and secular influences deriving from them, usually pass under the code name "Judeo-Christian." Some critics see that hyphenated term to be nothing more than an invention of Americans who needed it to support interfaith harmony. Yet it still does designate a cluster of religious emphases born of the biblical tradition. "Judeo-Christians" unite at least in stressing faith in "the God of Abraham, Isaac, and Jacob," a God of history who creates and gives meaning to history. Protestants do not seek Nirvana outside history or see history as revolving through cycles of existence. History appears to follow a kind of arrow or trajectory that leads believers to think of beginnings, purposeful moments, and climaxes of history.

Third, Protestantism belongs to *western Christianity.* That means two things. First, it is distinct from Judaism, on which it builds. It regards the Hebrew scriptures, the book of the Jews, as the "Old Testament" in a Bible which it sees consummated in a "New Testament." While Protestants have often been anti-Semitic, it is a fact that in America many of them have pioneered in establishing better relations with Jews, whose spiritual heirs and cousins they remain. At the same time, the arrow of their history comes to its target or the trajectory of faith comes to its apogee in the figure of Jesus Christ. This Jesus of Nazareth in the Jewish heartland was indeed a rabbi of the Jews, but Protestants see him also as the chosen one of God, the anointed of Yahweh, the Messiah and fulfiller of history—as Jews do not see him.

Second, if they are thus Christian over against the Jewish element in western religion, they are also western over against the eastern. Some individuals of Greek or Russian descent may turn Protestant in the United States, but Protestantism does not trace its family tree to Eastern Orthodoxy, which led a life separate from western Catholicism since the eleventh century. The modern ecumenical or unitive Christian movements do lead Protestants and Orthodox to find kinship and communion of many sorts, for example in bodies such as the World and National Councils of Churches, to which Roman Catholics do not belong. Yet the typical Protestant knows little about the life of the Christian church in Greece and Russia or elsewhere in the East. Its arguments are family quarrels with the western or Roman Catholic church, from which it split during a sixteenth-century reform and revolt. It is from that western church that Protestantism has taken many of its terms and observances. Many Protestants like to say that they perpetuate the best in that Catholic tradition, whereas Rome diverted from its responsibility to carry forth that full truth of God which traces back to the revelation in Jesus Christ and the disciples.

Such a claim leads to a fourth element in Protestantism: it is a *biblical* faith. With Judaism, Islam, and the rest of Christianity, its members are "people of the book," but few bodies of believers make more of the centrality of the Bible than do most Protestants. Islam's devotion is to the revelation in the Qur'an. That book speaks of various biblical figures including Moses and Jesus, but it has little to do with the Hebrew scriptures and the New Testament. Judaism rejects the New Testament and has been shaped by some sacred writings that developed after biblical times. Eastern Orthodoxy sees truth perpetuated through tradition under custodianship of bishops. Roman Catholicism adds to that the authority of a chief bishop, the Pope at Rome. Protestantism in almost all its forms rejects such notions of custodianship, although parts of it may retain bishops, sometimes conceiving them to be in "succession" back to the apostles of Jesus. Protestantism has no place to go for its sources, norms, and authorities than to what it calls the Old and New Testaments of these sacred scriptures. Most Protestant disputes have been battles over how to interpret the Bible. Whether they have been settled or not, these arguments and differences on Protestant soil have to be addressed by reference to the Book.

Protestantism is a *God-centered* faith. That is another assertion which most observers would take for granted, yet it needs saying. There are world religions, including many forms of Buddhism, which do not have a clarified experience of or witness to God. There are also polytheisms and paganisms, in which many sacred figures receive devotion. In practice many Protestants may seem to give loyalty also to Mars, the god of war, or Mammon, the god of money. Yet when they are serious of purpose, they concentrate all their faith on the God of the Bible, the "Yahweh" of the Hebrew scriptures who is also seen by them to be the Father of Jesus Christ. Most Protestants welcome the language of ancient creeds with their expression of faith in the Trinity. That creed sees God as a Creator or, in male imagery that transcends human sexual metaphor, God is a judging and caring Father. This God is revealed and embodied in a special way in the Son, Jesus Christ. God is also active and being made present in and as the Holy Spirit. Typical Protestant congregation members would find it confusing and difficult to have to spell out the meanings of this Trinity as it was defined by early and usually Greek-influenced Christians. They do, however, take for granted the results of such definition.

In most respects, Protestantism should be seen as eagerly *monotheistic,* sharing with all Christians and Jews a faith that God is One and that there are no others who merit trust and devotion. In its trinitarianism, Protestantism finds company with Eastern Orthodoxy and Roman Catholicism. The God of this faith is regarded as being active in two chief ways. On the one hand, there is a note of transcendent justice, as someone has called it. This note witnesses to the perfect holiness, righteousness, and justice of God. Without this witness, it is argued, the world would be only a chaos devastated by relativism. People could live by faith in gods they would invent. They would be free to pursue any course of action they found congenial. The God of justice, however, is absolute in setting forth certain demands: thou shalt not kill; thou shalt not steal; thou shalt honor parents—such phrases from a King James Version of the Ten Commandments are part of the mental makeup of most Protestants.

This God remains mysterious in so many ways. How, for example, does evil originate and how is it permitted to live on, to afflict even God's faithful? Yet God is anything but mysterious in another aspect. God is patently gracious. That is, God creates and sustains life, even where creatures abuse it and do not give obedience to God. Where they fail, God forgives their failures and sins, for God has given Jesus Christ, the Son, to the world. In both his life and sacrificial death Jesus reveals what God is like and makes possible new relations to God. Protestants differ considerably as to exactly what transaction went on in the death of Jesus. Some, using medieval Catholic language, see Him delivered up like the sacrificial Lamb of the Hebrew scriptures. Thus he "takes away the sins of the world" and is offered up to satisfy a just God's demands for goodness. Others find such language to be biblically based but uncongenial to their pictures of what God is like. They see the death and rising of Jesus as a victory by God over forces of evil. Liberal wings of Protestantism have often tended to stress Jesus as the authoritative teacher. He is an embodiment of divine love, the great example of sacrifice. Such liberals have had more difficulty calling Jesus the unique Son of God, as some other Protestants do. Here it is only important to note that Protestantism is somehow a "Jesus" religion: Jesus Christ, who gives the name to all Christian faith, is the focus and center, the constant theme in Protestantism.

What none of this does is to show how within western Christianity Protestantism is *distinctive.* With all Catholics most of Protestantism witnesses to the Trinity, to a just and graceful God, to the authority of the Bible and the centrality of Christ. In fact, efforts to find something that all Protestants can unite in and hold uniquely against all other western Christians sounds like a negation. They do not give obedience to the authority of Rome and the Pope, who since 1870 has been formally seen by Catholics as infallible in respect to faith and morals. Protestants want to see this rejection of theirs in positive terms. They believe that to see authority consolidated in a single human and a single office in the church is an inadequate way of assuring freedom and faithfulness. In the modern ecumenical age they may respect the person of the Pope: many are even willing to envision a church of the future in which they would regard the bishop of Rome as "the first among equals." They have never been able, however, to envision the day when they would be able to see the custodianship of truth and tradition consolidated in his office. They reject the authority with which the Pope speaks as the deputy of God, the Vicar of Christ. To be under the papal obedience is to be a Roman Catholic; to be a Christian of this western and Catholic tradition but to reject such obedience ordinarily is a distinguishing mark of Protestantism.

Protestants are *worshippers.* While some of them see their faith as highly individualized, most of them come together for prayer, to hear preaching, and to celebrate the sacraments and rites of the church. All but a few of them baptize people in order to initiate them into Christian membership, although they differ over the age at which to baptize people. They also argue over whether the baptized must first be aware of having "come to faith" or whether they may be baptized as infants. There are disputes over what form the application of water may take—whether the new members are to be immersed or simply to have water poured or sprinkled over them. Most Protestants—here the Quakers and Salvation Army are rare exceptions—celebrate a common meal called, variously, Holy Communion, the Lord's Supper, the Eucharist, and the like. They differ widely in interpreting these acts: do they impart grace, or signify grace; are they done in response to divine commands as acts of obedience or are they expressions of a life of grace and a celebration of the divine presence? Most Protestants also make much of preaching in their worship. Preaching is announcing the story and message of the God of justice and love, the God known in Jesus Christ, with an end to increase faith and trust and inspire good action in the world.

Protestants are an *ethical-minded* people. That is, they share with Judaism, Eastern Orthodoxy, and Catholicism a strong impulse to try to live by commands or in response to the love of God. This living demands that they organize their lives in such ways that they work for justice and peace. They are expected to care for the needy, to live lives in which selfishness is overcome by love of the other. They may pursue these disciplines by church attendance, usually and especially on Sunday. They devise patterns for nurturing their young. Most of them claim to depart from merely worldly ways, although it must be said that most observers find most of them acting pretty much as their neighbors who are not Protestant do. Yet to say Protestant is to imply a kind of moral earnestness, an impulse to be faithful to the commands of God, a desire to improve and reform the world.

Much more could be said about some distinctives of Protestantism, but to do so would change the character of this story to a kind of encyclopedia of options. This is a story of Protestant *people.* That reminder demands one other task before the stage is set for Protestantism on American soil and especially in the life of the United States over more than two centuries. Who are they, where did they come from, and how did they get to the United States?

In the late Middle Ages in western Europe, chiefly in its northern lands, there were signs of increasing diversity in Roman Catholicism. Presumably united, it began to generate competing philosophies and outlooks. Catholicism nurtured universities in the cities of Europe. At universities many kinds of human learning developed which led scholars to question some of the old claims of faith. Different schools of thought developed. Some of them led to a criticism of papal policy. Others showed that some papal claims rested on forgeries. Still others, often called humanist, began to recover ancient languages. Using Greek and Latin, they began to find fault with Bible translations and doctrines based on these. Rising nationalism led some to be grudging about financial support of the papacy, which was, among other things, a military power among the powers. There were doubts about the way the sacred rites and ordinances were conceived and used. There could be magical overtones in people's approach to these; the papacy could then prevent people from receiving salvation and hope of heaven through the sacrament. Thus they exerted power over rival rulers. Popes, bishops, monks, and nuns, departed from the ideals of faithfulness and piety and often lived scandalous lives that shocked the pious laity. Most of all, it was believed that Catholicism had turned into a religion in which one was to earn or merit the grace and favor of God, not to receive them as gifts. If they were to be earned, how could one be secure in faith? If there was insecurity, could not and did not the church exploit the fears of people and begin to sell salvation through very gross and materialistic transactions?

While many Catholics began to ask such questions, they had a hard time finding a forum to spread them. It was possible for the Church to suppress debate and silence the questioners. Sometimes an institution called the Inquisition—which was designed chiefly to be used against heresy, especially in the case of people like Jews who had converted to Christianity— came to be feared by would-be reformers. Little maverick sects like the Waldensians, Cathari, and Albigenses, had long hidden out in remote areas, but now a generation of thinkers wanted to be in the cities and markets, the universities and churches. Some reformers used councils of the

Church in the fourteenth and fifteenth centuries to state their case. They soon became tangled, however, in the issue of the authority to call councils: could bishops do so, or were conclaves called or cancelled at the will and whim of the Pope alone?

These stirrings were truly international. At the beginning of the sixteenth century Spain was the scene of reform, but of a sort that was contained largely in the Roman church. Italy had some scholars and occasional preachers like Girolamo Savonarola, who was eventually burned. It was north of the Alps and away from the papacy that permanent and eventually breakaway reform movements had a better chance. In 1415 at the Council of Constance the Czech reformer Jan Huss was executed. In England John Wyclif inspired critical movements. The Popes were distracted by their own excesses, their desires to aggrandize Rome, their need to fend off the Muslim Turk who had captured Constantinople in 1453 and now gave signs of moving against western Christian Europe.

On that landscape early in the sixteenth century the Protestant movement, thus named at the Diet of Speyer in 1529, "broke out." The movement got its negative sounding name for rather accidental reasons in respect to a document signed at that Diet. Most Protestants thought of themselves instead more positively as "evangelicals." This meant that they saw themselves as promoting the evangel, the Gospel or good news of God's grace, against a Roman system that they saw to be fearsome and legalistic. Yet Europe was a crazy-quilt of principalities and emerging nations, and the evangelical movement took different forms in different places. Often its various forms were named after leaders or polities like the episcopal or congregational.

The best-known Protestant pioneer was Martin Luther, one of the young university teachers who, while studying the Bible, found in it a special way of viewing God's grace. What spoke to his heartsick soul he then preached gladly. Luther gathered other professors, preachers, protectors among princes, and laity. Across the river in Switzerland Huldreich Zwingli, one of the university humanists and a scholar who could take the sword and did die by it in battle, undertook a less conservative reform than Luther started. Of more influence was a French lawyer in Geneva, John Calvin, the most systematic thinker of the movement. Zwingli and Calvin admired Luther, but their Reformed party and the Lutherans parted over the meanings of the Lord's Supper and other teachings. The Reformed movement spread through parts of France and the Netherlands.

Protestants of Lutheran and Continental Reformed background were in America from early times. Some Reformed came to New Amsterdam, today's New York, after 1624. There were Swedish Lutherans at Philadelphia and in Delaware soon after. While the Reformed remained strong in the Hudson valley and New Jersey, more Lutherans came early to Pennsyl-

vania. Significantly, these minority groups from the Continent chose to settle in the middle colonies, since the northern and southern already had
established churches shaped by English Protestants who did not always
welcome these continental Europeans. These English Protestants demand
more notice.

In England, the spread of the Bible had its influence in shaping Protestant sentiments. Scholars at Cambridge and Oxford were like their counterparts at Germany's Wittenberg or at the Swiss schools. Yet the English
Reformation depended more on the crown than did most continental
movements outside Lutheran-turning Scandinavia. King Henry VIII,
named "Defender of the Faith" by the Pope for his attacks on Luther, was
soon thereafter to chafe under Roman obedience. His marital difficulties
and the Pope's unwillingness to sanction the arrangements he would make
in respect to divorce and remarriage helped lead him to a break with
Rome. Soon monasteries were being burned, and churchly lands were
turned over to secular hands. English Protestant liturgies and practices
developed. Yet the Church of England or Anglicanism was, like Lutheranism, a conservative Reformation. It kept many practices that were later to
look "Catholic" to dissenters, even as they were proudly seen to be Catholic by Anglicans. Among these was the retention of bishops in the apostolic succession, which means the office was traced back in continuity to
the apostles of Christ. Bishops claimed direct authority through the ages
from Christ's commissionings. For some time in the sixteenth century,
England bounced back and forth between Catholic and Protestant loyalties
in a set of moves that meant great risk of life and sometimes loss of life
and the expression of courage by church leaders on both Catholic and
Protestant sides. Then England became permanently Protestant.

Meanwhile in Scotland, under the stormy John Knox, a form of Protestantism developed which kept more of the character of John Calvin's Swiss
movement. It rejected the episcopal, or bishop-ruled, polity of the church
and, because it would be governed by lay elders, adopted the name based
on the Greek word for elder, presbyter, and became Presbyterian. This
Presbyterianism became the established church in Scotland as Anglicanism was official in England and Lutheran and Reformed faiths were on the
Continent.

Establishment meant privilege. The established Church had the sanction of law behind it. It was to be supported by the public whether all
people believed in its teachings or not. This privilege meant that there
were close ties between throne and altar, bishop and prince. That did not
mean that there were no tensions. It did mean that those who believed in
"unestablished" ways were despised, sometimes harassed, suppressed,
and persecuted.

Once the Protestant movement broke out, however, its impulses could
not all be contained in established churches. More radical reformers

thought that God's justice could be effected only if ties between throne and altar were broken. God's grace could be assured only if the state had no say in its imparting. Some of these reformers rejected the staid ways of a Luther in Germany or a Thomas Cranmer in England. The "Lord's Supper" of these established reformers looked all too much like the Catholic Mass. They were also social conservatives who gave little hope to emerging peasants and urban radicals.

On the Continent these movements, persecuted by Catholics and established Protestants alike, received many names. Sometimes they were Anabaptist, because they baptized again those who had already been baptized by others. Some were Mennonites because they followed one Menno Simons. Still others became Dunkers because they immersed in baptism, or Brethren because they wanted apostolic simplicity. Hounded around Europe, many were to take refuge in Pennsylvania and other colonies. These colonies allowed the sectarian and often peace-loving people who would mind their own business a place to practice that business.

In England the main dissenting movement tended to be led by educated people, often lawyers and other leaders from Cambridge, Oxford, *Puritans* and other centers of learning. They came to be called Puritans. These people tended to be at the same time robust and disciplined, sometimes severe, reformers of the church. Not all of them wanted to leave the Anglican church, but they would reform it, rejecting bishops and simplifying ceremonies. They would give first attention to the Bible and preaching. Puritans called for some sort of experience of faith, an owning of the covenant in which people of warmed heart acknowledged they would keep their part of an agreement with a demanding and still graceful God who saw them as the elect.

Puritanism was to be a part of a revolt in the middle of the seventeenth century. It was, in any case, the introducer of still more instability in England. Soon there were radical spinoffs: Levellers, Diggers, Fifth Monarchy Men, and others who would take history into their own hands against established religion and authority. The Quakers also emerged on this soil, as did various Separatists, people who saw final authority in the congregation.

England in the early seventeenth century was described as teeming or swarming with restless adventurers, capitalist investors, religious dissenters, unwelcome lawbreakers, and people of profound vision for a new society. Out of these cohorts came the people who were to settle the eastern coast of what became the United States. To their south were Spanish Catholics, *conquistadores* and missionaries, who reached latter-day Florida, Louisiana, Arizona, New Mexico, and California. To their north were French Catholics, often fur traders but also missionaries, and, in Protestant eyes, agents of the Pope. The settlers on the American shores wanted nothing to do with these people. Whatever else the colonists were, they were certainly anti-Catholic. Except in Maryland after 1634, the colonists were largely able to exclude Catholics and to begin fashioning colonies that were some day to become for a time a Protestant empire. We shall meet the settlers again in Chapter 3 as empire builders, but it is helpful to anticipate them now.

The first of these pioneers were Anglicans who came to Virginia after 1607. While they are not usually seen chiefly as religiously motivated, they did bring along a priest and gave privilege to Anglicanism. Eventually that faith was legally established in Virginia and the other southern colonies. This circumstance later led to major battles over separating church and state. Meanwhile, some of the Separatists, remembered as Pilgrims, after having lived in exile in the Netherlands, came to Plymouth colony in 1620. They were followed by more staid Puritans who formed Massachusetts Bay and then New Haven and Connecticut colonies. They established Puritan Congregationalism in those colonies, where they welcomed no dissent.

Some of the more radical Separatists, often people who came to Anabaptist convictions and were called Baptist, settled Rhode Island and were hospitable to many faiths. The Quaker William Penn founded Pennsylvania. After some experiments with Dutch Reformed establishment in New Netherland, today's New York, that colony, in order to be free for commerce had to be free for people of many faiths. There and elsewhere in the middle colonies no establishment endured.

These pioneers came to America to continue the Protestant Reformation, or just to be Protestant. Most people, we must presume, simply wanted to live out profitable existences and create happy circumstances for their families. Yet the church came to be prominent in their lives. These separate groups of Protestants had little to do with each other from colony to colony for a time. Certainly they did not see much value in forms of Protestantism other than their own. But by the 1770s, when they began to work for independence, and soon after, when they won it, they began the debates that centered on questions of how to protect faiths, whether to give privilege to some churches, how to keep religious and civil authority or "church and state" separate. They were on the way to their empire, but it was always to be one with great internal diversity and diversion. The Protestants were, in short, ready to act out a drama of faithfulness and conflict, one that has not yet ended.

2 · Clearing Space: The Removal of the Native American

The American Indian

Empires occupy space. Citizens of the United States spent a century completing the conquest of their land and of the people who had been there before them. The Protestants who provided the religious impulse for the conquest seldom raised questions about the rights of those native Americans. Almost never did it occur to them that these people, misnamed *Indians* by Christopher Columbus, had values—including religious systems—which needed to be understood.

The conquering Protestants regularly employed imperial language. As early as 1610 Virginia colonists were connecting missionary work with conquest and barter. If the Indians could not be converted "apostolically, without the helpe of man," they would have to be approached "imperiallie, [as] when a Prince, hath conquered their bodies, that the Preachers may feede their souls." The English would "marchandize and trade" the natives' "pearles of earth" for "the pearles of heaven."

The apostolic note was often forgotten as the colonists preferred to move "imperiallie" or by "marchandizing." For their more aggressive movements, they needed justification, and these were provided them by divines who accounted for the natives' presence in largely negative terms.

The colonists were conscious that they had been a chosen people and were fond of quoting verses from the Bible which assured the chosen that the heathen had been given them for an inheritance. But when the heathen resisted and when animosities and warfare resulted, stronger language was needed. The influential Harvard-bred Boston cleric Cotton Mather had written in 1702 that "we may guess that probably the *Devil* decoyed those miserable savages hither, in hopes that the gospel of the Lord Jesus Christ would never come here to destroy or disturb his absolute empire over them." The poet-cleric Michael Wigglesworth, in 1662, pictured this demonic empire as "a waste and howling wilderness/ Where

13

none inhabited/ But hellish fiends, and brutish men/ That Devils worshiped."

In the nineteenth century more moderate views of the natives' origins were to be developed. The most romantic and, to people of that day, most tantalizing was the guess that they were heirs of the ten tribes of Israel who had been carried off to captivity by Assyrians in 422 B.C. Elias Boudinot, the statesman who adopted a Cherokee son, published *A Star in the West; or, A Humble Attempt to Discover the Long Lost Ten Tribes of Israel,* in 1816. Through fanciful connections between the languages and practices of ancient Hebrews and contemporary Indians he hoped to provide a charter for positive attitudes toward the first Americans. Protestant Bible-readers found such an approach appealing. In their world of revivalism it was hoped that this would inspire Americans to treat wandering tribesmen well. *The Book of Mormon* also connected people described in the Hebrew scriptures with pre-Columbian America.

Whatever the natives' origins, most colonists and citizens found them unattractive and threatening. In any case, they occupied space which an expanding nation needed. They had to be dislodged. The early expansionists did not always develop theories to justify their activities. Few could have anticipated that the United States would expand from Atlantic coast to Pacific coast within a century, and in the race for land the natives were not the only ones whose rights were neglected. But they suffered most. The Reverend Mr. Jedidiah Morse, geographer and missionary, quoted an Indian chief who understood the imperial process well: "Where the white man puts down his foot, he never takes it up again."

Resistance was inevitable, and it lasted for a century after the birth of the American nation. In 1866 Chief Bear Rib, a Sioux, asked, "To whom does this land belong? I believe it belongs to me . . . I cannot spare it, and I like it very much . . . I like it and I hope you will listen to me."

The political policies through which natives were displaced regularly received clerical support. In both the War of Independence and the War of 1812, most natives had been on the British side. After 1812, of course, they could no longer count on British protection. On their own they were divided, ill-organized, outnumbered, underarmed. For a century after American independence they were strong enough to make some trouble for expansionists, and they did. As early as 1786 it was beginning to be evident that the final solution to the Indian problem would eventually come to rely on spatial segregation of the natives' reservations. Never during that century were they to be free to become United States citizens. The Constitution treated their tribes along with foreign nations.

In 1789 the Congress promised that "utmost good faith shall always be observed towards the Indians; their land and property shall never be taken from them without their consent." Sometimes for reasons of conscience and often for the sake of legal fictions the conquerors would pay a pittance for preempted land. Indian resistance was fought off from Fallen Timbers in Ohio in 1794 through the Seminole Wars of 1816–1818 to the last stand east of the Mississippi, the Black Hawk War of 1832, and then through fifty more years of mopping-up operations in the West.

In 1830 the Indian Removal Bill set the terms of policy. A few religious leaders protested. Three missionaries identified themselves with the Cherokees and were arrested, chained, degraded, and eventually sentenced to four years in the Georgia penitentiary. By the time of the Mexican War in 1846, it was becoming clear that removal policies often included programs which allowed for extermination.

A religious people could not take such extreme steps without religious rationales. Senator Thomas Hart Benton provided one by arguing that whites alone used the land "according to the intentions of the CREATOR." As late as 1870, the governor of the Colorado Territory invoked the Creator: "God gave us the earth, and the fullness thereof . . . I do not believe in donating to these indolent savages the best portion of my territory. . . ." Governor William Henry Harrison asked whether America was to remain "the haunt of a few wretched savages, when it seems destined by the Creator to give support to a large population."

In the course of colonial and national history a number of options had been present. The first of these was coexistence. By the time the nation was formed, few continued to believe in this possibility. Too many atrocities had been committed by both settlers and natives; too many interests had clashed.

The more enlightened Protestants joined and even led those who argued for a second approach: the natives could best be absorbed and assimilated through intermarriage and by living among whites. They prepared various programs which would combine the task of civilizing and Christianizing Indians. No one improved on the formula of Virginian William Byrd (d. 1744) who combined business with pleasure in his droll comment that he could not see why there was not more intermarriage. He pondered the strange fact that a good Christian should have "refused a wholesome straight bedfellow when he might have had so fair a portion of her as the merit of saving her soul." Sexual fears of the kind that were directed to blacks were less frequently related to native Americans. Yet intermarriage in settled communities was frowned on. When Elias Boudinot's Cherokee son married a white girl a little Connecticut town reacted in rage and the event led to the closing of the mission school where they had met.

Two of the chief advocates for assimilation were Protestant clergy. Jedidiah Morse, who wanted the government to take care of Indians, protested policies of extermination and pointed to the values in Indian ways of life. More explicit was missionary Jeremiah Evarts who two years later, in 1829, wrote articles against President Jackson's removal policies. A Protestant empire-builder himself, he foresaw a world under Christian influence, but one in which people like the Cherokees could take their place as part of America. Chief Justice John Marshall considered this "the most conclusive argument that he ever read on any subject whatever," but it was not to prevail.

A third option allowed for the segregation of the natives. Whites would have their empires, but the first Americans could either have a state of their own—an idea which never gained much favor—or they could be placed on reservations. Establishment of reservations turned out to be the predominant policy, and the majority of Protestants favored it. The tireless missionary Isaac McCoy felt that for the Indians' own good they would have to be placed beyond the range of whites. He fought Jackson over what he saw to be phony promises to natives. In 1823 he was still hoping for a western state where they might know the "privileges of *men,* and the prospects of a settled home," but later he argued only for reservations.

The removal-reservation plan was followed at the expense of the natives' privileges and dignity. They were moved from place to place, depending upon whites' interests and needs. Eventually Chief Spotted Tail of the Sioux asked in weariness but with wit, "Why does not the Great Father put his red children on wheels, so he can move them as he will?"

An option that was compatible with both absorption and removal centered on religious conversion. Many Protestants argued that whether or not these disciples of the devil or lost tribes of Israel were to be blended into the nation or be segregated from it, their lives would be enhanced if they came to accept the Christian faith.

The idea of Christianizing the natives had been among the earliest stated objectives of the colonists two centuries earlier. The Virginia Company in 1610 propagandized: "The principal and main ends are first to preach and baptize into the Christian Religion and . . . to recover out of the arms of the Devil a number of poor and miserable souls. . . ." The colonial missionary record of Protestants was not impressive. By 1622, after the massacre at Henrico, the Virginians largely lost taste for evangelizing. In New England a few lonely enterprisers set out to convert natives, but their yield was small. By the end of the American Revolution, only about twelve such missionaries were active and the venture had been all but abandoned. The company of those who had made an effort did include some of New England's stalwarts: Roger Williams, John Eliot, David Brainerd, and even Jonathan Edwards. Their efforts had been of little avail.

Men who carry concepts of empire ordinarily believe that their values are superior to those of others. Protestant leaders combined faith in God with faith in their own virtues. The American Board of Commissioners for Foreign Missions, an agency that shared a desire to resume missionary work, stated as late as 1856 that Indian missions were "instituted for the spread of scriptural self-propagating Christianity. This is their only aim.

Civilization, as an end, they never attempt." Yet, argued the outliners of the policy, civilizing inevitably went along with Christianity. A missionary confided to his diary in 1828 that the savage was to be turned into what looks like a Yankee type: "Industry is good, honesty is essential, punctuality is important, sobriety essential." In 1854, one evangelist wrote to another that the Christians were to show natives "Yankee enterprise—go-ahead determination."

The Protestants, full of go-ahead spirit as they were, were never so successful as Roman Catholics had been in their efforts in the western hemisphere. Catholic missionaries, being celibate, were more mobile. They had held a somewhat more tolerant attitude toward Indian ritual and custom than did the evangelicals, who insisted on rigorous discipline and whose religion virtually demanded some literacy.

For a time, even while their fellow citizens and fellow believers were busy removing and exterminating natives, numbers of Protestants set out once again to convert and minister to them. During the early years of the nineteenth century, America was experiencing widespread revivals of religion. Many spoke of the days as a time of a Second Great Awakening, not unlike the awakening which had enlivened religion in the colonies seventy years earlier. The revivalist impulse was to be carried to all, including nonwhites.

As part of the awakening, missionaries banded together in societies. By 1787 the first of these had been organized. At the turn of the century the Northern Missionary Society of the State of New York worked among the Oneidas, and efforts among Wyandottes followed in Massachusetts in 1811. Some evangelicals were working as far west as northern Illinois by 1823 and Eleazar Williams, one of the more devoted representatives of the faith, also knew some successes in Wisconsin that year. In the South after 1801 efforts among Cherokees were frustrated by governmental policies against these Indians, but Protestants continued to work among them wherever they were pushed through the 1820s and 1830s.

Most amazing of all, by 1834 Jason Lee had gone overland to Oregon, the territory where two years later two famed couples, the Marcus Whitmans and the Henry H. Spauldings, arrived to work the territory. Through misunderstandings about the work of Whitman, a medical doctor, Indians reacted and attacked the mission in 1847, killing the couple and twelve other people. The mission was closed. But the Protestant empire, frail as it was in this effort, had reached from coast to coast sixty years after independence.

To speak of a single empire may seem misleading, for in this as in all its endeavors, Protestantism was frustrated by its disunity. If the Indians had tribes, so did the Christians. Alfred Brunson, author of *Western Pioneer* (1872), reminisced in terms of demonstrable untruth: "The Heathen to whom we ministered never knew from us the differences between denominations." A few Protestants did act charitably toward each other, even if sometimes they did so in order to fight off Roman Catholics. Most of the time they went their own ways. Curiously, the natives who responded reproduced some of the subtler features of Christian disunity. Mixed-bloods of better education and moderately high status became part of the upper-class church groups while full-bloods and those who had had fewer opportunities to advance themselves joined the simpler, more primitive, lower-class white churches.

Since the missionaries could not unite in faith, some urged that they should divide the territory. Thus Cyrus Kingsbury of the Connecticut Missionary Society wrote in a letter of 1820: "I have long been satisfyed that in converting the Heathen World . . . different denominations must occupy different portions of the great field and not blend their exertions and thus interfere with each other and distract the attention of the Heathen."

Internal competition was complicated by still another factor, the appeal of overseas missions. While America was expanding its domestic empire, an advance guard of missionaries had begun to carry the Christian gospel and Yankee go-ahead determination to many parts of the earth. Recruits for native missions were scarce. More glamor was associated with work in Burma than in the midst of despised and hateful local nonwhites. Gordon Hall, a noted missionary in India, stated the case for work in the East over that in America. Efforts in India would cost less and offer more. The agent could acquire a single language that would be used by many people, while American Indian dialects were spoken by few. His "in the east, Providence seems to have set an open door rather than in the west" was a strange reversal of the general prowestern mentality of the century. And Hall inserted a realistic aside: "From the situation of the Indian tribes a mission among them would be attended with greater perils and sufferings. . . ."

Work on Indian reservations was difficult and unrewarding. The missionaries had to cooperate with governmental agents, many of whom could not disguise their disdain and hatred for their subjects. Potential converts understandably had difficulty distinguishing missionaries from these despised agents. The conversion-seekers had to be a rare breed of people who would devote themselves to learning languages, building churches, holding revivals, instructing the young. Jedidiah Morse urged that "education families" be sent to live with natives to teach them religion and values. "I give this name to those bodies which have been commonly denominated *Mission Families*. . . ." These were to form the core of a community. They represented one of the few original aspects in the whole movement. But, said Morse, these pioneers would need a government that "should be in its nature *paternal-absolute, kind,* and *mild.*" The first two adjectives applied. The other two did not, and therein lay the root of many problems.

During the decisive century of nation-building most of the missionary efforts failed and church after church gave up. Almost no one boasted of successes in this field, even though the representatives for the Protestant empire were given to much boasting. It was determined that the cost per soul had become too high; the mission was not paying off. The books did not balance. The Rev. Mr. William H. Milburn wrote the epitaph in 1860: "The Indian must perish." The natives were still "an utter hopeless prospect."

Two other options remained. Until 1863 it would have been legally possible to do what empire-builders had done for ages, to enslave their victims. But Indians made poor slaves. They were freer than blacks to engage in reprisals. As a matter of fact, they sometimes even created a novel problem for antislavery evangelicals when they themselves held black slaves.

Finally, there was extermination. The young nation and its churches did not lack advocates of what today would be called genocide. Using instruments of war, disease, and degradation, the conquerors cut into the native population. While at the time of Columbus there may have been 900,000 people in the area that was to become the United States, only about 280,000 were left by 1876. In 1782 the Pennsylvania jurist Hugh Henry Brackenridge called for "extermination" of "the animals vulgarly called Indians." Over a century later, Theodore Roosevelt said, "I don't go so far as to think that the only good Indians are the dead Indians, but I believe nine out of ten are, and I shouldn't inquire too closely into the case of the tenth." Not a few church leaders joined in these sentiments. Massachusetts missionary Timothy Flint, acknowledging wrong done by both sides, appealed to laws of nature: "In the unchangeable order of things, two such races can not exist together. . . ."

For all these policies, American consciences had been informed and soothed by Protestant representatives, lay and clerical, who assured the United States that it could clear space by removing or exterminating natives, and that this could be all in line with laws of nature and the will of God.

Few had ever listened to the Indian. At the time of the birth of the nation, a few theorists at the fringes of the churches had placed high values on the natives' way of life and seen their religions virtually to be on a par with Western religions. Now and then a Jedidiah Morse would publicize some positive features in the lives of the first Americans.

By the time Indians found voices, it was too late. Chief Joseph surveyed the spiritual damage: the Christians "will teach us to quarrel about God as the Catholics and Protestants do on the reservation . . . We may quarrel with men sometimes about things on this earth, but we never quarrel about God. We do not want to learn that."

One fragment from a nearly forgotten past served to remind later citizens of the meaning of the clash of empires, viewed from the aspect of the loser. Seneca Chief Red Jacket spoke to a Massachusetts missionary in 1805. "Brother, our seats were once large, and yours were very small; you have now become a great people, and we have scarcely a place left to spread our blankets; you have got our country, but are not satisfied; you want to force your religion upon us." He went on, "We do not understand these things; . . . We also have a religion which was given to our forefathers . . . We never quarrel about religion . . . Brother, we do not wish to destroy your religion, or take it from you. We want only to enjoy our own."

Under the authority of the Continental Congress, the *Apocalypse de Chiokoyhikoy, Chef des Iroquois* was published. A piece of propaganda, anonymously "translated"—perhaps by a missionary—it was claimed to be an old Iroquois prophecy. In 1777 it was released to counteract British agents' promises to Indians. The document shares with much Christian propaganda the vision of a great future in America; in this case, the Indian was represented as prophesying that "a new people" (Americans) will come on the scene to conquer European nations. These new people "are destined to become, in the hand of the great OKA [the highest Deity], the agent of a blessed revolution, which is to bring peace, prosperity, innocence to the new world, and to restore all their rights to the true masters of that world; the savages [or aborigines]."

The restoration did not come. An impassioned Helen Hunt Jackson looked back 104 years later and spoke of *A Century of Dishonor.* One hundred years after the *Apocalypse,* President Rutherford Hayes spoke of "broken promises and acts of injustice on our part." His magnificent understatement also summarized the involvement of Protestant empire-builders during that century and the one which was to follow.

3 · The Builders of Empire

The White Anglo-Saxon

The white Americans who set out to develop a national empire after 1776 grew increasingly conscious of their self-image. Their task demanded heroism and sacrifice. They knew that they needed to be clear about their identity as well as their purpose. By the time of independence they had had one and a half centuries of experience on which to build a concept of themselves. Their achievement is incomprehensible unless and until their racial, national, and religious make-up and symbolism are understood.

They took for granted whiteness, Almost any white Protestant spokesman during the first century of national existence would have agreed with a chapter-heading in a standard geography book of the 1860s: "The White Race the Normal or Typical Race."

The normal or typical race had been given license to clear space and to take it over. Its leaders found no difficulty relating divine purpose to such a mission. The superior people would move at the expense of the inferior. The school textbooks of the era are one of the best indicators of the public picture. One published in 1793 argued that "nature has formed the different degrees of genius, and the characters of nations, which are seldom known to change." Children in school in 1813 could read: "The religion of nature, the light of revelation, and the pages of history, are combined in the proof, that God has ordered that nations shall become extinct, and that others shall take their places." One hundred years after the Constitution, children still heard that it was a "well-established law of nature, that causes an inferior race to yield to a superior when one comes in contact with the other."

The new United States had been formed geographically within a kind of pincers that had been wielded by people who, the Protestants were sure, had been rejected by God. To the south were Spanish and Portuguese Catholics. God had somehow permitted them to take the southern half of the hemisphere and they even had made inroads into the southwest and southeast of what would later be the United States. To the north and west were French Roman Catholics, who occupied Canada and some of the old Northwest Territory. The English Protestants on the eastern coast of North America at the time of the beginning of expansion needed to develop a sense of destiny over against these religiously hostile forces.

When in doubt, these religious founders invoked the doctrine of Providence. A foreknowing God had seen to it that the better part of the western hemisphere would not be explored until the Protestant Reformation was well under way in Europe. Providence had played games with the Catholics, allowing them to plunder the gold of the south while hiding from them the land of promise in the north. Such were not merely backwoods opinions, born for an early death. At the end of the nineteenth century, Leonard Bacon, as sophisticated as any American church historian of his time, was fully convinced of this version of God's rationale.

"By a prodigy of divine providence, the secret of the ages had been kept from premature disclosure," he wrote. Had the discovery of America been achieved even a single century earlier, the transplanted Christianity would have been that of the church of Europe "at its lowest stage of decadence." Bacon was generous enough to remind his readers that the Catholicism which was supported by earlier colonists had been that of the sixteenth, not of the fifteenth century. Thus it was the heir of a "reformation *of* the church" (Catholic style) and not merely "reformation *from* the church" (Protestant style).

Bacon reserved his greatest enthusiasm for the thirteen colonies and their English-speaking heritage. He even found virtues in the religious divisions within them. He reasoned that their division, which was almost in its "ultimate stage of schism" would, in a "worthy possible solution of the mystery of Providence in the planting of the church in America" turn out to produce liberty and unity. Only those philosophers who forbade Americans to find in history the "evidences of final cause and providential design" would disagree. In all these sentiments Protestants stood in continuity with New Englander Francis Higginson, who was said to have extended farewell to England in order to "practise the positive part of church reformation" in America.

Church people and the unchurched alike thought of the new republic as a Protestant domain. Geographies, spellers, and readers from 1804, 1806, 1817, 1835, and 1846 included charts delineating the religions of the nations of the world. The United States was always listed as Protestant. The basis for the listing was never made clear. Only a minority of the people were members of religious groups. Officially the civil authorities were to be neutral toward religion. By 1846 significant numbers of non-Protestants were on the scene. But by observation and instinct Americans had come to call their territory Protestant.

Land, people, and nation were beginning to be seen in a kind of mystical unity. When an elementary school reader in 1828 first used the word "nationality" it had to explain that while the term was used by "some writers in America" it is a "new word and not to be found in the dictionaries." But for some time to come, Protestant apologists also found it useful to transcend nationality and to see the empire in racial or international terms. Thus the great church historian Philip Schaff could explain to continental readers as late as 1855: "I doubt whether the moral influence of Christianity and of Protestantism has more deeply and widely affected any nation, than it has the Anglo-Saxon."

While the church historian Leonard Bacon in 1898 foresaw a simple blending of Protestants and while the German-trained scholar Philip Schaff was expansive enough to include all kinds of national experiences in Anglo-Saxonism, in their day-to-day life the Americans found reasons to account for ethnic, religious, and geographical differences. In the mood of *E Pluribus Unum,* they had to fashion a unity, and did so by beginning with the dominant groups. Others were to be assimilated into these, measured by them, or rejected by them.

The census of 1790 is revealing for an understanding of the way races and religions were to be graded. The new nation was overwhelmingly English: the census takers reached a population that was 83.5 percent English in background and orientation. The Protestant chroniclers tended to value the non-English on a scale that corresponded remarkably to the proportions of representation in 1790. Second came the Scotch, with 6.7 percent, to be followed by Germans (5.6 percent), Dutch (2.0 percent), and Irish (1.6 percent). As the nineteenth century progressed, more and more Irish Catholics came, and this complicated the earlier positive appraisals of the Irish component.

Much of the later drama within the Anglo-Protestant empire in the United States can be anticipated by anyone who looks further to see how nineteenth-century immigration worked against the proportions of the first census. In 1850, 42.8 percent of the foreign-born in America were from Ireland, 26.0 percent from Germany, only 13.7 percent from England and Wales. Later, southern and eastern Europe were to send millions who would cause the old English–Scotch proportion to dwindle. But at the birth of the nation, the people virtually had only the problem of how to live on the basis of outlooks associated with English Protestantism, since so many were represented by it.

They began by doing what people in search of a usable past conventionally had done: they made a liturgy out of their history. The Deuteronomist in the Bible set a pattern for this religious style when he quoted Moses advising the people, "And you shall make response before the Lord your God, 'A wandering Aramean was my father . . . and the Lord brought us out of Egypt.'" Governor William Bradford spoke in this mode in lines that have been called the greatest in all New England's literature: "May not and ought not the children of these fathers rightly say: *Our fathers were Englishmen which came over this great ocean, and were ready to perish in this wildernes; but they cried unto the Lord, and he heard their voyce, and looked on their adversitie. . . ."*

"Our fathers were Englishmen." Two British Christians asserted after their visit to America in 1836: "Blot out Britain and America from the map of the world, and you destroy all those great institutions which almost exclusively promise the world's renovation." On the positive side, "unite Britain and America in energetic and resolved cooperation for the world's salvation, and the world is saved." Professor Schaff made clear that in tying on to England, Americans automatically bought an imperial and dominating spirit. "The Anglo-Saxon and Anglo-American, of all modern races, possess the strongest national character and the one best fitted for universal dominion," in part because of their shared Protestantism.

The English Protestant bond was tested both by the Revolutionary War and the War of 1812, yet the racial and religious ties were deep enough to survive these crises. They did force Americans to face the question of their own identity, however, for from the beginning they had to justify separate existence and soon were legitimating their ideas of their own superiority.

For these purposes, Americans had to rate England and Europe negatively. At the beginning of the eighteenth century, Cotton Mather, a spokesman of the old order, set a tone for historians in subsequent centuries: "I write the *Wonders* of the CHRISTIAN RELIGION, flying from the Depravations of *Europe,* to the *American Strand.*" The founders were English. But England and the Old World had become depraved, and pure men or positive church reformers had to come to a new strand. How could one account for American religious superiority? The answer was consistent: the founders had been tried, tested, and sifted by persecution on religious grounds in England. The best features of national character, according to orator Edward Everett in 1824 (and according to preachers before and since) "are to be found on the side of the oppressed few, and not of the triumphant many." Their ordeals had purified the founders and their faith.

During the first half-century of nationhood, while the English Protestant population overwhelmed all others, religious leaders spent their energies luxuriating in their freedom to make distinctions within this element. Most of them followed South–North lines. Since more of the literary activities were to go on in the North, the point of view of its representatives worked its way into the textbook tradition. The influential geographer-cleric Jedidiah Morse set a pattern in 1791 when he reminded children that "there are but few religious people in these southern states; those who make any pretensions to religion are remarkable for their piety." Other writers criticized southern religionists for their laxity. In all southern states, there is a very numerous body of people who "are literally as to religion NOTHINGARIANS." In contrast to the depravations of Europe, however, the southern American strand still came off better. Such minor compliments were small comfort to southern spokesmen who, needless to say, found occasions to match Morse's rhetoric in defense of their own case.

Among those not explicitly English, the Scotch-Irish were most lauded. They had come to the colonies much later than the English, but for the most part they were highly regarded. These were Protestant heirs of a situation in the British Isles in the seventeenth century, when England had tried to squeeze Catholics out of northern Ireland. Tens of thousands of Scots went to Ulster to live on expropriated land (almost four million acres). But these venturesome Protestants came upon bad times. The established church hemmed them in and the government's import regulations hurt their woolen and food business. A century after they had begun to move to Ulster they began to come to America. Unwelcome at Boston in 1718, they settled in the middle colonies, especially in Pennsylvania and New Jersey, where they were free to set up presbyterial polity—and to be welcomed into the American mainstream.

Ruth Miller Elson, student of nineteenth-century textbooks, finds that these books are unanimous in rating the Scottish people highest among the nations. A geographer in 1848 gave them the ultimate accolade and showed how much a part of the empire-building community they were: "Like the inhabitants of New England, the Scotch are religious, moral and industrious." The Scotch-Irish, having endured oppression from the English hand, were the best of this breed. The Germans, although less well represented, also rated highly in the schoolbook tradition. German-Swiss Philip Schaff showed how the admired Germans could be grafted into the Anglo-American Protestant tree. They are "in fact off-shoots from the same Teutonic root." The Germans were religiously more inward while the English were more activist: they could blend well into America, but these Germans would have to adapt to the largely English environment, the generous Mr. Schaff advised.

The trickle of French Protestants (Huguenots) were well spoken of by the Anglo-Saxons and Teutons, but they were seen as a spent historical force, and were absorbed into non-French churches. French Catholics were, of course, not part of the new empire and their nation—despite its aid to the colonies and in part because of French revolutionary excesses— was, after 1794, among the lowest-rated of European nations or of potential contributors to the American population. France was the home of infidelity and Catholicism; the two forces were seen to feed off each other, and neither brought promise to America. Through the whole first half-century (and even more after the great immigrations of the 1840s) the Catholic Irish were even more to be despised.

Protestant England, the Scotch-Irish, and to a lesser degree Germany and the Lowlands, had made their contribution to that nation which Schaff

[handwritten margin note: Catholics / despised / all status / based / on / Eng. / Protestant]

was later to say was "the country for average intelligence, average morality, and average piety," *average* being a positive term in his antiextremist vocabulary. In 1783 Ezra Stiles, president of Yale College, predicted that the American Christian future would be about equally divided between Congregationalists, Presbyterians, and Episcopalians. Those who heard or read him would have had little reason to question this prophecy or vision. In the new nation these three clusters did predominate. They shared the virtues that had been endorsed for empire. Their subtle variations could be blurred, however heated their ancient arguments had been, for the sake of average or mainstream Christianity. While they were soon to yield the first two places statistically to Baptists—a colonial minority—and to Methodists, who were just forming during the first ten years of national life, they were to survive as representatives of typicality in American religion. Others could be added to their mainstream in the American strand, but it was most difficult for any one to force them out of it.

First among these three groups in order of priority were the southerners, the English Protestants who followed episcopal polity and who through the whole colonial period were related to the Bishop of London. They had come to Jamestown with the first settlers and made up the official religion in most southern colonies at the time of independence. By 1780 there were 406 churches of this obedience—the fourth largest number of any church in the colonies. Neglected by London, suffering from identification with the establishment, the Anglican church became in many places little more than the religious expression of the southern aristocracy's way of life. The Great Awakening in the colonies had done little to warm or purify this church. The southern church suffered during the Revolution because so many of its clergy remained faithful to their vows to the king and were Loyalist or Tory.

Many Episcopal laity were, fortunately for the future of their church, founders of the republic. After a decade or two of crisis and after the church no longer knew legal privileges, there was considerable recovery, and nineteenth-century Episcopalianism was to survive and prosper in average American Christianity.

The Congregational-Presbyterian cluster predominated in New England. Historians who complain that too much of American history has been explained in terms of Plymouth Rock and Massachusetts Bay can find reasons for this when they review the religious drama of New England. Followers of what they called "the Congregational Way," people who advocated complete autonomy for each local gathering of Christians, were among the motivators for early seventeenth-century settlement. They made up much of the oligarchy. Civil and religious authorities were fused in unimaginably complicated and profound ways through much of the colonial period. Religious leaders there were notably articulate and conscious of their traditions. They recorded and preserved for later generations a body of literature that almost overpowers the historian. When numbers of American religious leaders joined forces to produce the first interreligious history in the United States in 1844, the spokesman for Congregationalism could boast, "At the present day, probably in no portion of the world, will fewer infidels, or openly immoral men be found, than in the New England states." Like it or not, other Americans were taught to accept the image of New England's religiosity and dominance.

Ezra Stiles, in an autobiographical fragment which combines naïveté with tolerant wit, reported on the way one could come to a view of New England's superiority even if religiously tolerant as Stiles was. "From the cursory View I made of Ecclesiastical History," he confided, "I thot all the protestant Churches as well as all the Xtian Churches since the first Age, had many Usages and Doctrines which I did not find in the Bible." Yet he spotted sincere good men in all churches, so he adopted and professed an extensive and universal charity: "I readily saw the Mode of Worship in the New England Churches was as conformable to the Bible as any in the World, and I thot more so."

Between the episcopally-oriented South and the congregational North were the middle colonies. For most of their history no religion was established by law. Here was the stronghold of those who preferred presbyterian forms, although many of the New England churches had also adopted the polity in which elders ruled and local churches met in synods. If the congregational-style churches still were first in number, with 749 in 1780, those of presbyterian preference were coming up fast with 495 to second place. More and more of these were of Scotch-Irish stock. These churches profited from a magic blending, as Leonard Bacon could observe after a century. They represented in their ministry and membership "the two most masterful races on the continent, the New England colonists and the Scotch-Irish immigrants." They needed little help beyond that fact to be typical, average, mainstream representatives or agents of empire. But they did have much else in their favor, including great profit from the Great Awakening of the 1730s and 1740s, a strong identification with the winners in the American Revolution, and a good record in the quest for religious freedom for all Americans in the early years of the republic.

Of the right racial stock, although originally suspect in both southern and northern colonies, were the English congregationalists who were called Separatist in outlook. They formally separated from the Church of England, having abandoned hope of reforming it as the more moderate Puritans intended to do. Because many of these insisted on strong church discipline they expected an adult affirmation of faith, and those who linked this affirmation with baptism were called Baptist. Their churches numbered 457 by 1780 and only a serene Yale graduate like Stiles could have overlooked this third-place cluster in his prophecy for the American future.

The Baptist founders had been persecuted in New England. They found refuge in Rhode Island, a colony set up by Roger Williams, John Clarke, and others on the basis of separatist principles. More of them moved down south to become irritants there after the eighteenth-century awakenings. Still more found the charters of Pennsylvania and New Jersey congenial. Their growth, their participation in the Revolution, their aid in the search for religious freedom, and their success in early nineteenth-century revivals were to bring them (along with the Methodists) to first place among American churches by as early as 1820. Citizens of the United States were not in a position to argue with such success, especially since these churches were made up of people with the proper racial credentials and historical background. They, too, were allowed to be average.

As all these grew, the proportion of Quakers declined. Agents of William Penn in his colony of Pennsylvania in 1682, they had for a century worked to keep the tolerant Penn's "Holy Experiment" in religious liberty and commonwealth alive. But their colony was host to so many other persecuted religious groups that they were overwhelmed. Many left the old ways and not a few chose the less rigorous Anglican mode of worship without falling from grace in the Philadelphia elite. The Quaker peace policies were regarded as unsuccessful in the face of the Indian and unpatriotic in the presence of the British. However, the English background and the generosity of their intentions assured their continuing if dwindling presence in average-typical Protestantism for some time to come. Observers of the American scene were later to say that they wielded influence "far beyond their numbers."

The middle colonies provided a home for the largest number of what Schaff called "un-English" churches. Most of them came from Protestant parts of Germany or from the Netherlands. This meant that they could be smuggled in as Teutonic cousins if not Anglo-Saxon siblings, and their connections with the Reformation almost three centuries earlier made it possible for them to present proper credentials. The fact that so many of them spoke Dutch or German was the most serious handicap to their growth and impact. Centering in Pennsylvania, New Jersey, and New York, by 1780 they formed 328 Reformed (Dutch and German) and 240 Lutheran churches—fifth and sixth respectively, so far as numbers of congregations were concerned.

In addition to these six large English and un-English Protestant clusters, there were fifty-six Roman Catholic churches in the colonies. Almost all were in Maryland and Pennsylvania. Many estimate that they numbered only 20,000 people in a new nation of 4.5 million. But as local representatives of European depravation they were almost universally mistrusted. Only now and then were individual Catholics of wealth, like the members of the Carroll family, permitted to be filtered through the anti-Roman screen to face positive public regard. The occasional contributions to religious liberty in colonial America made by Catholics in Maryland and New York were regarded as exceptional or were forgotten. By the time of the Civil War, Catholicism was to be the largest single communion in America, and most of its communicants were not of accepted racial stock.

At the moment when thirteen colonies were beginning to form one nation and when eastern seaboarders began to move across the mountains into the west, Protestantism of English and what people then called Anglo-Saxon, Teutonic, or Caucasian stock set the terms for the religious dimensions of empire. Because they were divided in their churches and because they came from different nations, earlier traditions and racial theories almost inevitably had to be appealed to so that the many could be included. The first major American church historian, Robert Baird, spoke for people in these early decades in 1844: "In a word, our national character is that of the Anglo-Saxon race," and people must study "Saxon institutions, and Saxon laws and usages." The German and English, "essentially Germanic or Teutonic," are "the chief supports of the ideas and institutions of evangelical Christianity," and hold "in their hands the theoretical and practical mission of Protestantism for the world." The United States was to be the base for that mission, but its internal empire had to remain secure and securely white Protestant. On that the white Protestant majority, whether its members went to church or not, could agree for many decades after 1776.

4 · The Overlooked Protestants

The Black American

On July 4, 1776, Benjamin Franklin, John Adams, and Thomas Jefferson were appointed to be a "Committee to prepare a device for a Seal of the United States of America." Numerous suggestions were offered. Franklin advocated a design which featured Moses. In the background, the troops of Pharaoh would be seen drowning in the Red Sea: "Rebellion to tyrants is obedience to God." Jefferson's suggestion contained elements that were to be included in the adopted seal. The children of Israel in the wilderness were "led by a cloud by day and a pillar of fire by night." While this biblical content nearly evaporated by the time of final adoption, it is significant that these statesmen—in so many ways uneasy themselves about the Jewish-Christian heritage—drew upon the Bible for symbols which could unite and interpret their peoples' experience.

In the years to follow, Americans would again and again read themselves into the stories of the biblical Exodus and deliverance from tyranny and slavery. For most people the acts of coming to America and becoming independent were completed acts of freedom and deliverance. For a very large minority, however, the use of such symbols was expressive of vague promise and desperate hope. They were in America, but not yet fully of it. They had not been rescued or liberated. And when these black Americans would evoke the symbols of Exodus they looked subversive to those around them. Not for one hundred years did most of them have even a minimal legal experience of liberation. They were to know many a Moses but were denied a promised land.

The Protestant empire was built at the expense of black inhabitants. They were either overlooked, intentionally neglected, enslaved, expatriated, or exterminated. But if they were an acted-upon people, they also were agents in American history. They relate to grand and tragic themes of the national epic. The historic limits imposed upon them have revealed the obsessive concerns of some thoughtful whites and have elicited the hatreds and rage of countless millions of others.

30

The story of black Americans differs from that of other migrants in that they alone were systematically deprived of their heritage, including their religion. The white majority came on its wilderness errands and empire-building tasks in the name of religion, or at least was free to exercise and develop it. Not so with the millions who traced their lineage to the west coast of central Africa. Religion played little positive part in their coming, mainly because in almost every instance theirs was a forced departure from the old home. Beginning in 1619 when twenty black "indentured servants" arrived and continuing through the decades after chattel slavery had become the policy, they were consistently uprooted from their old communities.

1619 – 1st black slaves

Almost nothing of African religion survived. Well and good, said the whites, who saw little in what they called "fetishism and animism" at best and heathenism or degradation at worst. With an instinct that bordered on genius, they seemed to know that one way to break persons was to destroy the religious dimensions of their communal experience. The sense of "life force" prominent in so much African religion could be denied when tribal and communal patterns were shattered. The family was destroyed. The horrors of midpassage eliminated many through death and initiated for others that process of cultural uprooting which was designed to keep them from being a people. As slaves, they became commodities without rights, unable to develop memories in continuity with their religious past.

"Our fathers were African." Had blacks wanted to speak in tones like those of their white contemporaries, they would have had to restore old African religious or cultural elements; they had lost continuity. Their enslavers knew how, deprived of a history, blacks could be deprived of identity and community.

At the time of American independence, then, it was hardly possible to speak of blacks as "a people." Their community had been atomized, and amnesia had been imposed on them. The outsider to their community set the terms of definition, and as might be expected, those terms were then almost uniformly negative. A Harvard student on the debating team of 1773 had no difficulty justifying slavery on the grounds that the black was "a conglomerate of child, idiot, and madman"—a quotation so representative of its time that it needs little parallel or supporting documentation.

Not that no white Christians took interest in the Africans' plight. Moravians and Quakers worked carefully to minister to them and to improve their image and their hopes in white communities. The Society for the Propagation of the Gospel, after 1741, began some systematic missionary activity. The few who had cared about the souls of native Americans also cared about those of African Americans. Thus John Eliot set out to carry the Gospel to them and even Cotton Mather, whose record on red men was ambiguous, to say the least, had a positive view of missions to blacks.

Those who took action to let blacks become a people met difficulty on all hands, beginning with even the simple points of Christian experience. Should they be baptized? In New England whites were reluctant, for baptism conferred the franchise, and it was unthinkable that the child-idiot-madman should vote. First redefine baptism so that it did not automatically confer rights on them and then let them be baptized. So be it, and so it was done. In Virginia the issue was debated on similar terms: would not the rights of baptism (or the entering of marriage contracts) turn blacks into legal entities and persons? Some theological gerrymandering seemed necessary to work around the problem. By 1667 Virginia had discovered ways.

Baptism, it was argued, brought psychological benefits which blacks would misuse. To white worriers, the Reverend Hugh Jones was as reassuring as his words were revealing: as for baptizing blacks, "several of the people disapproved of it, because they say it often makes them proud, and not so good servants." These objections were easily refuted, "for Christianity encourages and orders them to become more humble and better servants, and not worse, than when they were heathens." Jones was careful to agree with those who feared that literacy would lead to insurgency, however. So far as the other sacred issue of property was concerned, the Bishop of London settled that in 1727: "Christianity does not make the least alteration in civil property." It brought blacks freedom from bondage of sin and Satan, "but as to their outward condition they remained as before, even after baptism." With such an all-clear signal, missionaries and slaveowners could go ahead, extending elements of Christianity to these partitioned-off Protestants-to-be.

The number of blacks grew. By 1710 there were perhaps about 50,000 in the colonies and by the time of the Declaration of Independence this number had grown tenfold; at the time of the War Between the States there were about four million. As coinhabitants if not fellow-citizens with the white majority, they went through some experiences similar to that of the majority. When there was a Revolution, they fought. When white Protestants formed what came to be called religious denominations, the free minority among blacks did so with similar celerity and talent. When evangelicalism was warmed up early in the nineteenth century, blacks took to revivalist techniques with ease. When whites looked West and had dreams of empire, so did blacks. But their dreams were to be denied at the hands of their fellow-believers in the larger society.

Blacks have always formed one of the largest of all Protestant elements, and most blacks who were religious were Protestants. From the point of view of Christian theology there should have been the experience of a single "people of God" in America, but practically there were two such sets.

The blacks' relation to dominant Protestantism was ambiguous. On the one hand, the degree to which they accepted evangelical Christianity, adapted it, and lived by it, was an impressive compliment to its spiritual power. Much in the faith worked well and rang true to them. On the other hand, every aspect of the black-and-Protestant bond was conditioned by the fact that only parts of the evangelical experience were permitted them. Even these parts were transformed by the white experience. The Jesus around whose name they gathered seemed to be an Anglo-Saxon. The traditions that were parcelled out to blacks with such guarded care were white translations of an historical religion that had not been born on Anglo-Saxon, Teutonic, or Caucasian soil.

That blacks had parallel or imitative experiences is clear from the readiness with which free blacks developed denominations. Some of the more established and conventional churches prevented such formation and welcomed blacks to the edges of their denominations and conventions, segregating them in galleries of the largely white churches. The more evangelistic and free-form churches like the Baptists allowed for autonomous development of all-black local churches, and the highly structured but down-to-earth Methodist church was to see and in some ways to encourage separate "African" parallels.

These were early developments. Richard Allen, for example, had converted to Christianity while a slave in Delaware. With currency depreciated by the Revolution he was able to buy his freedom. He became an itinerant preacher under the tutelage of Bishop Francis Asbury. After the war he settled in Philadelphia but his successes at St. George's Church led to reaction. At a "kneel-in" in a communion service Allen and his associates William White and Absalom Jones were physically removed from the Lord's Table. The independent Free African Society was the result and, with the encouragement of notable whites, Allen persisted in seeing to the development in 1816 of the African Methodist Episcopal church. Another major denomination was the African Methodist Episcopal Zion church, a result of a secession in New York.

Life in these free northern churches paralleled that in white counterparts. The preacher became a man of status. Some experience of freedom and promise came with the presence of these institutions that blacks could in part control. They carried their work briefly into the South, until reaction to slave revolts in 1822 and 1831 led to suppression there. They joined in benevolent endeavors and set up religious presses. For some of them, identification with free America became quite complete. Just before his death in 1831 Allen was to write, "This land, which we have watered with our tears and our blood, is now our mother country."

Northern whites often played games with these churches. Many Protestants encouraged their development because they seemed to portend no harm and because their existence kept blacks from worshipping with white congregations. But others saw that the control of religious institu-

*more
suspicion
in South*

*cotton
gin*

tions represented aspiration and hope and could lead to the sharing of empire. These black churches were watched.

Watching became nearly a full time business in the South, where the career of Africans in America took a new course with the invention of the cotton gin in 1791. Now there was a step-up in plantation development. Slavery was to live on for seven more decades. During those decades religious and racial doctrines developed while whites justified their enslaving activities. In those years it was only natural that the Protestant missions and churches would be the most closely supervised of all black activities and agencies.

In the South, free blacks were eventually not allowed to preach to whites, as a few had done earlier. In many cases, blacks were not to meet except in the presence of a stipulated number of white supervisors. Numerous plantation owners grumbled about the wasted days and dissipating activities they saw to be associated with Sunday trips to towns and churches, so they set up services for blacks on plantations. Great numbers made no spiritual provisions at all. Sometimes this was done through oversight, for early Americans were not always very religious and did not feel it important to impart to others what meant little to them. Just as often blacks were systematically kept from Christianity. It was feared that they would get ideas of freedom if they read about Moses leading God's people out of slavery in Egypt. They would get delusions of pride if they would read St. Paul talking about the equality of bond and free in Christ. How could they be trusted to be content with the biblical passages that allowed for slavery? How could one be sure that they would read the Bible through the Bishop of London's spectacles, so that they would know that freedom for them (unlike that of Moses' people) was to be internal and spiritual only?

Literacy, then, was feared if not always prevented or discouraged. Since few blacks could write or were free to do so, most of our glimpses of plantation religion come through the eyes of those who oppressed them at worst or who were paternalistic at best. "I would that every human being have the gospel preached to them in its original purity and simplicity," said one quotable slaveholder. "It therefore devolves upon me to have these dependants properly instructed in all that pertains to the salvation of their souls." His punch line was revealing: "In view of the fanaticism of the age it behooves the Master or Overseer to be present" whenever religious training was imparted by a "suitable person."

Now and then visitors would report on the charm evident inside paternalistic Protestantism. "Upon one plantation I visited in Mississippi," the visiting agriculturalist Solon Robinson was to report, "I found a most beautiful little Gothic church, and a clergyman furnished with a house, provisions and servants, and a salary of $1,500 a year, to preach to master and slaves." How effective the ministry to slaves was can best be determined by the sense of mystification one slaveowner expressed when after years of orthodox catechism training one of his slaves replied to the question, "In whose image were you made?" "In the image of de debil, master." He had gotten the point not from the catechism but from the ethos that came with his religion. In 1836 a travelling missionary described the end result of oppressive Protestantism: "The Gospel ... teaches [the black] obedience to God, and faithfulness to the interests of his earthly master."

Not always. The Gospel also taught many blacks obedience to God through faithlessness to the interests of earthly masters. Those who feared that the Bible and Protestant prophecy were subversive messages for the blacks were not wholly misguided. Again and again there were slave revolts, and in most cases they were based in part on a reading of biblical passages on freedom. Rebellion in Haiti, the American Revolution, the tantalizing doctrines of equality and freedom dangled by the Declaration of Independence and implied by the Constitution were compared by blacks with the brutal and degrading slave system. Their churches provided catalysts and centers of organization. Late glimpses of white mistrust still came from urban centers in the 1830s and 1840s, after the main slave revolts had been put down. In 1840 New Orleans newspapers printed complaints that a vicious and designing "black fellow in black" held forth with "pernicious doctrines;" six years later the black Protestants were still accused of inflammatory sermons. While the noise of the assemblies was often the superficial basis of grumbling, "*other* and *graver*" reasons having to do with insurrection were at the heart. The great fear, declared a number of Charleston, South Carolina, citizens in 1847, was that religious instruction would give blacks "plenitude of freedom of thought, word and action in the church" so that they would establish "organized community."

These whites spoke out of a quarter-century of experience which had crested early in Charleston with Denmark Vesey's revolt and with Nat Turner's in Southampton, Virginia, in 1831. Even as early as 1800 there had been a revolt near Richmond. Thomas Prosser's slave Gabriel Prosser, who was imitating the biblical Samson, had been taught to read and had read of freedom in the Old Testament. "I had heard in the days of old when the Israelites were in service to King Pharaoh, they were taken from him by the power of God and were carried away by Moses." While God had blessed Moses with an angel to go with him, "I could see nothing of that kind in these days." His revolt was aborted, but its spirit lived on among blacks who in the early nineteenth century were in this respect the most consistent freedom-seeking Protestants on the American scene. Prophecy and protest in explicit biblical terms became part of the program of the discontented.

Denmark Vesey, an enigmatic and violent man, came to hate passive blacks as much as he did oppressing whites. A carpenter who won money in a lottery to purchase his freedom, he used the African Methodist church to spread doctrine and amass organizational support. His group wanted to seize Charleston, but they were betrayed and thirty-seven of them were hanged; more repression followed. In preparing for the insurrection, Vesey had come to an astute understanding of the ambiguity of religious symbols and acts. On the one hand, they could be used for designated causes while, right under the noses of the oppressors, a different hearing could be given the reading of the scriptures and a different use of the religious gatherings could be developed. "And the children of Israel sighed by reason of the bondage, and they cried, . . . And God heard their groaning." But God's people would have to take direct and violent action. "He that is not with me is against me," declared the messianic Vesey. He wanted no one to be spared his wrath, and quoted the Bible in support: "And they utterly destroyed all that was in the city, both man and woman, young and old" (Joshua 6:21).

No less biblical was the rhetoric of Nat Turner, who led the best-known and, to whites, the most threatening of all insurrections. He and sixty followers killed fifty-seven whites in the belief that they were setting in motion a Mosaic activity of liberation. Public reaction in Turner's Virginia matched that in Vesey's Carolina: backlash led to new oppression and an even closer scrutiny of church activities. At a Sunday meeting Nat Turner had been jolted by the preacher's text, "Seek ye first the kingdom of heaven and all these things shall be added unto you." He would devote his life to heaven *and* all things, including freedom for his people. After his escape from slavery he spent thirty days in the woods, praying and reflecting. "I had my wishes directed to the things of the world, and not to the kingdom of heaven . . . I should return to the service of my earthly master." But he moved beyond such servile thoughts and in explicit imitation of biblical protest and revolt he carried on his insurrection until it met its inevitable doom.

On a more intellectual but no less forthright plane, a free black and an advocate of black rebellion, David Walker, published an *Appeal in Four Articles* in Boston in 1828. The pamphlet was disseminated throughout the South, where it produced great fear and reaction. Walker argued his case on American republican grounds, grieving over the respected Thomas Jefferson's inability to assign a rightful place for blacks. Once again: "So far, my brethren, were the Egyptians from heaping these insults upon their slaves, that Pharaoh's daughter took Moses, a son of Israel for her own." Walker derided Americans for calling Turks barbarous while "thousands of them will absolutely beat a colored person nearly to death, if they catch him on his knees, supplicating the throne of grace." While he criticized the Christianity around him, he appealed, "Have we any other master than Jesus Christ? Is he not their master as well as ours?" Some might allow that to be true, but they were less ready for his talk of the land; "This country is as much ours as it is the whites', whether they will admit it or not."

Many of the whites who regarded themselves as humane wanted to preserve a white empire by removing blacks to Africa. The imperial sense was always strong in colonizing activities. The distinguished physician Benjamin Rush hoped that the black Protestant churches he was supporting might "be the means of sending the gospel to Africa, as the American Revolution sent liberty to Europe." But if his was a missionary interest, others saw colonization as a problem-solver for the white empire. Patrick Henry had asked: "Our country will be peopled. The question is, shall it be with Europeans or with Africans?" It did not occur to him or other worriers that a Euro-African or an Afro-European people could intermarry and share the space. Or when it did occur to them, they were frightened. The only prominent advocate of such mingling was Samuel Stanhope Smith, who surprisingly advocated a policy "to bring the two races nearer together, and, in a course of time, to obliterate those distinctions which are now created by a diversity of complexion." Not so liberal was Thomas Jefferson, as he programmed empire for the continent. He looked forward to distant times when "a people speaking the same language, governed in similar forms, and by similar laws" would hold domain, but—speaking of blacks—"we cannot contemplate with satisfaction either blot or mixture on that surface."

The American Colonization Society worked to help Protestants set up the state of Liberia in Africa. Only a few blacks went to live there and by 1831, despite a long afterlife, the policy was regarded as a failure by whites even as it was despised by most blacks. The latter saw it as a "miserable mockery" designed not to benefit the retransplanted blacks but only to "benefit the slaveholding interests of the country," or to get rid of dangerous free blacks.

"I know this scheme is of God," said an advocate. Negro rejoinders, printed in William Lloyd Garrison's *Liberator,* argued otherwise. "Be it known, that we are not all such misguided, deluded mortals as to be duped by your plans." "Make but the attempt in consecrating a portion of your time, talents, and money upon us here, and you would soon find the cause of Africa's injured race vindicated by her descendants." "We consider the United States our home."

Despite the imposed passivity that characterized so much of blacks' lives, they often developed and saw to the retention of religious forms that did minister to their needs. It has often been pointed out that about half of the black leaders whose names are remembered from the early decades in the United States were preachers. The Bible, interpreted Protestant style, was the unifying book and bearer of symbols for the developing black community. "Spirituals," themselves to be interpreted ambiguously—as otherworldly *and* as freedom songs—give some glimpses into that community life.

The emotionalism that whites saw in black religion derived both from the African past and from the evangelical present. The American black was in the empire but he was not free to participate in sharing its benefits. Religion sustained him in his frustration when all seemed hopeless. As a worshipping, suffering, experiencing member of a community he was able to keep alive aspects of Protestant witness which successful and victorious white empire-builders forgot. But the price for both peoples was very high.

At the root of it all was the question of conscience. Ex-slave J. W. C. Pennington, a Presbyterian minister, asked the unanswerable question that troubled the divided Christians: "Who has authorized the division of the church of God into *white* and *black* divisions? I have come in contact with prejudice almost at every step, and God is my record, that I regard the haters of my people only with pity."

The community of reconciliation taught America how to divide, for it was an early agent of segregation in all its forms.

Dr. Hugh Williamson published a justification for making America a white country in 1811. A quintessential Protestant, an American nationalist, an imperialist by instinct, he worried about the black person's presence and used natural philosophy and biblical revelation to make his point to his own satisfaction: climate and environment shaped people. Over a long, long period of time "the constant, universal agency of the God of nature" would alter blacks so that they would become white. America would solve the racial problem by developing whiteness.

Religious support of oppression, in the meantime, led to national tragedy and left scars and open wounds. The slaves kept getting the message of a gospel of freedom, and were able to remember and reproduce what the preachers had told them. But so deep was the division that even death would not end it. A slave remembered that he was told at church, "You slaves will go to heaven if you are good, but don't ever think that you will be close to your mistress and master. No! No! There will be a wall between you; but there will be holes in it that will permit you to look out and see your mistress when she passes by. If you want to sit behind this wall, you must do the language of the text. 'Obey your masters.'"

II · THE LAND

5 · A Charter for Empire

The Civil and Religious Settlement

Religious wars are the bloodiest conflicts. When people invoke the name of God on their side and against the enemy, they tend to license outrage and atrocity. Especially when many religious parties are contending in crusades or to effect change, one expects bloodshed. The American colonists, as they formed the new nation, could have been expected to go through religious wars. Within a half-century they inaugurated one of the most drastic changes in public religion in western history. While the event was not without drama, it occurred without warfare. Few, if any, shots were fired. Not many were imprisoned, harassed, or—except in a couple of colonies—greatly inconvenienced during the time of change.

Shortly before independence, the Americans were still living off a 1,400-year-old charter. This charter went back to the emperor Constantine, in the fourth century; its theoretical base had been provided by St. Augustine. According to this reading, religion was established by law. Establishment meant official favor and status. The government encouraged one religion and discouraged or persecuted all others. The civil authorities saw to it that somehow there would be fiscal support for religious institutions. In turn, the civil powers found that their rule was then blessed by religious authorities. They were able to claim rule "by divine right." In such a combination—and it tended to prevail almost everywhere that Christians were present in any numbers for 1,400 years—the dissenters were either driven out or hemmed in.

Most of the colonists had come to preserve the old way. Even if they had been dissenters in England and even if they came for religious free-

39

[handwritten margin note: dissenters become establishment]

dom for themselves in the New World, most of them soon found that they had become an establishment. They liked what they were. They invited dissenters out of their colonies to a few hostels for troublemakers, like Roger Williams' "Rogue's Island." The dissent that was to cause minor trouble to the new kinds of established churches was often homegrown, the result of revivals and awakenings of religion in the colonies.

[handwritten margin note: ?]

After 1776 and certainly after 1789 it was clear that the two-party system of establishment *versus* dissent within the churches was doomed. Here were thirteen small "nations" becoming one out of many. Nine of them recognized official establishments of religion. All of them had a significant number of dropouts and dissenters. No single church body was strong enough to prevail in the new United States. What some called multiple establishment, official support of several faiths, was soon seen to be unworkable. Only one choice remained. The churches had to be cut off legally and fiscally from support by civil authorities, and many in the churches wanted to prevent the government from disturbing them. The result was the drawing of what James Madison called a "line of separation between the rights of religion and the Civil authority." With disestablishment came "voluntaryism." People could choose a church or choose no church, and churches were put on a pay-as-you-go basis of support by their clients and members.

[handwritten margin note: disestablishment of Maine for details]

Later Americans have taken this solution for granted. It has seemed natural and necessary. Yet the people who effected it must have known that they were innovators. If they were friends of religion they knew some risk was involved in their ventures. The new pattern had been virtually untried. It would have an impact not only on religious institutions but also on government everywhere. Sanford H. Cobb, an expert on the history of religious liberty, claimed that the American pattern of religious freedom was "the most striking contribution of America to the science of government." Many would agree. Because the change has often been described as epochal it has also always been seen as the result of deep struggle. Yet if one looks for religious conflict in American life, it will be found more within the terms of the new charter and not over the adoption of the charter itself.

Old battles, it is true, can look like minor skirmishes to people who did not have to fight them. But the record makes clear that in only three of the thirteen original states was there enough resistance to produce any kind of drama at all. In most other colonies the change was made as if with a sigh of relief, in a spirit of tidying up, and with only whimpers of reaction. One hundred years after the great innovation, in 1888, British visitor Lord Bryce wrote the summary that is so often quoted: "It is accepted as an axiom by all Americans that the civil power ought to be not only neutral and impartial as between different forms of faith, but ought to leave these matters entirely on one side." Less noticed is his next sentence: "There seem to be no two opinions on this subject in the United States."

No two opinions. But there had obviously been at least two interests, proestablishment and prodissent. They somehow had to be fused if there was to be a charter that all Americans could accept. The members of the huge nonchurched majority in the new nation had to find a way to assert their freedom to be neutral and disinterested. The few radically antireligious people had to discover ways to oppose "priestcraft and superstition." On the other hand, the people in the significant churchgoing minority had to find a way to belong to churches without embarrassing themselves or inconveniencing others. And the few passionate defenders of religion needed a formulation which they could endorse enthusiastically. Eventually, all these interests came to be satisfied. Americans succeeded in creating a legal nonestablishment, even as they saw to the development of a *de facto* establishment whose security lay in the ethos, customs, habits, and practices of popular government.

Why, if the change was so great, was it made with such relative ease? The historical record reveals at least four reasons. The first was already implied by the variety of practices prevailing among the thirteen colonies. Indeed, shortly before independence these presented a blur of paradoxes, contradictions, ambiguities, and compromises. Many leaders of official churches openly "connived"—and *they* used the term!—with dissenters to buy off discontent. And dissenters joined with practical politicians to bring about so much change that instability resulted. A new charter was needed if for no other reason than to bring some sort of order out of chaos.

The church leaders were as divided as were civil authorities. There were only about 20,000 Roman Catholics, and Jews made up but one twentieth of 1 per cent of the citizenry. Native Americans and blacks were overlooked. This meant that all the contention was going on between white Protestant heirs of northwest European (and overwhelmingly British) traditions. The evangelicals were simply carving up their own territory. They knew they were in competition and needed ground rules so that competition would not result in conflict. The public needed protection from them. They were in the process of inventing or developing the unit called the denomination which was later to assure that conflict could be channeled into comfortable and secure paths. They needed help from outside to come to the new situation.

James Madison took comfort from the division of the churches. He could see they would not be able to mount warfare against each other. "Security for civil rights must be the same as that for religious rights; it consists in the one case in a multiplicity of interests and in the other in a multiplicity of sects." But if society was safe from the sects, they were not safe from each other. "The sects in this country . . . required . . . more guards against the oppression of each other, than they would in Turkey against the oppression of the Grand Seignior," mourned Daniel Webster. The Great Awakening of the 1730s had demonstrated the need for church leaders to move from colony to colony to carry on their work. In that setting, as in others, it was clear that intrareligious tensions had to be checked in some official and face-saving way. Dissenters were eager for a new charter and many leaders of official churches had no heart to fight them.

To these reasons must be added a third. The churches were very weak and in no position to look for better terms than what they got as the new nation was being formed. While religion was deeply stamped on colonial institutions and minds, few bothered to be observant. Later Americans would often be supplied a mythology which paraded the founders as intense Christians. Citizens were often told that there had been a great fall from a golden age when those who formed the nation had all believed and worshipped passionately. Just the opposite was the case. At no other moment in the 200 years of national experience were religious institutions so weak as they were in the first quarter-century after independence. It is difficult to establish reliable statistics, but some guesses suggest that only about 10 percent of the people were formally church members—about one sixth the figure of twentieth-century America.

Even though few belonged to churches, not many wanted to harm religion. Apathy, not antipathy, was the rule. Those who fought the establishment in Virginia were often so lackadaisical that they had to be coached and even provided with sectarian names when they came to register their dissent. The colonial and revolutionary wars had taken their toll. People were preoccupied with nonreligious aspects of nation-building. Mild forms of deism and similar kinds of thought were imported as novelties from Europe. Their respectability in the circles of the nation's founders demonstrates the fact that then—as never again—the support of heresy or dropping out of conventional religious institutions were not acts that brought political liabilities. Thomas Jefferson, James Madison, George Washington, Benjamin Franklin, and most of their colleagues and peers were quite discontented with orthodox Protestant teaching and practice.

Religion and the churches did survive, however, and they did produce some people who cared about a charter for religious freedom and expansion. With the revivals that began around 1801, many more were to care much more. And these second-generation citizens found the patterns of disestablishment and voluntaryism to be congenial and useful. One reason for this was that the new charters carried over much of the religious heritage of colonial dissent. There was, in short, a Protestant theological base for the new nation's formulas and, while few had stood on that base before nationhood, most American Protestants did so in the nineteenth century.

Put most simply, people who shared this religious point of view came

to the issue of disestablishment for an opposite reason to that advocated
by Jefferson. Whereas Jefferson wanted a line drawn to keep clerics from
meddling in civil matters, those in the lineage of Roger Williams wanted
to be sure that civil authorities would have no say in matters of conscience
and belief. The clergy won most: it has been more difficult for government
to intrude on religion than for clerics to intrude on civil territory. Roger
Williams dreamed of the day when God would restore His garden (the
church) and paradise; if so, "it must of necessity be walled in peculiarly
unto Himself from the world." Not all of Williams' expressions were so
defensive; he and many other colonial dissenters also often spoke in positive terms of religious freedom for the sake of the world.

A review of the way change was brought about in the various colonies
and later in the states reveals little drama—if one brackets and isolates the
special case of Virginia. Often overlooked is the fact that the real innovation had gone on long before in the four colonies that never had established the church. Rhode Island, Delaware, Pennsylvania, and New Jersey
had always seen themselves as hosts to dissent and to varieties of religion.
Not that their leaders were wholly secular in their outlook. Some, like William Penn and the Quakers in Pennsylvania, seem to have thought that the
religion of the pure spirit would soon overwhelm people—that people of
good will, given a good reception in Quakerdom, would soon become
Quakers. But no matter on what grounds, these four colonies did not find
it necessary to support the 1,400-year-old Christian practices.

In addition to these four colonies, a number of others either removed
civil support from religion or set up multiple establishments well before
the time of Virginia's final controversies. Such was the case in Maryland,
North Carolina, Vermont, and South Carolina, although in South Carolina's
constitution of 1778 it was declared that "the Christian Protestant religion
shall be deemed, and is hereby constituted and declared to be, the established religion of this State." In New York the final outcome had been
assured as early as 1752 and 1753 when some lawyers resisted efforts to
give the Church of England privileges there.

Three colonies kept their official arrangements until well into the nineteenth century. New Hampshire, after some tension, made the change in
1819, a year after Connecticut made its move toward disestablishment. The
last gasp was, appropriately, in Massachusetts. This most rigorous theocracy had also been the first. The establishment lived there for 203 years.
Massachusetts' religion experienced few assaults from infidels outside the
gates. Internal difficulties helped bring about the eventual end. For decades before the end, the Massachusetts version had been so congenial and
compromising that the establishment no longer provided much of a target
for anticlerical or dissenting opposition. As the old churches turned from
trinitarian congregational orthodoxy to Unitarianism, the old defenders
came to see that state support went to heresy and they, too, lost taste for

such support. The ease of the delayed victory was visible in the voting: 348 to 93 in the House, for example, in 1831, and 32,234 to 3,273 when the public was asked to ratify disestablishment.

When new states were formed, they followed the experience of those which had come to voluntaryism in religion; thus Ohio's Constitution in 1802 argued "that all men have a natural and indefeasible right to worship Almighty God according to the dictates of conscience." No person "shall be compelled to attend, erect or support any place of worship, or to maintain any ministry against his consent."

What drama or conflict there was, then, must be found in Virginia. This struggle has taken on epochal dimensions because its chief agents chose to see it that way. They came to operate with the serene confidence that two thirds of the Virginians would side with dissent. The established church, never strong or too wellstaffed and thousands of miles away from a rather heedless bishop, had become very unpopular because so many of its clergy had chosen to side with the king during the revolution.

The strongest support for continuing the old official status for a minority church did not come from the clergy. Not one ordained minister is regularly remembered as having spoken up forcefully and from the front ranks during the controversy. Instead, numbers of laity who associated that church with their way of life, with privilege, with venerated ways of doing things, stated the case. Some, like Patrick Henry, the last great diehard, were genuinely concerned about the low estate of religion in Virginia and seemed to fear that removal of civil props would mean the demise of the church. To a lesser extent, a mildly impassioned George Washington was also reluctant to see the end of privilege.

New forces were on the scene in Virginia, however. During the Great Awakening of the 1730s and 1740s, dissenters from New England came down to begin work in a new backwoods. Many of them were revivalist in approach and fervid in temper and manner. They were sincerely committed to a theology of religious freedom and were personally inconvenienced by the old order. When prerevolutionary political issues came to the fore, religion was always tangled up with them and dissenters exploited them. In 1759 the Two-Penny Act was the tinder. Anglican ministers saw their salaries slightly cut into, and protested. The Bishop of London wrote in their support, blaming dissenters for attempting to "lessen the influence of the crown and the maintenance of the clergy." That triggered reaction. "The preservation of the community is to be preferred" even to the preservation of established clerics.

The Virginia transition is remembered as a deep conflict not only because of the records left by frustrated dissenters, but also because of the passionate involvement of gifted leaders like Thomas Jefferson and James Madison. While their official documents are classics of restraint and eloquence, their private words were often angry. Jefferson, a nominal Anglican, remembered the battles after the Virginia Constitutional Convention of 1776 as "the severest contests in which I have ever been engaged," because although "the majority of our citizens were dissenters . . . a majority of the legislature were church men." Until the end of his days he could speak of the clergy as being tyrannical and ambitious, hierophantic and prone to persecute others. Madison knew that some dissenters were in jail and shrieked about the "diabolical Hell conceived principle of persecution" that was raging. Madison, it must be remembered, was more congenial to traditional Christianity than Jefferson, but he could not endure religious intolerance.

The Virginia citadel, then, was being subverted from within by dissenting parsons and laypersons and from without by "infidel" political leaders. For the sake of understanding the nineteenth-century uses of the charter by evangelicals, it is important to note the quality and character of the sentiments described as infidelity by their foreparents. Many of the Virginia leaders were attracted to a kind of thought associated with the Enlightenment, a genial and tolerant deism. They believed in a divine order in the universe, in natural law and natural rights, and in the moral significance of acts for which people would be rewarded or punished. They cared less for revealed religion, miracles, and the supernatural. A familiar phrase came up in their regular advocacy of "reasonable Christianity."

Jefferson was most militant against orthodoxy and sectarianism, but he spent evenings cutting and pasting moral and nonmiraculous elements of the Gospels together in a multilingual *The Life and Morals of Jesus of Nazareth*—while in the White House! James Madison, angry as he was over diabolical persecution, had been formed in part by Protestant teachings on religious freedom and remained a nominal Christian. George Washington seemed to want to avoid explicit reference to Christian doctrines, but he saw himself as religious and remained a vestryman and even a mild defender of establishment.

These Virginians were heirs of a specific kind of Enlightenment. Theirs was moderate, shaped by Protestant Christianity, not informed by a long history of anticlericalism as Voltaire's or D'Holbach's was in France. They were not so skeptical as David Hume in England. While the deist fashion was to decline with American reaction to French revolutionary excesses and was to be swept away when the new revivals began at the turn of the century, it surfaced just long enough to make possible the introduction of some needed language of natural rights into America's charter documents.

Dissent was often very orthodox and deism was obviously very heterodox. But the two formed a not uneasy if temporary alliance to effect change. The most noted infidel and the most active dissenting clergy spoke in similar terms. Thomas Jefferson could say, "It does me no injury for my neighbor to say there are twenty gods, or no god. It neither picks my pocket nor breaks my leg." His preacher-cohort John Leland defended the First Amendment because it permitted "every man [to] speak freely without fear, maintaining the principles that he believes, [and to] worship according to his own faith either one god, three gods or no god or twenty gods, and let government protect him in doing so."

Dissenters and deists were allied with most of the people, but there was residual defense of establishment in the Virginia legislature, and ten years were to pass before it collapsed entirely. In the Virginia Constitution of 1776, after Jefferson's strong draft of an article was rejected, a Declaration of Rights by George Mason was incorporated. One can learn the tendency from it, but handwriting on the wall is one thing and handwriting in the lawbooks is another, so men sought legal change. On December 5, 1776, dissenters were exempted from supporting the established church; the fiscal beginning of the end had come. The act was endorsed in 1777 and 1778 and made permanent in 1779, one year before dissenting ministers were granted the right to perform weddings.

Not all was clear even then. Jefferson's Bill for Establishing Religious Freedom of 1779 did not meet ready acceptance, and in 1784 counterforces almost succeeded in introducing a tax for teachers of religion. This would have led to a kind of multiple establishment. When Jefferson went to France, Madison had to take over the leadership. His Memorial and Remonstrance has rightly earned fame. Its fifteen articles against the assessment bill are full of both practical matters and arguments based on ideals and ideas. Even Madison noted that "a considerable portion of the old hierarchy" hurried to sign up with him when he reintroduced Jefferson's bill and saw victory on December 17, 1785. It became law on January 19, 1786. Only negligible vestiges of establishment remained, and legislative acts in 1802 renewed these. Patrick Henry had fought for "the old hierarchy," which lacked an effective legislative mouthpiece when he became governor. Although Massachusetts' final action was forty-seven years in the future, after Virginia one can say that the charter had been completed.

The evangelical empire-builders in the early nineteenth century built on it at once. They were pleased to see that the Declaration of Independence, now being enshrined in national lore, included references to "Nature's God," the "Creator," the "Supreme Judge of the World," and "Divine Providence." While the author did not mean what revivalists meant, these Protestants could easily translate to their own satisfaction. The United States Constitution was part of the charter. New and radical in that it was silent about commitment to God, only a clause forbidding religious tests for public office was included. The Constitution was supplemented by a First Amendment which forbade federal establishment of religion and guaranteed free exercise of religion. The national seal blended traces of Judeo-Christian religion with other symbols. The new flag, it has been pointed out, was startling and novel because it lacked explicit religious symbols like crosses or fasces. Soon this flag was taken into the churches' shrines.

A *de facto* establishment grew where the old legal one had fallen. Later Americans of many persuasions from antireligious to fanatically proreligious have lived with and claimed the charter. As late as 1892 Supreme Court Justice Brewer could say, "This is a Christian nation," but as early as 1796 in a treaty with Tripoli the administration had said that "the government of the United States of America is not in any sense founded on the Christian religion." Even within a single document the two interests relating to the one opinion coexisted. The Supreme Court of Maine in 1854 declared that the state "knows no religion" and cited eight religions to prove that all possessed equal rights—but then went on to uphold the reading of the Protestant King James Version of the scriptures in public schools, even though Catholics were protesting the practice. Daniel Webster said that "Christianity—general tolerant Christianity—Christianity independent of sects and parties—that Christianity to which the sword and the fagot are unknown . . . is the law of the land," even though the authors of that law had studiously avoided Christian reference.

The antireligious have been relatively secure because of legal disestablishment and freedom to be nonreligious. The religious have been secure because of *de facto* establishment in an ethos that has transformed the founding documents and translated a charter. The evangelicals who built an empire in America could not have asked for more. There was little occasion for anticlericalism. No other minority was receiving special favors. Protestants could compete with each other without danger to society. They could even yield on some issues (like the "Jew-clauses" in state constitutions and blasphemy laws) because they had so much else working in their favor.

Protestants had provided many bases and roots for religious freedom; many of their fathers had been either dissenters or acquiescent "old hierarchs." The deists had disappeared and the spirit of fervent religion was sweeping the land. Most of all, as not a few believers pointed out, the new charter worked. Churches, thrown on their own resources, were much more effective than those had been which depended upon the largesse of civil authorities and the grudging assent of the citizenry. Had they read the charter closely, they would have found many uncomfortable ideas. But for the new day, effects were to matter more than ideas, and ideas could be transformed. Indeed, they were.

6 · Enlarging the Territory

From East to West

The few Protestant church members in the first generation after independence devoted their energies to survival, regrouping, and writing or understanding their charter. This charter freed them from the control of civil authority, and, in effect, licensed them to compete with each other on equal terms. By almost any standard of measurement, religious institutions were at their lowest ebb in the first decades of national life, commanding the devoted attention of only the approximately ten percent of the people who were church members.

In the second generation, all this was changed. Having a charter, the leaders began to use it to rouse people from apathy and to build community. A strong sense of place was fused with their sense of mission and destiny. As had their predecessors, they regularly resorted to scriptural imagery to define themselves. In the colonial era the image of the wilderness prevailed. Now the familiar term was "the Promised Land," and they were the Israelites who were called to conquer it.

Lyman Beecher, spokesman for so much of evangelicalism in this era, wrote *A Plea for the West* at the end of the generation, in 1835. His text was from Isaiah 66:8: "Who hath heard such a thing? who hath seen such things? Shall the earth be made to bring forth in one day? Or shall a nation be born at once? for as soon as Zion travailed, she brought forth her children." So successful were the orthodox at making the identification with Israel that the larger literary community was able to build on it. Herman Melville could expect assent when he, far from conventional Protestantism, would remind readers: "We Americans are the peculiar, chosen people—the Israel of our time; we bear the ark of the liberties of the world."

At times the Americans were generous; sure that they were chosen, they would ask, "chosen along with whom?" The answers were ambiguous. The only other contenders were Protestants of northwest Europe and England, the people who helped make up what many of them called (after 1843, when the term entered currency) western civilization. On racial, religious, and historic grounds England was most favored, even though the United States was to fight it in 1812.

48

One of the best known and certainly most representative attempts to keep the North Atlantic ideal alive in Protestant mission was a correspondence in the *Home Missionary* of June 1849. The author surveyed a half-century of achievement and saw the growing ascendancy of England in China and the Asiatic islands just as Americans were reaching California; the pincers movement "completes the control of the four great coast lines of the northern hemisphere, by two Protestant nations, speaking the same language, and one in all the great features of their character." He linked this to the contemporaneous rise of steam and commerce, and hoped that people would see that "herein a great trust is committed to us by Providence, for the benefit of a new empire." God had kept the Pacific world "for a people of the Pilgrim blood; He would not permit any other to be fully developed there." The biblical cadences rang again and again: "In the fulness of time, when a Protestant people" had been brought to the continent, God committed the shores to England and America. Needless to say, England was secondary in the evangelicals' thinking. But the more thoughtful of them, when they reflected on the task of winning a world, looked for whatever help they could get.

Much had to happen to give plausibility to such talk by the people of the 1840s. The *Home Missionary* writer referred to one cluster of events: the development of new means of transportation and communication, the rise of industrialism, and the impetus for world commerce. With these came also the need for an opened American West. Land was provided through the Northwest Ordinance of 1787, although not many moved into the upper Midwest until after the battle of Fallen Timbers in Ohio in 1794, when the Indian threat was beginning to be removed. The Louisiana Purchase in 1803 added millions of acres to the territory. From the mid-South, settlers began the trek to the Southwest, to West Virginia, Kentucky, Tennessee, and beyond. From New England and the middle colonies the migration moved across Ohio, Indiana, Illinois, and across the Mississippi. Through ports like Baltimore and New Orleans thousands and thousands of new immigrants would come from Britain or European inlands to the American inland without a coastal interim. In 1790, 94 percent of the people lived in the original thirteen colonies; in 1850, about half of them did.

To these factors must be added a third, the rise in Protestantism's consciousness of a worldwide mission. From Protestant beginnings in 1517 to about 1792, thought about missions or expansion on the part of reformed Christians was rare, and action taken in support of such thought was even rarer. The continental movement called Pietism had inspired a few forays into India and elsewhere early in the eighteenth century, but these were slowed as Pietism waned. And the Enlightenment and rationalism sapped churchly energies by calling into question the idea of intruding on the areas of other religions.

Suddenly, just as the American chosen people were asking what were the uses of chosenness, Protestantism was inspired with a desire to convert people, to spread its civilization, to expand and conquer. The evangelical awakenings uniformly inspired them to share the saving word of Christ's Gospel, and new developments in transportation made their dreams feasible. The movement is usually dated from the impulse of a British layperson, William Carey, who felt called in 1792. Exactly ten years later an American young man, Samuel Mills, was the first to experience a similar call and ten years after that, in 1812, with the effort of Adoniram Judson in Burma, American evangelicals joined the movement to send missionaries.

The means were there, and two milieux, the American West and the rest of the world, were ready. For the tiny minority of active Protestants in America to take on the new tasks, a grand concept was necessary. They found it in the idea of empire, which was a kind of public and semipolitical counterpart to the religious ideal of the Kingdom of God. The reality of empire had to be tied very closely to the formation of a strong national unity. Few men had anticipated such unity; in England, Dean Josiah Tucker rejected the idea: as far as the future of the grandeur of America was concerned, "its being a rising empire under one head . . . is one of the idlest and most visionary notions that ever was conceived, even by writers of romance." He was sure that when people thought of the immense regions to be conquered, they would come to consider "the highest probability that the Americans never can be united into one compact empire under any species of government whatever. Their fate seems to be . . . a disunited people till the end of time." The evangelicals did not accept such terms; they saw themselves as agents of one nation, one people, having, as Princeton's Charles Hodge put it in 1829, "one language, one literature, essentially one religion, and one common soul." How could they help but exert "a greater influence on the human family than any other nation that has ever existed"?

This nation was, of course, "the principal nation of the Reformation," as Jonathan Edwards, the colonies' greatest theologian, had seen it. In new ways churches and nation were bonded; the editor of *Harper's New Monthly Magazine* wrote in 1858, a century after Edwards: "A national Church is one thing, a national Religion is quite another; and in nothing are they more unlike than in their capacity to awaken the sense of Providence in the breast of a people." The churches were assigned a specialized role, while "a national Religion," Protestant in provenance and tone, would take care of Providence and the people.

The unlikely troubadour who celebrated the rise of this bonded empire was the pretentious president of Yale College, Timothy Dwight, who in *The Columbian Muse* in 1794 wrote:

As the day-spring unbounded, thy splendour shall flow,
And earth's little kingdoms before thee shall bow;
While the ensigns of union, in triumph unfurl'd,
Hush the tumult of war, and give peace to the world.

"The influence of the Old World has been frittered away," argued Charles Hodge, "from the fact that it has never had Unity." European power passing into American Protestant hands "comes to *one people.*" Lyman Beecher's son Edward asked how a social architect might create "not the infidel or transcendental millennium," but the "true, Protestant, scriptural" paradise on earth. The implied answer lay in the simplicity of American political and religious institutions. "Every thing . . . will be simplified." The scholarly Baptist minister William R. Williams in 1836 pointed his readers to this unified, simple base for empire in "the expansive and self-sustaining energies of the gospel." Not military or political impositions but "the evangelical character of our land is to tell upon the plans and destinies of other nations."

Admittedly, these leaders represented an evangelical oligarchy. They were poor reporters; the states were struggling with the concept of national unity and the churches were more divided in the United States than anywhere else in the world. But they were cheerleaders, coaches, and prophets, pointing a direction—and for decades they were well on their way to providing it. The means, as cleric Horace Bushnell, one of their greatest leaders, kept reminding them (in *Barbarism, the First Danger*) was "to fill this great field with Christian churches and a Christian people." This would "present mankind the spectacle of . . . a religious nation." The purpose of it all, wrote Calvin Colton, a politician who had been a cleric, was "to *reduce* the world, and the whole world, by a system of moral means and agencies." For once, *The Home Missionary* reminded readers in 1845, an empire was making its conquest peaceably. "The past history of the world has been that of wars and animosities. When converted to God, it will be the unfoldings of Christian love. The transforming process is going on. Who would not be an actor in it?"

People of such self-confidence needed a firm sense of the superiority of their religion and their culture. That they thought their religion to be superior is a fact which needs no documentation. When people go out to all the world as missionaries, in the spirit in which these were sent, and with full knowledge that other religions prevailed in that world, they certainly needed a negative view of those religions and a supremely positive view of their own. Their sermons, tracts, pamphlets, and letters constantly focus on that theme.

Cultural superiority was closely related to the spiritual claim. Christianity—Protestantism—in the hands of Anglo-Saxons purged by the American ordeal, was perfectly poised for an imperial spread. While not a few of the clerical and lay leaders were aware of American inadequacies in the artistic and literary realm, they shrugged these off as being secondary in Christ's empire. Aware of moral faults, they used the missionary mandate as a motive for citizens to correct these in order to keep their credentials in order.

The sociopolitical realm was the sign of cultural superiority. Here in America were free institutions which allowed for the opportunity of free people. Not a few used the model of New England, whether or not that had been their base, and enlarged on it for all humanity. The historian Hollis Read (1850) saw that the Puritan element was softening, melting, and fusing the rough-and-tumble people of the American West's varieties and "running them into the New England mould." *The Home Missionary* editors wanted "a large portion of those Western states" to be made to become "what New England is now (and if so much, then much more) a land of churches, and schools, and charities, of pious homes, and great religious enterprises. The world is to be converted at the West."

If one's own model was superior, that meant that all others were inferior. The leaders had little difficulty inspiring the masses who were joining their churches to see that. Both the American West and the world left much to be desired. The West, for all its varieties, was pictured as a kind of spiritual vacuum, to be filled by those who got there first with the most and who worked most strenuously to win people. The West, in the earlier decades of the national period, was still described as a wilderness, full of dark terrors and threatening natives. By the time of the Jacksonian years, the natives in these descriptions had been mysteriously replaced by Catholics and infidels. Of Catholics there were few, since the Irish immigrants were attracted to industry, and for the moment that was concentrated in Boston, New York, and other eastern cities. The Germans did not want to and could not compete with slave labor in the South and so settled in the upper Midwest, where they were soon to share most features of the Anglo-American evangelical empire except its language.

Conservatives like Samuel F. B. Morse, moderates like Lyman Beecher, and liberals like Horace Bushnell joined in the massive Protestant attempt to make a bogey out of the minuscule Catholic presence. The evangelicals were constantly hearing rumors that the Pope was to concentrate Roman energies on winning the West, having failed so miserably in the original thirteen colonies. They were glad to pass these rumors on, for those who heard them were then better prepared to pay for and staff the new missions and churches of the West. The American Bible Society urged evangelicals to counter "His Holiness, the Pope [who] had, with eager grasp, already fixed upon" the Southwest.

No less ominous and almost as invisible as the Catholics were the infidels—that ragged band of village atheists, stray French utopians, maverick freethinkers, and other dropouts—who were lifted out of insignificance by the evangelists who had to raise money to fight off the first danger, barbarism. In 1829, the leader of the Disciples of Christ, Alexander Campbell, debated the socialist Robert Owen in what was then a citadel of the new West, Cincinnati; national publicity served to notify Protestants that Owen and his kind were out to subvert the Christian empire. Wherever Lyman Beecher looked in the West he spotted infidels, and Prairiedom's Primate, the colorful evangelist Peter Cartwright, entertained and inspired people by his accounts of physical bouts with blasphemers and infidels.

In 1855 Edward Beecher summarized the half-century of endeavor in a philosophy of history which proved that the West would be "the field of Armageddon," the "Waterloo conflict of the globe," the "one more conflict, and that the last." Good and evil would collide in the West, and at the right time Puritanism and God would link forces to smite evil so that "its convulsive dying agonies" would be felt in every land. "This work belongs to God alone; it is his last and greatest work before he reigns on earth."

"Every land." "Earth." Those terms reminded the evangelists and special pleaders for empire that they and their followers were confronted by evil and unbelief in the systems of bad religion all around the world. The impression of other religions' inferiority was stamped on people's minds and remained effective. The advance guard of missionaries—like the sacrificial and well-intentioned Adoniram Judsons—would make the first American cultural contact with a new Asian or African nation. In the Judsons' case, it was with Burma. At the beginning they would be lonely and friendless, heroic but still frightened strangers in a land that was full of people who were at first uncomprehending and later hostile.

These missionaries would meet frustration; it might take years before they would make their first converts. In the meantime, a stream of letters to the sending agencies and other folks back home would describe the obvious evils in unreformed world religions. Adoniram Judson's wife Ann spoke of the Burmese, for instance, as "heathen," "sunk in the grossest idolatry," beyond the reach of Christian principles that could have lifted them above the "wicked inclinations of their depraved hearts." They are "given to every sin. Lying is . . . common and universal." These evils would be formalized and exaggerated through repetition—nineteenth-century tracts and sermons often make lurid reading on these themes. The missionaries, and again Judson was typical, would meet misfortune. Sometimes as a result of antiimperial military conflict, sometimes through counterreligious reaction, and just as often for trivial or incomprehensible reasons, the missionary would be persecuted or jailed. His wife would report back on "the diabolical cruelty" of the jailers. Frustration over failure led to rage and abuse on the part of missionaries, whose weapons were words. The picture of others' cultural inferiority was thus deeply impressed.

Later visitors, whether for commercial, scientific, or even partly self-critical missionary reasons, often came upon the scenes and, in taking a second look, began to see nonwestern cultures from within, as it were. Their more positive appraisals could never catch up with or counteract the original, more negative, pictures that had already come to be accepted. This pattern of rejection was later still to have import for American foreign policy. At the moment, isolated as East was from West, its impact was strongest on motivation for carrying Christianity into all the world.

With a West and a world to win, the representatives of evangelical empire had several needs, all of them easily fulfilled. First was an appropriate ideology or theology. They found this in a rather simple adaptation of the older Calvinism, or in another system which many called Arminianism. The then-current version of American Arminianism had arrived chiefly through the influence of the Wesleyans, who were stressing God's benevolence, humanity's freedom to respond to God, and the fact that Christ had died for all—not just for the elect. Such a theology committed people to evangelism and activism. Like the relaxed Calvinism of the period, it provided a large role for human participation in the divine plan. Those who huddled with Samuel Mills under a haystack during a storm near Williams College condensed the necessary element of this theology in a simple phrase: "We can do it if we will." The Haystack group, as these pioneers came to be called, never meant to arrogate to themselves the initiative in history. They had a strong sense of Providence and divine purpose. But their approach to religious thought allowed much human cooperation. It honored those who responded, were converted, and undertook action in line with the plan of God.

Later scholars have seen the cultural and social effects of their work to be so obvious that they find difficulty recalling that at the heart of the endeavor was the equally simple goal: to save souls. The sense that they were involved in a transaction with God over the fate of humans in the face of heaven and hell was overpowering to them. All the rest—education, health, charity, cultural benefits, civilization, nationalism—was secondary. But these ideas of conversion and salvation were held by people whose bodies occupied space in the world, whose activities were influenced by the civil order, and who came to care greatly about the secondary effects. Where once upon a time Calvinism had provided the integrating context for all of life, now the American civilization itself was beginning to do this. All great eras of prosperity to the church, commented Lyman Beecher as he studied Isaiah 66:8, "have been aided by the civil conditions of the world." "There is not a nation upon earth which, in fifty years, can by all possible reformation place itself in circumstances so favorable as our own for the free and unembarrassed operation of physical effort and pecuniary and moral power to evangelize the world."

To evangelize the world—that was the great goal of empire. Once a theology had been fashioned or, better, while it was emerging in a course of action, energies and activities had to be summoned. Ministers, fundraisers, foreign missionaries, heads of benevolent societies, revivalists, and circuit riders were the new heroes of kingdom and empire. Some leaned toward the extravagant in their language. The biographer of one of these in 1853 wrote that the circuit rider merited "a veneration second only to that [accorded to] the Saviour."

These agents could not, of course, undertake their work without extraordinary means of support. In 1801 the two New England old-line denominations overcame their hostilities enough to form a Plan of Union which lasted until 1852. It was directed toward joint work for extending the evangelical realm. The years between 1801 and 1852 saw the rise of a network of interdenominational and often laity-led societies for home and foreign missions and, later, denominational replacements or competitors. These societies showed great innovative spirit in their means of raising funds and attracting people to represent the cause. During these decades women won their way into minimal acceptability. At first they were allowed to raise funds. Later they were cast in heroic molds as missionary wives and widows. By midcentury some of them were allowed specialized forms of representing the mission overseas.

The bastions or citadels for the expanding empire were often the new colleges. Many well-reputed liberal arts colleges west of the Alleghenies served to keep the faith pure, to encourage learning, and to represent evangelical values. DePauw, Oberlin, Knox, Denison, Wabash, and scores of other western schools were founded to match eastern counterparts like Amherst, Williams, Colgate, and other colleges founded for evangelical purposes. The quality of western society, it was argued, exposed it to "vehement and brief excitements, to epidemic delusions and agitation," to demagogues "not only in politics, but in religion and all social interests." Colleges were to provide "principles of stability" and constant influences, according to a report in 1855. They did so by blending ministerial training with what today would be recognized as, in outline, the curriculum of a liberal arts college.

To many people the most dazzling and the most puzzling achievement was the ability of evangelicals to keep their eye on the West and the world at the same moment. Starting from a small base in the population, preoccupied with surviving and developing forms and theology, they were concerned not to see the empire divided spiritually between home and foreign missions. At the root was the genuine desire to see *all* people saved, however pretentious it might seem to set out on such a goal. The two aspects of empire were in constant interplay. When work among native Americans became unattractive, many were drawn to the glamor of foreign fields. On the other hand, foreign work served to build up the home front.

The leaders would welcome support for any field: *"Christians of our country are more ready to contribute donations for the heathen than to labor in connection with Tract distribution for souls at home . . . ,"* complained the American Tract Society in 1835. But this kind of language was balanced just as often by reports that on the whole support for the two fields grew together. Lyman Beecher coauthored an appeal for missions which almost overlooked the pagans: "The direct and powerful effect of foreign missions has been to give estimation and extent to the institutions of religion in our own land." A Reverend Henry Mandeville spoke (in 1847) of "The Reflex Influence of Foreign Missions." This reflex "electrifies the whole man" and "creates a difference between him and other Christians." "Unity of spirit" then begot "union of effort, and union of effort" reacted to strengthen the unity of spirit that gave it birth.

Any movement so magnificent in scale as this expansive endeavor was destined to face problems. Most of them came from within, for few in the West bothered to oppose these combined religious forces from outside. The world religions were in a somewhat quiescent stage during the high decades of missionary endeavor.

One group of western Protestants called themselves antimissionary, and thus represented to others the highest kind of heresy. They opposed expansion for a variety of reasons. Some were put off by the enthusiasms which accompanied the easterners' efforts to promote mission. Some were Calvinist and felt that God would save those he wanted to save, whether humans made efforts or not. More were primitivists, who were mistrustful of the educated clergy who manned many outposts. Most of all, they united in their opposition to "human agencies" and organizations which united the local churches, entities which they thought should be fiercely independent of each other. One Illinois Association in 1830 declared "an unfellowship with . . . missionary institutions." Antimission forces remained generally small.

Inner competition worked both ways: sometimes it stimulated the mission and sometimes it offended people and kept them at a distance. The language of competition was virulent. But the churches could unite against common enemies, and their sages saw unities in the "common religion" of the Protestant nation.

The characteristic spirit of competition followed James B. Finley's lines: "I plainly told my brethren I had nothing against the Presbyterians; I loved them, but I loved Methodism more, and as we had a shop of our own, we would not work journey-work any longer." The competition was a sign of success and success stimulated more competition. By 1837 many interdenominational agencies were falling apart. Each group wanted to be in on the harvest in these rich fields, each wanted a cut of the pie, a place for the towers of empire, a share of the hearts and minds of the people.

The deepest division in the empire was one over which evangelicals could not have full control, nor was it stimulated by their religious enemies. While East and West were increasingly interactive, North and South were dividing during the peak years of evangelical empire-building. The Reverend James D. Knowles preached a Fourth of July sermon in 1828, one which set the stage for a new act in the empire. He worried over the sectional feelings which were sometimes more powerful than patriotism and asked: "Could local jealousies and jarring worldly interests ever lead the disciples of Christ to think of each other as enemies?" Could Christians in Missouri and Alabama ever imaginably "willingly consent to a dissolution of the national compact" and, worse, "meet each other with hostile bayonets in the field"?

They could and did, with benefit of clergy.

7 · Dividing the Territory

North and South

The evangelical empire was fatefully divided on geographical lines. That there were strong bonds between religion and localism is not surprising. Religious defenses of the way of life of various states or even of regions in the new nation were common. Practical interests also caused people to see the Protestant kingdom as divided geographically. There was always tension between the westerner, who was facing new territory, and the more settled eastern dweller.

In no case did regional tensions interrupt the forward movement of the Protestant empire so much as they did when the North and the South went their separate ways. The early nineteenth century saw a progressive worsening of relations between these sections. At every step along the way religious arguments were invoked and Christian symbols were used to identify God's part in separate causes.

An initial glance at the end of the period, marked by the beginning of the War Between the States, reveals two ways in which religion was implicated. On the one hand, it was used to charter an ideological base for the two-nations idea. A typical expression came from Benjamin M. Palmer, a leading secessionist cleric, who like most of his colleagues saw messianic purpose in southern separation. If the South "has the grace given her to know her hour she will save herself, the country, and the world." In another message he urged: "We have vainly read the history of our fathers, if we failed to see that from the beginning two nations were in the American womb."

Associated with the theological argument was a practical one. Just as some imperialists had argued that colonization could take blacks back to Africa as missionaries, so now some found virtue in the necessity of separation. The New Orleans branch of the Young Men's Christian Association in 1861 asked its northern counterparts, "Has it not occurred to you, brethren, that the hand of God MAY BE in this political division, that both governments may effectually work out His designs in the regeneration of the World?"

Two nations in one American womb, both working for world regeneration—such a concept had not dominated either the political or religious leaders of the late eighteenth century. Its development became an early-nineteenth-century obsession, and the states that were to become part of the Confederacy plus some border states were full of ministers who made their contribution to it. In this instance as in so many others, religion served to justify a people's course of action, and its symbols gave legitimacy to their particular purposes. Even the most sacred imagery could be introduced, sometimes to a nearly humorous effect, as in the instance of the Tennessee preacher who reminded his hearers that Jesus Christ himself (a Judean) was a southern man, as were all of his apostles, who seemed like authentic Confederates. There was one exception: the northern betrayer, Judas Iscariot.

The consequence of the two-nations theory for the Protestant empire was temporarily devastating. One set of symbols was being employed by the two sides. There was one Bible, one heaven, one hell, one Jesus Christ, one path of salvation. Yet this set was used for opposite causes. Thoughtful people were disturbed over the weakening of confidence in the truth of a religion that could be devoted to such mutually contradictory purposes. How could God be the God of the South against the North and of the North against the South? How could he have chartered slavery, as southerners were to see it, and opposed slavery, as northerners often contended? How could he have invested his truth in the system of southern orthodoxy on the one hand and in the patterns of northern experiment and development on the other?

Two whole styles of ecclesiology began to emerge within the evangelical empire as two sets of people, with the help of clerical sanctions, set out to divide the territory. The sequence of steps by which southern religion developed demonstrates the degree to which evangelicalism was threatened and tested.

The first chronological step in the rise of southern national religion involved rejection of one of the roots of the South and the nation. The broad and relaxed semideist thought associated with "the American Enlightenment," the working faith of many founders from the South and the religious rationale for many American institutions, had to be opposed and finally to be destroyed.

Tidewater Virginia had to be forgotten. Not that all old Virginians were deists or heresiarchs. To some later historians, in fact, people like Thomas Jefferson, George Washington, and James Madison have appeared as mavericks or mutations against the background of appallingly ignorant and dreadfully backward Virginia neighbors and their parsons. To some extent this may be true, especially when one remembers that all people of genius are mutations and mavericks. Still, at the time of the founding of the nation, there was at least as much expression of heterodox Protestant philosophy in Virginia as there was anywhere in the North.

When reaction to deistic thought came with the rise of new revivals, not a few northern Federalists set out to make the point that the Enlightenment lived on chiefly in the South. Thomas Jefferson, the infidel, was a living example, as was his friend Thomas Cooper. Not only did infidelity survive on the coast, it was making its way west into what some came to call "liberal Kentucky." Numerous infidels and Unitarians were spotted around Lexington in the last decade of the eighteenth century. In 1794 a Baptist of Unitarian tendency, Harry Toulmin, became president of Transylvania University, which was technically a seminary at that time. As late as 1818 the liberal and antiorthodox religious faction there was powerful enough to appoint a distinguished Yale heretic of Unitarian leanings, Horace Holley, to the presidency. "All sects, even the Episcopal and Associate Reformed, threw open their pulpits to him." Lexington became known as the Athens of the South.

A man of Holley's point of view was not destined to last, as the systematic attack on vestiges of Enlightenment went on. Kentucky turned out to be a scene of mopping-up operations by the southern revivalists. Holley was accused of being a frequenter of racecourses, theaters, and ballrooms, of holding "sabbath evening parties,"of attacking evangelical doctrines, and of opposing "Christianity in every form." By 1827 he was gone and southwestern infidelity had been virtually exterminated.

Only one celebrated survival of the American kind of Enlightenment in the South lasted longer. Thomas Cooper had left England in 1794 because people thought he sounded too much like French Revolutionaries. A friend of Thomas Jefferson and the chemist Joseph Priestley, he eventually was appointed professor of natural science and law at the University of Virginia in 1811. But the orthodox clergy hounded him for his deism and he had to resign almost at once. By 1820 he was president of South Carolina College but he was singled out as an anticlerical and antireligionist. There was no room for him in the evangelicals' South and he was in effect tried for atheism. He resigned in 1834.

Cooper's writings give as well as anyone's a picture of early nineteenth-century southern religion from the viewpoint of one of its victims. He was most vulnerable in his attack on defenders of the literal character of the book of Genesis, which he found to be full of "absurd and frivolous tales." Cooper made the best of his sense of isolation and even claimed that it stimulated his research and motivated his persistence. In 1829 he wrote: "I should live here more comfortably if this land & the people were not so theologically ignorant and bigotted, but altho' very unpleasant it gives me stimulus to constant exertion in opposition."

Cooper lost, and continuity with the religious freethinking of colonial Virginia died with him. From 1830 until long after the Civil War, almost no southerner of note found it useful or advisable to go his own way and make a point of attacking the evangelical synthesis which had bonded with southern culture.

The second breach of continuity with the colonial past in the early national sequence came with the relative demise of the old established church in Virginia. Bishop James Madison had viewed its remains and concluded that it was "too far gone ever to be revived." Never very vigorous, separated by the Atlantic from its bishop, poorly administered and often weakly staffed, it suffered by identification with loyalist and Tory causes during the Revolution. Demoralized and yet traditionalist, its leaders did not readily adapt to the revivals which picked up new recruits for dissenting churches during the latter half-century. While recall of the good old days of Virginian religion lived on through the plantation period wherever people invoked a "Cavalier myth" of gracious and gentlemanly courtliness over against pushy Yankeeism, the Episcopal church dwindled.

Rather than trace the years of what was coming to be a minority church, it is sufficient to look at its relative position on the eve of the War Between the States. While there were strategic Episcopal churches in the cities to attract people of that faith and of fashion, and while some dotted the rural and village landscape, they had yielded place to more assertive churches. According to best estimates, by 1860 the whole new southwestern area was only 1.6% Episcopal in its identification. Methodism had taken over first place, with the loyalty of one third of southern church members at its command, just as one fourth of the people were Baptist and one fourth were Roman Catholic. Presbyterians and Disciples of Christ made up the remainder. In Arkansas and Kentucky the old colonial church held less than 1 percent of the population; in Mississippi, Missouri, and Tennessee fewer than 2 percent were Episcopal; Alabama, Louisiana, and Texas had the largest elements, but in none of these did it reach 3 percent. With such small statistical presence and because of vast changes in the ethos, one can safely speak of the gradual dissappearance of an effective Episcopal voice in the experience of most of the newer southerners.

This review of the failure of southern colonial Protestantism from the Virginia Tidewater and the old establishment to win the West prepares us to understand the next phase in southern religious development: the sweep of the South by new-style revivalist churches. The new stirrings that were later to become "the Second Great Awakening" were first evident in the South on Presbyterian campuses in Virginia; Hampden-Sidney students were responsive in 1787 and not long after Washington College recognized signs of religious renewal.

The great push came with the beginning of the new century and with the southwestern movement. While Presbyterians continued to take part and to adapt, the strongest forces were now Methodist and Baptist, as well as, some decades later, Disciples of Christ. In Logan County, Kentucky, Presbyterian James McGready had stimulated revival in 1797, and at Red River in 1800 the outlines of a new religious force for a new century began to be clear. The accent here as elsewhere was on personal salvation. The new techniques included the well-known camp meeting, which worked its way into the national mythology as a distinctively southern invention. In 1801 Cane Ridge, Kentucky, saw a camp meeting with over 20,000 participants. Baptist and Methodist revivalists often stimulated high emotion and welcomed physical signs of response.

Indications that the Holy Spirit was active needed extraordinary endorsement, and southerners found these in the signals of nature. The lettered and the unlettered alike shared a world view in which the elements themselves were connected with the happenings associated with conversion. When by 1810 the original revivals were spending themselves and disaffection and apathy were setting in, signs occurred in the heavens. A bright comet appeared from March 1811 to August 1812. In December 1812, earthquakes followed in the Mississippi valley. Was God dealing with his people? Life seemed especially frail and eternity was imminent. People had to come to a decision. Here was the "direct agency of Jehovah." The Presbyterian Synod of Kentucky took proper note of the events, thanking God for "providential dealings such as Earthquakes and War" because these led men to attend to scriptures and the means of Grace, so that "many additions have been made to the Church the last year—that some have returned to our Communion . . . that Infidels in general have been more silent."

These revivals were the root experiences for backwoods southern religionists, and they contributed so much to the southern and Protestant tradition that ever after their effects had to be reckoned with. The accent on conversion was so strong that through much of the nineteenth century many southerners saw the act of turning to faith as the be-all and end-all of religion.

Polity was important for the development of the revivalist bond with the culture. The Methodists used one approach, *connectionalism,* which meant that congregations were connected through an elaborate system, yet the church was not centralized. The Wesleyans were superb organizers—mobile, adaptable, and ready. Despite a deep schism in the 1790s, their churches prospered and rose to first place. The circuit rider was the advance agent. New forms of organization were developed at once: a *class system* that assumed intimate life because it organized all members into "classes" or cells, and *superintendency* were the means of supervising, staffing, and synthesizing these churches. Yet localism was strong. On the new terrain people were isolated from each other and the church was one institution they could use to develop social forms and fellowship. It was under local control. This was even more true in the Baptist–Disciples of Christ orbit, where local autonomy was proclaimed with fervor and defended with passion.

The southern churches did not develop completely distinct institutions. At the turn of the century, northerners were busy inventing denominations, a new kind of parish, Sunday schools, benevolent societies, and foreign missionary work, and the South prospered along the same lines. The distinctiveness of southern religion in the period is found elsewhere.

During the years when the North was beginning to urbanize and receive the first foretastes of industrialism, the South was taking an opposite trend. Some historians like to write the history of the War Between the States as a consequence of different timetables of industrialization. Whether or not one can place so much emphasis on this one process, it is true that southern religious leaders saw themselves as the defenders of the plantation in the rising Cotton Kingdom after 1830. These leaders extolled rural and village values over against urban; their heroic images were agricultural, and spiritual life was seen—even more than in the rural North—as tied inextricably to the soil.

Significantly, revivalism and ruralism stamped black and white southern religion alike. By 1859 about 12 percent of blacks in the United States were estimated to be church members. Almost all of them were Methodist (215,000) or Baptist (175,000); exactly 100 years later the four largest black denominations were still in this lineage. What many later whites thought were distinctive features of black races of Africa were largely inheritances of the revivalist-rural religion which first reached both slaves and free people.

During the years of the Cotton Kingdom, the association of religion with race came to be a distinctive feature of southern preoccupations. By 1830 it was the dominant feature and the old issues of Enlightenment religion, old Episcopalianism, and even revivalism began to be secondary. If this was not always the case in the formal deliberations and in the sermons of the churches, it did show up constantly in the public and civil forms of religion as evidenced in political decisions, newspaper reports, and literary accounts.

During the three decades before the war the American South became increasingly isolated not only from the North but from much of the rest of the western world, where strong judgments against slavery were being expressed. This isolation led to a self-defensiveness and to obsessive concerns. Harriet Martineau, a visitor from abroad in the 1830s summarized: "A magic ring seems drawn around those who live amidst slavery; and it gives a circular character to all they think and do upon the subject. There are but few who think within it who distinctly see anything beyond it."

Southerners did see attackers and threateners beyond their magic ring or circle. When people experience moral stigmatizing, they need strong justification for their actions. Protestantism was expected to provide this and did so with almost no ambiguity. Until around 1830 there had been room for dissent on the slavery issue. Before that date, there were more antislavery societies in what was to become the Confederacy than there were in the North. But slave rebellions, the self-preserving plantation economy, the decline of procolonization societies, the rise of militant northern abolitionism, and the increasingly felt judgment of the world made dissent against slavery seem treasonous. Many clerics, for example Episcopal Bishop Leonidas K. Polk, were slaveholders, and they made pragmatic defenses of the institution. But practical appeal was not enough. Theological justification of the institution had to be forthcoming, and this was increasingly linked with racial or racist doctrines to produce a semipermanent antiblack religious ethos for many southern whites.

At the root of the southern defense was the fact that the Bible did not proscribe slavery. Sometimes it allowed for enslavement. The apostles lived with slavery in the New Testament era, although they sought reform within the system, as many southern ministers also set out to do. Many connected slavery and racism by claiming that Noah's son Ham, cursed to be a slave, was the father of the black races. The distinguished southern theologian J. H. Thornwell relied on the New Testament arguments, however: "The Scriptures not only fail to condemn Slavery, they as distinctly sanction it as any other social condition of man."

While some argued that the Bible committed people to a political defense of slavery, many others used the opposite argument. In this reading, the church ministered only to otherworldly interests, working for spiritual concerns. In no instance were there to be a blurring between these goals and human politics or reform. Thornwell himself could reason on both sides of this case and argued that the church "has no commission to reconstruct society." Such an approach, thought the theologian, could help whites remain untainted and free to minister to blacks and thus to serve as a check on the kind of racism which saw Negroes as animals: "We are not ashamed to call him our *brother*."

With the defense of slavery over against a disapproving world, southern church leaders were more and more concerned to resist religious change. Whereas at the beginning of the century southern Protestantism was almost as varied as was the northern counterpart, by midcentury those inside the "magic ring" were the most rigidly orthodox Protestants in America. From Europe and in the northern seminaries came the first signs of recognition that the Bible was to be subject to historical criticism. In the South clerics became ever more literalistic about the Bible. The church's tradition included some antislavery elements; these were rejected in favor of "the Bible alone," since the scriptures allowed slavery.

Along with biblicism and the accent on conversion and salvation, southern Protestantism held to an even more rigorous and legalistic moral code than did the more varied northern churches. The great Methodist Bishop Francis Asbury had spoken in personal terms: he would have a holy people, or he would have no people. The quest for holiness, however, came to take a very individualistic line in the first half of the century. The accent was on vices of persons, not evil in the forms of society. Reform meant change in the individual, not the tearing up or modification of a social contract that had been religiously approved. In 1843 in New Orleans defenders of the clergy spoke of them as being "not political crusaders, but simple and guileless teachers" of the Gospel who would not "dogmatize on the civil relations or rights of individuals" but would be "chiefly concerned with the heart and conscience."

When the War Between the States came, southern religionists were as ready as their northern counterparts to justify their cause as being God's. Superorthodox southern clerics were not alone, however, in their appeal to God as on their side. The best-known northern liberal of the day was Horace Bushnell, who during the war reminded the public that "we associate God and religion with all that we are fighting for." The northern cause "is especially God's and so we are connecting all most sacred impressions with our government itself." He could be militant: "God, God is in it, everywhere . . . every drumbeat is a hymn, the cannon thunder God, the electric silence, darting victory along the wires, is the inaudible greeting of God's favoring work and purpose."

With such bloodthirsty enthusiasm coming from a genial liberal whose cause was finding moral endorsement across the Atlantic, we should not be surprised to find beleaguered and defensive southern ministers sounding even more strident. The churches more than any other institution sustained southern morale and justified its causes. In Rome, Georgia, the Reverend J. Jones cries, "If the rescue of the holy sepulchre from the infidel Moslem, induced three millions of men to lay their bones in the East, shall we not willingly contend to snatch the word of God from the modern infidel?" "Nature and nature's God has marked us out for two nations," said a colleague.

The Georgian T. R. R. Cobb asked the church to stay with the Confederacy and used significant terms: "She should not now abandon HER OWN GRAND CREATION. She should not leave the creature of her prayers and labors to the contingencies of the times, or the tender mercies of less conscientious patriots. *She should* CONSUMMATE *what she has* BEGUN." And the chair of the military committee in the Confederate House of Representatives said in 1865 that "the clergy have done more for the success of our cause, than any other class. They have kept up the spirits of our people. . . . Not even the bayonets have done more."

Several major denominations divided over North-South issues beginning around 1836–1838 and continuing on through the 1840s. But even where there was no formal division, separate forms of Protestantism were growing in South and North. As Abraham Lincoln, who sometimes looked like the only Protestant on the scene, was to remind both sides: "In the present civil war, it is quite possible that God's purpose is something different from the purpose of either party." In great contests each party claims to act in accordance with the will of God. "God cannot be *for,* and *against* the same thing at the same time." Both sides prayed to the same God—yet both could not win. Lincoln did not draw the ministers' conclusion: that they could prove that their cause was God's. He wanted people to try to conform to what they knew of God's will, rather than claim God as their own.

South and North were eventually to be reunited by force of arms and later by other bonds, and their religious forces gradually came back together. The South introduced the tragic sense of life to the Protestant empire; it had lived with despondency, despair, and defeat. But in another sense, it did not lose its place in the empire. Its biblicism, individualism, conversionism, salvationism, orthodoxism, and numerous other "isms" lived on and were carried to the North. Even its racism tended to be victorious. And although in the early nineteenth century protest diminished so much that the South looked like the least Protestant part of the nation, later years were to show that the statistical weight of Protestantism would remain in the South, the most Protestant part of the nation—and the empire. American evangelicals have always known that the South is where bodies are, and these people exert their weight.

III · THE EMPIRE

8 · The Invention of Forms

Denomination, Parish, Education

The first half-century of national life saw the development of evangelicalism as a kind of national church or national religion. But within that informal context a formal pattern of church life developed. Within the empire, ministers and lay leaders served as the custodians of faith and values. They busied themselves gathering followers, organizing them into effective units, ministering to their needs, judging their ways of life, and exhorting them to take their place in the world. For such activities it was necessary to invent new forms or to radically rework old ones. The result was a network of denominations, local churches, educational institutions, revivals, and agencies.

The attempt to assess the potency of these forms necessarily leads to some chronological retracing of steps, for these inventions began with the birth of the nation, especially in the light of that charter which disestablished churches and put congregations on a voluntary basis apart from civil authorities. If it is true that nothing so basic as this change had occurred in the administrative side of Christian church life in 1,400 years, there should be no wonder that stresses and strains should be felt in the small units of church life. Few historians have been able to look back without a sense of wonder, however, at the speed and finesse with which religious leaders adapted and accommodated themselves to new circumstances.

At least not since the birth of Protestantism three centuries earlier and probably not since the beginning of Constantinianism in the fourth century was there such a sudden flowering of new forms as occurred in the

67

northwest European and particularly the Anglo-American orbit. The political revolutions ("the death of the king" and thus the death of the "God of divine right") and the Industrial Revolution together changed the situations of all people there, and religious institutions changed with them. For one half-century, they not only adapted but they often set a pace.

The result of these stirrings in what is often called the Wesleyan era, after the English religious genius John Wesley, who had so many intuitions concerning the character of people in his age, was a set of forms which churches at least in the United States were to live to the present day. When twentieth-century Protestants curse the complexity of their own day and look back with nostalgia to "the good old days," they often describe a way of life associated with the forms from this Golden Age. Ironically, no sooner had these new forms been developed than their rationale was removed from under them. In the second half of the nineteenth century, industrialism and the urban setting were so enlarged and their impacts so intensified that very little of the earlier forms applied directly to the world of factories and cities. Yet people continued to cling to them, lacking their parents' inventive power to come up with institutions which would serve as well in an urban and ecumenical age as these did in a rural-village and competitive age.

One other generalization is necessary before a survey of these forms is undertaken. The success with which Protestants developed denominations, local churches, Sunday schools, revivals, and benevolent agencies came at a high price. These institutions grew larger and larger, but their goals encompassed ever narrower portions of life. Something of a division of labor went with the birth of these forms. In order for them to live their own lives, to be supported, and to be effective within a limited sphere, church leaders had to abandon involvement in area after area of people's lives.

Legal disestablishment was only the most dramatic symbol in this pattern. Disestablishment and the presence of a godless Constitution only meant that in its final logic, the role of the "priest" had changed. The priest was no longer needed to serve as the official interpreter of the civil order for all people in the society. But the adaptation went far beyond this legal minimum. More and more, the minister was asked to serve only those transactions involving humans with heaven and hell. Anything that had to do with tearing up or rewriting a social contract for this life would be at best a spillover. At worst, it would represent a threat. As a middling definition, it would at least be considered meddling in affairs which should be beyond his range.

So the evangelical churches as churches were increasingly content with the business of saving souls, rescuing individuals out of the world, and ministering to private, familial, and leisure worlds. By the time they discovered the implications of this institutionalized divorce between faith and the surrounding world, they found that the society at large was eager to honor the new informal contract. In effect, church leaders were told: "You stay within your narrowed sphere, and we will sanction you. Step out of it to discuss society's discontents; involve yourselves in the grand issue of slavery or oppose our wars or call into question our ways of arranging society, and we will destroy you." The attempts to overcome the division of labor that was accepted with the new forms has taken the energies of major church leaders through most of the ensuing century.

The first of the great inventions, and the one which determined life in the others, was the denomination. Denomination is a studiously neutral term, a "nothing" or noncommittal word. It imposed itself as if its logic were irresistible and its scope predestined on all churches. Many Protestants did not want to be denominated in such sociologically neutral terms. They wanted to speak of themselves as the church and of all the false churches around them as sects and cults. They were free to do so, but if they wished to communicate in the larger society they were forced to accept the denominational mode of speaking. The denomination assured groups that they could remain free to pursue their private truths so long as they accepted society's legal pattern of toleration.

The denomination, then, was the way in which jurisdictional matters were settled in the evangelical empire. In colonial America there had been a host culture, the established church, and a guest culture of dissent, welcome or unwelcome. In the United States, all churches were on the same footing. This meant that the old hosts had to do the most adapting.

The denomination that suffered the most was the Anglican church in the South. Not a few observers felt that it could not survive in the United States. Some of its early leaders thought it would die out with the end of the great landed families of Virginia.

Maladministration, doctrinal latitude, clerical lassitude, loyalism and Toryism, the villain role in disestablishment—what more could a church have going against it? But in 1784, only one year after the Treaty of Paris and the end of the Revolution, the entrepreneurial Connecticut cleric Samuel Seabury was off to England, hoping to become the first bishop for the Episcopal denomination in America. He had to settle for consecration by Scottish bishops. More acceptable and more effective was William White, who chaired two meetings in New Jersey and New York the same year. These meetings led to a General Convention in Philadelphia in 1785. From it, the modern Episcopal church in America can date its rebirth and new life. White became one of two bishops consecrated in England in 1787. Dwindling statistically, small, weak, and torn, Episcopalianism had begun to reorient itself in the new nation and by 1811, when Bishop John H. Hobart began his work, the church's survival in the American mainstream had been assured, although its power centers had moved northward.

Congregationalism had not suffered; its good name had been enhanced during the Revolution. But it was plagued by internal doctrinal difficulties as the urban New England divines in the Enlightenment era radically reworked the old Calvinism. They spoke of reasonable Christianity, a benevolent deity, natural as opposed to revealed religion, and eventually of Unitarian ideas of God. By 1825 a split had come. What had once been *the* established church in New England was now two smaller denominations, Congregationalism and Unitarianism.

The third beneficiary of colonial establishment, Presbyterianism, also came through the Revolution on the side of the angels and was poised for the denominational era. The Presbyterians reorganized soon after the war, and in 1788–1789 formulated the doctrines and polities which were to sustain them through much of the national period.

The drama came with the new cluster of denominations. Methodism was most successful. It had been only a "connection" or emphasis in the Church of England until the Revolution. In 1784 at a Christmas Conference its leaders set forth a discipline and a program which was to bring Methodism as a denomination to prime at the side of the second group, the Baptists. No church profited more from the transition from dissent to denomination than did these fiercely autonomous and ready-to-go churches. They were joined around 1809 by people who were reluctantly to form another denomination, the Disciples of Christ (or the Christian church, depending upon where one stood and what one's accent was) under the leadership of Alexander Campbell. These churches were at first a loosely organized cluster that grew out of schisms in Methodism and emphases in Baptist and Presbyterian churches. Professing to speak where the Bible spoke and to be silent where the Bible was silent and thus to seek primitive simplicity, they steadfastly refused to be known as a denomination. They were not granted an exemption by their neighbors, however, and had to play the denomination game, too. Churches of continental background adapted similarly.

By the end of the first decade of the new century, the Protestant leadership understood the new rules of the game. They had been playing it ever since the Second Great Awakening came to boost their churches' fortunes, around 1800–1801.

Absence of holy war between these groups did not mean absence of unholy rhetoric, and the verbal conflict between denominations has created an impression of great tension. Unquestionably, to those who cherished the idea of Christian unity and good manners, the competition was disturbing. Thus evangelist Peter Cartwright would speak of non-Methodists as heathen and rejoiced when their representatives would meet physical abuse. He said he "did not hesitate to enter the pulpit of another denomination and there assail its theological teachings." "What had he to do with ministerial courtesy or denominational etiquette which denied his right—his call—to attack [a] slayer of the souls of men?" asked his biographer. Down deep, Cartwright was a charmer who saved his fistfights for infidels. The outsiders, who would have had plenty to worry about in interchurch warfare, could chuckle and enjoy the contrived, controlled, and, to them, irrelevant verbal jousts and bouts of evangelical hucksters.

In a sense, the denominations could be compared to price-fixers sharing a single market. They were representatives of different brands who had formed an informal union to protect themselves from outsiders. If one wants to see how safe denominational conflict was, just look at how churches reacted once or twice in American history when a church violated their terms of consensus. The second of these instances was the controversial Jehovah's Witnesses. The first was the Mormons in the 1840s. The Mormons, not regarded as Protestant or even Christian ("Mormonism, the irreconcilable foe" of both Catholicism and Protestantism, snorted historian Philip Schaff), was that rare exception, a church whose pretensions led to holy war. Various publics asked that they be "exterminated or driven from the State." Their leader, Joseph Smith, was martyred at Carthage, Illinois. They had to migrate from New York to Ohio, to Missouri, to Illinois, to Utah.

The mainline Protestants joined in support of a brief shooting war with the Mormon militia in Utah in 1857. "This," said President Buchanan, "is the first rebellion which has existed in our territories, and humanity itself requires that we should put it down in such a manner that it shall be the last." The Mormon contrast reveals the otherwise safe character of denominational conflict.

While internally, theological differences seemed important, the denominations could always unite for practical and strategic purposes. They perceived themselves as a family of Protestant churches. Some worked for an Evangelical Alliance and began to enjoy an international alliance in 1846. Many made informal family charts of denominational unities. Robert Baird clustered them around two poles, "evangelical and unevangelical." Philip Schaff could do no better than "English and German." All lived with "white and black" as an apparently predestined distinction. Within each denomination, then, people lived a private church life; only what the groups held in common was important outside them. People were invited to "get religion"—a new American coinage—by joining "the church of their choice." The practice has endured, and the terms remain.

The second invention was a corollary of the first. Whereas for many centuries, the parish had meant the single local embodiment of the established church, in eighteenth-century England and America dissenting congregations were becoming as licit as the establishment's local representative. When denominationalism was born, the old territorial parish system died, and local churches became freely competitive. With this change, control passed more and more into local hands, as it had already begun to do in the establishment which followed "the Congregational Way" in colonial New England. The implications for polity and politics were vast. Whether or not churches were episcopal or presbyterian, in many senses they were at base congregational.

In the new local church system, ministers took on a new status. In effect, they were hired by a clientele. They remained effective if they were acceptable and popular. If they stepped too far ahead or too far out of line, the people who had chosen to join their church could withhold contributions or make life unpleasant or run them out of town. The freelance cleric tended to be the maverick; the congregations' pastors had to engage in a subtler politics between pulpit and pew.

Difficult as it is to write a brief history of something so varied and sprawling as the new local church system, one can take some snapshots that represent early nineteenth-century realities. In most of these, the minister would be central. American evangelicals prided themselves on their lay orientation and their assent to the doctrine of the priesthood of all believers. They did not favor the trappings of clericalism and minimized visible distinctions such as clerical garb. Ministers were often recognizable for threadbare clothes. But in a growing middle-class society, professionalism was inevitable. While others were off at work, ministers alone were on hand to cajole their flocks into existence and manage their affairs. They might be preacher-farmers or preacher-teachers; economic survival was always a problem for these sacrificial heroes of faith; but they represented a distinctive role and were usually called "Reverend" or "Preacher."

The number of clergy enlarged. While between 1832 and 1854 the population grew by 88 percent, the numbers of clergy increased by 175 percent. Not a few claimed that this growth was for monetary reasons, but the more one examined the circumstances of "the hireling clergy," the less plausible is the charge. Units were smaller, the churches were growing in numbers and favor, ministry was becoming more specialized and professionalized. Many ministers were undereducated and in the evangelical ethos some of them were taught to despise higher education. Seminary was an illicit word in many denominations.

The antimissionary minister Daniel Parker argued on these lines: "Christ, when he was about to send out preachers, he called them, whether they had learning or not, and gives us no account that a Seminary of learning was essential to the ministry." Protestants professed to despise the honors that went with ministry in some circles. Thus Peter Cartwright could criticize "all the sapient, downy D.D.'s"—even though, in 1842, he was himself glad to accept the D.D. Urban or rural, educated or not, status-conscious or not, poor or not (and probably poor) the minister increasingly represented the local church.

The congregational idea had been to keep matters simple by keeping them local. Even the building was to demonstrate simplicity of purpose; the Methodist Discipline of 1784 urged: "Let all our churches be plain and decent; but not more expensive than is absolutely unavoidable; otherwise the necessity of raising money will make rich men necessary to us. But if so, we must be dependent upon them, yea, and governed by them. And then farewell to Methodist discipline, if not doctrine too." Some did become subject to the rich, but for the most part they were tied to middle-class aspirations. Simplicity was left behind as clienteles prospered.

The programs also lost simplicity. Diaries of colonial clergy revealed that many had almost no churchly duties apart from the Sabbath sermon. The rise of "the activity church" meant that the minister ran an ever more complex organization. As the interdenominational agencies were increasingly crowded out by denominational directorates around 1837, pressures were placed on local churches to be productive in the competitive society. In the end, just as denominations competed with each other, the local churches were also called upon to do so—even within a single denomination. The success motif prevailed.

The competitive practice secreted an ideology. God had, in this interpretation, always wanted churches to be fiercely independent of each other and under local control. Values from the outside were screened out. Religious opinions surrounded the people's basic beliefs with such power that it was difficult for the prophetic note of judgment against society to emerge. A typical critical visitor, Harriet Martineau, looked for judgment during her visit to the American South in the early 1830s. "I found the more quiet and 'gentlemanly' preaching harmless abstractions—the four seasons, the attributes of the Deity, prosperity and adversity, &c." With one exception, "I never heard any available reference made to the grand truths of religion, or principles or morals." While she found the American clergy absolved from the common clerical vices of ambition and cupidity, she did find them guilty of "the idolatry of opinion." They were "self-exiled from the great moral questions of the time." On slaveholding, the most guilty class of the community in her eyes was not the mercantile but the clerical.

A liberal, religious-minded father told her, "You know the clergy are looked upon by all grown men as a sort of people between men and women." She was disturbed to see that the minister was expected to be "the faithful guardian" in the world of female middle-class virtues. There is no reason to take Harriet Martineau's word by itself. The judgment can be corroborated, with a few impressive exceptions, by a study of the subjects on which ministers of local churches chose to comment. The judgment can be understood and the minister can be sympathized with if one perceives how subjection to clientele prejudices was built into the local church system in the early years of the voluntary church. The local congregation was exceptionally expressive of the racial, ethnic, and economic interests and needs of the people gathered in one place through one style of ministry. Rarely could it transcend those interests and limits.

The third great invention at the end of the eighteenth and the beginning of the nineteenth century was the Sunday school. Originally designed to bridge sacred and secular worlds, it came more and more to serve the religious world in a private way. Originally born in an undenominational context, by 1830 it had been increasingly absorbed into the denominational system and became part of the competitive pattern.

The Sunday school was born in 1780 in England, where a philanthropist named Robert Raikes wanted to provide at least minimal secular and religious education to new classes of people, people who were victims of, but potential agents in, the rising industrial order. Just as the transformation of the territorial parish to competitive local churches was instantaneously international, so was the Sunday school movement an immediate Anglo-American instrument. In 1785 William Elliott established one in Accomac County in Virginia. During the next several decades Sunday schools spread rapidly, despite opposition.

Because they were new and because they represented a threat to conventional modes of church life, they were often frowned upon by ministers and church leaders, and at the beginning thrived on what amounted to virtual persecution. Many ministers were threatened by every kind of innovation. Lay teaching jeopardized clerical preaching; religious and secular subjects were blended; women acquired new roles in the churches. We are told of ministers who chased female Sunday school teachers with sticks and brooms, calling them servants of Satan. In Nashville, Tennessee, in the early 1820s, one congregation posted a sign, "No desecration of the holy Sabbath, by teaching on the Sabbath in this Church" would be permitted.

The Sunday school was destined to prevail, for it was an effective instrument of evangelical values and a useful means for inculcating agreed-upon virtues. One slightly jaundiced commentator remarked on the curriculum: it was made up of Bible, catechism, spelling books, readers, and "dull, prosy biographies of unnaturally good children, who all died young." Many evangelicals advertised that the Sunday schools were great democratizing influences. Children of poor and rich alike were welcome. Actually, they met on middle-class terms. The poor were welcome, but countless observers in the 1830s reported how much stress was placed on having children scrubbed up and starched for their appearance at Sunday school. There they were brought into the context of evangelical moral values, the ethic of production and aspiration, and the simple manners. Without doubt, this institution did help lead to the birth of the democratic public schools in America.

The rise of the public schools meant that Sunday schools had to concern themselves less and less with teaching reading, spelling, and other secular subjects. In this way, too, the Protestant meaning-system was separated and segregated from the larger world. Subjects which related to daily decision were removed from this realm.

Dedicated laymen and laywomen, working outside the church organizations, were so successful that the churches adopted their efforts. In Boston, the Sunday School Union was formed in 1816; in Philadelphia one was organized in 1817. (In the early nineteenth century Sunday schools were primarily urban institutions). In 1824 the American Sunday School Union was chartered. In 1830, it announced its intention to institute "a Sunday School in every destitute place where it is practicable throughout the Valley of the Mississippi."

In such ventures, the Union and its denominational counterparts were successful. The Sunday school won acceptance. Religious education in the home never was able to compete with it, and the rise of Sunday schools seemed to many parents to relieve them of responsibility for religious education. Protestants (with the exception of some Lutherans and Seventh-Day Adventists or small Reformed groups) never set up parochial schools on a proportionate scale comparable to that of the Catholics. Other experiments in the twentieth century, for shared time or released time, never effectively challenged the Sunday school.

An institution, then, born in a barely literate society to introduce children to both religious and secular worlds outside the context of competitive churches became normal and normative. All other experiments were to be measured in the light of this evangelical success. Its character changed because the world around it changed. A literate society with mass public education left only an hour for private religious interests to the Sunday school. The church school became the instrument for transmitting the viewpoints and interests of separate denominations and local churches to a new generation.

By the 1830s, the churches' adaptation to the voluntary system of church life was virtually complete. With a genius that defied logic or programming, they had accepted their foreparents' charters for free religion in a free society. They had successfully tied this charter to the competitive ethos and had found the forms for perpetuating the faith and supporting the surrounding culture. In the process, they had permitted themselves to be boxed-in practically and ideologically excluded from major areas of public moral and ethical decision. Needless to say, evangelical thinkers and reformers were not content to be boxed-in in this fashion, and they spent their years interpreting and serving the empire that lived in part off the fruits of their stewardship. They did want to save souls. They were restless to do more.

9 · The Command of Christ, Interpreted

Theological Interpretation

In 1851, Mark Hopkins, president of Williams College, summarized the half-century that had seen the great expansion of Christ's empire. He was not a profound philosopher, but he was an enthusiastic reporter. Christianity had always proposed to herself "the subjugation of the world," but had fallen back, in part because of ignorance of her field.

At about the commencement of the nineteenth century, according to Hopkins, "when the command of Christ, interpreted by modern discoveries, began to work in the heart of the church, a new direction began." The work was not finished, but God's plan was at last being worked out. Hopkins was enthusiastic about the subjugation of nature through inventions which were "taken up in the Divine plan as means to a spiritual end." Material instrumentalities were to be transformed into "the objects of the spiritual kingdom."

Just as important was the worth of the person, centering in liberty and rights and based in the "value which Christianity puts upon the individual." Nothing could stand in Christianity's way. Hopkins also stressed the reform movements which were supposed to "bring human conduct and institutions into conformity with the idea of right." In the end there would be a "triumph of Christianity in which alone the perfection of society is involved."

In a few paragraphs he had summarized the prevailing Anglo-American evangelical concept of mission and empire. By stressing the way changing times called for changed interpretations, he also condensed something of what American Protestants in his century undertook in the name of theology. Theology in the formal sense is in the hands of monks, bishops, or professors who relate the word of God to the world of humanity. But on the informal level, preachers, writers of tracts, and diarists also write theology.

The evangelical empire and the people in it needed guidance and interpretation. To think of this activity as "doing theology" seems confusing to many people. In their model, theology demands great minds. It is difficult to make a case for the presence of many religious geniuses on the American scene between Jonathan Edwards and Josiah Royce, William James, or Walter Rauschenbusch over a century later. Among the church leaders, perhaps Horace Bushnell alone is much read a century later. At the fringes of religious life an occasional spirit like Ralph Waldo Emerson attracted notice.

If giants of thought were not present, neither was there much effective theological work on the conventional European model. Those who hold that model look for bookishness, intellectualism, abstraction, analysis of traditional documents. European theology toward midcentury was in a period of great fertility, as thinkers coped with historical relativism, biblical criticism, and radical social thought. By contrast, American thought seemed bland and unpromising. There seems to have been little trans-Atlantic contact. Almost no one in Europe read American theology and not many Americans were up-to-date on the writings of Coleridge or Schleiermacher. At Mercersburg, Pennsylvania, the Reformed theologian John Williamson Nevin warned Americans that they should prepare to face drastic thought of the kind that prevailed in Germany. "It is preposterous to suppose that in the most speculative portion of the whole Christian world" errors stand "in no connection with the general movement of the world's mind." But that encounter was postponed. The Darwinian challenge was also still in the future.

Lacking giants or European types, Americans came up with little theology that deserves reading in anthologies of masterpieces of Christian literature. But they did what was needed: they set out to interpret their world. The assumption that they were all mindless activists hardly does justice to the amazing variety of enterprises during the half-century after the Second Great Awakening. The American project was almost a reversion to the concrete Hebraic mode. Christians would reflect on the meaning of their own history as a people. They would face the actual problems of their life together, rather than retrace historical controversies.

Jonathan Edwards, capable of grand-scale theorizing, had long before set such a theological project before himself when he announced that he had on his mind and heart "a great work, which I call a 'History of the Work of Redemption,' a body of divinity in an entire new method, being thrown into the form of a history." He would study events in the church of God and revolutions in the world of humanity through all ages, centering in Christ, concentrating on his own contemporaries, and having an eye on the future. Unfortunately all we have is a posthumous collection of sermons from 1739, printed in 1774 as *The History of the Work of Redemption*. Edwards' successors took up his task, whether they were conscious of the precedent he had set or not.

To understand the religious thought of the evangelical empire, it is necessary to see what could be assumed, what had gone before. No one in the tradition questioned the legitimacy and appropriateness of the Bible as the fountain and norm of their teaching. They all accepted the Protestant Reformation with enthusiasm, although they might argue over its details. Luther and Calvin were heroes to many. More stood in the lineage of the English Reformation and its Puritan purifications, as carried to America.

The American refinement early added the federal or covenantal note, an enlargement of John Preston's ancient word, "God hath made a Couenant with you, and you are in couenant with him." God had dealt and would deal with God's children in the light of a covenant, particularly the new covenant of grace in Christ. (The "federal" idea came in through importation of the concept that Adam stood at the head of the race as representative human.) Adam had been a "public person," who anticipated all his progeny and whose descendants' acts, in turn, related to his own.

The covenant idea had received at least one major transformation as a result of the First Great Awakening in the 1730s. Jonathan Edwards and his colleagues preached for decision, conversion, the regeneration of humanity. The potentially faithful were told that their decisions were fateful for their personal destinies and for the shape of community. And, at about the time of the Revolution, the idea was on the verge of being translated beyond recognition in the religious forms of what might be called the American Enlightenment. Natural reason, natural law, natural order now stood at the side of (or as a challenge to) revelation. Christianity was made reasonable, and Christ was not so much a redeemer as an example. But the theology of the Awakening and of the Enlightenment both were designed to honor the human and bring him or her closer to a God who was more benign or benevolent than John Calvin's aloof sovereign had seemed to be.

These strophes describe what had gone on before that half-century of enterprise which had led Mark Hopkins to rhapsody. In the year in which he wrote, an American Home Missionary Society fundraiser, the Reverend David Riddle, called American Christians, (who "in the nature of the case" knew they must be a great people but "not necessarily or universally a holy people") to filter their experience through Protestant devices. "Let no man delude himself with the dream, alike contrary to fact and philosophy, that without evangelical influences and institutions, any thing else, however excellent, will preserve us as a people from ruin." Inventions of the kind Hopkins praised, and doctrines or institutions which he had celebrated, would be meaningless unless seen through evangelical spectacles and blessed by the grace of God "and wrought into the heart of every man."

The burden of theologians between 1801 and 1851 was to bring humanity and God together in a fresh synthesis. The agency and activity of humans were stressed, as was the condescension or benevolence of God. But these could not be accented without difficulty, for most evangelicals stood in traditions where human corruption and human guilt imputed because of Adam's fall lay heavy on the race, while God was majestic, holy, sovereign, and remote. How could people build community unless the covenant could be clearly interpreted? How would they know who was in it or out of it unless God could, in Perry Miller's term, be a "chained God," could assuredly be accountable to humans?

A canvass of the main movements of people who set out to answer these questions could give misleading impressions. Not all religious thought in America was devoted explicitly to these concerns. There were people who ruled themselves out or who were ruled out from the efforts. First among these were the people called "unevangelical" or "nonevangelical" by Robert Baird and others. These also stood in the Protestant tradition. Frederic Hedge, a Transcendentalist minister, argued that Unitarianism represented "the Protestant idea in its last development and fullest extent"; beyond it lay only the fully free Church of the Future. These people to the left of Unitarianism were not acceptable to the evangelicals, and they were free to pursue a somewhat different agenda.

The hundreds of thousands of black Protestants found no interpreters to speak as Hopkins had to the whites. Free or slave, they were systematically barred from having access to inventions. Rights and liberties of individuals were virtually unheard of among them. They were not permitted much of a part in the benevolent and reformist enterprise. The progressivism and optimism of the period's white theology meant little to people whose only hope was otherworldly. Black Protestants did share many features of life with whites. Their interpretation of life also accented decision, conversion, and morality. But freedom to form community or to participate in interpreting the empire was denied them.

A third group does not easily fit into the preoccupations of the Anglo-American evangelicals. They were safely Protestant, and in the nineteenth century the place of none of them in the empire was questioned. But something in the thought of each element of it limited their usefulness to the custodians of the culture. They shared the Christ-centeredness of evangelicalism, but either were of the wrong national stock or else insisted on some peculiarity or other which could not be "evangelically assimilated," as Lyman Beecher would say.

Of proper stock were the Presbyterians at Princeton or the Episcopalians under "High Church" influence. Princeton defined itself in creedal terms and devoted itself to the standards of sixteenth-century Reformed and Presbyterian Christianity. That meant that its Archibald Alexanders and its Charles Hodges were faithful Calvinists who wanted to be untainted by flux and change. Hodge bragged that no new idea had risen at Princeton during his tenure, and in this as in so many matters he had the credentials to speak with assurance.

High Church Episcopalians gravitated to men like Bishop John Henry

Hobart. Their Christian orthodoxy could not be denied, but to outsiders they looked suspiciously papist. They shared what seemed to be the pretensions of the British Oxford Movement, flirted with Gothic architecture and formal liturgies, devoted themselves to bishops, and in countless other ways went a separate path from that taken by revivalists.

The Protestants of continental lineage had several handicaps. By the 1840s they were absorbing new immigrants. Many were isolated by their languages. Reformed and Lutherans alike insisted, as did the Princeton thinkers, on adherence to sixteenth-century formulations. The Reformed gathered at a small backwoods seminary at Mercersburg, Pennsylvania. They also were accused of smelling of the Oxford Movement. Some of that movement's romantic views of the continuity of the church and the organic relation of its elements were attractive to them. Some of the Lutherans, under people like Samuel S. Schmucker at Gettysburg, Pennsylvania, worked to fit into the evangelical scheme and were ready to forego loyalties to some distinctive teachings in order to share the mixed benefits of Americanization. But others, under midwesterner Carl F. W. Walther, who arrived in 1839, wanted to resuscitate safe and settled orthodoxy.

These groups varied among themselves and were accepted or rejected periodically by the mainline ·evangelicals. Their permanent contribution to American church life came through their insistence on the integrity and identity of the church, uneroded by forces in the environment. They were, by the way, as ready as any of their contemporaries to tie God to the nation's purposes and to inculcate support for religious nationalism. Most of them also participated selectively in many of the humanitarian and reform programs of evangelicals.

More important statistically and for their immediate impact than all of these were those religious groups whose theologians interpreted the command of Christ in the light of the attempt to bring humanity and God together on new terms in a new community for pursuit of a new empire.

First in the sequence of interpretations was the movement in New England toward acceptance of elements of the Enlightenment's world view. Though it was prior to the others, it was also—from the viewpoint of the orthodox—the most radical and least satisfying adjustment. In the later decades of the eighteenth century urban Congregationalist clergy in New England began to question their Calvinist past and rejected almost all of it. Charles Chauncy, who made an effort to hold revivals during the Great Awakening, soon learned that such agitations were not for him (nor was he successful at being a revivalist), and became the revivalists' antagonist. Surrounded by other literate critics, Chauncy attacked both the prevailing doctrines about human nature and God.

The movement in New England was often called Arminianism, in a somewhat accidental reference to an earlier Dutch theologian, Jacob Arminius. The name had earlier been applied to a movement in the Church of England which rejected Calvinism. The New England trend was in continuity with that spirit of rejection. Informed by deism but not itself deist, drenched in Enlightenment thought but not "infidel," its proponents conceived that Calvinism threw people into infidelity. How could anyone rely on a covenant between an absolutely arbitrary God, defined in ancient Greek terms, and an absolutely corrupt humanity, as stigmatized by archaic Latin theologians?

The Arminian party stressed the reasonableness of Christianity in what has been called a spirit of "supernatural rationalism." Jesus was the exemplary person who brought together a benevolent and reasonable deity with humans who were full of potentiality for good. By 1805, when Henry Ware, who belonged to this faction, was appointed to the Hollis professorship at Harvard, it was clear that many of the most prestigious elements at the urban centers in Massachusetts and to a lesser extent Connecticut had made the move. Ware's anthropology was uncomplicated; the human is "by nature . . . innocent and pure; free from all moral corruption, as well as destitute of all positive holiness . . . He is by nature no more inclined or disposed to vice than to virtue . . . He has natural affections, all of them originally good, but liable by a wrong direction to be the occasion of error and sin."

By the time these church leaders had formed a denomination in 1825 they were called Unitarian, after their emergent doctrine of God. The God who could bring the best out of good natural affections had to be benevolent and cooperative. The great leader of Unitarianism, William Ellery Channing, more than anyone else formulated "The Moral Argument Against Calvinism" in 1820: "Calvinism owes its perpetuity to the influence of fear in palsying the moral nature." Humans are subdued by terror and become so confused that they "even come to vindicate in God what would disgrace his creatures." The Unitarian movement never became statistically significant and was on the defensive in the midst of nineteenth-century revivalism. But it had captured the strategic congregations of New England. Bypassed and rejected by evangelicals, it served for many Americans through these decades to help them fuse the rationalism of the eighteenth century with a more romantic view of humanity and community in the nineteenth century.

A more moderate revisionist party in New England worked out of Connecticut (and thus more conservative) strongholds. For the evangelicals this second force, often called the "New Divinity," was more important. These moderates crucially weakened the old Calvinist view through what looked to later generations like abstruse and technical arguments about human depravity and the imputation of sin.

Most of the New Divinity thinkers, like Jonathan Edwards the Younger and Joseph Bellamy, failed to draw large congregations. But in Timothy

Dwight, president of Yale College and an instigator of the eastern phase of the Second Great Awakening in the first years of the new century, it found a spokesperson. Conceiving himself to be equidistant from infidel Unitarianism on one hand and obscurantist Calvinism on the other, he began to help soften Calvinism's austerities. But "Pope Dwight" contributed less than Samuel Hopkins, whose doctrine of "disinterested benevolence" inspired missionaries and humanitarians, or Nathaniel William Taylor, the finest mind in the movement.

Taylor modified the old Calvinist predestination (which seemed to limit human agency) by enlarging the concept of human free moral potency. People could look back on an action and see that what had looked fated to them at the time was really a matter of choice. "They always had, in other words, full power to the contrary, even though God knew in advance what they would do." Historian Sidney Mead summarized Taylor's effort as a sophistication of what revivalists talked about when they said, "whosoever will may come." Another way to put it: the revivalist kept on saying, "You must." But what moral sense did it make to say people must unless they could? So Taylor devised a doctrine of human nature in which it was clear that one could rightfully assure another, "You can." Taylor's famous address, *Concio ad Clerum,* at Yale in 1828, was the high point of this effort at formulating a modified Calvinism. A similar trend in Presbyterianism in the hands of clerics like Albert Barnes and Lyman Beecher stood over against Princetonian intransigence and Old School resistance. Between 1835 and 1837 the stresses in the Calvinist stronghold became too strong and on these and other issues—including, in complicated ways, slavery—the Old School and the New School split.

The New Divinity and the New School were the more or less refined intellectualizations of the revivalists' motifs. They helped inspire the reform and benevolence movements. Armed with the reassuring congratulations extended to humanity and with a comforting doctrine of God, all against the background of implied orthodoxy, people of God could move freely out into the empire. Calvin Colton observed them in action: "They go to work," he wrote in 1833, "with as full and as undoubting confidence, as men apply themselves to any enterprise whatever, and in the career of which they have realized repeated and uniform earnests of success."

Even more self-confident and much less concerned about their ability to preserve the old theology were the revivalists in the mold of Charles G. Finney on one hand and the Wesleyans on the other. These leaders rarely sat down to formulate theology in bookish ways; they were constantly on the go. But they could not engage in radical innovations in Christian practice without resort to theory, and the commands of Christ, newly interpreted through them, were channeled out to the American millions.

This revivalist interpretation, which might well be called histrionic theology, born of a theatrical spirit which could dramatize destiny through rhetoric, was not without a touch of preplanned body English. The successful New York evangelist Finney even formulated a theology of gesture: "Gestures are of more importance than is generally supposed. Mere words will never express the full meaning of the gospel." Ministers should throw themselves into the meaning of the biblical writer so as to adopt his sentiments, "embody them, throw them out upon the audience as a living reality." Those who called this theatrical or letting down "the dignity of the pulpit" were bidden to remember that theaters were thronged every night ("the common-sense people *will be* entertained") while the serene and stodgy ministers were preaching "sanctimonious starch" to small audiences.

Finney had large audiences, and they welcomed his histrionic rejections of the past. He knew that people were shopping for new syntheses; in his colorful language they were in a state of "betweenity" in the decade 1825–1835. They were "halting and doubting whether they should reject" Calvinism. Finney made rejection easy. Licensed to be a Presbyterian, he claimed to have assented to the basic Westminster Confession without having read it; later he had had to study it. "I was absolutely ashamed of it . . . I could not feel any respect for a document that would undertake to impose on mankind such dogmas. . . ."Such language from a respected leader was calculated to help people out of betweenity. Their new home was in the revivalists' camp, where "New Measures" were set up to bring people to a point of agitation and decision. In Finney's world, all people possessed a "natural ability" to choose the right. A loving God was waiting for their choice. "You must" had easily become "You can."

The Wesleyans, whose Methodist church was outstripping almost everyone else on the scene in the early decades of the century, worked with a similar concept of potent humanity and benevolent God. They, too, were called Arminian, although they were far more orthodox than the Arminians-turned-Unitarian and in style were closer to Finney and his colleagues. So attractive were these revivalist elements that they seemed to many to have swept the field. Historian Robert Baird could overlook Old Schools and High Churches, Mercersburgs and backwoods Lutherans, to report that, niggling theological interpretations aside, all "agree that . . . a revival is an inestimable blessing: so that he who should oppose himself to revivals *as such,* would be regarded by most of our evangelical Christians as *ipso facto,* an enemy to spiritual religion itself."

A fourth school of interpreters of the command of Christ contributed to the evangelical synthesis by accenting simplicity. Baird believed that American Protestants were tending toward "the simplest and most scriptural Christianity" with their "glad tidings to all men." No one better formulated the concept of simplicity than did Alexander Campbell and his fellow Disciples of Christ or members of the Churches of Christ. Formed out of a number of schismatic groups after 1809, these primitive movements wanted to contribute to the American concept of community. They rejected complexity and religious development. People would find God and be found in God if they could overlap nineteen centuries of the Fallen Church and restore first-generation biblical Christianity. "Where the Scriptures speak, we speak; where the Scriptures are silent, we are silent." Historian David W. Noble has spoken of the custodians of America's past as Jeremiahs, constantly calling people back to the innocent and the primeval. They were "historians against history." In the same mood, these Christians were "traditionalists against tradition." While they consolidated the biblicistic principle into what eventually became a denomination, the concept of innocence and simplicity went with most revivalism and evangelicalism.

The culmination of all these movements came in the inventive synthesis of Horace Bushnell, a Hartford, Connecticut, cleric who was later looked to as the pioneer of evangelical liberalism in America. Bushnell took on the problems they had all wrestled with: how to have a dependable theological charter for covenant and empire and how to bring together God and humanity. Bushnell blurred nature and supernature with a romanticist's finesse. The marks of optimism and progressivism colored his theology. A gentle man who never wanted to be an iconoclast, Bushnell carried the interpretation of human agency further than others by continuing to weaken the old doctrines of corruption and depravity. Yet he did not want to place himself outside the biblical and even the orthodox traditions. In 1844 he wrote, "Nor is our view any infringement upon the doctrine of depravity, in whatsoever manner it may be held. It only declares that depravity is best rectified when it is weakest, and before it is stiffened into habit." Bushnell accented human responsibility and grace through *God in Christ.* Not much remained of the old precarious covenant. God and humanity could now easily come together. God, in Miller's terms, was more chained than ever, more observable, more to be counted upon.

The implications of this trend in newly interpreting the command of Christ for community and empire are clear. While evangelicals may have preached laissez-faire economic doctrines and stressed individual conversion, they could do anything but let unsaved people alone or let saved people go it alone. The Gospel, wrote a *Spectator* author in 1829, could "renew the face of communities and nations. The same heavenly influence which, in revivals of religion, descends on families and villages . . . in like manner, when it shall please him who hath the residue of the Spirit, [may] descend to refresh and beautify a whole land."

Bushnell, the evangelical liberal, never tired of making the point that the whole land was Christian at midcentury. Already in 1835 he wrote, "What nation ever did as much in fifty years, to soften the condition of man, and prove the faith of the cross?" At the end of the Civil War he boasted, "We are the grand experiment of Protestantism! Yes we—it is our most peculiar destiny—we are set to show, by a new and unheard of career of national greatness and felicity, the moral capabilities and all the beneficent fruits of Christianity and the Protestant faith."

At one end of the log was Mark Hopkins, rejoicing in the new interpretations of the command of Christ; at the other was Horace Bushnell, reminding: "God even reserved a world for [Protestantism's] development . . . God sent us hither to make a signal experiment." The American environment itself had, in a fusion with evangelicalism, become revelatory and redemptive.

10 · Forays for Reform

Means of Reforming and Serving

The Protestant leaders often looked at the empire which they had created and called its design very good. The first half-century after independence saw them busy regrouping, consolidating their positions, establishing themselves as the custodians of the spiritual aspects of nationhood. They celebrated the new United States, pointing out how the founders in the colonial era had provided the religious force which was wedded, after 1776, with political institutions for the good of humanity.

So close was the bond, so deep the union, that a basic attack on American institutions would have meant an attack on Protestant Christianity itself. Positively, defense of America meant a defense of the evangelical empire. The most widely accepted Protestant political and economic theorist of the period, Francis Wayland, wrote one year before the nation's jubilee in 1825: "Popular institutions are inseparably connected with Protestant Christianity. Both rest upon the same fundamental principle, the absolute freedom of inquiry." Economic gain had come to the many because of the "pious zeal of Protestant Christians." He spoke for his generation. In the nation's golden anniversary year, the American Home Missionary Society's Constitution announced that it was "doing a work of patriotism, no less than that of Christianity" by carrying on missions in the nation. The more Protestants, the better the nation; the stronger the nation, the better were the chances for Protestantism.

The embrace of the Protestant empire on the part of church leadership was a positive unifying factor on a scene which otherwise could have meant only division. The redoubtable Lyman Beecher called for pious, intelligent, enterprising ministers throughout the nation, people who could establish educational centers, develop common habits, and "institutions of homogeneous influence." These would produce "a sameness of views, and feelings, and interests, which would lay the foundation of our empire upon a rock. Religion is the central attraction which must supply the deficiency of political affinity and interest."

During this half-century, a strong consensus about what was permissible in public realms developed. Foreign visitors by the scores carried away as a first impression the "sameness" which Americans brought to the major institutions and values of their society. The best known of these, Alexis de Tocqueville, remarked that "the majority draws a formidable circle around thought. Within its limits, one is free: but woe to him who dares to break out of it." Religion, he saw, was a major element in the formation of this circle. He believed there was no country in the world where the Christian religion retained a greater influence over the souls of people than in America.

Yes, the design of creation was very good. But the details of America were not perfect, and evangelicals by nature could not be content with less than ideals of perfection. Not all people were converted to the faith as yet; in fact, only a small minority of the people by 1826 were formally committed to the care and custodianship of the evangelical leaders. There was much soul-saving still ahead. More than this, converted and unconverted people alike did not always act up to the ideals of those who had drawn that formidable circle which defined the acceptable and the proper. By the beginning of the Jacksonian era the Protestant leadership, lay and clerical alike, had undertaken the building of great engines for reform and had begun an almost fanatic crusade for reform. In a progressive spirit and with revivalist fervor, they set out to improve the moral situation and to engage in mopping-up operations against the residual forces of evil in their empire.

To people of their day, such activities came so naturally that it is difficult to think of them apart from their reformism. They also needed reform talk in order to justify their mission. The denominational system, allowing as it did for so many competitive views of truth, had made it impossible for the Protestants to sell themselves as guardians of theological truth. Denominationalists thought of themselves as guardians, but the public could not trust them, for they disagreed with each other. Many of the world's religions would gladly be judged on the basis of the beauty they espouse, the grace they impart, the philosophic serenity they provide. American religion, legitimating itself to a public, chose to do so on moral grounds.

People who came to these shores to complete the "positive side of church reformation" found themselves, then, eager to complete the reformation of manners and the reformulation of morals. While their mentors regularly sent them out on evangelistic missions with simple injunctions ("all you have to do is save souls") they made equally clear that holiness was to be a follow-up to conversion. People whose hearts were changed were to produce new kinds of actions. This view of reform was integral to the evangelical view of the world. It was urgent as a step toward saving humanity by "giving universal and saving empire to the kingdom of Christ," as the *New York Evangelist* put it in 1831 when it called for support of crusades against the pleasures of a corrupt world.

Those who listened to the evangelical reformers in the late 1820s would have heard remarkable accord on a number of themes, each of which would explain why leaders wanted to remake a world which they already claimed to have made once before. They were, first of all, people who stood in the biblical tradition but who regarded it through Puritan eyes. They thought of themselves as Puritans, and later generations would type their actions in that lineage.

As latter-day Puritans, they followed their fathers in the habit of tending to claim a monopoly on morality. William S. Plumer said in 1830: "The very essence of every system of manners, morals, and religion, not evangelical, is corruption—gross, foul, deep, total corruption." However much they adapted Puritan theology, they kept this negative view of the nonevangelical world around them. By this standard, all humans failed. The church leaders knew this of themselves and attempted to be scrupulous in their judgments on themselves—although many saw their self-judgment itself to be prideful. When they tried to impose their views on the whole society, they often looked oppressive. Frances Trollope, visiting just before 1831, grumbled that "the absence of a national religion" in the constitution had not kept people from developing a religious tyranny which was being exerted very effectually without the aid of the government. The mores and the ethos could impose what laws never could do.

The Protestant leaders were taken seriously, secondly, because enough people in their environment shared their basic claim, that the way people acted in daily life had ultimate meaning. The decisions in the here and now affected destiny there and then. Their manners and morals were related to the primary transaction going on between humans and God and having to do with heaven and hell. Lyman Beecher was a typical father when he wrote to his wayward son Edward (who later was himself a reformer): "Oh, my dear son, agonize to enter in. You must go to heaven; you must not go to hell!"

In addition to their Puritan heritage and a heaven-versus-hell motivation, evangelical leaders reveal a source for moderate reform in their personalities. The tracts, sermons, and propaganda materials of the time often obscure what the diaries people left or the impressions they created on others reveal. The autobiography of Lyman Beecher, for example, reveals a warm and loving father, a figure often obscured by the same man's public posturing. Many of these severe people were also warmhearted and benevolent. Their empire had as much of a humanitarian and charitable makeup as it did a reformist character. But that gentler side showed chiefly in private, to members of families and the circles of the initiated. The public posture was stern. The names of their societies often had a negative sound ("The Massachusetts Society for the Suppression of Intemperance," came more naturally than "The Massachusetts Society for the Encouragement of Temperance"). Sometimes they showed more rage against lazy slaveholders than they did love for enslaved blacks.

Through the whole crusade, the evangelical leaders were seen to be opposed to pleasure and amusement. As long before as 1793 Nathaniel Emmons, a man who trained scores of clerics in the reformers' generation, had said in this mood that "all diversions, whether more mean or more manly, are the grapes of Sodom and the clusters of Gommorah [sic]."

So sweeping were evangelical concerns that a critic from within the ranks, Calvin Colton (who moved from ministry to politics), labeled the approach *Protestant Jesuitism.* In a rambling tract of that title published in New York in 1836 he noted that "in less than the period that belongs to a single generation, the economy of society in this country, in all that pertains to moral reform and religious enterprise, has been formed on a model entirely new to ourselves, but not without type in history."

Colton could reach for no more stigmatic comparisons than those he did: the crusaders resembled Catholics—and Jesuits at that. A few people who stood at the head of moral and religious organizations were ambitious for power and to spread their views. "Their eyes are everywhere; they see and understand all movements; and not a whisper of discontent can be breathed, but that the bold remonstrant will feel the weight of their displeasure." He saw the whole community, on whom they rely, to be "marshalled and disciplined to their will." Most readers of Colton subtracted a few points for his prejudices and then went on to concur with his general complaint. The most familiar charge made against these Protestant Jesuits by outsiders was their ability to overlook great societal flaws and to maximize minor personal vices. Few were as passionate about this charge as was James Russell Lowell just before the Civil War. He believed that American Tract Society members did not care for the sufferings of the blacks who danced to the music of the cart whip, "provided only they could save the soul of Sambo alive by presenting him a pamphlet, which he could not read." Protestants, he said, were shocked at a dance or a Sunday drive but were silent about the separation of black families, the selling of Christian girls for Christian harems, and other vices that went with slavery.

A final and perhaps the deepest source for reform came from the postmillennial accent prefigured by Edwards and voiced by Finney and his followers. America was to be remade as part of the plan anticipating Christ's Second Coming and the inauguration of a thousand years of justice and peace. To prepare for this, each person was to be holy and to work for an improved world. A certain optimism about America as the milieu and the means inspired these church leaders. They were led to establish agencies and forms to carry on their work.

Intoxicated by their gains while soul-saving during the Second Great Awakening, evangelicals spent the second decade of the century setting up organizations for reform and humanitarian causes. The rise of the Jacksonian spirit, the movement west, and the calls for decision about the destiny of new people in new territories, provided eastern-based empire-builders with opportunities and causes. Working in an axis with British evangelicals, they concentrated in urban centers around New York, Philadelphia, and Boston. Their energies were drawn to fund-raising societies which would publish materials or send out people in support of causes.

The societies were the key to it all. Captain Marryat, one of the ubiquitous foreign visitors, confided to his diary in 1837 that "Americans are Society mad," and they carry on their work with zeal and fanaticism. Church leaders may have profited from a general societal madness. One can just as well make the case that they taught others, pioneering in the establishment of voluntary agencies for countless purposes.

The names of the societies give some view of their scope and tone. A sample includes: the American Female Moral Reform Society; the Association for the Relief of Respectable Aged, Indigent Females; the Connecticut Society for the Suppression of Vice and the Promotion of Good Morals; the Philadelphia Society for the Encouragement of Faithful Domestics; the Penitent Females Society—and even an American branch of a British society to aid the Ruptured Poor. Once established, these agencies constantly took on new programs. The masthead of the *New York Evangelist,* for example, demonstrated the constant increase in scope. Asking for "the emancipation of man—the intellectual, political and moral emancipation of the world," its editors in 1831 claimed to be "Devoted to Revivals, Doctrinal Discussion, and Religious Intelligence Generally" but in 1835 and 1837 they also included "Practical Godliness" and "Human Rights." According to the *Quarterly Register of the American Education Society,* by 1830–1831, the thirteen leading societies had gathered $2,813,550.02. The figure looks small by later standards, until one realizes as did the Education Society that from the birth of the nation to October 1, 1828, the nation itself had spent only $3,585,534.67 for internal improvements.

These agencies were at first led by lay people and were nondenominational in outlook. Throughout the pre-Civil-War period enough homogeneity remained in Protestantism so that nondenominationalism could well mean the sameness for which Lyman Beecher had stumped. One glance at religious statistics gathered by Robert Baird and Joseph Belcher (1855, 1857) shows why it is that we can speak of a rather small family of denominations as having the most power. By the mid-1850s, black and white Methodists and Baptists claimed 2,682,560 members; the older colonial triad of Congregationalists, Presbyterians, and Episcopalians had 908,673 members. Who was left? Only 350,346 in German-background groups, most of them Lutheran and Reformed—and many of them sharing general evangelical sentiments on these causes; in addition there were 247,096 in a cluster of "strays": Universalists (100,000), Unitarians, Friends, Swedenborgians, Shakers, and others. At least three and three-quarter million of the four million listed Protestants could be thought of in the evangelical aggregates, and these provided the power base and the common point of view for the churchly custodianship of morals in the empire. Each of these groups had to be guaranteed autonomy, in order to keep the integrity of their doctrines. The American Tract Society in 1830 typically made clear that members were to "come to their work with the solemn and honest stipulation to be each the protector of his own peculiarities." Denominationalism grew to create structural problems. It did not much change the moral or benevolent point of view, however, and to most victims or beneficiaries of the system, denominational differences were irrelevant and often unrecognizable.

The presence of these societies followed several false starts made by evangelicals before they finally found appropriate ways to work. At first some had wanted to retain theocracy. Disestablishment had meant, however, that they were to be formally and legally cut out of official civil affairs, and most of them willingly accepted some separation of realms. A few tried to overcome the problem by weight of numbers. The best-known instance was the call by Ezra Stiles Ely, a Jacksonian cleric, who proposed "a new sort of union, or, if you please, *a Christian party in politics.*" If the major Protestant groups would unite their citizens, they "could govern every public election in our country." Not many rose to the call. Agreed as they were on a general Protestant doctrinal consensus and in a common view of morals, they had too varied partisan commitments to be attracted to such a fusion. The more reflective feared the implications of such a combine. Not much came of it.

Perhaps the best way to think of the normative activities of Protestant leaders, then, is in the language of the foray: they moved out from their secure or "formidable circle" of institutions and sentiments into the larger empire. There they would attack, take some spoils, and return to security. The clergy suffered somewhat from their partly sequestered status. In Tocqueville's analysis, this resulted from the fact that American religion was legally a distinct sphere, "in which the priest is sovereign, but out of which he takes care never to go." In the narrower sense this was true, but ministers had a way of defining religion broadly so that their distinct sphere of sovereignty could be enlarged for specific purposes.

When they went on such forays, they usually spoke first in terms of rescue (to save people from sin and a corrupt society) to be followed by repair of society through rescued individuals and finally through reform. Reform could come about as a result of changed hearts, organized pressures, and often of legislation. Religion *was* a sphere distinct from civil authority and Protestants *had* eschewed a Christian political party, but that did not mean that they could not bring weight to bear on the lawmaking process.

Lyman Beecher outlined the program that became widely acceptable.

Call attention to a problem. Involve the religious people, "the better part of the community." Educate the young. Finally, there was "the indispensable necessity of executing promptly the laws against immorality."

With remarkable consistency, the Protestant leaders defined what were the matters that fell into their distinct sphere and those that lay outside it. Within it were reforms having to do with personal vices and moral problems over whose direction the single individual could have some control. Outside it were any attempts to change the whole fabric of society, to rewrite the social contract, to call into question basic institutions. Deviations from these lines of distinction were rare.

The moral problems that kept the empire from reaching perfection included duelling (at a time when duelling was becoming less common), profanity, theatergoing, card-playing, and more major problems. The most glamorous and appalling at once was prostitution, and not a few evangelists took interest in the various Magdalen societies which opposed the practice, sought to rescue its practitioners, and to rehabilitate its victims. The revivalists, often ready to preach on this lurid theme, were effective in raising funds to face the problem and were selfless in their personal devotion to the cause. The towering revivalist of the era, Charles G. Finney, according to the *Advocate of Moral Reform* in 1835 made the curious contribution to the Female Moral Reform Society of a "cot and mattrass [sic]."

The moralists wanted to impose their view of the Sabbath on the public. They felt that American virtue depended upon observance of the Lord's Day not merely as a day of rest but as a day of worship, on which work and amusements should be prohibited. Through the second decade of the century, controversy centered on the practice of transporting the mails on Sundays.

Equally obsessive was the crusade against intemperance. In 1808 the first Temperance Society was formed at Moreau, New York; by 1831 more than 4,000 such societies existed. The antiliquor campaign was the best known and longest lasting of the legislative efforts by the church people who went out on forays to reform society. In the twentieth century their heirs were to pass a constitutional amendment in support of prohibition of liquor. The crusade began as a matter of legitimate social concern. Both on the rural frontier and in the new urban centers, a father's addiction to alcohol could mean the ruin of the family. Through the years, therefore, many evangelicals—whose religious antecedents usually had not opposed moderate use of liquor—moved toward temperance positions. These turned out to be unsatisfying. In a young nation given over to emotion, revivalism, and conversion experiences, the teetotal rejection of alcoholic drink was most satisfying and on it the highest premiums were placed. Eventually the temperate were to be judged along with the intemperate, and a social reform program came to be a campaign of intolerance and hatred against drinkers as often as it was a sympathetic move for those who suffered from their practices.

All of these moral problems in the evangelical empire were regarded as controllable personal vices. They could be met within the context of existing instituitons without radical changes and thus belonged to the religious leaders' "distinct sphere." Beyond that, their forays were limited, timid, and even prohibited. Francis Wayland spoke for the mainline evangelicals when he criticized those who were "very much bent upon taking the social fabric to pieces" to build a new one. Their doctrine committed them to support of existing political and social arrangements. Albert Barnes, a major theologian, reminded followers; "Submission to government and to law is a duty of God." As soon as their approved Revolution of 1776 was over, the leaders closed ranks against further and future revolutions.

On the negative side, they saw that most radicalism was in the hands of people like Robert Owen and Frances Wright, self-proclaimed infidels who were stirring up working people in New York and elsewhere, helping them organize against employers, against natural order, and against the law of God. Ely called for a Christian political party against infidels, which in his vocabulary included even the nonevangelical but otherwise very respectable Unitarians. Virginian William S. Plumer saw the root of societal evils lie in the infidelism of European freethinkers. The threat of infidelity consistently served as a bogey to rally support for the standing order.

Tearing up the social fabric was against the law of God and was favored by enemies of God. Those features by themselves should have served to keep the Protestants in line. But the leadership had much more than this going for it. Most white Protestants and almost all of their leaders were themselves aspirants in that middle class which offered people great opportunity. Why destroy such an effective and promising system? They were dependent on what Beecher called "the better part of the community." This better part was not only religious. It was also economically and politically cautious and often quite wealthy. Much of the leadership of the voluntary societies was in the hands of men like John Wanamaker and Arthur and Lewis Tappan, men of wealth who sought security. Merchants, clergy, and professional people wanted to hold on to what they had. Support of moral reform would guarantee that they could. Support of social revision could threaten it. Lewis Tappan reported and warned at once, in a letter written in 1827: "He who scoffs at christianity, or attempts to subvert what are deemed the foundations of the social fabrick, is considered as an enemy to public peace."

The radicals asked the revivalists who engaged in occasional forays to the edges of their distinct sphere whether there were not *basic* wrongs in society, evils that individual moral reform could not counter. As rich in opportunity as America might be for the middle classes, significant numbers of citizens were poor. What comfort was there for the hopeless poor in the evangelical ethic which was coming to be formulated in a celebrated book of Francis Wayland's in 1837: "It is necessary that every man be allowed to gain all that he can." Two years earlier he had written, "Each has a right to use what is his own, exactly as he pleases."

The revivalists regularly preached charity to the poor; that was true. But such charity, however well meant, was negligible. It was usually done in a paternalistic spirit. The radicals were told that efforts to eradicate the roots of poverty were futile ("the poor you have always with you"), and the attempts to help laborers organize contradicted the law of God. People could preach to the poor, give to them, dignify them, save their souls, or do whatever they would personally, but they could not change the social fabric to improve their condition.

The status of women, argued the radicals, needed improvement. Women had few opportunities and were subjected to every kind of indignity with the support of biblical warrant adduced by evangelical ministers and lay leaders. Many of the more extreme social reformers and socialists were women. Women began to tie feminist causes to other unpopular agitations like the abolition of slavery. According to all accounts, evangelical clergy were virtually unanimous in rejecting the feminist cause. They opposed efforts to extend the franchise to women or to almost any others who did not then have it. Feminists who were religious were so repelled by conventional Protestantism's opposition that they drifted off to Unitarianism or to some of the new free religious groups to gain moral support.

Only on one issue was there a partial exception, some stretching and tearing of the social fabric. Some evangelicals advocated abolition of slavery. In the South such antislavery activity virtually disappeared from the churches after 1830, when the whole clergy lined up in support of their section and, with varying degrees of enthusiasm, in support of its offending institution. In the North, much abolitionism grew up within evangelicalism but later moved out of it. By the early 1840s William Lloyd Garrison had largely purged the mainline Protestants from the American Anti-Slavery Society. Some moderate abolitionists like Theodore Weld remained in the evangelical orbit and worked with great effect. People of his point of view were subjected to much harassment and ostracism, but remained faithful.

Most were to feel, as one anonymous reviewer said, that evangelicals were "between the upper and the nether millstones of a *pro-slavery* Christianity, and an *anti-Christian* abolitionism." Until 1830 they had supported the colonization program, not so much with a sense of blacks' rights and equality as with a desire for a humane-appearing solution to a white societal problem. But the African colonization scheme fell apart during the 1830s, and procolonization sentiment could not easily be converted into proabolition activity.

Most of the northern church leaders generally despised slavery and many of them took courageous action. But their record over all does not detract from the generalization that for the most part the clergy and agency leaders were careful not to disrupt the republic they had inherited, to tear up the social contract, or threaten the fabric of society. This became clear in their virtually unanimous support of the War Between the States, even though many of them had been for peace when society at large was for peace.

Just before the Civil War a lay revival in 1858 saw the encouragement of moderate reform programs, through instruments like the Young Men's Christian Association. The proreform spirit of some leaders in this revival was transformed a half-century later by "social gospel" advocates. By the time of the war, however, it was clear that the reform spirit was still limited to forays out into the environment, activities which would not threaten the security of the society or, certainly, of the churches which lived in a distinct sphere within it. Initiative for dealing with basic questions about society and the condition of people in it passed out of the evangelicals' hands. They continued to save souls and to try to reform individuals.

IV · TESTS OF EMPIRE

11 · The Protestant Majority

The Struggles of Women

Through the nineteenth century, Americans gained perspective on themselves by reading reports by foreign visitors. Alexis de Tocqueville, Harriet Martineau, Frances Wright, and Francis Grund were only a few among the many who came to America, returned eventually to Europe, published their observations, and found themselves read back in America. Almost all such observers took note of religion, since they were curious as to how it would prosper when there was no support by the state. Most of them were puzzled to find it thriving, even if they were bewildered by changes wrought by the American scene. One common observation they shared: in almost every religious gathering, the majority of people present were women. What is more, the presence of this majority colored the character of congregations and not too subtly influenced the personality and approach of the clergy.

Had women not always been the Protestant majority? It is impossible to know what base these visitors used, given their European experience. It is possible to find many pages in which they commented on the ways women made up the charity and reform groups through which the voluntary system in religion worked. Harriet Martineau decided that only "women and superstitious men" made up the audiences for preaching, but she was a biased onlooker.

The clergy did concur about the character of their supporters. Some resented this feminizing. They chafed when the men who supported "muscular Christianity" or who resented its atrophy made fun of the clergy. The liberal and the conservative or revivalist churches were alike in these respects. When the Reverend William Gage moved from the Unitarian to the Episcopal church he looked back and remembered that his former church "was almost without male members," but he was not to find a very different situation in his new church. By the end of the century little had changed. The group that was to make up latter-day fundamentalism claimed that, far from reaching the shakers and movers, liberal clerics attracted chiefly older women, but not many men nor youth of both sexes. Congregationalist Howard Bridgeman put the nervousness into print with an article entitled "Have We a Religion for Men?" He smiled as he concluded that "women naturally gravitate to the prayer-meeting, and men as naturally to the penitentiary."

The clergy did dote upon the women and some became emotionally and sexually involved with them. Frances Trollope, writing on manners in America in the early 1830s, sneered that "it is from the clergy only that the women of America receive that sort of attention which is so dearly valued by every female heart throughout the world." Yet if women were so loyal and acted upon, they were not free to be the actors up front. Throughout the century most churches barred them from pulpits. From the vantage of a later day it may seem curious that few aspired to clerical leadership or made arguments for it, yet nothing in the culture would have led them to entertain the idea that they should.

The numerical presence of women did not mean that there were *no* men, only that these were outnumbered. Men by the hundreds of thousands gave attention to preaching, took leadership roles in congregations, and headed the reform organization network. They did come to recognize, however, that women were beginning to use the church as a means of larger expression. Of course—and some "of courses" can never say enough—it was expected that the women who attended Protestant churches should excel as submissive spouses, contented homemakers, and responsive nurturers of children in their own homes. Their influence on American culture is immeasurable. The evidence of their strength and talent is available to anyone who takes pains to trace through biographies the influence of churchly mothers on their daughters and sons.

Increasingly, however, as laborsaving devices became more available and servants more affordable, women had time and energy for activity outside the home. The early forms they put to work were women's auxiliaries and support groups. As "city mission societies" grew in New York, Boston, and Philadelphia, women could be counted on not only to engage in the works of love under male direction. They soon learned the language of reform and they used it, to raise funds, inspire action, and impel others, women and men alike, to join them in service activities. R. Pierce Beaver was able to point, in *All Loves Excelling,* to great amassments of energy and creativity by women.

Latter-day celebrators of women's roles may look back and see this antique world of auxiliaries to have been a world of great limits. Why should the men be paid to be ministers while women must always volunteer? Yet men also were volunteering in a religious society that always had need for more free-time workers than it could afford salaried staffs. And if people in a later age can indulge in condescension over these limits to women's roles, it is valid to note that everything begins somewhere. Women's movements for reform, to spread temperance in the use of alcoholic beverages, to visit the sick and free prostitutes from their servitude, and yet to work for abolition of slavery, as did pioneers Angelina and Sarah Grimké: all worked to help women break old bounds.

Sometimes the process was almost amusing. The Grimkés were South Carolinians of a notable and reasonably humane slaveowning family tradition. Bred in one church, converted by revivalism to another, they first sought out and found a little Quaker meeting in Charleston, only to find that its members were two old men who did not speak to each other or to them. They made their way north, using avenues opened by humanitarian Quakers, only to find their goals frustrated even there because they were women. Like so many others in abolition movements, they moved to the edges of the conventional church, although they were to depend on churchly energies and to dabble with new forms of religion all their life. Angelina married Theodore Dwight Weld, a major revivalist-abolitionist figure.

At the margins of ordinary church life, they found their way to the lecture platform. Remarkably, Angelina got to address the Massachusetts legislature. She helped arrange for the building of a hall for abolitionist speeches in Philadelphia but saw it burned down by its enemies almost at once. Male antiabolitionists so hated the antislavery cause and abolitionists so welcomed eloquence and energy from people like the Grimkés that it was the sisters' position on slavery which won them notoriety and support. Only after a second glance did it sink in that these were women on the platform, speaking not only to women but to mixed company, *to men*. By then, these pioneer women were proving that they were capable of speaking and wielding influence.

The attempts to keep women from leadership and to suppress their voices in churches, as in society, was not born simply of contemporary male motives to dominate. The women themselves found their role circumscribed in the Bible. There they were told that they were created later and derivatively, from a rib of the male. In the New Testament the church as the bride of Christ was to be submissive, as women were to submit to their husbands. In the writings of Paul there were directions that women should keep silence in the church.

Some Protestants carried the Pauline command to extremes. At least in the New Testament church there had been some exceptions. In the same letter to the Corinthians in which the apostle Paul told women *not* to preach and pray publicly he also told them that when they *did* preach and pray, they should do so with heads covered. These letters, the Protestant feminists were quick to note, also paid respects to numerous women in leadership and apostolic positions. Had not Paul chiefly been accommodating his message to a culture in which Christian women should not take on the burden of transcending its sexual stereotypes? Was he fighting against a culture where priestesses in pagan religion connoted or practiced immorality? All these reservations began to be noticed by women who wanted change.

One of their problems was the acceptance of limits by some strong pioneering women. For example, Catherine Beecher, the daughter of Lyman Beecher and sister of Harriet Beecher Stowe, was a true pioneer in the education of women. She helped found academies and inspire other women to teach. Yet she opposed other women who favored suffrage, other kinds of equality with males, or the right to be ordained and to preach.

Gradually it became evident that women were finding their way up from the congregation to the front of the sanctuary. Some put their energies into teaching in the Sunday school, that new invention of Robert Raikes in Gloucester, quickly imported from England. Yet older-fashioned New England clergy went out of their way to reject such intrusions on their domain and all but treated some devoted female teachers as witches or heretics. The women stayed and, through work in Sunday schools, played a great role in shaping the Protestant generations.

Another sphere in which women began to break beyond the bounds of their past was foreign missionary activity. The process was evolutionary. First, women made their way into auxiliaries and support societies. In 1814, Baptist Luther Rice, back from India after one of the very first round trips by missionaries, rejoiced: "Indeed, the great number and rapid increase of these laudable FEMALE INSTITUTIONS cannot fail to create emotions the most lively and gratifying—hopes and anticipations of the most ardent and animating nature." The women were bringing the pennies and collecting more that would send more Luther Rices to more nations.

Then came a first advance. Protestant clergy were not celibate, and those who embarked on dangerous and lonely ventures to convert the heathen could not be expected to travel alone. Women who married them, often after the men's assignments and in the full knowledge that they might never again see their friends and families, had to be a special breed. Their husbands could gain purpose and meaning by conceiving themselves as servants of Christ in direct contact with pagans and new Christians in

India, the Sandwich Islands, Burma, or wherever. The women, meanwhile, were soon expected to be homebound, caring for the children of their unions.

These women were not content with simply fulfilling such expectations, as they came to share their husbands' vision of need and their missionary zeal. They were attentive to their children's needs and came to run rather complex domestic staffs of servants. Through these contacts with servants, they came to hold views of personal life which men dealing with congregations often lacked. They saw the need for clinics, schools, and welfare agencies, so they started them, staffed them, taught and eventually preached in them. In 1816 three Baptist wives wrote from their Ceylon-bound ship: "If not deceived in our motives, we have been induced to leave our beloved friends and native shores, to cross the tempestuous deep, from love to Christ, and the souls which he died to purchase. And now we are ready, waiting with the humble hope of being employed, in his own time and way, in building up his kingdom where he is yet unknown." In scores and then hundreds of instances their hopes were fulfilled. They were to be civilizers as well as converters, and their Board believed that "the decencies of civilized life, including a just appreciation of the female character, can never be introduced among the heathen, unless by the aid of females who have been educated in a Christian country."

Sending agencies remained grudging in their acknowledgment that they were getting two missionaries for the price of one. They were slow to confer status on the women. Yet other women, then other support society members, and finally congregants, observed the many functions of these women as they read their letters or listened to speeches by those who did survive the tempestuous seas and dangers to health, to return for furlough and to gather support. Harriet Atwood Newell was only nineteen years old when she became the first American missionary to die overseas on the Isle of France after expulsion from Calcutta. Many years later short accounts of her life were still moving other women to emulate her zeal. In numerous cases, when a husband died overseas, the widow carried on the work and kept his support network, thus being accepted and rejoiced in by men and women alike.

A third phase came when never-married women were sent out for missionary careers. In 1820 the Society for the Propagation of the Gospel among the Indians and Others in North America commissioned three women to serve Indians, if not "Others," and soon larger numbers were going to the dangerous and unattractive native American mission fields. More accepted the glamorous and safer assignments overseas. One Daniel C. Eddy was awed as he observed Baptist Eleanor Macomber work in Burma. He included her in a book of such heroines. "No husband helped her decide the momentous question [about whether to go into missions], and when she resolved, it was to go *alone.*" So "she crossed, a friendless woman, the deep, dark ocean, and on soil never trodden by the feet of Christian men, erected the banner of the cross." Widows had found it easier to gain support, but nonwidows were also ready.

It appears that the first single nonwidow to be sent was a Betsey Stockton. It may be that she was chosen because not only her sex but her race put her beyond the zone of convention in the first place. "Betsy Stockton, colored woman, *Domestic Assistant*" was her listing when she went with a family to Hawaii in 1823. Two years later, when she returned, the reports were out that she had "well run" a school. Having earlier served the president of Princeton College as a domestic servant, she had learned well and was "qualified to teach school and take charge of domestic concerns." Little is known about her subsequent career, but the pioneering had begun, long before women were given such leadership posts in America.

Moves for ordination of women and licensing them to preach to Americans, male and female, were at first tentative and often frustrated. Pioneers included liberal denominations like the Unitarians or those which had very broad views of ministry, like the Quakers. Yet in both cases, while roles of women were honored, these clerical appointments were far from what most Protestants conceived of as professional, ordained, "set aside" ministerial vocations. To the surprise of many who have more recently begun to explore the roots of women's ordination, it turns out that often the revivalist traditions and those who embodied values of the "old-time religion" did the pioneering.

One can trace much of the ministerial activity back to the evangelizing of Charles Grandison Finney. Finney went from town to town, city to city, in the 1820s and 1830s, preaching a Gospel about a benevolent God who empowered people to carry on his work. If once upon a time the converts-to-be were pictured as passive members of the elect who would be won if God so willed it, Finney turned things around. The Spirit of God was encompassing and energizing. Whoever used the right techniques and had the right impulses could be converted and convert. The result was an understanding which stressed human capacity. Finney thought that if one was converted, he, or she, should pass it on, and set to work by word of mouth and with hands of action to convert others and turn them loose in the fields of the Lord. By 1835 he had moved to Oberlin, Ohio, where a new college was inspiring evangelists, missionaries and, soon, attracting evangelical abolitionists. Among those attracted to the classes and meetings at Oberlin were converted women, who wanted to gain techniques and vision to be put to work. Finney, already under fire from staid clergy for his flamboyant and experimental ways, may not have anticipated this response, and should not be described as an intentional encourager of women in ministry. However, his theology lacked a clear measure that would put a damper on women's ambitions, and Finney finally had little taste for suppressing them.

Student Lucy Stone said that "men came to Oberlin for various reasons" while women came "because they had nowhere else to go." Stone had a friend and eventual sister-in-law named Antoinette Brown. Brown soon learned about limits, for there was, she said, "considerable difference of opinion on the woman question among the faculty, still more among the students." Yet when she came to Oberlin in 1846 she had signed up for theology courses. She completed her college career in 1850 but was not given a diploma or support for ordination. Brown was to find her way eventually to leadership positions, especially in abolitionist causes; to others were left the Oberlin battles.

Evangelical feminists look back on Phoebe Palmer for the breakthrough. She was a Methodist lay person who preached a Gospel of "entire sanctification" or "perfection" after the model of one school of Methodists. God was the agent of conversion, but converted people could and should aspire to be respondents to the divine, people who were coming toward perfection. She took this message on the road in camp meetings and then took up issues demanding social reform. In 1850 she started a Protestant welfare house at Five Points in New York. While she said little on the controversial subject of slavery, Palmer was in front of many other causes. Although technically never ordained, she filled most ministerial roles better than did many men in the Perfectionist movement. By her personal example she made the idea of women in ministry more acceptable.

When the Salvation Army, another Perfectionist denomination, came into the spotlight, it was evident that women were in its leadership. Indeed, the Army's cofounder, Catherine Mumford Booth, who defended Palmer's ministry back in England in 1859, saw to it that women would be preachers in the Army from the first day. No one looking at Wesleyan Perfectionism or the Salvation Army would confuse it either with Unitarianism or liberalism, yet among them were women who were in advance of those in the more staid if theologically more moderate groups.

It is possible to claim that attention to the ordination of women shows a clerical bias. Therefore it does not do justice to the lay character of Protestantism or to the sheer weight of numbers in the laity. Yet historians who trace female ordinations do know something about how power has been focused in the ministerial office, and they have properly seen the symbolism of the office. Thus when organized feminism got its impetus in a meeting at Seneca Falls, New York, in 1848, the women there gathered quite properly expressed resentment about the office of ministry as then constituted. "Exclusion from the ministry" was one of their complaints, for thus man "has usurped the prerogative of Jehovah himself, claiming it as his right to assign for her a sphere of action, when that belongs to her conscience and to her God." More than a century was to pass, however, before women in most Protestant denominations were ordained and admitted to ministry. And this admittance by no means assured instant status full and equal to that of men or full and equal use of their talents.

Energies went at once into other causes which were more immediate in the lives of most women. The most urgent one for the women of Seneca Falls and their heirs for seventy years was woman suffrage. The right to vote seems to be a merely secular affair, a matter of state. Yet it belongs in religious history because many of the attitudes that limited women in the public sphere grew out of interpretations of biblical themes. These dealt with women's place. Much of the eventual support of women's rights by men came from the clergy: they reread the Bible and found there other texts that urged a larger role for them.

In the matter of suffrage, it was not the case that only conservative men put up and kept up the bars. Progressives also had a blind spot. At the turn of the century, as the suffrage cause mounted in intensity, the progressive Protestant social gospel was in its prime. Yet its leaders had a blind spot in respect to suffrage. Their chief metaphors had to do with male imagery about the fatherhood of God and the brotherhood of man. They were typically Victorian in their celebration of women, who were to be homebound. Thus they would serve church and society as wives and mothers, but not express themselves in the tainting fields of politics and public life. Thus the leader, Walter Rauschenbusch, disdained feminist causes. He thought women should continue the Christianization of the family by staying at home, thus fulfilling their God-assigned destinies. Women had to make it on their own, without much Social Gospel help. Only one woman, Vida Scudder, who was an Episcopalian socialist and novelist, was in the front ranks of progressive Christianity.

Curiously, when suffrage did come, it arrived first under antiprogressive auspices in very conservative western states and territories. Utah entered the union in 1896. Its delay to that date was occasioned by the fact that in this Mormon kingdom polygamy was practiced. Yet Utah already had woman suffrage after 1879, even though Mormon outlooks on women have always assigned them circumscribed roles. Colorado followed in 1893 and Idaho in 1896, while Wyoming entered the union six years before Utah with a woman suffrage clause as old as 1769 which was included in the constitution.

Population was low in these territories. Newcomers were often lawless and drifting male railroad workers, miners, or ranch hands. It was feared that they might gain power to pass licentious and lax laws and thus disrupt the peace for the long-term settlers. By adding woman suffrage, the "old stock" people with their recall of Puritan ways would hold firm power longer. In these states and territories it was often Methodist and other clergy who supported woman suffrage. Clergy tagged on to the suffrage issue allied causes: temperance and then prohibition. Those who opposed the Anti-Saloon League were not entirely wrong to see it, in the words of one critic, as "Protestant political supremacy" asserting itself one more time. Much of the leadership of the Woman's Christian Temperance Union, as the second word of their group's name suggests, came from Christian, especially Protestant, impulses. Prohibition was not at first seen as pecksniffian or a righteous striking out at individual drinkers. It was a social cause, since the liquor interests often took advantage of miners and workers in factories, depriving families of care and financial support. In a society with little governmental support of welfare, this meant victimizing families and turning them to helplessness and poverty. Protestant women of the old stock joined forces with men in ministry and other partisans to advance progressivist Prohibition.

There was no denying that as these women's causes grew they had to take on the biblicism of clerics and others, including laywomen, who felt that the Bible allowed for no other sphere for women than the home. Just as the Bible had earlier been used by southern literalists to support slavery, so now it was used everywhere to oppose suffrage. This meant that people had to work their way around the Bible. This was a hazardous task which a few firebrands took on at expense to the movement in an America that cherished the Bible. Or they could neglect some texts and lift out others, for the Bible certainly did show women as judges, preachers, evangelists, agents of good works—anything but constant homebodies, no matter what St. Paul wrote about them some days. Third, they could work to reinterpret the whole Bible in the light of modern knowledge.

It happened that while arguments for suffrage were expanding, there was also developing a school of biblical criticism. This criticism was not meant to destroy faith in the Bible but to employ the same techniques of analysis one would use on any literature, techniques from which the Bible had earlier been exempted as God's inspired work. Now importers from Germany and England began to teach how to get at the essential message of the Bible by seeing its contexts. Now people could strip away the accidents of culture in Paul's world and discern the kernel of biblical truth.

Most of the women leaders employed only moderate forms of biblical criticism, but a few took the cause recklessly into their hands. Elizabeth Cady Stanton, tired of hearing clergy wave the Bible at suffragettes, waved a book back. She and a committee prepared commentaries that issued in the *Woman's Bible* just before the end of the century. The more politic leader, Susan B. Anthony, cautioned the agitators, "No—I don't want my name on that Bible Committee—*You* fight that battle—and leave me to fight the secular—the political fellows." Anthony did not want to be evaluated by her views of the Bible. It turned out she was astute. There *was* backlash against Stanton and her *Woman's Bible* for its heresies. The moderates had to recover their ground. They chose to do so by continuing to reinterpret the cultural settings of biblical statements about female subordination.

Some leaders made strong use of the Bible. The Reverend Anna Howard Shaw stressed that the life of Jesus showed him working for the full expression of the rights and talents of all people, men and women. Such language was effective. In no other profession were there as many supporters of suffrage as there were in the office of Protestant ministry. Clergy fought each other over interpretation of the texts. In the course of the decades they gave strong levers to those who wanted to help create a new sense of freedom for women, A cultural context would emerge in which the ageless message of the faith would find new voices, new public voices, those of women.

Most of the time we can tell the story of the Protestant empire without lifting out the names of these rare women who somehow were able to make their way as abolitionists, feminists, clerics, suffragettes, missionaries, and reform workers. Yet they represented the Protestant majority in the mainstream and the revivalist-minded churches.

As for the groups at the margins of the Protestant empire, movements that did not fit the patterns of respectability, here were places where women excelled. Mother Ann Lee was a British visionary who helped establish the celibate Shaker sect in America. When Adventism suffered as a result of founder William Miller's bad calculations about the date of Christ's return, it was a woman who picked up the pieces. Ellen Gould White combined her health interests with Miller's millennialism and sabbatarian interests. She could be thought of as the real founder of that still prospering denomination called Seventh-Day Aventism. Madame Helene Blavatsky promoted Theosophy in the 1870s, just as the Fox sisters of New York spread Spiritualism at midcentury. Best known of all was Mary Baker Eddy who developed a movement on Protestant soil, a "science and health" accent called Christian Science. If the conventional male leadership, with female acquiescence, ordinarily denied women a place of power outside the home in the Protestant empire, women would find other ways to lead, and they did. Those at the cultural margins eventually helped make the figure of the woman religious leader more plausible. They also did their part to help the cause of seeing the Protestant majority find a voice.

12 · The Great Transformation

The Present City,
The Industrial Beginnings

During the prime years of the evangelical empire, toward the middle of the nineteenth century, Americans were called upon to weather one of history's great transitions. Not since prehistoric people invented or discovered agriculture or village life had anything happened on such a grand scale to change all the physical and many of the psychic aspects of life.

The modern city, first commercial and later industrial, was developing. It replaced the old pastoral image and reality with which colonial Protestants had grown up. Evangelicals had to transform their ministry to the people during these years of growth. Because of their strength and location, the church leaders were well poised to interpret the changes urban and industrial life were beginning to bring. They did so with effectiveness but also at considerable expense. They had to leave behind codes of ethics relating to economics, politics, and communal life, codes that had developed over many centuries in Christianity, Protestantism, and the American colonies.

Between the Revolution and the Civil War, the great physical transformation became increasingly visible. From village and farm to city; from a green landscape to the gray and red of concrete, smoke, and brick; from a world of isolation webbed in a minor way by roads to a world of connections implied by railroads; from a world of animal power to a world of steam—these were the manifest signs.

Historians may argue about the details of the urban and industrial revolutions. They may not agree on the question of their long historical roots. But they have little difficulty documenting the new perceptions of people in the United States in the second third of the nineteenth century. In 1776 only five colonial cities had grown to 20,000 or 30,000 in population and at the beginning of the century only New York had reached 60,000. By 1860 New York numbered 600,000 people, and numerous other cities were thriving. The agrarian realm on which Thomas Jefferson had relied for republican values was passing. Person-to-person market affairs were being replaced by impersonal and corporate contacts. The limitless space that had always terrified and comforted colonists (Timothy Dwight at Yale still thought that God had permanently set aside the West—Vermont and New Hampshire—for infidels and immoralists) was being overcome.

Western Europe was going through a transition at the same time. England was somewhat in advance, but Germany, France, and the United States moved together, and in many ways the North Americans outpointed their trans-Atlantic competitors in the race for mastery over the processes and products of nature. In western Europe the change evoked great ideologies. Socialism, Marxism, and communism served to explain the industrial process. In the United States the transformation seemed to be less burdened with ideology, but the evangelical leadership did play a strategic role in converting the old symbols to help society adapt to the new world. If the leaders sometimes did this inelegantly, it must be pointed out that no one did so with finesse. If they accommodated themselves and their symbols at the expense of old meanings, it should also be noted that other interpreters were in the same business.

To understand the evangelical interpreters, it is well to recall how poised they were for their task. By the 1830s they had spread into all the inhabited areas of the United States, dotting the landscape with churches and staffing them with circuit riders, revivalists, lay leaders, and stable clergy. They operated through a network of interactive and interdenominational agencies. Their literature had a monopoly in many areas. Their values dominated in the school textbooks. Their sermons were often the only examples of public speaking many people heard.

While in adapting to modernity they had accepted responsiblity chiefly for private, familial, and the leisure areas of life, Protestants' desires to save souls and lead them to holiness spilled over into other aspects of society. They dabbled in politics and legislation, usually in indirect ways and occasionally directly. They tried to build community, even if the ground rules of life in a pluralistic society kept them from officially imposing their view of a biblical covenant on a Christian commonwealth. They would win back in the mores or ethos what they had lost or given away in the laws.

Many of them stood in the tradition of John Wesley, who could say that "Christianity is essentially a social religion; to turn it into a solitary religion is indeed to destroy it." They were willing to expose it so readily that a man like Lyman Beecher had to worry "whether the tendency was not to make religion worldly rather than the worldly religious."

The evangelicals' impact can be assessed when one reads their own boasts and complaints, when one listens to the awe with which European visitors regarded their effect for good or for evil, or when one gives attention to the wailing of the nonevangelical critics. The whole story cannot be told simply by listening to gifted representatives in these three groups, but when the subject is the historical study of transformed symbols, it is valid to pay heed to the controllers, manipulators, or interpreters of symbols. Here they shall be noticed first for their attention to urban change, then to industrial beginnings, and finally, to the ways in which they fused the two and transfused them with new Christian meanings.

The city was a necessity in a time of rapid population growth; in 1812 the United States had only 10 million people; by the beginning of the War Between the States, this had trebled to 31 million. The industrial labor force increased over 125 percent between 1820 and 1840, and more and more of this force was in cities. In 1800, farmers outnumbered urbanites fifteen to one; by 1830, this figure was cut to 10.5 to one, and in 1850, to 5.5 to one. If the wilderness and the farm beckoned to take the overflow from the cities, far more people moved from frontier and rural areas to towns and cities, there to join or clash with hosts of newer European immigrants.

The move from rural toward urban life did not come as a total shock to the American evangelicals. They could read of the birth of the church in ancient cities like Jerusalem and Athens and Rome. They knew of its survival in the few moderately sized cities of medieval Europe. They saw that it had made its way despite the breakdown of intimate community in colonial Charleston, Newport, Boston, Philadelphia, or New York. But cities did represent many novel features to them, and this brought about a crisis and demanded interpretation. During the 1830s and 1840s the ministers regularly discussed the spiritual temptations that the urban condition brought. Most of the language of Protestant piety and devotion was rural in origin. The contact between the person of holiness and the soil was accorded almost mystical status. Not only the ministers saw spirituality in these terms. The intellectual community, as personified by the Transcendentalists, by the Emersons and the Thoreaus, either affected dislike of the city or were ambivalent about what population clustering did to the soul.

More dramatic was the effect of the cities on the forms of church life which had been shaped just decades before. The new kind of parish, being the result of revivalists' appeals and not mere territorial carvings, demanded person-to-person contacts and at least the illusion of stability. But the growing cities were impersonal and full of mobile people who moved to the places where their kinds of expertise were needed. In the colonial or frontier village, the white meetinghouse or church tower dominated the green. In the industrial city even the visual symbol of the steeple was lost in the chaos of factories. People came and went.

The Protestants did not wholly turn their back on or despair of the new cities. Every downtown crossroads was marked by numbers of competing churches, and as people moved from the cities' cores, the churches followed. Some people, at least, understood the dynamics of urban organization. However much the evangelical benevolent, reform, and missionary empire was directed to the West and to the primitive world, it was run from Boston, New York, or Philadelphia. The mixed benefits of urban and technological life were immediately brought into the service of the Gospel by the more inventive lay and clerical leaders.

The revivalists in particular had to make a response to the challenge of the city. The revival had had a rural and communal context, and the language associated with revivals preserved this. The camp meeting, the gathering at the river, the sawdust trail, all portray the older setting. But by the time of Charles Grandison Finney in the 1820s, the need to take on the cities was evident. Finney had moved from towns to the small cities of upstate New York with only slight decreases in effectiveness. But he could not avoid the metropolitan areas. His friend Theodore Weld warned him away: "Don't be in too great haste to get hold of the cities . . . Kindle *back fires* . . . over the interiors." But even Weld hoped the cities were ripening for eventual revival. By 1828 and 1829 Finney was adapting to New York, Boston, and other cities, not without some success. Revivalism took on some urban color early, while it retained a rural ethos and language. But in making its move, it had to be content with that aspect of the city which best preserved village values of stability, order, and aspiration. Evangelicalism was wedded to the middle classes, even while the cities were becoming havens for thousands of lower-class workers and the poor. "The business, the bustle, the dissipation, the etiquette and a countless number and variety of things seem to stand in the way of good" in the city, warned Finney's correspondent George W. Gale in 1830. "There is a kind of moral atmosphere so to speak even in the religious world in such places which seems to taint and transform everything about them." It became the churches' tasks to create the kind of setting where better etiquette and order could prevail.

With the city there arrived another feature, industrialization. The pace of change came so fast that in fifty years the United States virtually accomplished what John Adams had not envisioned happening in a millennium when he prophesied to Benjamin Franklin in 1780, "I say that America will not make manufactures enough for her own consumption these thousand years." Few of the Protestant founders would have written a different script for the future. They knew and cherished preindustrial society, and their faith and its forms were adapted to it. Industrialization called for transforming of faith and forms.

Change came early. In 1829 a Massachusetts physician, Jacob Bigelow, coined a new term in his book title *Elements of Technology* and spoke with prescience of a gap in centuries. Industrial change "declared the independence of the nineteenth century from the eighteenth—of the practical, materialist, hardheaded, utilitarian age from that of ideology and benevolence." For one or two more years, more manufacture went on in homes than in factories, but that was to change in the 1830s. There were only 77 patents in 1800; there would be 1,000 in 1850, for invention had to keep pace with the demands of machines. The first American railroad began operation in 1829; by 1860, 30,000 miles of track linked cities.

The human change that went with smoke and steel has often been chronicled. A new premium was placed on practical science. People moved further from the need to use God to account for forces of nature and history. The United States, at least to its Jeremiahs, was taking on complexity and thus rejoining Europe. The loss of innocence meant inevitable corruption. People were valued for their production and not for their persons. People moved from quiet and traditional communities to pluralistic centers where a variety of religious and nonreligious temptations beckoned. The pattern of life on Sundays changed with the new leisure for some and the need for more days of work for the victims of industrialization. The city allowed freedom for escape from the opinions and pressures of others, as Nathaniel Hawthorne noted in his comment on "our New England villages, where we need the permission of each individual neighbour for every act we do, every word that we utter, and for every friend that we make or keep." If God worked through social pressures in intimate villages, people were free of God in industrial centers. Religion was threatened.

Many evangelicals welcomed the city without industry and industry without the city. Men like Lyman Beecher in Cincinnati or Charles Finney almost anywhere knew how to reach merchants and commercial leaders, and knew how to employ them in the mission of the church. They feared the industrial workers whose values would be eroded and whose church ties would not survive urban contacts. On the other hand, many mid-nineteenth-century people saw industry and technology to be a gift of God for human dominion over nature, but they wanted factories to remain in sylvan settings. Jefferson, suspicious of cities, liked the earlier manufacturers who were "as much at their ease, as independent and moral as our agricultural inhabitants." The southern industrialist William Gregg as late as 1845 could still contend that "a cotton factory should not be located in a city." "There it would be impossible 'to control the moral habits of the operatives, and to keep up a steady, efficient, and cheap working force.'" Most of all he feared overcrowding and "attendant lapse of morals." Evangelicals often prevailed on manufacturers to provide churches and to force workers to Sunday school and church. But successful factories attracted large populations, and cities grew almost everywhere to fuse with industry and provide a dual problem in the evangelical empire.

Industry brought new worshippers to the shrine of science. People were distracted from theological pursuits. The colleges which once had trained ministers now had to begin devoting themselves to practical learning. The evangelicals were alert to the threats of these new idolatries. But more crucial to them was the problem of new classes of people who came with the beginnnings of urban industry. The immigrant who was Catholic was viewed almost purely as a threat. The laborer who was being reached by radical organizers was viewed with suspicion as a potential subverter of the evangelical empire, a system which had no room for workers' organizations.

In the late 1820s dozens of workers' groups and unions were organized in New York and Boston, and scores of newspapers communicated their interests. The Protestant clergy had discouraged such unions and lost (or had never held) touch with the people who joined them. Blacks were not free to respond, so black churches were not part of the picture. White churches were tied more to the middle class, and their practices bred new doctrines of property and individualism. So the workers were often abandoned to radicals and freethinkers like Frances Wright and Robert Owen. By the time of the panic of 1837—after which these organizations fell apart for several decades—support of labor was tied to outright infidelity in the Protestant mind. The *Boston Atlas,* a conservative voice, spoke for many in 1834: workers "from the halls of infidelity and atheism; from the dram shops and dram cellars . . . are loud in the praises" of those who catered to their interests.

Against these infidels and their followers, Robert Baird was ready to remind European critics of evangelical clergy. These ministers imparted a "conservative character" to ordered life, especially as they had to "resist the anarchical principles of self-styled reformers, both religious and political." Churches which had known how to regulate colonial economies, oppose usury, restate doctrines of fair price, or at least to teach stewardship to individuals and honesty to over-the-counter transactors, did not know how to cope with anything like collective bargaining.

The great transformation of the middle third of the nineteenth century, then, saw Protestant church leaders reacting to urban and early industrial change by huddling up to the self-made citizens of the middle and, when possible, the upper classes. Most of the ministers came from these classes, had most successes with them, shared their values, and tried to help people make their way upward in them. What they did not notice was that many in their clienteles were only giving lip service to Christian teachings, following them where convenient and discarding them where they did not serve to justify new and non-Christian modes of living.

The church born among the poor and developed for their passion and their solace was coming to despise the outcasts. The church born to be suspicious of riches licensed unregulated gain. The Protestant churches, shaped in a colonial America which had fostered commonwealth concepts, chartered individualism. A tradition which had exalted persons over property converted and justified absolute rights to property on the part of the industrious. The ideal of organismic community was overshadowed by a religion which largely accepted the laissez-faire competitive enterprise system. Church leaders sought to soften the system by injunctions to charity and benevolence, but they would not tamper with the social pattern itself, coming to see—despite both the long and the recent Christian past's pronouncements—that these had been ordained by God.

The Reverend Jonathan Mayhew Wainwright, descendant of a distinguished colonial family of ministers and later a bishop who officiated at wealthy John Jacob Astor's funeral, spoke for the new elitists: "The unequal distribution of wealth we believe to be not only an unalterable consequence of the nature of man, and the state of being in which he is placed, but also the only system by which his happiness and improvement can be promoted in this state of being." He went on: "Once touch the rights of property, let it be felt that men are imperilled and harassed in their efforts to obtain it, that its possession is insecure . . . and you immediately stop enterprise." Stop enterprise and you stop the progress of knowledge and "also of virtue—and then where is the happiness of such a community?"

A Marxist would be tempted to say that the ministers were captive of the class they served, but not many served the Astor-Vanderbilt classes. Nor were many of them personally wealthy and thus they were not guarding their own property. Many were simple, honest people of the frontier who perpetuated rhetoric of distrust of riches. Others were struggling citizens of the middle class who honestly believed that the "room at the top" ideal of aspiration best trained people to self-discipline and thus to virtue. They came to believe that what they perceived to be socially necessary and psychologically satisfying was actually foreordained in the plan of God and commanded in scriptures.

In the twilight years between the old merchant or commercial economy and the beginnings of the new industrial one, the middle classes passed an informal but binding new social contract, and did so with benefit of clergy. During the last of the pre-Civil-War revivals in 1857–1858 William Aikman was to ponder the lessons of a financial depression: "GOD IN COMMERCE, is the interpretation of the history of those years." The interpretation matched the enterprise of the decades. "NO ADMISSION HERE, EXCEPT ON BUSINESS" seemed to be the motto over the "one gigantic workshop" that was America to visitor Francis Grund. Gustav Unonius from Sweden visited Rochester, New York, and reported the surprising combination of "*churches and banks*—evidence . . . of the greater intensity of both spiritual and material activity" in the newer American cities. In every block there were temples "erected for the worship of either God or Mammon."

Practically, said Henri Herz of a visit in 1846, "in America, trade and religion often give each other mutual support," for churches were rented for secular occasions and halls were used for churches. But some argued that trade and religion *could* be effectively separated in the American mind. Karl Griesinger, writing in 1848, said that the churchgoer would be deterred by neither rain nor other elements from worship. All week long they may "do things from which the worst infidel would shrink with disgust" but on Sunday they are off to church. "Where else on the face of the earth do you find such piety?" The piety had nothing to do with heavenly manna. "The preacher is dealing not only with listeners but with customers" and the clergy must meet competition and be businesslike themselves. (Griesinger may be counted as a prejudiced witness; he once grumbled that boredom itself would bring people to church. No trains moved and no entertainments were open on Sunday. "People who make such laws must be half crazy.")

What the foreign visitors found with rare unanimity, the evangelical church leaders contended for without subtlety. Contrast the attitudes toward riches and poverty before and after the evangelical transformation. Early in the nineteenth century the rich were envied and despised and were certainly not to be emulated. Gardiner Spring would preach in 1830: "Do not envy the rich!" The poor cottager lived in poverty and rags and earned daily bread with the sweat of his brow but his piety "spreads a charm around his humble dwelling you may well envy." But for the rich worldling, wealth "ensnares his soul" or presents an obstacle to eternal salvation, throwing "mountains in his way to heaven."

Spring's point of view was dying, and only lip service would be paid to it later on. Already by 1836 the Reverend Thomas P. Hunt in *The Book of Wealth,* argued that "No man can be obedient to God's will . . . without becoming wealthy." Charles Finney, a transitional figure who lived in a world of fixed economic laws and who was setting his sights on conversion of the wealthy, could still moan in 1833, "O this money that destroys a man's spirituality; and endangers his soul!" and could write that "the whole course of business in the world is governed and regulated by the maxims of supreme and unmixed selfishness." But Francis Wayland was less negative and in *The Moral Law of Accumulation* (1837) said that "God intends that man should grow rich," though he softened his laissez-faire obsession with Christian doctrines of stewardship.

As the rich played a bigger part in the economy of God and empire, the poor inevitably were increasingly stigmatized. Marcius Willson's *Second Reader* in 1860 was a throwback to much earlier evangelical teachings about static orders. School children "should be very thankful that [their] lot is better" than that of the urban poor, but they should not be proud. "It was God alone who has made our lot to differ from the lot of theirs." Horace Bushnell had asked all, and especially the poor, never to be dissatisfied with their calling. "Choke that devilish envy."

But such a predestining view of poverty was unsatisfying in the world of competitive enterprise. If God willed all people to be rich, he no longer willed them to be poor. If they were poor, this was the result of their own fault, usually a moral fault. "The first lesson a boy is taught on leaving the parental roof," reported a Fall River, Massachusetts, labor leader in 1846, "is to get gain . . . gain . . . wealth . . . forgetting all but self." He had plenty of clerical support. Aspiration had built the empire, and God would bless the person who transcended poverty by efforts, even if at the expense of others. Michel Chevalier visited the Lowell factory workers and studied the system to find that among these "nuns," "the rigid spirit of Puritanism" was "carried to its utmost."

The American's business creed was reaching a new stage of development. The minister and theologian of evangelicalism progressively identified with competitive individualism at the expense of community.

No old creeds were denied. No old confessions of the churches were deserted. Few admitted that they were making changes. They did what accommodating interpreters often do. They made things come out right in a world of inevitable change and, blessing change, became agents of it by the way they evoked symbols of continuity to disguise change. The same God, same Christ, same Bible, same heaven and hell, the same sense of calling were preached in the early 1860s as in the 1820s, but new meanings were read into them. The uneasy were given a good conscience, the indolent were jostled and prodded, the victims were extended charity, the system itself was not tampered with. It was identified with the laws of nature and the only plan of God.

13 · The Fire from the Fringes

Protestants Beyond the Evangelical Churches

The custodians of the Protestant empire at midcentury would have argued that all evangelicals belonged to their churches. The reason for this is simple. Evangelicalism is based on the relation of persons-in-community to Jesus Christ, a relation expressed only in the churches. But Protestants have not successfully been able to confine the Protestant spirit to the Protestant churches, and the first half of the nineteenth century saw many embodiments of protest outside ecclesiastical institutions or at the far fringes and borders of evangelicalism.

The Protestant spirit, in this context, implies prophecy and protest. It is based on the idea that the church represents but does not embody the Kingdom nor exhaust all that is implied in the reality of the Kingdom of God. Such a spirit suspects institutional claims for divine right, shuns idols, protests too close a bond between a symbol and the divine reality behind it, and rejects a simple blending of the finite and the infinite in human organizations. Whenever the Protestant churches made extravagant claims about their hold on truth or justice, people who followed the logic of Protestantism radically had to speak from the boundaries, to fire from the fringes. The period between the War of Independence and the War Between the States saw numerous examples of protesters who had come to judge Protestantism.

The first of these, as we have already seen, came through the moderate Protestant-based version of the American Enlightenment professed by people like Benjamin Franklin, James Madison, and Thomas Jefferson. Shaped by biblical lore, grateful for earlier Protestant contributions to human freedom, resentful of Christian dogmatism but respectful of its higher morality, they often found themselves at odds with the churches. Their heresies were selective. Few of these eighteenth-century people could have accepted anything like doctrines of original sin or God's act of foreordaining people to hell. They minimized or disregarded supernatural claims, even as they studied ways to apply the moral demands of Jesus in the new society.

Because this kind of Enlightenment was not anti-Protestant, it was possible for the evangelical minority in the first quarter-century after 1776 to relate to it and even to fuse with it. Historians have often stressed the resultant parallels and cross-influences between Protestant Christianity and nonecclesiastical and especially governmental traditions in America. In such a reading, Christianity in its Protestant lineage and the democratic faith joined in their "enlightened" faith in moral law, which resembled Protestant witness to the Kingdom of God. Constitutionalism perpetuated Calvinist ideas of the restraint of evil. The free individual in American republicanism paralleled the free Christian of evangelical regeneration. The ideas of progress in the republic were reminiscent of millenarian Protestant hopes. The democratic faith and Protestantism alike called people to mission in the world. Both fed each other's sense of destiny. Both shared positive belief in God and in "the people," and brought the two together in a faith that somehow God's will could be known. Both believed that that will could be determined as part of the truth that emerges from conflict.

Much of the conflict crossed the lines between holders of republican creeds and evangelicals. The former claimed that the latter made arrogant and self-righteous claims, while the church members charged that the democratic faith could easily become a new form of Christless infidelity. So they were often ready to shout "Infidel!" at others or to label fringe churches, at the boundaries or beyond the boundaries of orthodoxy, nonevangelical or unevangelical. The Unitarians who had absorbed motifs of moderates in the earlier Enlightenment era drew and returned most of the fire in the first decades of the new century. "Calvinism is giving place to better views," wrote William Ellery Channing in 1820. The people he referred to as Calvinist did not give way, so far as the statistics of church membership were concerned. Unitarianism remained the official faith of an elite few. But its Protestant spirit perpetuated much of the Enlightenment faith in reason which had helped form American institutions and constitutions.

These moderate para-Protestant traditions have been more significant than their own contemporary radical protest forces. In the generation of the founders, people like Ethan Allen, Elihu Palmer, or most notably Thomas Paine were iconoclasts. Insisting that they were not atheists on the one hand and were far from orthodoxy on the other, their militant deism picked up notes from Protestantism. They believed somehow in a God beyond the control of priestcraft and a deity beyond superstitions and of human ritual. They believed in reason and the free individual. They blasted institutions like churches which claimed to represent the full plan of God on the basis of revelation. Their extremism and ineptness, coupled with American fears of infidelity after revolutionaries set up cults of reason in France around 1793–1794 set them up for a fall. Timothy Dwight led the hosts of evangelicals to victory against them in the Second Great Awakening around 1801–1802. The church leaders, in fact, gave them notice far beyond their significance. They did this in the interest of exaggerating the evils that would go with rejection of the standing order.

The spirit of radical antichurch Protestantism revived briefly in the late 1820s, beginning with the coming to America of the Scottish philanthropist, community builder, and socialist, Robert Owen. Owen teamed with the fiery Scottish-born reformer, Frances Wright, Abner Kneeland, and numbers of communitarian freethinking groups to attack the growing hold of evangelicals on American institutional life and the national character. In their debates, like those between Owen and Alexander Campbell at Cincinnati in 1829, they chose to attack the idolatries and clericalism of even the most primitive and anticlerical of the evangelical leadership. They conceived of themselves again as working out the logic of Protestantism's faith in freedom and reason to its extreme.

These iconoclasts found a target in the alliance between evangelicals and other defenders of the political or economic existing order. They complained that the Protestant churches were justifying the system of slavery, even though church leaders had often pointed to incompatibilities between Christian teaching and human slavery. The reformers identified with the new urban workers who were being neglected or put down by the established evangelicals, clerical and lay, and helped organize parties and unions for laborers in the late 1820s. They criticized the ties between clerics and people of wealth or of middle-class aspiration, in the interest of primitive Christian-style simplicity or authentic human community. Robert Dale Owen said that Christianity ruled in America only "for her utility as an engine of state policy." It gave tools to the powerful and enslaved the weak and ignorant, preventing reason from coming on the scene. "This is the secret of Religion's success. She supports the throne, and the throne supports her." Abner Kneeland laid his axe at the foot of the tree of civil and economic power intertwined with clerical might. Fanny Wright regularly unrolled the Declaration of Independence and showed how clerical custodians of empire prevented actualization of its tendencies.

Miss Wright made distinctions in her attacks: "I am said to make war upon the clergy, and to hold them up to the hatred and derision of the people: it is not so. I have denounced the system, not the men." By 1830 she felt "warned, for a reason, to retire," and withdrew. Robert Owen allowed for good people in the religious field, but claimed that evangelicalism was run by lower types. He, too, protested in the name of pure and high religion against cheap compromises between American churches and enslaving powers.

Like their predecessors before the turn of the century, these men and women of the Jacksonian era failed in part because of their own utopianism and impracticality. But more important in their downfall was a new counterblast by Charles G. Finney, Lyman Beecher, and a new generation of revivalists who found the infidels useful when they wanted to conjure images of terror or to drive people to support of the churches. The first two victories belonged to the evangelicals.

The third and most dignified intellectual and spiritual assault on Protestantism was more successful. It came to a climax in the late 1840s and early 1850s, out of the left wing of Unitarianism, in the Transcendentalist movement, and in the impressive flowering of American literature. Thoreau's *A Week on the Concord and the Merrimack* (1849) was followed a year later by Nathaniel Hawthorne's *The Scarlet Letter* and the next year by Herman Melville's *Moby Dick.* In 1854 Thoreau repeated with *Walden* and the next year saw publication of Walt Whitman's *Leaves of Grass.* For two decades before this Ralph Waldo Emerson and Theodore Parker had issued a steady stream of addresses, sermons, and essays.

Like many talented people, these authors and speakers were not representative of all the interests of their day. Nose counters can point out any day that statistically the revivalists had far more people in range of hearing. The common people adhered to the old faith. But if one measures the hold these nonchurched leaders had on the imaginations of influential people and the ways in which they have been enshrined in the American school textbook tradition, it is easy to see the kinds of victories they had over the evangelicals. They represented what may have been the first successful post-Protestant generation in the United States. From then on, the intellectual and academic communities were increasingly divorced from Christian sources. After them, those who fashioned or controlled the symbols of community for the nation were free to ignore the Protestant context. After the Transcendental era, people would always be surprised to see expressions of loyalty to orthodox Christianity in the literary community. A schism had occurred in the national soul and psyche.

This literary generation came on the scene at a crucial moment. The evangelical churches were in a period of still-increasing growth and strength. Divided over the issue of slavery and on geographical lines in the 1840s, they still found many bases for unity and confidence within their main geographical and political regions or sections. The frontier was open; the California gold rush was inspiring new westward moves. Cities were growing; the industrial process was being accepted and even sought. With so many changes in people's physical circumstances, people were "in a shopping mood" for ideas or symbols which would help them interpret reality. For many, the old creeds could simply not bear the strain or carry the weight.

At such a time one would expect to find many options, and the student of America in the quarter-century before the Civil War will not be disappointed. Transcendentalism, romanticism, utopias, millenarian visions, ideas of innocence and primitivism, pantheism and paganism, doctrines of Over-Soul and Absolute Spirit, dreams of community and contentions for socialism all vied with conventional evangelicalism and the political or economic old order.

Many of the attackers considered themselves to be the pure Protestants who would sever the ties between grasping ecclesiastics and enslaving establishmentarians, and many later historians rank these gifted leaders as Protestants. They regard it as a truism to state, for instance, that Emerson was a Protestant who valued Christianity's guidance for conduct but not for belief. His expressions against the Lord's Supper were an attempt to carry Protestantism's wariness about idolatry of symbols to extremes. Orestes Brownson spoke of his work as a "protest against Protestantism." Perry Miller has introduced Emerson, Thoreau, Brownson, Alcott, Parker, and others among *The American Transcendentalists* with the reminder that they were "Protestant to the core" but they turned their protest against the Protestant ethic. Daniel Aaron has seen the early progressives, beginning with Emerson and Parker, to be derived in part from an "unorthodox Protestant Christianity more urgent and more fiercely evangelical than the bland reasonableness of the Enlightenment." They were born at a time when a righteous minority protested against the human damage of the urban and industrial era and the exploitation of victims at the expense of republican ideals. To carry on their vigorous protest, they often had to move outside the Protestant churches.

The new spokespersons were united in their justifiable sense that they were moving from one epoch to another. Emerson saw the change as well as any and expressed himself better than most as he pointed to the gaps, breaches, and schisms. The party of the past had been warring against the party of the future since 1820. In a lecture delivered near the end of his career he remembered the war between intellect and affection; a crack in Nature had "split every church in Christendom into Papal and Protestant; Calvinism into Old and New schools." "Men grew reflective and intellectual. There was a new consciousness." On this scene appeared reformers, not with "the fiery souls of the Puritans," but gentle souls in a "time when the air was full of reform."

At the moment of this crack or schism, the literary figures united in recognizing the breaking up of the old Christian interpretation of life. "Forget historical Christianity," urged Emerson. Many did not have to work to forget; they merely reported on the slippage. In his essay on Jonathan Edwards, Oliver Wendell Holmes, the science-obsessed Harvard medic who spent his life working his way out of Calvinism, wrote: "The truth is that the whole system of beliefs which came in with the story of the 'fall of man' ... is gently fading out of enlightened intelligence," to be replaced by new sciences.

Sometimes observers of the dying empire and system spoke with measured regret, mingled with hope. Emerson could remember a debt to "that old religion which, in the childhood of most of us, still dwelt like a sabbath morning in the country of New England, teaching privation, self-denial and sorrow!" "The spirit's holy errand through us absorbed the thought." He asked, somewhat nervously, "What is to replace for us the piety of that race? We cannot have theirs; it glides away from us day by day." Parker was predictive and devastating: the traditional faith was in a stage of "the last glimmering of the candle before it goes out."

The writers and lecturers protested against the vestiges of old Protestantism and called for the emergence of the new. George Ripley wanted to effect a theological transition: "The time has come when a revision of theology is demanded. Let the study of theology commence with the study of human consciousness." Emerson wanted to retrieve and enlarge the idea of love: "This great, overgrown, dead Christendom of ours still keeps alive at least the name of a lover of mankind. But one day all men will be lovers."

The call for a replacement to the old Protestant order was easily made; finding the replacement was more difficult. The transitional leaders were haunted by the terrors of unbelief at midpassage. Here as so often, Emerson was most eloquent: "A new disease has fallen on the life of man ... our torment is Unbelief, the Uncertainty as to what we ought to do; the distrust of the value of what we do." One could not be content only to be the iconoclast, and he complained, "Our religion assumes the negative form of rejection." He compared the age's distemper to the world of the colonials who walked in the world and went to their graves tormented with "the fear of Sin, and the Terror of the Day of Judgment." "These terrors have lost their force," only to be replaced by unbelief.

Not all the writers were as content as Parker and Emerson to leave behind the web of symbols to which the ancestors had responded. Nathaniel Hawthorne and Herman Melville, throughout their lives, agonized over the cosmic themes which had animated the old Protestantism. While the revivalists gloried in their statistical successes and overlooked slavery and industrial victimization, and while evangelicalism turned optimistic in its glorification of the trivial, authors like these pondered the old Protestant witness to the tragic dimension of life. In the midst of progressivism, bravado, and boasting, these were the new Puritans who wrestled with the deep, dark underside of the human venture and the national experience. One might go so far as to say that one half of the Christian message about man's nature had gone underground, to be neglected by evangelists who made conversion easy and who promised too much. Protestantism lived outside the churches, and many a colonial theme can best be revisited not in Beecher or Bushnell but in Hawthorne or Melville.

Rather than write a long aside on American literary history, it is more to the point to quote Melville's essay on Hawthorne, published in 1850. He spoke of blackness, of "a touch of Puritanic gloom" in his colleague's writing. "This great power of blackness in him derives its force from its appeal to that Calvinistic sense of Innate Depravity and Original Sin, from whose visitations, in some shape or other, no deeply thinking mind is always and wholly free." Melville argued that no thinking person could permanently weigh the world without at least sometimes throwing in "something, somehow like Original Sin, to strike the uneven balance." Hawthorne did so with greater terror than others. "This black conceit pervades him through and through."

Not all those who saw old Christendom dying were able or willing to reexplore Protestant witness to the depths of the human story. At the opposite extreme were people like Walt Whitman, whose new religion would be a celebration of democracy, a kind of pagan-pantheist rejoicing in creation. Whitman would repudiate precisely the themes that so "fixed and fascinated" Hawthorne and Melville.

These outsiders, freed from ecclesiastical ties if not yet liberated from Protestant obsessions, had found numerous vantages from which to judge and condemn the custodians of the evangelical empire. The elder Henry James, attracted to Swedenborgianism and at home with technology, envisioned a communal world which, as he wrote in 1847, was most opposed by the Protestantism which at that time had no room for a social gospel. "As at present constituted, it is the citadel and shield of individualism, or the selfish principle." Three decades after this he could still think of Protestant Christianity's "insane habit of regarding human life as PERSON-ALLY and not as SOCIALLY constituted."

Theodore Parker turned his Protestant spirit against the villains in this selfish drama, in *A Sermon on Merchants* in 1846. They had taken the place once held by fighters and nobles, to control politics. "This class is the controlling one in the churches . . . in the . . . way it buys up the clergymen. . . . The clergymen will do its work, putting them in comfortable places." Parker observed what became a notorious activity in decades to follow: "The merchants build the churches and endow theological schools; they furnish the material sinews of the church." Metropolitan churches had become as commercial as shops. Parker could hardly restrain himself when he saw how the church tied itself to the people of wealth who had scrambled for it adroitly and with vigor. In no country in Christendom was life so insecure, "so cruelly dashed away in the manslaughter of reckless enterprise." He reminded believers that Jesus had said that one who would be "the greatest of all, must be most effectively the servant of all." The whole economic ethos of evangelicalism supported people who stood in total contradiction to this ideal. "Ecclesiastical blowbags" supported the inspiration of the Bible to shore up their "hospital of fools, the resort of rooks and owls." Of the church: "The one thing it does well is the baptizing of babies."

The maverick reformer Orestes Brownson underscored the point in an article on *The Laboring Classes* in 1840. He also struck at the obvious practical and emotional tie between successful aspirants and their clerical advisers. The exploiting employer, not the enslaved worker, is praised as the good man, as a worthy Christian. Why should he not be, "since our *Christian* community is made up of such as he, and since our clergy would not dare question his piety, lest they should . . . lose their standing, and their salaries?" In a truly Protestant spirit he remarked that not a few of the churches rested on Mammon for their foundation, and their clergy were raised up, educated, fashioned, and sustained by the exploiters.

Brownson was speaking of "free labor," which he seriously but with an extremist's touch and tone argued was more dehumanizing and frustrating than the slave labor which he also abhorred. But the problem of slavery was still another which demanded the raising up of Protestants outside Protestantism; most of the antislavery and abolitionist leadership that was not working in a church context had grown up on the materials fed to the evangelical conscience. Abolitionists were often sons and daughters of conventional clergy who believed that they acted out the logic of their parents' positions, even if they had to repudiate their parents and their churches.

The flaw in the Protestant defense of slavery in the South and its general rejection of abolitionism in the North was that before it had become impolitic to oppose slavery or politic to oppose abolition, most churches had gone on record to criticize human enslavement. The opponents of slavery who turned against the churches had only to remind many clerics of their earlier positions. What had changed? Had they been wrong from the first? This few of them would have been ready to admit, for they had tied their opposition to slavery to basic biblical teachings. Had slavery softened, become more humane? Hardly. Their critics protested that the clergy had simply compromised for the sake of popularity and to keep their enterprise going. So the moral assault had to move outside the churches and even had to work against them.

As early as 1780 the Methodist Episcopal Church, then in infancy, had condemned slavery as "contrary to the laws of God, man, and nature . . . contrary to the dictates of conscience and pure religion." By 1836 southern Methodists had undergone a complete change, criticizing any who would try to interfere with master-slave relations. Presbyterians in their General Assembly in 1818 called slavery "a gross violation of the most precious and sacred rights of human nature; as utterly inconsistent with the law of God." Significant numbers of Presbyterians denied this teaching during the time of their schism, 1836–1838. The third major group with a large southern membership, the Baptists, found pronouncement-making more difficult because congregations and associations were autonomous. There was less national organization. But enough Baptist leaders had early spoken against slavery, only to turn silent or become prudent apologists when the Cotton Kingdom demanded their assent and support.

William Lloyd Garrison, best-known of the radicals, turned on the churches and eventually purged his part of the movement of evangelicals, who led churches that were "the most implacable foes of God and man." The most "intense abhorrence should fill the breast of every disciple of Christ" in their presence. They were inhabitants of "a cage of unclean birds and a synagogue of Satan." Garrison remained Protestant, even when in an anarchic mood he nominated Jesus Christ to Presidency of the United States and the world.

A final realm in which a Protestant spirit outside the evangelical churches had to rise to judge Protestants was that of national chauvinism. Emerson, although ambivalent on this issue, called it silly, for "every nation believes that the Divine Providence has a sneaking kindness for it." While the Beechers and Bushnells, the Waylands and the Finneys, were ready to tie the purposes of God to the details of American empire and mission, others had to speak the note of reservation. The climax of the Protestant-beyond-Protestantism movement in the nineteenth century came through the activity and witness of Abraham Lincoln.

At times he could engage in an almost uncritical act of devotion to the state, regarding the Union with the fervor of a religious mystic. But this man, shaped by evangelical culture, who never joined a church and found himself at home with no particular creed however much his language and thought were formed by the Bible, could also be reflective in judging his nation. Protestant in his reliance on God, he was not overconfident that he could interpret precisely what the will of God was for the nation. He spoke of America not as Bushnell had, but rather of its populace as an "almost chosen people."

"The will of God prevails. In great contests each party claims to act in accordance with the will of God. Both *may* be, and one *must* be wrong." Another time he reminded, "Both [Union and Confederacy] read the same Bible, and pray to the same God; and each invokes His aid against the other." "The prayers of both could not be answered." "The Almighty has his own purposes." People should try to do God's will as well as they could determine what it was for them, rather than claim God for their purposes. In such sentences Lincoln kept alive a Protestant witness to the limits of national pretensions at a time when almost no Protestant leaders North or South felt free or willing to do so.

If the evangelicals, then, were so adapted to their empire that they had lost the critical note and fallen into what looked like fatal compromise or idolatry of ecclesiasticism, competitive individualism, or nationalism, the United States on the eve of the Civil War did not lack iconoclasts who would wreck their altars, and was not short of gifted spokespersons and leaders who did something more creative. They raised doubts about the pretensions and confidence of the people who invoked the highest religious symbols for the widest variety of human causes.

14 · The Beginning of the End

Stresses and Strains Before the Civil War

Trustees of empire, even those devoted to gentle purposes like winning souls for Christ and spreading holiness, always had to be vigilant. Threats from within and without disturbed their peace. The history of Protestantism in America in the early nineteenth century was an almost continual record of protection and attack, of conflict imagined or real. The obvious warfare, that between denominations, occupied the energies of many church members. But these verbal skirmishes, full of animosity as they may have been, neither terrified nor gave promise to outsiders. The real defense of empire went on elsewhere; a review of the Protestant successes sets the scene for an account of the circumstances which led to the end of the empire.

Those who were promoting the Kingdom of God in America were for the most part of similar ethnic stocks and, although their differences seemed vast to them, they held to a broad evangelical consensus of opinions. Their homogeneity was most visible to foreign visitors, latter-day immigrants, infidels outside the churches, or victims of their united actions.

To achieve the position from which this unity could be exerted on the environment, they had engaged in recurrent waves of revivalism. Starting almost from scratch, on a frail colonial base and with little popular support, they could number as revivals the Second Great Awakening in 1800–1802 and a follow-up after the War of 1812; the late 1820s, "the Finney era," saw consolidation of new strength, and from about 1837 to 1857 revivals remained a characteristic way of spreading the faith. The lay renewal of 1858 was the last in the sequence.

Throughout this period the evangelicals had to beat back opposition. They were abandoning fields of service to Indians, trying to forget the mission to the native Americans, and took pains, whether under the system of slavery or among free blacks, to assure that blacks would not share actual

126

power. The infidel assaults had been put down in the 1790s, the 1820s, and with less success, around 1850.

Heretics had come again and again to disturb the peace. In the early years of the century the Unitarians were first to be tabbed as unevangelical, because of their denial of central Christian doctrines. Soon after, a more rough and tumble group, one made up of less elite classes and thus more ready to compete on the revivalist front, the Universalists, who denied eternal damnation, served as a foil for evangelists who were looking for immoralists or blasphemers in every village. In the 1820s a Unitarian-style schism among the Quakers (the Hicksite faction), and some of the "Christian Connexion" in the broad Disciples of Christ and Church of Christ element, looked suspiciously unorthodox because of their unwillingness to accord full divinity to Christ. Labelers regularly placed them all among the nonevangelicals, along with infidels and socialists. Most of the orthodox held fast.

The evangelicals had even contained their own too-orthodox, the Princeton scholastics, the Mercersburg "Puseyites," and Bishop Hobart's Episcopal High Churchmen, so that these did not cut too much into their ranks. All these groups wanted to impose doctrinal, liturgical, or hierarchical standards from the past, and their rigor or rigidity could have been a threat to evangelical unity. Alertness on these fronts had not kept them from adapting to two of the great sea changes in human history. They had survived and helped bring about a revolution, the end of the divine-right claim for kings and the beginning of the postcolonial era. Evangelical doctrines and visions were transfused into republican institutions and democratic faith. Half a century later the even more profound change implied by the words "urban" and "industrial" did not completely upset them. They provided rhetoric, symbols, and motivation for interpreting the new world.

In the process, the Protestants had invented durable forms for religious life, revised Christian theology top to bottom, embraced new economic creeds, won the West and begun to win the world. They coexisted across increasingly hostile North-South lines.

The key to what Lyman Beecher had called the "exuberant glorious life," was the virtual monopoly that the white Protestants had on spiritual and moral formation in the culture. No one else was so well located or so well organized to leave a stamp on all institutions and on the mores. When their monopoly was challenged, as it was from two directions, they reacted strenuously, exuberantly, but often ingloriously.

The lesser challenge, and one which did not haunt the evangelicals so much in the decades to come, came from other Protestant-style religious groups who thought of America as their unique Zion. The other, and the one which eventually brought an end to the empire, came from the monopoly-destroying immigrants who insisted on a point and eventually made it: America was a pluralistic society. Her charter did not permit religious monopolies, did not establish hosts to welcome (or shun) guests, did not license empires within the republic.

Beginning in the late 1820s, the United States was filling up with numbers of groups who rejected existing forms of community. They served to test the limits of consensus, and came to encounter either total ostracism or actual persecution and martyrdom. Many of these were small, ephemeral, and unsuccessful groups, and they need not concern us long. Zoar and Oneida, Amana and Aurora, Hopedale and Bishop Hill, were names of communities begun by various groups: Rappites and Shakers and Transcendentalists. Their systems always included spatial separation. Thus it implied control of lands exempted from the disciplines of moralists in the evangelical empire. Now and then church leaders could really rise to the challenge, as in their condemnations of Oneida's John Humphrey Noyes' "complex marriage," with its overtones of free love and a holiness beyond the law, in the late 1840s. They were always on their guard against European infidel intrusions at the hands of Saint-Simonians, Fourierists, or Owenites.

None of these communities were as disturbing as the religious communions which grew out of the evangelical environment, transforming Protestant visions of the future into what seemed like disturbing realities. The best known and most frightening of these was Mormonism. This religious movement began in the western part of New York, which had been "burned-over" by revivals. It seemed to exaggerate and caricature the evangelicals' millennial sense of attachment to the American land. Mormon teaching included polygamy, because "the Lord commanded it." Thus it violated the most sacred of the middle-class Protestants' ethical canons. And the Latter-Day Saints wanted land, a place apart.

In the articles of faith the official dogma reads: "We believe in the literal gathering of Israel and in the restoration of the Ten Tribes; that Zion will be built upon this continent; that Christ will reign personally upon the earth; and that the earth will be renewed and receive its paradisaical glory." Founder Joseph Smith, shortly before he was martyred, gave evidence of his brand of patriotism: "The whole of America is Zion itself from north to south." Here were the real American religionists, the ones whose revelation focused directly on the national landscape. They exemplified many of the Protestant virtues, including thrift and optimism.

The evangelicals were unable to destroy them, despite political-religious clashes all along their route to Utah. Of all the groups whose dogmas challenged Protestantism, the Church of Jesus Christ of the Latter-Day Saints has come closest to perpetuating the imperial idea. In Utah, southern Idaho, and most of Nevada, Mormon majorities live as conservative Protestants had hoped to do a century and a half earlier.

Other religious groups were seen to pose challenges but these were seen to be minor as time passed. Mother Ann Lee's Shakers, a simple group with strange forms of worship, was to be only a brief threat. The Millerites, followers of New York state resident William Miller, gathered twice in 1843 and 1844 for a literal return of Christ. But when after these embarrassments and disappointments they dispersed to regather under the leadership of Ellen Gould White, they began to blend back into the Protestant family of acceptable churches. Their observance of the Saturday Sabbath and following of Old Testament dietary laws set them apart, but doctrinally only their millennarian views seemed extreme. They did not seek land or a space apart and posed no permanent threat. Only the Mormons succeeded in developing a theocracy inside the empire, in occupying an area where "Gentile" evangelicals never were able to extend their dominion.

The other great factor which began to spell the end for the men of the Protestant estate came to have great significance in almost all areas of the nation, particularly the urban. This was the succession of waves of Continental and Irish immigrants who began to find a way to American shores in the 1830s. Religion was almost always a factor in rejection on the part of the older settlers, although ethnicity also had to be reckoned with.

These waves included Continental Protestants and infidels, Roman Catholics, Jews, and later Eastern Orthodox citizens. The Jews made little impact on the national consciousness before the Civil War. While through their Bible studies many Protestants came to hold views which might be classified as theologically anti-Semitic, the Jews were too small a presence (about 3,000 people in 1815) to represent encroachments on the spread of empire. They had been in America since colonial days, and by 1848 numbered only about fifty congregations. Anti-Semitism became a social reality in the 1880s and even more in the twentieth century. It was a feature of the early post-Civil-War Ku Klux Klan. But in the prewar days, American Judaism attracted little general Protestant attention. To be classified among the unevangelicals in the books on religion meant only that Judaism kept some very good and some rather weak company in the minds of the classifiers.

The major Continental immigrants around midcentury came from Germany. Some of these were fairly well off and were soon accepted in America. Others came to oppose political religion in Germany and chose to remain aloof and geographically isolated through the rest of the century. But the majority came in waves that represented reasons for concern to the Anglo-Americans. Some of them were failed revolutionaries who found Europe uncomfortable after the Revolution of 1848. Many were apathetic about religion. Most were Catholic, Reformed, and Lutheran.

Germans had been well-regarded in the textbooks on which nineteenth-century American schoolchildren were brought up. Contrived racial theories found that Anglo-Saxon democracy was born in the forests of ancient Germany. Modern Germans were cultured and struggled for nationalism. They were comprehensible. But coming in droves as they did, they were hard to absorb or comprehend. They were the first group of numerous newcomers who could not speak English, and they often gave little evidence of hastening to learn.

The record of the century shows that German isolation need not have led to such a sense of threat to the old settlers. But many expressions of distrust and suspicion survive. Most Germans became superpatriots and wanted to share a love of the land which those of British provenance had expressed. Yet they seemed to have a reserve clause whenever they made clear that they thought their faith and culture, German culture, were united. A liturgy that Lutherans used in Pennsylvania in 1786 asked God who had been pleased "chiefly by means of the Germans, to transform this state into a blooming garden, and the desert into a pleasant pasturage," that he should "help us not to deny our nation, but to endeavor that our youth may be so educated that German schools and churches not only be sustained but may attain a still more flourishing condition." Such a culture within a culture, unassimilated and conscious of separate identity, was to be frowned upon.

Under the leadership of Samuel S. Schmucker of Gettysburg, Pennsylvania, a large element of the older eastern settlements among the Lutherans were on the point of Americanizing and becoming a part of the evangelical movement when another faction came to withhold consent. Thousands of new "old Lutherans" settled in the Mississippi valley and they withstood efforts to be amalgamated into the evangelical consensus. Old-line American revivalist denominations then considered them fair game for proselytization. A Methodist mission superintendent announced: "The Germans almost all belong to some church, and are strongly attached to what they call their faith. Hence we have to preach their religion out of their heads in order to preach Bible religion into their hearts." In the numerous expressions of this type it was clear that "what they call their faith" was not acceptable in the common evangelical vision.

The peak year for German immigration was 1854, when 215,000 arrived. Germans were most visible when their non-Pietist majorities gathered for social purposes. They were given to beer drinking and other robust entertainments. Worse, they chose to celebrate on Sunday. This observance of "the Continental Sabbath" was abhorrent whether in the hands of Lutherans, Reformed, Catholics, "Forty-eighters," or the religiously uncommitted. Ethnic and cultural factors dominated so much that in such circumstances the fact of being a Protestant availed German-speaking people little.

During the 1830s and 1840s German separatist movements developed. These were designed to perpetuate German culture and education, but in some cases calls for separate German states alarmed their fellow citizens. Reaction was not long in coming. In 1849 Kentucky Congressman Garrett Davis argued for restrictions on German immigration. His speech reflected a widespread attitude directed against the "myriads" who were pouring in from the "German hives" to establish ominous enclaves. They live "in isolation; speaking a strange language, having alien manners, habits, opinions, and religious faiths, and a total ignorance of our political institutions; all handed down with German phlegm and inflexibility to their children through generations."

Davis foresaw the day, less than fifty years hence, when the upper Midwest would be "essentially a distinct people, a nation within a nation, a new Germany." Davis then evoked racial appeals of the kind that carried so much weight in those decades. "In a few years, as a distinctive race, the Anglo-Americans will be as much lost to the world and its future history as the lost tribes of Israel."

The Germans did eventually find alliances in the existing American political structure. More important, they dispersed so much that talks of separatism became politically unfeasible. Large elements of the German population were trained to be submissive and obedient to all higher authority and found it easy to transfer loyalties to the American government. Only German Catholics long continued to suffer formal exclusion from the circle of evangelical acceptability, but German Protestants had served to help break the simpler ethnic bonds which had held the empire together.

The final test for those who argued that the American republic demanded religious homogeneity came with the arrival of millions of Roman Catholics. Those who insisted on the "one national religion" concept on a Protestant base were to be overwhelmed by these millions. But they did not go down without a battle, and the three decades before the Civil War saw the height of the only interreligious conflict which, when blended with ethnic and political concerns, led to some bloodshed.

The leaders of the Protestant kingdom knew very well what was happening as the Irish, German, and other Catholic "hordes" began to make their way into United States ports in the 1830s. They were to spend years in agitation for immigration laws, in attempts at legal limitation on Catholicism, or in efforts to make life so uncomfortable that other potential immigrants might be dissuaded from coming. A few tried to convert people from Catholicism, hoping to assimilate the immigrants. Such a program proved unpopular in part because it was unsuccessful and in part because too many Catholics were not of proper racial or ethnic stock to become acceptable even if they did become Protestant.

The anti-Catholic preachers and pamphleteers (who seem often to have been more prejudiced than the laity) had deep reserves of suspicion on which to draw. The original colonists had felt themselves beleaguered, with French Catholics to the north and Spanish-Portuguese Catholics to the south. They had emotionally protected themselves against Catholic intrusions into the thirteen colonies. Where possible they isolated the Catholics, mostly in Maryland. Where necessary they began to accept them, as in the case of prestigious families like the Carrolls. But with few Catholics on the scene, it had been easy for colonial parsons to exaggerate stories of Catholic superstition and horror; no one was around to refute them. People could thus constantly reaffirm the prejudices their foreparents had brought with them from England and elsewhere across the Atlantic. The Dudleian lectureship at Harvard was established to provide pseudointellectual substance for anti-Catholicism. While not many Americans were churchgoers by the time of independence, they saw Catholicism to be a religio-political combine that boded only ill for the republic.

As the 20,000 or 25,000 colonial Roman Catholics grew to a body of 40,000 at the beginning of the century and multiplied forty times by 1850 to 1,606,000, there were ever-increasing levels of animus and threat in the Protestant rhetoric. In 1816 there had been 6,000 Irish; by 1850 there were 961,719. The peak years for Irish immigration were 1845–1847, during the horrendous potato famines.

Catholicism was always represented as a political religion which had its designs on world subjugation through coercive means while evangelicalism had similar designs but would use persuasion only. The Catholic immigrant was often pictured as a person of low morals and bad habits, racially inferior, congenitally alien, and historically unable to understand or contribute to free society. It is true that nineteenth-century Catholicism was making noises which gave political anti-Catholicism a certain plausibility. Some Protestants misread the signs of the times and exaggerated Catholic power in Europe. In their argument, Catholicism was merely trying to spill over into North America to extend its strengths. Others were more aware of the fact that political Catholicism was "on the ropes," and that in the pontificate of Pius IX at midcentury, Catholicism was struggling for survival in most European states. Almost everywhere the new nationalisms worked against Catholicism.

The First Plenary Council held in Baltimore in 1829 can be seen as the event from which organized anti-Catholicism took its rise. That Council demonstrated that Catholics were in the United States to stay; that they liked it there; that they were organizing so they could extend their ministry and mission. Baltimore was an early center of American Catholicism. Not a few Protestant divines were convinced that the basement of the cathedral was an arsenal and a dungeon, and made a point of warning against this citadel in widely published reports.

The first major anti-Catholic pamphleteer and one who stirred as much conflict as any other in the half-century was a failed artist and the inventor of the telegraph, Samuel F. B. Morse. Few have been able to explain his bias and animus; given his esthetic nature and the appeal that Catholic and especially Italian culture had for this nature, it is hard to see how a man of his talents would devote his life to the cause. Many have dated his crusade from a minor incident in Rome in 1830. Morse was observing a papal procession when "without the slightest notice, my hat was struck off to the distance of several yards by a soldier, or rather by a poltroon in a soldier's costume." His instrument was a gun and a bayonet. The man's officer, said Morse, had been responsible for the incident. No doubt anti-Catholicism would have been as intense without Morse, but from that year on he devoted himself to providing uniting symbolism.

Morse provided the catch phrase: here was a *Foreign Conspiracy* to take over America. The immigration was not merely an accidental result of European overcrowding and famine. It had been designed for the overthrow of America. The old Holy Alliance had been resurrected, now to work through the Jesuits. In Morse's work, published in 1834 and 1835, he asked for anti-Catholic unions against Catholic balloting power. "Our religion, the Protestant religion, and Liberty are identical, and liberty keeps no terms with despotism."

That a clash of empires, the coercive Roman and the persuasive evangelical-republican, was involved was clear from the frequency with which territorial imagery was presented. The Methodist bishops in 1844 said that "Romanism is now laboring, not only to recover what it lost of its former supremacy in the Reformation, but also to assert and establish its monstrous pretensions in countries never subject either to its civil or ecclesiastical authority." They called for unity against Catholic extension in the invaded Protestant communities. Three years later a *Protestant Annual* editor asked, "Have we not reason to believe that now, while popery is losing ground in Europe, that this land presents to the Pope a fine field of operations . . . ?" The Pope would use his fiendlike purpose so that he could "make a grand a triumphant entree into this country when he shall be hurled from his tyrannous and polluted throne in Europe." At midcentury a secret nativist "Know-Nothing" party was formed; some of its literature envisioned the day when American presidents would "go a-toe-kissing" and have to expiate rebellious deeds by standing in the wintry weather outside the Pope's chamber. "Then there would be a rare time for shaven monks—an imperial field of plunder and rapine."

Entrepreneur Lyman Beecher seized the opportunity to try to organize energies for missions in his *Plea for the West.* Horace Bushnell warned of *Barbarism, the First Danger* in the West in 1847, while Albert Barnes thought that the Mississippi valley would be "the great battle field of the world—the place where probably more than anywhere else the destinies of the world are to be decided." The *Home Missionary* in 1839 said "the cause is the cause of the West." "There the great battle is to be fought . . . between Christianity . . . and the combined forces of Infidelity and Popery on the other."

Now and then a voice of sanity would come forth, like that of Henry A. Wise, an Episcopal layperson in Virginia in 1855. He calculated that Catholics were outnumbered twenty-one to one: "Now what has such a *majority* of numbers . . . to fear from such *minorities* of Catholics . . . ?" But the conspiracy theory was used to reply to his kind. As early as 1834 *The Protestant Vindicator* was spreading the "ascertained fact that Jesuits are prowling about all parts of the United States in every possible disguise . . . to disseminate Popery." These disguises included "puppet show men, dancing masters, music teachers, peddlers of images and ornaments, barrel organ players, and similar practitioners." Against such disguises, a majority might well be powerless.

The Nativist and Know-Nothing parties consolidated political sentiments against Catholic immigration and expansion. A convent was burned at Charlestown in Massachusetts in 1834; there were riots and some deaths in Philadelphia in 1846 and minor skirmishes elsewhere. The Protestant public was ready for every kind of palpably phony and lurid disclosure like the *Awful Disclosures of Maria Monk* in 1836. People would believe any tall tales of what went on behind convent doors. Nativism and Know-Nothingism were too extreme for even a passionate people and they began to be dissipated before the time of the distractions of the Civil War. By then so many Catholics were on the scene that their presence was also felt positively. Their loyalty was largely unquestionable. The Protestant majority was to spend most of the next century learning to live with them. As Protestants did so, they picked up a new understanding of the American religious charter, even as they began to lose their dream of a homogeneous evangelical empire.

PART TWO

From Evangelical Empire to Protestant Experience *1877–*

V · A COMPLACENT ERA

15 · The Failure to Bind

Reconstruction and After

The War Between the States and the ensuing period of Reconstruction represented permanent problems for those who had sought to advance a single Protestant program for America. That program had been rather clear and consistent for almost a century. Using the raw material from the covenants of colonial history, church leaders had set out to win people's souls for Christ, to make them holy. They were determined to present God and humanity with a reformed dominion, whose citizens could help fulfill his purposes by spreading the Gospel into all the world.

For these tasks they had recognized that, despite what seemed to them to be valid differences on denominational lines, they had to contribute to a single national religion, and many of the leaders touted the virtues of "sameness" in the design for the republic's spiritual life. During that century, however, divisions deeper than those between Protestant church bodies were developing—even within Protestant churches themselves. Those which most frustrated the attempts to perpetuate the evangelical empire followed the lines of the Civil War (between North and South) and of one of its most visible issues (between whites and blacks).

The failure to mend and heal in the 1860s and 1870s shaped the destiny of Protestantism for the ensuing century. There were, of course, other plaguing problems to the custodians of empire. They failed to bring together the older Anglo-Christians with the later Continental intruders. They were surrounded by non-Protestant immigrants, especially in the city. They found that much of what they had considered to be distinctively Protestant was blurred in the American environment. They chose to divide over issues of religious thought and social action. But the North/South and black/white issues were the greatest predestining factors for the second national century, and they deserve first attention.

The Union had won the war, and, although President Lincoln wanted his compatriots to aid in binding and healing, vindictive policies were eventually to win out during the dozen years that ended with 1877 and the close of the era of Reconstruction. The South was set back economically. Its factories and transportation facilities had been destroyed. Morale was low. Worst of all, the South had lost many of its young men. And new problems presented themselves, many of them centering around the issue of the blacks freed by the Emancipation Proclamation of 1863. Suddenly a defeated section had to cope with the problem of four million largely untrained free people. Not to educate them meant that they would remain passive and inert. To educate them meant that they would become economic threats in already depressed areas.

For southerners, the recovery of pride was essential. One way to regain it was to make monsters of northerners, who often rendered that task simple by their punitive and vindictive actions. William A. Dunning, the major southern historian who gave his fraternity the basic picture of Reconstruction with which many worked for decades, was to define the episode as "the struggle through which the southern whites, subjugated by adversaries of their own race, thwarted the scheme which threatened permanent subjection to another race."

Making devils of the northerners was not by itself a sufficient basis for new self-esteem. The religious people of the South had a more difficult problem. They had seen their cause to be a moral one, chartered by Providence itself. God had led them to slavery as a peculiar institution, to secession as a policy, and to battle as a means for defense of both. Now they had been defeated. Had they been wrong? Had God failed them, or had they failed God? There were varieties of answers to these questions, but few answers led to the kind of soul-searching out of which new concord with the North, including northern Protestants, could have come.

In the time-honored evangelical manner, some preachers and editorialists in southern Protestantism sought and found the answer to their questions about southern defeat in the individual vices and sins of their people. Thus they could attack these private problems of manners without having to acknowledge that something had been basically wrong with the shape and the fabric of their empire. Beyond this, they could only make references to God's will. God, wrote a Georgia Baptist editor in 1866, "has done what he thought best." He may have "laid his hand heavily upon us; certainly we are deeply smitten, but in the midst of it all, we rely on his goodness, and would not, if we could, interfere with the workings of his Providence." A Virginia editor could not believe that God would have designed the Civil War to overthrow slavery, an institution which God "ordained, established and sanctioned" forever. God could not have intended that an "inferior race might be released from a *nominal* bondage and endowed with a freedom which, to them, is but another name for licentiousness, and which must end in complete extermination." He concluded: "It was Satan that ruled the hour" of emancipation. Earlier the same paper had said that the war settled problems of power, not of morality. Expressions such as these were widespread, and they provided almost no base for reunion.

The northern church leaders, especially those who had been ardent for abolition of slavery, spoke in opposite terms. God had vindicated their cause and therefore, it was presumed, God could stand with them in support of repressive policies against the defeated South. The tones of moral self-righteousness were strident. The war had settled matters not simply of power but also of morality. The period after the war gave them an opportunity to try to extend their empire into the South. They would carry on missions to whites and blacks in the region. Often they were motivated by genuine concern for the emancipated blacks, and even some of their misguided and ineffective policies of education, reform, charity, and soul-saving grew out of good intentions. But they were thoughtless about the problems they created for people in the southern churches, to whom the new missions looked simply like an invasion of territory.

The old language about land, space, and territory, a language with which Americans had become familiar from the lips of those who had earlier spoken of a single Protestant empire in America, reappeared in the context of this invasion. "Parson" Brownlow spoke in territorial terms from his base in Tennessee. Trading upon the Unionist sympathies of people in some areas of that state, this itinerant preacher gained the governorship and expressed rabid Radical Republican positions against the secessionist heritage. "The Devil is in the people of the South. . . . If we are to have another war, I want a finger in that pie. I want your army to come in three divisions, the first to kill, the second to burn, and the third to survey the land into small parcels and give it to those who are loyal in the North."

Short of a war, the churches could carry on spiritual imperialism, and it was recognized as such by many southern leaders. An editor in Virginia in 1866 claimed that northern churches were "far more . . . political organizations than . . . religious fraternities, and, being such, are already much too strong for the public safety." Methodist bishops in 1869 complained that some northern Methodist missionaries and agents "who may have been sent into that portion of our common country occupied by us" came with the avowed purpose to "disintegrate and absorb our societies."

As a result of this ongoing struggle, it was impossible for the major churches to reunite across the Mason-Dixon line. Smaller groups like the Lutherans, who had few churches in the deep South, and the Episcopalians, who had only a small minority presence in the Confederacy, had never split on sectional lines and these had less difficulty rebuilding. The northern Episcopalians, for the most part, had never wanted to acknowledge that a political and military division had torn their church apart. In 1862 at the General Convention the northern-based church even read the names of southern bishops in roll call, and only six months after the war the southern bishops were reinvited to the General Convention.

The churches which had served most of all as guardians of religion in the Confederacy had greater difficulties with their northern counterparts. The Baptists made sporadic postwar attempts to come together, but almost nothing came of these and the localism which always enhanced, or afflicted, Baptist life in America sapped the motivation for a united church. By 1870 it was clear to all that southern churches did not want to reunite with the North. From that day southern Baptists have gone their own way, to remain the majority faith in the South and to overwhelm statistically their northern brothers.

While their organization would have permitted reunion more easily, the Methodists were equally torn and equally uninterested in re-forming a national church on the lines of the one that had been divided in 1845. Not until 1939 was there to be a reunion of Methodism. Methodists shared with Baptists a statistical predominance throughout the South, particularly in the border states.

The third group, and the theologically most sophisticated, were the Presbyterians. Their divisions had formed a crazy quilt of New School and Old School in North and South, beginning around 1837. The Old School was doctrinally more rigid and, in the South, inclined to proslavery tenets; the New School was made up of moderates, chiefly in the North; they were also moderate on the abolitionist issue. They continued to divide on sectional lines within and across these schools during and after the war. One part of the Old School divided during Reconstruction in the border states, as northern Old and New Schools were working for reunion. This was effected in 1870. But a southern Presbyterian Church, separate and equal, was the result of these schisms and reunions, and it was to live an independent life for the century to come.

The northern churches concentrated on educational missions among southern blacks. Often overlooking the developing patterns of segregation and racism in their own territory, philanthropists, educators, missionaries, and agents of northern churches spoke in judgment of the spiritual vacuum left by southern churches. It was true, there was an exodus from such churches. In 1860 there had been 207,000 Southern Methodist blacks, while in 1866 only 78,000 remained on the registers. The Presbyterians saw a 70 percent drop in the few war years and the years immediately following. The decline was to continue; in 1861 there had been 31,000 southern black Presbyterians, but by 1916 this number dwindled nearly to the point of nonexistence, to 1,322.

One of the favorite northern philanthropies was in the field of higher education, as colleges and universities like Hampton, Fisk, Atlanta, and a score of others were developed in the years of Reconstruction. Many of these grew out of the efforts of a nondenominational group, the American Missionary Association. At the same time, each denomination carried on its own work. Methodists set up Paine College in Georgia, while the Baptists sponsored Spelman for girls in the same state. Presbyterians and Episcopalians, to a lesser extent, paralleled these activities. But few of these efforts were regarded with favor by southern churches, who saw in them simply more tentacles of Radical Republicanism, prideful judgment, and the creation of black elites who would threaten them in their already deprived circumstances.

Reconstruction, then, saw the setting up of permanent problems for any who had ever dreamed of a continuing single dominion for Christ in the hands of Protestants. One glance at the religious map of majority churches by counties in twentieth-century America makes clear how deep the geographical divisions themselves have remained. Except for a few Catholic counties in the delta of Louisiana and in extreme southwest Texas, virtually the entire deep South is made of up of counties with Baptist majorities (black or white), interspersed with an archipelago of Methodist counties. The Methodists grow stronger the farther north one moves, and dominate in a long band of counties stretching from West Virginia through the southern Midwest in Ohio, Indiana, Illinois, Iowa, Missouri, and Kansas. Very few counties in the Northeast, the Great Lakes area, the upper Midwest or the western half of the nation have Methodist or Baptist majorities. Except for Mormon territories, only Lutherans in the upper Midwest (Wisconsin, Minnesota, the Dakotas, Iowa, and Nebraska) predominate throughout a region—and the Lutherans, chiefly of Continental origin, were not assimilated into the Protestant empire.

While Baptists, Methodists, Mormons, and Lutherans reigned in their own parts of the country, the colonial big three, the Congregationalists, Episcopalians, and Presbyterians, dwindled in statistical significance and were a minority presence in a kind of thin spread across the nation. Almost nowhere did any of the three have statistical predominance in a county and none of them held enough clusters of counties to represent anything like a regional empire. Without some comprehension of the deep territorial divisions resulting from the schisms in denominations and the disagreements over the ethos, the later history of American Protestantism is virtually incomprehensible. The old Anglo-Protestant denominations of the North have never been able to call for support in theology, mission, or politics from the parts of the country where the huge Protestant predominances are: the Baptist base, the Methodist midsection, and the Lutheran arm. And not often do members of churches in these latter sections feel united with the mainline northern churches left over from the evangelical imperial years. If there had ever been a chance of having all the Protestants regain the common vision of a single destiny for America and its churches, the war and Reconstruction ended it.

Reconstruction not only led to continuing division between churches; it left a spiritual stamp upon the South. For a fanatic few, it gave birth to white supremacist organizations like the Ku Klux Klan, organized on December 24, 1865, with a mishmash of Protestant biblical justifications and eclectic liturgies from the lore of secret societies. This organization was to rise from time to time to give militant expression to the most spiteful sides of the argument for a white Protestant empire. While a frightening menace to both blacks and to whites of good will in the South, it could hardly be called typical of the fruits of Reconstruction.

Among these fruits was the tragic sense of life which lived on in southern churches in the years when northern leaders were developing and demonstrating ideas and programs based on progress and optimism. Southern pastors had to minister to more people who were in abject poverty, for whom this world held little or no hope. Thus they continued to accent the deferred benefits in the life to come, in a heaven won for believers by Jesus Christ, while northerners could continue to pick up the post millennial line of the evangelical empire and talk about the ways the American environment itself could be transformed into the Kingdom of God.

The southerners throughout Reconstruction had to continue to justify the eternal design of slavery, a case they had made on the basis of an infallible and inspired Bible. Thus they tended to continue to make literal use of biblical passages to justify their ongoing translations of the Southern Way of Life. They had to resist even moderate acceptance of developmental views of revelation or cautiously critical attitudes to the formation of the Bible in the years when many northern church leaders had begun to accept such positions and opinions. The South, in reality and in later mythology, was to be seen as biblicist and conservative, and much of what came to be called the Bible Belt had its home there. It was an inerrant Bible that provided heavenly solace for people who had to look to eternal life for happiness and victory and who had to find ways of judging the northern invaders during and after Reconstruction.

Changes in the understanding of blacks' religion and church life and later patterns of white racism also developed as a result of Reconstruction. Were one to continue the narrative of the first half of this history, he could expect a script that would read something like this: While slavery had been accepted for a long time, and with it an implicit view of black inferiority, the emancipation and Union victory changed all that. After 1863 blacks came to be awarded some of their rights and the Fourteenth and Fifteenth Amendments to the Constitution brought more. During Reconstruction blacks even held office throughout much of the South. Since almost all blacks who were religious were Protestant, the trustees of Protestant dominion in America took advantage of the situation. They greeted these as their brothers and became partners in continuing their mission to America and to all the world. No problems of theology and few problems of polity stood in the way, since these blacks held to the southern majority religions (Baptist and Methodist) and in the North these faiths were also strongly represented.

Anything but that happened. Reconstruction and its aftermath in South and North alike drove whites and blacks further apart, and no instrument played a larger part in institutionalizing and justifying this separation than did the complex of Protestant churches. Before the war, blacks and whites—for all the gulf slavery had implied—at least felt some sort of spiritual bond. The whites took responsibility for some religious education and development, even on the plantations. But after the war, the black exodus from southern white churches was sudden, nearly total, and virtually always welcomed. The black was seen by southern church leaders to be an ally of the Radical Republican of the North, the partner of the hated conqueror, the instrument of his subjugation. Fears of miscegenation and rape were evoked. The mission to blacks was largely abandoned by southern church leaders. They established the policy of segregation in religion as well as in the rest of life. Ironically, they sold this pattern to the North and in this area of life at least, the South "won" Reconstruction.

Curious new kinds of racism were both the bases and by-products of the new separationist policies. No such drastic ideologies could have been developed in religious America unless religious people had been ready with justifications. Providence, which had been called upon to justify colonization, extirpation or removal of Indians, extension of covenants and charters, slavery and antislavery, now was reinvoked ot legitimate segregation and racism. The society hardly needed preachers to make the claims for divine warrant. Politicians and publicists could do the same. Pennsylvania's Congressman John L. Dawson saw race prejudice itself to have been "implanted by Providence for wise purposes." Prejudice would prevent miscegenation and other unwise policies.

Near the end of the war a Boston cleric, Increase N. Tarbox, wrote *The Curse; or, The Position in the World's History Occupied by the Race of Ham,* a reflective discussion of the religious roots of racism. Americans of his own time, he mourned, had picked up "by inheritance from our fathers, a set of ideas and opinions, which in the unquestioning period of childhood we were easily made to believe, and which have been and are still firmly held by multitudes as undoubted truths." They passed with a "halo of antiquity" through ensuing generations. "If you venture to disturb their faith in these old traditions," complained Tarbox, they "will start back instinctively as if you were trying to unsettle the foundations of everlasting truth." Precisely. And if this was true in prewar New England, it was doubly true during the period of negativity and fear in the southern Reconstruction. The racist had a firm religious base on which to build.

If Providence had implanted prejuduce as something salutary, so God had also taken care to make the black inferior. In the white Protestant scheme of things, while this was predestined, yet man was somehow responsible. And responsibility for black inferiority, slavery, and segregation, lay with one of the sons of Noah at the time of the biblical flood. Those who accepted the Bible literally had no difficulty seeing this son, Ham, as the father of the black races and the head of the negative covenant by which his heirs were to occupy inferior status to the end of time. The suggestion that the black's descendancy from Ham could not be demonstrated was shrugged off or met as an attempt to "unsettle the foundation of everlasting truth."

Many historians suggest that full-blown racism did not prevail in the South until around 1890, but that among the institutions which pioneered in its development by this time was the church. Here was Christian separating himself from Christian, Protestant segregating Protestant, evangelical defining another evangelical as inferior. Few went so far as Charles Carroll in his well-known *The Negro A Beast,* published in 1900 by the American Book and Bible House in St. Louis. He carried the curse of Ham all the way to the point of saying that the Negro was subhuman, beastly, without a soul. Significantly, this book met with a more favorable reception around the churches or at the fringes of membership than it did from responsible leadership, and some clerics took pains to condemn it. But many of them had helped prepare the climate in which Carroll's type of diatribe could find a hearing. Some spoke in the mood of a writer in the *Presbyterian Quarterly* in 1887: "The color line is distinctly drawn by Jehovah Himself." People dared not tamper with it. Such writers as the editor of the *Southern Presbyterian Review* feared a generation earlier that if "the patent fact of the essential inferiority of the black race is denied or even ignored," educators and religionists would only contribute to difficulties.

While southern moderates strove valiantly for some time to prevent segregation in church, they failed. While they tried to limit the overt racism of the crusaders and the fanatics, they were silenced. The northerners could for some time parade the justifications for their invasion and mission in southern territory by referring favorably to their own home areas, where slavery had long before been abolished and where racism was covert. But as the decades passed, it was clear that the black was not much more highly regarded in the North and that patterns of segregation developed in the South were being eagerly imported and quietly sustained all over the North. Northern Protestants were pleased to see the expansion of purely black religious organizations and not a few took pains to point out that blacks themselves preferred to "run their own show" and go their own way as equals in separate churches rather than as late-starters, minorities, or inferiors in integrated churches.

During these decades, uneasy advocates of segregation and white supremacy did not have to turn only to the churches for support. Curiously, the rise of the sciences and secularization of higher education were also boons to them. A generation of anthropologists, sociologists, and historians in major universities were proving to the public that the black was indeed inferior by any number of measures. Even southerners suspicious of godless science were able to select from the findings of scientists those teachings which confirmed their view of the scriptures, and segregation along with white supremacy were among these. Where scientists failed, politicians North and South could contribute; as late as 1906 President Theodore Roosevelt, who later confessed that having Booker T. Washington as a guest at the White House dinner was a mistake, could write of blacks that "as a race and in the mass they are altogether inferior to the whites."

A summation of the theology of racism would include elements such as these in its composite: God had made humans of one blood but of a number of races. The difference between these races was obvious, but the difference between blacks and whites was even further complicated by a specific historical event: the curse of Ham. Christ died for all, including blacks, and all could be saved and would somehow share heaven as a result of Jesus' work, should they accept his sacrificial death. Yet God had also implanted racial prejudice to help people overcome whatever temptations they might have to share intimate elements of mortal life. And among these elements was a spiritual coming together in the personal bonds which religious life in the congregations of those days implied. So the same God who had chosen the white Anglo-Saxon to carry on a mission to blacks and other inferiors around the world had also chartered separation of whites and blacks in both North and South. Blacks would be free to develop their own organizations.

Develop them they did. In the decades following the war and Reconstruction, the black churches remained as they had been before the war, the single most important institution under the control of blacks. While the Gospel preached in them paralleled that in the white Protestant churches and while the polity was similar, there was little interaction between the two. The black churches were called upon to perform functions appropriate to their communities. Through their educational system the more significant black leadership in politics, business, and education emerged. The local churches provided centers of meaning in a world of frustrations; systems of status in a world of general lack of fulfilment;

locales for interpersonal experience in a bewildering world; settings for celebration in a tragic world; and bases for power in a world that left them no other outlets.

Growth was dramatic. About 12 percent of the blacks in the United States (one-half million out of four and one-half million) were church members in 1860. In the following ten years, the African Methodist Episcopal Zion Church grew from 27,000 to 200,000 and the African Methodist Episcopal Church grew in the South from zero to 400,000 members around 1880. The blacks were divided in their "freedom" as they had been divided in slavery. Still predominantly rural in the nineteenth century, their churches knew little interaction. Denominational lines predestined them to go separate ways. The exodus from Presbyterianism led to the formation of a dwindling Cumberland Presbyterian Colored Church while Episcopalianism, one of the few churches that did not see formation of separate bodies, did develop separate congregations and rendered the Blacks even more powerless.

Blacks did remain Protestant, however. Roman Catholics made few inroads, and fifty years after the war not more than 1 percent had been won to Catholicism. Most of the blacks chose to make America the setting for their destiny. The appeals for emigration to Africa by Henry M. Turner, a bishop of the African Methodist Episcopal Church in Georgia, were hardly heeded. Most blacks welcomed dubious benefits of partial freedom in America to the uncertainties of return to Africa. Many were simply outside the range of appeals for return and had to cope with life before them.

In any case, black churches developed an independent life, to the general relief of southern and later northern whites. The Protestant empire of people's dreams a half-century earlier was disintegrating from within because Christians could not transcend the political and racial themes of war and Reconstruction; northern and southern, black and white Protestants all went their own ways.

16 · A Decorous Worldliness

Popular Protestant Accommodation

If white Protestants in the South were charged with giving solace and providing explanations for a depressed and defeated section, no such problems afflicted white northern Protestants. They had supported the militarily victorious side and it no doubt entered their minds that Providence had thereby given the sign that the political and moral positions of the Union had been vindicated. The best-known minister of the post-Civil-War years, Henry Ward Beecher, spoke in typically prideful terms of the ongoing empire.

"We are to have the charge of this continent." The South "has been proved, and has been found wanting. She is not worthy to bear rule." After noting how the old Confederacy had lost the sceptre in the nation and the several states, he continued in the conventional imperial terms: "This continent is to be from this time forth governed by Northern men, with Northern ideas, and with a Northern gospel." He was as sure as a thousand other ministers could be that the continent was to be cared for by the North simply because "the North has been true to the cause of Christ."

Not for nothing were these religious leaders later to be characterized almost automatically with the adjective "complacent." The North, its Protestant churches, and their ministers were in a new situation of power and pride. How the religious forces were to act in such circumstances was to determine many elements in the relation of the churches to the environment in America for decades to come.

The most famous sentence summarizing their stance comes from the pen of historian Henry F. May, who took a long look at America in its centennial year and near the end of Reconstruction and concluded: "In 1876 Protestantism presented a massive, almost unbroken front in its defense of the social status quo." Later historians may be tempted to be revisionist about their predecessors' judgments on the American past, but it is difficult to find documentation that would lead one to alter May's judgment.

In classic Christian terms, one should defend the world situation if it was congruent with the biblical pictures of the Kingdom of God. If not,

147

Christian leaders were called to be uneasy with it, to pronounce some sort of judgment on the way their world was put together, and to point it to a course which would make it look more like the promised Kingdom. While the Protestant clerics still continued to denounce individual faults of people in and around their congregations, they were even more at ease with general societal trends in the late 1870s than their grandparents had been in the 1830s.

The world of 1876 has seldom been looked back upon by people of any substantial political group as a time of the "good old days." The decades surrounding that date are usually remembered with pejorative terms like "The Great Barbecue" or peopled with a rising new group of "Robber Barons" who took advantage of the poor in the "The Gilded Age." Those were years of Reconstruction, with all its faults and failures; of high-level political corruption; of unchecked growth of personal fortunes at the expense of helpless millions; of general moral flabbiness and growing self-centered nationalism. Prophetic Protestants should not have been expected to confuse such times with life in the Kingdom of God, but not a few were on hand to christen them, to name them in terms acceptable to the Christian tradition.

In retrospect, one can best understand the Protestant identification with the world around the churches by trying to comprehend the pace of change in the western world and in the United States. It was difficult to cope or keep pace with the change. Clerical interpreters of culture had to help their people understand this world.

Reconstruction brought unprecedented problems to a nation suffering the wounds of division. The dash westward, partly interrupted by the war, was resumed. How lands should be acquired by individuals, railroads, or trusts, and how the frontier should be civilized were vital issues only a few years before historian Frederick Jackson Turner was able to transform a sentence in a Census Bureau report into a philosophy of history: the frontier was closed. The imagery of a threatening and beckoning wilderness and prairie would lose its magic. America was being filled up.

The trends toward the rise of factories and the growth of cities, noticeable already forty years earlier, were accelerated when the factory cities, the urban industrial centers, spurted. A whole new mode of human organization, almost all its details ominous to people of traditional habits and values, called for interpretation. To fill these cities, millions of new arrivals to America, almost all of them not part of the Protestant old stock, had to be assimilated or withstood and segregated. Labor, frustrated four or five decades earlier, had now come to the point where it was ready to organize. The new phenomenon, the strike, threw terror into the hearts of the conventional and the complacent. Women, often put in their place by evangelicals and a generally male culture before the war, began to assert themselves in groups for various causes, including most notably the rights of women.

In the idea-patterns of the churches, much change was forthcoming. From England announcement of Darwinian theories reached America, where people found that age-old views of human origins and development and of the integrity of Scripture seemed to be jeopardized. At the same time, Continental ideas about the origin and development of Scripture were beginning to be accepted by elitist religious thinkers in the North. Such acceptance threatened the basis for old-line evangelical thought about the national covenant. Evangelism was changing from its rural setting to the urban milieu in the hands of gifted revivalists like Dwight L. Moody, then in his prime. A new class of celebrity clerics was developing in the cities, people who attracted large followings because of their messages and modes of delivery. New religious groups like Christian Science were being formed and older exceptional groups like the Mormons were proving that they could not be put down. Roman Catholicism, the faith of so many immigrants, was coming to a new position of power in the cities and seemed to be a threat to the public schools, institutions which were coming to be a kind of junior branch of the established religion of the American Way of Life.

In the midst of these changes, it is little wonder that religious trustees of old American values would have trouble relating critically to trends which they saw to be in continuity with those old values. They defended personal property, endorsed individual rights to acquire wealth, congratulated those who aspired and achieved, and enlarged America's sense of mission and destiny in the world. Before the Civil War the presence of people of great wealth like the Astors or Girards was a rarity. After the war it became commonplace, and not a few of the 4,000 millionaires who were coming on the scene in the quarter-century after the war could feel that their course was being ratified at every turn by the major leaders of the Protestant churches.

In the face of such changes, one might have expected that many ministers would have eschewed the task of religious interpretation. With such an alteration of the environment around the churches and with so many challenges to their thought patterns, hermitages or ghettos could very well have seemed to be an attractive alternative. Or ministers could have taken seriously what their predecessors had announced that they themselves were doing, but rarely did—avoiding comment on the public world. Many did. Preaching on the cross of Christ was often undertaken only in the isolated context of soul-saving, and men like Dwight L. Moody made a genuine attempt to speak in such terms. But more characteristic were the new popular preachers. Among them few stood taller or attracted more followers than Henry Ward Beecher, whom we have already met as defender of the North's right to continental empire. In 1862 he announced that it was the duty of the minister of the gospel "to preach on every side of political life. I do not say that he *may;* I say that he *must.*" What had been seen as accidental or incidental to ministry came, in Beecher's time, to be integral to many a preacher's tasks.

There were more and more pulpits from which to speak, and there were ever more people to hear. Contemporary historians Robert Baird, Joseph Belcher, and Charles C. Goss left statistics from which can be gained the general sense of growth. During the ten years that ended wtih the conclusion of the war, Methodists grew by 22 percent, Baptists by the same amount, Presbyterians by 24 percent, Congregationalists by 34 percent, and Episcopalians by 46 percent. Even if one allows for gross inaccuracies, it is easy to see at least that the lines on Protestant graphs were not turning downward. So far as membership, attendance, and support were concerned, these churches were not in trouble. Here was a "churchgoing" America on an unprecendented scale. It was a church-building age. Church property holdings, mostly in white Protestant hands, were reported to have grown from $171 million to $354 million between 1860 and 1870.

The choice of celebrity clerics as representatives of the churches' culture needs some defense or qualification. No attempt is being made to say that every parson spoke as Henry Ward Beecher did about this world. He was marked as a kind of maverick, eager to empty the old Calvinism of its last embarrassing traces. Beecher and his contemporaries, Phillips Brooks in Boston, Russell ("Acres of Diamonds") Conwell in Philadelphia, T. DeWitt Talmadge, a Brooklynite as Beecher was, and a score of other interpreters do not make up the whole of the clergy. The frontier people and westerners and the revivalists' rural leaders would also have to be studied if the interest here were in polling and nose-counting. The attention to the accepted popular phrasemakers is warranted, however, because these gave public shape to a Protestant culture. They were widely quoted as authorities and chosen as custodians of the national religious symbols by readers of magazines and newspapers, by critics of religious change, and by large congregations of influential people in whose hands much cultural destiny lay. They do not represent the whole picture, but they did fill a distinctive role and deserve attention for the ways they filled it.

That role might be termed "transformer of symbols." A complex society is held together by certain common assumptions and shared beliefs. The people who made up the America of 1876 and thereafter had more in common than merely shared physical space within national boundaries. Large groups of people do not organize themselves simply around abstractions or philosophical concepts. These become concrete in certain traditional slogans, promises, and threats. Much of what was concrete in American hopes and dreams had been fashioned under religious auspices. How one regarded the nation, one's job and wealth, the poor, people of other races, origin and destiny—all these were interpreted and in a way regulated by reference to symbols like God, Christ, Holy Spirit; heaven and hell; moral purpose in the light of the Ten Commandments and the Sermon on the Mount.

The symbol-manipulators in the pulpits had to help their followers see purpose and meaning in a new way of life. They did so not by depriving these followers of rootage in the past. Indeed, Henry Ward Beecher used almost all the symbols his father Lyman Beecher had invoked half a century earlier—but he transformed them, robbed them of some old meanings and invested them with some new ones. In the process, his hearers could feel the security of knowing they were affirming the good in what had put together a fortunate country and a productive way of life, even as they could be reassured that necessary changes were approved by people who spoke for God.

Not everyone had to gather under pulpits to receive such interpretation of the common symbols of personal and national life. It was at once one of the strengths and weaknesses of Protestant preaching in the period that it was in general agreement with "what everybody said." Rarely was there anything abrasive or embarrassing to the sensibilities of the newly influential people in the culture. Ideas which ran counter to what middle-class and rich people of presumed good will held as common property were not often expressed. But the fact that numbers did turn to the pulpit and the religious editor or author does indicate something of the extent to which changes in the way of life were to be interpreted in century-old America. If the minister in the new industrial cities could help people turn with nostalgia back to the small-town life which they still regarded as normative and saving, so much the better.

The chosen area of clerical invocation or transformation of symbols in public life had to do chiefly with the economic order, with how people gained and spent or gave away dollars, with how they ordered their jobs, and related to their superiors and their inferiors. There was much less concentration on political life as such, and many ministers in effect turned from it because their preaching advocated a way of life in which the state would play a minimal role and the individual a maximal one.

While as the period progressed a minority of people were to fashion a social gospel which would stand in judgment on much in the industrial order, in the early decades after the war and Reconstruction, the ministers largely developed a kind of individual gospel which, they presumed, was exactly what their foreparents had preached. But whereas their ancestors had related this individualists' gospel chiefly to the destiny of immortal souls, the descendants—using the the same symbols but investing them with new meanings—turned from the spiritual to the material world and from eternal to temporal concepts of destiny. They came to endorse the American Way of doing business, as their forebears had begun to do, but then they took the dramatic step of applying this ethic to the more complex world of big industry.

Ministers catered to the affluent members who could build bigger churches. Staffs of what had once been peoples' churches were now often subject to the economic points of view of the rich on their boards. While outside muckrakers and occasional inside prophets would criticize such catering and such willing subjection, the ministers found it easy to go once again with the massive, unbroken front of support for things as they were. The old Wesleyan injunctions to gain and save wealth were ripped out of Wesley's old "love not the world" context and preached to people much at home with the world, with wealth.

As every student of the period knows, such worldly goods were coming into the hands of a few who could control the lives of the many. The poor had no access to the levers of power and acquisition, but clerics like Phillips Brooks minimized their number and their plight. Of course, he said, some poor existed. The rich could be charitable and the poor could do much more to lift themselves by their bootstraps if they only followed the gospel which taught that wealth was a sign of divine approval. The state was not to interfere or regulate in any way. People were not equal nor were they to have equality. God had predestined inequality, although God continued to hold the poor responsible for the sins which led them to poverty, even as the rich were called to accountability for the way they were to disburse their wealth.

Inequality, according to the Reverend A. J. F. Behrends, was "an original, ultimate, and unalterable fact." Government should not be "paternal and take care of the welfare of its subjects and provide them with labor." That was un-American, said Beecher. God "has intended the great to be great, and the little to be little." Russell Conwell preached: "I say that you ought to get rich, and it is your duty to get rich." Bishop William Lawrence of Massachusetts is still remembered chiefly for his aphorism, "Godliness is in league with riches."

The old biblical texts about the difficulties rich people would have getting into the Kingdom of Heaven troubled these transformers of symbols little. They always found a way to work around, surround, or reinterpret such embarrassments and to assure their hearers and readers that God had all along intended that the Kingdom should look like the newly affluent Americans' world. "In the long run," said Lawrence, "it is only to the man of morality that wealth comes. We believe in the harmony of God's universe. We know that it is only by working along his laws natural and spiritual that we can work with efficiency." He reverted to the older evangelicals' themes about the shape of the nation: "Material prosperity is helping to make the national character sweeter, more joyous, more unselfish, more Christlike."

Was such language new? Certainly some accents had changed. Whereas a half-century earlier, the poor had been told to be content with their status, they were now being judged as sinful because they were poor. Whereas the material quest of the rich had once been hedged by injunctions against loving the world, now the eternal judgment that threatened the rich had largely disappeared from the vocabulary of the preachers. But between these extremes, hearers could focus on what sounded rather familiar. The language of the gospel of acquisition had been fashioned a half-century earlier in a much different preindustrial culture. Americans were now passing into a new epoch in world history. The gospel of wealth being preached by clerics and industrialists like Andrew Carnegie did not strike the members of congregations or readers of editorials as being so new. In order to attract attention, representatives might often term it as being new, and it certainly was successfully adaptive to new circumstances. But an examination of the rhetoric reveals how regularly old familiar injunctions, once uttered in rural and village churches, were being rephrased in the new cities and in the audience of new classes of people.

Historian Eric J. Hobsbawm has pointed out in another context that the new industrial world had no pattern of life suited to the new age, so people more and more "drew on the only spiritual resources at their disposal, preindustrial custom and religion." He said of first-generation industrial workers what also might be said of industrial masters and America's huge new acquisitive class: "They looked backwards as much as forwards." The preindustrial custom and religion which these looked back upon was the complex fashioned or at least ministered to by the trustees of the evangelical empire, which predominated in the ethos in the first century of national life.

Seen in this light, the clerics filled a somewhat different role than first greets the eye. Their interpretation of life was not so simply being fashioned on the spot, to serve as an ideology to explain away the evils of an industrial order and to justify the lives of the new exploiters. Instead, this interpretation served to help inspire an industrial order, to give it momentum and pace, to hasten its rise and encourage its growth. Rather than serve as blinders for people who were slightly disturbed by the sight of victims of the new industrialization and the brutal life in the cities, it served as a charge to set the process of change in motion. The doctrines and ideals were waiting around, antiques from village and rural America, when person-to-person relations dominated. They needed only to be dusted, shined, arrayed, and employed in an impersonal world of industrial domination, trusts, stock markets, and speculations. Providence, election, working out one's salvation, proving God's favor, sharing his benefits, all features of the older evangelical ethic, were revalued in the emerging world. In the process they were deprived of much of the old backdrop of eternal rewards and punishments that had once accompanied them.

Not that no new features were gathered up into this gospel. Indeed, part of the ingenuity of the Protestant ministers and much of their success can be seen in relation to the degree to which they were able to absorb new theories. In a generation given to an awe for scientific explanation, they were able to appropriate selective elements of that scientific theorizing and make it part of their gospel. In the case of the early decades of the second American century, the mainline Protestant leaders bonded their old ethics with the new creed that is often styled Social Darwinism.

Social Darwinism came from sources outside the churches. Sometimes these roots had to be obscured, especially in the hearing of theologically cautious Protestants who feared the connotations of the word "Darwinian" or who resented some contenders for the creed, people like the tireless sociologist-lecturer Herbert Spencer or the exminister William Graham Sumner. The more one studies Social Darwinism the less one sees what was novel in it, little that was different from what was being propagated by celebrity ministers, or in contradiction to the Protestantism then so often publicly expressed. Social Darwinism may have been the means for secular-minded people to acquire much of the impetus of the transformed evangelical ethic, and it may also have been the way latter-day heirs of the ethic could sound up-to-date and scientifically sophisticated.

What Social Darwinism added to the vocabulary of the Protestant promoters was the purported scientific base for competition in the motif of "the survival of the fittest." An age hungry to reduce the random events of contemporary life to comprehensible laws, but one in which not all could relate to Providence, found that the idea of the survival of the fittest served to fit the random into the eternal scheme of things.

This antisocial teaching individualized the old Puritan-evangelical ideas about "election," ideas which were previously seen in the context of a covenanted community, and used them to justify personal economic competition as being guided by a principal of natural selection. As a result, many Protestants found themselves focusing on the material world and material processes as much as their Marxist opposite numbers overseas ever did with their "dialectical materialism." Spiritual language provided the halo for the new worldly talk, but it pointed to matters of implied secondary significance.

Survival of the fittest, whether in Protestant sermonic terms or in patterns described by Social Darwinist professors, meant elimination of the unfit. Christians were therefore placed in the novel situation of having to explain away the very classes of people among whom they conceived the Church to have been born and for whom the Gospel had been proclaimed:

the poor, the outcast, the downtrodden, the overlooked, the materially hopeless of the world. The rights of soul became property rights.

The ways in which the Christian Gospel provided the background for the gospel of wealth can best be seen in the career of William Graham Sumner, the most devoted and intelligent among the Social Darwinists. Sumner, who had a distinguished career as a professor at Yale after 1872, left behind his Episcopal orders and (he thought) his Protestant beliefs in support of the new theories of evolution and their application to a laissez-faire economic system. "I never consciously gave up a religious belief. It was as if I had put my beliefs into a drawer, and when I opened it there was nothing there at all," he was later to write.

What later students of Sumner noted as he, evidently, did not, was the degree to which the fittest of his earlier beliefs survived in his new sociology. He was more radical than most Protestant clerics in his formal rejection of the outer shell of Christian teaching and made a point of his disbelief in God and the Bible, in heaven and hell. But he kept his doctrine of morality and virtue, his ideal of the self-disciplined and striving model of character. Robert Green McCloskey has said that "he was the ideal parishioner in the church of Cotton Mather." He advocated "the idea of a divine plan with the divinity left out." God might not survive, but Order did. While Sumner's human did not need supernatural sanctions, the worshipper in the Protestant pew did. The effects and the ethics were the same in both cases. Stephen J. Field, the jurist who is usually mentioned in the same breath and category as Sumner, was also brought up in the Protestant context of New England. He was the son of an evangelical cleric and he also rejected the trappings of evangelicalism. Field kept more of a faith in the vestiges of deity than did Sumner, but he constantly worked to fashion a view of Order which would justify, explain, and give momentum to capitalist competition and acquisition. And the author of *The Gospel of Wealth,* Andrew Carnegie, revealed more than he knew about the sources of his Gospel even in negation: "I well remember that the stern doctrines of Calvinism lay as a terrible nightmare upon me." Beecher could have said the same, although his use of symbols was more subtle than Carnegie's.

The new Protestantism that was fused with Social Darwinism opposed state intervention. It attacked the rights of labor to organize and strike and advocated only the most modest and restricted charity to the poor. Revivalist W. H. H. Murray in 1870 argued that "undue importance . . . is attached to the connection of Christians one with another, and to the good or bad effect such connection has upon individual growth."

If the churches and the new worldlings offered the same substance, one might ask why anyone bothered to listen to church leaders, since the same ideas could be gained more cheaply elsewhere. But the pulpiteer offered symbols that suggested a "halo of antiquity" and ultimate motivations and justifications, and these were needed in a time of such dramatic changes. Later Protestantism produced its own critics and reintroduced a social note that had been increasingly neglected since colonial times. In the 1870s and 1880s prophetic criticism passed into the hands of the obscure, eccentrics, or relatively uninfluential people at the fringes of Protestant power. In 1880 J. B. Harrison noted that "the real religion of the people" had become largely "a decorous worldliness." Phillips Brooks rejoiced at the spillover from Protestantism to that world, impressed as he was by "the effort of men to do outside the churches and outside Christianity that which the churches and Christianity undertake to do." Conflict between church and world seemed to be disappearing.

17 · Perils–The City

A Bewildering Urban-Immigrant Environment

The Protestants in the second American century had more to do than keep on fighting the Civil War and keep on adapting to a new business and work ethos. As dramatic as the former problem and as far-reaching as the latter, was the new brute fact of the American landscape: it was turning urban. Few events did so much to weaken the evangelical empire in the United States as did the rise of the city.

Josiah Strong, a Congregationalist public relations agent whose best-selling book *Our Country* included a chapter on "Perils—The City" summarized the century of growth as perceived by people of his time. Observing the *Compendium of the Tenth Census, 1880* in his work published in 1891, he noted that in 1790 one thirtieth of the people had lived in cities of 8,000 or more people. By 1820 this element had been enlarged to one twentieth and just before the Civil War to one eighth. In 1880, almost one fourth lived there. While the whole population increased twelvefold, the urban population grew eighty-six-fold.

"The city," Strong noted, "has become a serious menace to our civilization, because in it, excepting Mormonism, each of the dangers" he had just discussed were enhanced. These perils included immigration, Romanism, change in the situation of religion and the public schools, intemperance, socialism, and wealth. On the last of these, by the way, Strong—as a marginal member of the social gospel movement—held more qualified views than did the celebrity clerics who had given it simple endorsement. He worried about "mammonism, materialism, luxuriousness, and congestion of wealth."

The author saw *Our Country,* the Anglo-Protestant empire, being overwhelmed by German and Irish immigrants. "Because our cities are so largely foreign, Romanism finds in them its chief strength." For the same reason, Strong saw the saloon and intemperance to be urban problems. Socialism thrived on "the social dynamite" of "roughs, gamblers, thieves, robbers, lawless and desperate men of all sorts" who gathered there. Were there conservative forces to save the country? "Here are the tainted spots

157

in the body-politic; where is the salt?" He observed that there was one Protestant church organization to every 438 of the population in 1890. But in Boston the ratio was one to 1,778 and in St. Louis one to 2,662. In Cincinnati the ratio was one to 2,195 and Chicago had only one to 3,601. True, urban churches were larger, but Strong could easily prove that the majority of the population was not being reached.

Education was a dire necessity. He argued that it took more intelligence to keep large populations republican than small ones. The writer foresaw Armageddon in the cities, having looked back on decades of minor threats: "The supreme peril, which will certainly come unless there is found for existing tendencies some effectual check . . . will arise, when the conditions having been fully prepared, some great industrial or other crisis precipitates an open struggle between the destructive and the conservative elements of society."

Protestants inevitably had to yield elements of empire in the city. They were not wholly unprepared for confrontation with urban life, but the urban-industrial mix presented overwhelming problems to them as it did to all the other nineteenth-century "powers that be."

American Protestants had been at home in the five colonial urban centers of 20,000 to 30,000 people each. More than is often recognized, they had appropriated many positive features of city life into their program early in the nineteenth century. But the towns of the pre-Civil-War period were still largely merchant cities, with comparatively homogeneous populations and an outline that Protestants could comprehend. Their village ethos and their small town mythology could carry them some distance in their task of interpreting and ministering in such cities. They had also welcomed industry and technology, but preferred to see their endeavors and evidences located away from large cities.

After the Civil War they could no longer prevent a combination from coming about: the factory and the city came together. And during the industrializing period, the farm—the familiar homeland of the evangelicals—dwindled in comparative economic significance. In 1870 farm income had outstripped that of factories by $500 million, but by 1900 factory income was $13 billion while farm returns were only $4.7 billion. In 1860 there were 141 urban (8,000+) sites in the United States, with 9 having more than 100,000. In the next half-century urban population would grow seven times in size and cities would multiply six times. By 1910, 597 cities had more than 10,000 people and there were 50 with over 100,000 people each.

However gladly welcomed by urban boosters, financiers, and competitors for public attention, the growth of cities was more rarely welcomed by intellectuals, writers, and spiritual leaders. The Jeffersonian tradition favoring agrarian life had become a virtual new covenant in American life, to which purists would return whenever they wanted to describe the good life. The literary traditions surrounding men like Ralph Waldo Emerson and Henry David Thoreau had deepened this tradition. Historians never tired of comparing innocent rural or village America with decadent and corrupt (because urbanized, industrialized) Europe.

Children in school were confronted with the conventional wisdom in textbooks which paradoxically boasted of industrial power but pictured village life as being normative. Their authors, often nostalgic sons and daughters of New England village parsons, returned again and again to the agrarian model, even though as the century wore on more of their readers were coming to be young urbanites. God had given the good, or rural, environment; humanity was spoiling it with an artificial, or urban, milieu. "The city for wealth, the country for health"; so taught a textbook of 1869. People would come to the city only with a fortune in mind or because there was no other place to survive. Virtue always resided in the innocent pastoral world: "The town for manners, the country for morals."

These values were nurtured beyond childhood, in sermons whose imagery was overwhelmingly rural. The best one could hope for was the dualistic kind of view typified in the famed Reverend Lyman Abbott's picture: "Every city has been a Babylon, and every city has been a New Jerusalem . . . and it has always been a question whether the Babylon would extirpate the New Jerusalem or the New Jerusalem would extirpate the Babylon." The Protestant view usually followed Josiah Strong's nervous lines about Babylon's potential victories.

One can compose from the sermons of the 1870s and 1880s a rather sophisticated analysis of the spiritual problems which sociologists and psychologists have later seen in the cities. The workers were divorced from their roots, from tradition, from each other. They found status in life only to the degree that they fulfilled a function. Unemployment had new terrors for people who could not depend for at least meager sustenance upon the soil. The temptations for government to be corruptible in the impersonal settings were especially strong. The tempo of life changed, for machines did not rest and demanded many shifts of work, shifts which confused the lines between night and day and between the day of work and the day of rest. People were dependent upon each other in complex new ways, but did not come into personal contact to receive the psychic benefits of interdependence.

All these were problems to all people, regardless of religious faith, in the cities. The more negative clerics avoided or scorned the city; the more creative ones did what they could to minister to them in the face of these problems. Because the threats represented challenges to the world of meaning in which Protestantism was at home, they threatened Protestantism itself. But there were other baffling urban realities which did even more to cause the old evangelical empire to yield, to adjust, and in many respects to crumble. The new urban immigrants simply fell beyond the range of Protestant outreach and attraction. Foremost among those were the Catholics and the Jews.

Josiah Strong provides representative texts on the problem of Roman Catholicism as perceived by late nineteenth-century Protestant moderates. Perhaps these writings did not generate the fervor shown before the Civil War during the period of Nativism and Know-Nothingism, during "the Protestant Crusade" against Catholic intruders. Perhaps the decline in fervor came about in part because it could be seen that the Catholic tide was irreversible and that those of Roman obedience could not be cajoled or threatened or forced to go back to Europe. The Ku Klux Klan had not yet made anti-Catholicism so much a part of its program. The American Protective Association, formed in Iowa in 1887, did not represent much of an anti-Catholic political threat. But Strong reveals to us the extent to which Protestants feared, mistrusted, and resented Catholics.

His bill of particulars was brief and clear. Catholicism opposed the bases of national life; it was critical of popular sovereignty, free speech, free press, free conscience, free schools, separation of church and state. Few Catholics would have recognized themselves in such charges, but Strong and his contemporaries could always point to embarrassing statements by popes and theologians to show what Catholics ought to enact and would pursue, if they ever became a majority—as they threatened to do in some cities already by 1891. Strong had heard the archbishop of St. Paul announcing the desire to *"make America Catholic."* This could not be done without bringing the principles of that church into active conflict with those of American government. All who remained loyal to Rome *"would necessarily become disloyal to our free institutions."*

When assessing Catholic prospects, Strong pointed to growth. How large was American Catholicism? Cardinal Gibbons in 1889 had counted nine million people while Bishop Hogan of Missouri ("But this is wild") placed the figure at thirteen million. Strong favored a figure under nine million, torn as he was between deciding on a scare figure, which would be high, and a low figure which would illustrate the continuing good sense of Americans as they repudiated Catholicism. He saw Rome "with characteristic foresight" concentrating her strength in the West, just as Lyman Beecher had foreseen a half-century earlier. Since his purpose was fund raising for western missions, he may have exaggerated the western influence, for most of his contemporaries were more concerned with urban Catholic growth—as he came to be in his chapter on the perils of the city. He duly noted the Roman peril in his chapter on that subject.

The Catholics were coming in large numbers. They were to be responsive to a papacy which (in the *Syllabus of Errors* of 1864 and in the decree of papal infallibility in 1870–1871) was speaking in tones that often frightened American republican Protestants. They were joining other Catholics in the cities and were coming to dominate some elements of urban life.

They were robbing the Protestants of their monopoly in the religious culture.

Between 1820 and 1900, nineteen million immigrants arrived, one fourth of them Irish and almost all of these urban. The cities were often the only place these transplanted agrarians could go. They had run out of money just purchasing a boat ticket and had no more funds to leave eastern seaboard cities like Boston or New York to seek fortunes in the West. They were lonely and stayed close together. It was their muscle that built much of the city, and many who had been lackadaisical about church in Ireland shared in penny sacrifices out of which were built the huge, gloomy, but somehow imposing edifices of urban Catholicism. The church was an institution they could control, and they gravitated to it just as blacks had done in their own time when they were denied access to other forms of social life or other means of finding status.

Catholics were a visible presence in Protestant areas because they did not keep the Sabbath, were seen by Protestants as intemperate, and—crowded as they were into shanties and slums—often were perceived as raucous rioters. On more sophisticated levels, they chose to build their own parochial schools when they found public schools to be too much under Protestant influence. This move was interpreted as a threat to public schools and misinterpreted as still another denial of the American Way of Life. The leadership of the Catholic church was necessarily rather safe and cautious. American Catholics were, until 1908, technically part of a mission. Not until then was their church removed from the Congregation for the Propagation of the Faith. In such circumstances, it was not advisable for the priests and hierarchs to draw attention or suspicion to themselves. In any case, conservatism came naturally to them. But when Cardinal Gibbons in 1887 refused to condemn the Knights of Labor, he in effect endorsed the right of labor to organize and gave tacit approval to Catholic participation at a time when many Protestants were still trying to prevent the rise of organized labor. This mildly progressive action, then, only made Catholics seem more un-American to conservative Protestants.

Catholicism became increasingly visible, not only through weight of numbers but also because of celebrated events. The Second Plenary Council was held in Baltimore in 1866. The Vatican Council of 1869–1870 was widely reported upon in the American press, in part because forty-five American bishops took part. In 1875 the first American cardinal was named and eleven years later the great Cardinal Gibbons was given the red hat. A Catholic university, under pontifical direction, was founded in Washington in the 1880s. Catholicism could no longer be hidden or repulsed. The Protestant empire was yielding.

Statistically less significant but not without problems for the Protestant psyche and status was the arrival in the cities of large numbers of eastern European Jews.

Jews had been in America since colonial times and because of their small numbers and cultural backgrounds had known only minimal hardship in the face of the Christian majority. There was never any possibility that Jewish faith could be regarded positively. But the background of the earlier Jews, from Spain, Germany, and western Europe had not been disturbing. The problems came when Russia engaged in pogroms in 1881–1882 and when the new Jewish migrations came from eastern Europe. These Jews were often secularized and sometimes politically radical. They did not adapt to rural life, despite the experiment of Baron Maurice de Hirsch to attract them to farms.

The Jewish presence, then, was always almost entirely urban. Many Jews came to practice what skills they had with needle and thread. Out of the sweatshops they came, within a generation, to control and make up huge garment-workers' unions. Others went into merchandising. They fashioned new-style synagogues and even new denominations of Judaism to meet needs in America. Organizations like the Young Men's Hebrew Association showed that Jews could profit from Protestantism's experience with American voluntaryism. Despite some hardships, they liked it in the United States. As some Charleston, South Carolina, Jews stated: "This country is our Palestine, this city our Jerusalem, this House of God our Temple."

Josiah Strong grumbled a bit about rabbis who complained that the public schools were implicit nurseries of Protestantism, but he directed little more attention to the Jews. Not until the twentieth century was anti-Semitism a big enough political problem to warrant the devising of Jewish defense organizations and Jewish-Christian interfaith amity groups. But even if attention was directed more to Catholics, the Jews were still another huge urban population that contributed to the downfall of the Protestant empire by chipping away at power centers of Protestant hegemony.

Not only Catholics and Jews created disturbances in the Protestants' views of the city. They also noted the presence of urban socialism, atheism, and indifference, and sometimes scolded their own sons and daughters for drifting away. Charles Loring Brace, a New York agent of a Children's Aid Society, complained (in a book on *The Dangerous Classes of New York* in 1872), that a person often lost his or her religious habits in the city. "If a Protestant, he often becomes indifferent. . . . Moral ties are lessened with religious." The city was large and impersonal. One could hide from supervising elders or spying friends and did not have to occupy a pew in order to retain status, as many had done in the village. The attractions of city life also pulled people away from the church.

Mammonistic pleasures were regularly inveighed against, but Protestants did more than warn against the perils of the city. When it was recognized that the city was inevitable, they began to adapt and some even went so far as to speak in positive terms of the city as a workshop for God's purposes. There were attempts to innovate, along with noble experiments, efforts to understand, initiatives for reform, and not a few institutional successes by Protestant valiants. Not all of them were in the hands of liberal Social Gospel advocates.

Yet for all the noble attempts, Protestantism did not come up with adequate or satisfactory new forms for ministry to the cities. The old preindustrial patterns, born just before the rise of the new cities, remained normative. On any rational plotting, the crazy quilt of denominationalism should not have survived the city, but it did and was enhanced there as new groups were constantly being formed. In the chaos, impersonalism, and pluralism of the city, people clung to what was familiar to them. The denominations had served to define doctrine and morals in the isolation of rural America, and they were rather tenaciously adhered to in the new setting. Not until early in the twentieth century did Protestant efforts at reunion in an ecumenical movement resume. The last half of the nineteenth century was largely a time of continued schism and competition.

If the denomination remained long after it had a charter, so did congregationalism. The defense of the local parish system, with congregational autonomy, remained strong in the "free churches," while Episcopal and Methodist (episcopal) or presbyterial and synodical churches were in effect also hypercongregational.

Such a polity would not have been devised by any who would seek an effective strategy for a whole metropolis. But it was inherited from village America, from its fashioning at the last possible moment before the rise of the industrial city. In the new city, the isolated and independent congregations could wallow in their riches, building splendid edifices—only to see these neglected as populations shifted in the face of immigration and industrial change. Or they could wither in their poverty, if they were outside the zones of affluence. Some tireless agitators tried to get church bodies to see that all the churches in the flux of the city would eventually share a single destiny. But despite timid and occasional experiment, the parochial model held the field. Similarly, no new educational patterns supplanted that heritage from preindustrial times, the Sunday school.

No one could survive in the city, however, without some measure of adaptation. The revivalist, the dominating figure from the early part of the century, lived on and tried to make his way in the city. Some evangelists did well; Dwight L. Moody perfected the urban style of evangelism. In many respects, his was a reenactment of rural rites in urban settings. Large elements of his audiences and respondents were middle-class Protestants of rural background, and not the hardened secularists he implied they were as he issued his calls for conversions. Despite both his efforts and his rhetoric, there is evidence that he did not penetrate the new Irish or eastern and southern European immigrant sectors, even insofar as these were made up of lapsed and indifferent Catholics.

Moody, at least, knew what had to happen. "Water runs down hill, and the highest hills are the great cities. If we can stir them, we shall stir the whole nation." Himself an urbanite who spent his prime years in business and then in preaching in Chicago, he carried the means and the message to major American cities as well as to the British Isles and was a widely recognized public figure who tried to bring the old gospel to new citizens of cities. His adaptations were only formal, however. Moody, like the popular preachers of the 1870s and 1880s, was conservative in his view of American society and avoided topics which would have shown him to be a tamperer with the society's way of life. He resurrected pre-Civil-War premillennial pictures of world history and did not expect to see the cities transformed toward the shape of the Kingdom. The Second Coming of Christ alone would bring in a new order, and Christians should occupy themselves in the meantime with saving others' souls and tending their own. By departing from the more critical and upsetting approaches of people of the Finney era, Moody drew revivalism with him away from progressivism and reform.

He had few programs for dealing with urban problems. During a New York depression in 1876 he recognized "great misery and suffering in this great city, but what," he asked, "is the cause of most of it? Why the sufferers have become lost from the Shepherd's care. When they are close to Him, under His protection, they are always provided for." Even those who would have agreed on the priority of soul-saving found little to respond to in such an approach, so far as desperate bodily needs were concerned. He bought most of the revised social ethic which Protestants were propagating on tracks parallel to those of Social Darwinists. The fittest would survive, and the fittest were those who like Moody himself were hard-driving, hard-working, carefully plotting aspirants. For all the attention, he did not reach the large unchurched masses nor did he contribute greatly to church growth. He spoke from inside the old evangelical empire to people who shared most of the circumstances of a new kind of city. Lesser evangelists imitated him. Many were less open than he to new thought currents. Only a few tried to relate to the new temporal needs of people in the cities.

Valiant attempts were made to create churchly forms that would directly relate to the city. The YMCA, a pre-Civil-War import, extended much hope and fulfilled many purposes in helping city-bound and lonely young men find a center of meaning and mission in the city.

Another reasonably successful import from England was the Salvation Army, a split from British Wesleyanism under the care of William Booth. It was evangelistic in intention but chose service to the urban poor as its most effective means. The Salvation Army became what looked to all like a tightly disciplined and structured denomination, which would stop at little to draw attention and which was more ready than most to send agents into parts of the city where they would have to roll up their sleeves and get their hands dirty.

The Army, which came across the Atlantic soon after its formation in 1878, was sometimes regarded as embodying an undignified, and even vile, approach. A prominent Methodist editor in 1891 was sure that men and women mingled in it to work out "schemes of iniquity." But the Salvation Army survived through tight discipline, Booth family control, and the wise decision to pick its shots: "Our movement is especially raised to help those who are the lowest fallen, the most depraved and the most neglected." Not many Protestants wanted to compete for tasks at the bottom of the urban social heap. Eventually some more staid denominations came to welcome the Army's chosen role and even began to support it. Often the butt of ridicule by uneasy urbanites, the Army was also widely respected for its efforts. Not a few aloof Americans became aware of the reality of the slums through the efforts of the Salvation Army.

More sophisticated were the newfangled "institutional churches" sponsored by experimenters who had at their disposal large urban church edifices and reasonably large amounts of funds. These institutional churches came as close as any form to representing a breakthrough in the metropolitan milieu. But they turned out, too, to be limited in their appeal and in their ability to find backing. Most Protestant churches did not follow the institutional route, therefore, in which all the needs of people were to be met through complex serving parishes which had some elements of the settlement house, the clinic, the school, and the recreation center to go with their more conventional inherited functions. The model in Chicago was formed in 1877 as the Pacific Garden Mission, located where it could meet the needs of urban outcasts. New York's Saint Bartholomew's Church sponsored some of the better-known rescue agencies in the city. Blessed with J. Pierpont Morgan's funds and only sometimes compromised by his influence, New York's St. George's Church was able to carry on unconventional ministries on the East Side, particularly during the tenure of reformist cleric W. S Rainsford, who could never be accused as Moody sometimes was of sitting around and letting the miseries of the city alone, awaiting the interruption of history by Christ's Second Coming. These churches took on problems of drink and prostitution, poverty and ignorance, boredom and unemployment. They were able to stir up distinguished enemies, among them Charles A. Dana of the *New York Sun,* who named Rainsford a "conspicuous representative of a school of unwise and mischievous social agitators." During the prime years of settlement houses, these institutional churches represented promise and filled many needs. But most Protestant parishes carried on business as usual and the instituional church movement remained fairly small.

It would be unfair to say that no experiment went on in the era of the Salvation Army, the YMCA, and the institutional church. In addition, some of the more urbanized bases for interdenominational cooperation survived and were improved on in the era. The Protestant approach to the city was anything but a dead loss. But it was at the same time not a representation of mastery of the metropolis. The brute physical facts of the city; the psychic damage they caused; the general apathy of church people; the overwhelming presence of new non-Protestant immigrants to the city—all these led to the further disintegration of the Protestant empire and gave even cool heads reason to continue an old American tradition of speaking of the city first of all in terms of its perils.

18 · A Private Place for Religion

Life in the Churches

Much of the time men and women participate in religious activities without being aware that they are part of the drama chronicled by historians. Late in the nineteenth century hundreds of thousands of American Protestants went to church once or twice every Sunday without necessarily being aware that in other parts of the country religious symbols were being invoked for the verbal continuation of the Civil War. Depending upon their location, no doubt most people who saw to the religious education of their children in Sunday schools, by now the normative Protestant pattern, were hardly aware of the deep divisions between blacks and whites in the South and, here and there, in northern cities—divisions reinforced by religious sanctions. Yet the religious conflict between North and South and between black and white "made history" while the churchgoing and Sunday school attending did not.

During the closing decades of the century, thousands of congregations left their mark on the record of American history in very visible ways. They contributed financially to see to it that great edifices for worship dotted the landscape. As they made these sacrifices, perhaps most of them would have seen their activities as an evidence of Christian self-denial. And as they erected fortress-thick walls, for fortress-thick walls were the fashion in the 1880s and 1890s, they might well have subscribed to the idea that they were thereby drawing a line between the sacred and the profane, the church and the world. Would they have recognized themselves in the historians' portraits which often depict the Protestantism of their time as having been given over to "a decorous worldliness"?

Protestant ministers, then as before, called on the anxious and sick and dying. They served to impose moral standards on the believing communities through stern sermons just as they offered the solace of the Gospel of Jesus Christ to the sin-sick and troubled. They often won loyal followings through their own examples of spirituality and service. They inspired giving for an ever-expanding Christian mission into all the world. Would their congregations have been as aware as historians are of the growing cleavage between the two sets of ministers and theologians? Were they aware that some believed that Protestant activity should be restricted to these private and individual Christian acts, while others were convinced that soul-saving and caring for persons could only go on in a world in which Protestants also concerned themselves with justice in the political and industrial realms, with the whole shape of society? Did the common people, those who did not get elected to attend church conventions and did not read theological journals, all line up on one side or the other of liberal-conservative party lines?

To pose the questions is to imply the answers. No, much religious activity goes on, as it were, in a private place, a personal sphere, far removed from the public realms which interest historians. Yet these sometimes apathetic and often quiet "voters" are constantly contributing to the public drama. Appeals are made to them. Eventually, theological changes in seminaries trickle down to them through the ministers trained at such schools. Over a period of years, the preaching of a Henry Ward Beecher, whether or not it parallels what they have heard at home, becomes a symbolization of positions to which they relate positively or negatively. As time passes, the social gospel is consolidated into such a visible force that those who favor it can rally people to their cause by positive references to the movement's leadership, and those who oppose it can rally other forces by using the term as a bogey, a scare word.

To take an example from later America: every Sunday tens of millions of American children attend Sunday school. Their going entails a great deal of activity affecting millions of families. Breakfasts are made, clothes organized, transportation arranged and, perhaps in very rare instances, lessons are discussed. What goes on in the cubbyholes where most Sunday school classes are held helps form the "mentally furnished apartment" in which maturing people make their choices about religion. Personalities of ministers and Sunday school teachers play a part in character formation. Yet almost all this activity is lost to historians unless they are interested in chronicling the statistics of growth and decline as a measurement of American Protestantism, or unless they are historians of religious education and study the changes in lesson plans through the years.

Yet on a particular autumn Sunday a bomb went off in a Birmingham, Alabama, Sunday school and several little black girls were killed. History was made on that day, and it was dutifully entered into the record. History was made because the occurrence was public, violent, newsworthy; it related to activities about which the whole society was insecure.

Most of this book (and of many other histories) is made up of reference to the public, the noteworthy, the exceptional, the result of shaping rhetoric or shattering activities. Yet a pause is in order, now and then, for a description of life in that private place which people set aside for religion away from the public world. It does contribute to history. In fact, the reality of personal religion in the late nineteenth century was itself part of the history that was being made. Colonial Protestantism involved believers in custodianship of the covenant for the whole community. Early nineteenth-century evangelicalism called people to trusteeship of a religious-political empire. But in the late nineteenth century there was a growing acceptance of a division of labor in religious life. Particularly among individualists in religion, there was a widespread feeling that to comment on politics, economics, and social issues as the Beechers did was to meddle in areas that did not concern religious people gathered as churches. To them, religion had to do with sequestered and segregated areas of life. The personal, the "spiritual," the familial, and that having to do with private life comprised the whole. The postulation of this sphere, then, represents the obverse side of "the religion that makes history" in these years.

The first noteworthy feature of institutional religion was its growth. In England the beginnings of decline in church participation, so evident throughout the twentieth century, had begun to set in. The British had not built enough churches to keep up with urban growth and had not figured out ways to appeal to the industrial workers; in a time of fashionable doubt, Victorian habits of churchgoing were beginning to be threatened. On the Continent, particularly in industrialized areas, church attendance and participation were declining and the huge new cities like Berlin, Germany, were becoming ecclesiastical disaster areas. Too few churches were built; too many members were nominally a part of enormous parishes. Ideological assaults on religion by intellectuals and anticlerical and antireligious labor organizations were drawing attention away from the churches.

In the United States, however, the churches were continuing to see ever-increasing participation. For all the inaccuracies in gathering and keeping church statistics, something can be learned from those that have come down to us. If in 1776 only about 10 percent of the people were on the church rolls, and in 1800, just before the Second Great Awakening, this had only grown by 1 or 2 percent, by 1850 the figure was 15.5 percent, and this number more than doubled during the next half-century, to 35.7 percent. It was to continue to grow past the 50 percent mark in the mid-1920s to near the two thirds level during the religious revival of the 1950s. Much of this growth did not belong to Protestantism. Roman Catholicism accounted for some of it. But allowing for all deductions, it is clear that growth in church membership has to be counted as one of the surprising and important historical events of the last half of the nineteenth century.

The lines on the graphs show proportionate growth for Catholics and Protestants through much of the period; that is, both lines go upward in parallel fashion. In 1860 there were about three million Catholics to five million mainline Protestants. In 1880 there were six million Catholics to match nine million mainline Protestants. In 1900 twelve million Roman Catholics were at the side of sixteen million members of the major Protestant groups. Growth in all the major churches benefited from immigration, evangelism, the appeals of the churches, and habits of the nation.

For Protestants, so far as can be learned from the patterns of church growth and the means of sustaining church life, most of the activity was in the broad middle classes. This is not surprising, for the century was seeing a great expansion of the middle classes. Yet it is remarkable that for all the language and efforts of mass evangelists in the cities, there was no great breakthrough to the new masses and classes that were changing the face of America and ending the dream of a Protestant empire. Typical of the charges or laments of the period was that of Oscar Fay Adams, in a celebrated article in the *North American Review* in 1886: "Say what we may, the Protestant Church has no place for the poor within its pale. The wealthy churches snub him till he leaves them for unfashionable churches or omits to go to church altogether." So much for the rich. As far as middle classes were concerned, "the churches which lay no claim to being fashionable are yet not overgracious to the poor worshiper who ought to be content with the religious cold victuals preferred his kind at the mission chapel."

Plenty of middle-class, "polite Americans" were always around to serve as a target for the denominations, which remained in competition. This was a Methodistic age in America, and during it the truth of a gospel was measured in part on the basis of the successes its propagators knew. Methodist historian Daniel Dorchester cited the spirits of progress, practicality, and success as tests of truth and never tired of compiling statistics to show the growth of Methodism and its cousins. It seems seldom to have occurred to these truth-by-numbers chroniclers to wonder whether Catholic growth might have been based on Catholic truth. The presence of new immigrants and the proclamation of a message of fear were the two factors that always were cited to account for growth in the camp of the enemy.

If there was more churchgoing, so, too, there was also some falling away and opposition. America did not have major "god-killers" like the Europeans Marx, Darwin, Nietzsche, and Freud—men who symbolized an assault on the old Christian views of life and destiny. The United States could not even produce many infidels of the Thomas Paine–Ethan Allen or Frances Wright–Robert Owen types it had known earlier. Robert G. Ingersoll cast himself in that role and was a celebrated and notorious platform speaker through much of the era. But the career of Ingersoll, the themes he treated, and the treatment he received only serve to document the church-attending ethos of his decades.

Ingersoll was the son of a revivalist Presbyterian preacher. As such, he knew Protestantism from within, so when he left the church, he knew in detail what he was attacking. A lawyer and Civil War hero, he entered politics and was a highly respected and thoroughly respectable moderate Republican politician, known for his "plumed knight" speech nominating

James G. Blaine in 1876. In the years when the rostrum was a favored focus for entertainment, he drew millions of listeners over a two-decade span. Church people were there to boo the villain, to be outraged, to have their faith confirmed by his denials, or to have a sense of being titillated or threatened. The "liberated" went to hear him confirm their reasons for opposing superstition and human-shaped deity. But Ingersoll was hardly more than an embarrassment or an inconvenience to Protestants. He formed no school, left behind no works of substance, and belongs more to the world of entertainment than to intellectual history.

At a meeting of the Evangelical Alliance in New York in 1873, Boston University President William F. Warren gave his account of why free thought was so weak in churchgoing America. American religious liberty "gives to American infidels important advantages over their European brethren, but this same liberty . . . deprives them of half of their power to destroy." In Europe, infidels were free to be inside the churches because of mass church establishment, while in America, voluntaryism meant that only true believers were members.

Henry Ward Beecher gave another accounting, in the *North American Review* in 1882, when Ingersoll was at his peak (and when Beecher was helping attract crowds by debating his religious antagonist and political ally). "The scoffing infidelity . . . is uncongenial to the temper and good sense of Americans of native birth, and of American education." In reporting as accurate as any he engaged in, Beecher noted that Americans "may tolerate change in [religious] institutions" and "amuse themselves with the wit of good-natured infidels." They may even applaud intelligent doubt, but Americans were too filled with "rational reverence" and "aspiring ideality" to waste their time with low skepticism. In those words Beecher also revealed how far mainline Protestant thought had moved from the days when his father saw dangers in every form of heterodoxy or infidelity.

If Beecher was a good reporter about the weakness of infidelity, Ingersoll was equally astute at observing the changes in religion and the national ethos. Near the end of his career he noted that a quarter of a century earlier, Americans had largely been orthodox but now they had "lost confidence in the supernatural and have slowly gained confidence in the natural." He resented the ways in which the lax and the changing were included in religious statistics and decried the statistical obsession which characterized the religion of his day. "At the last great day we can refer with confidence to the ponderous volume containing the statistics of the United States." He went on: "There may be more 'members' now than formerly, and this increase of members is due to a decrease of religion." The religious changes that Beecher applauded, Ingersoll derided; they left him no measure to determine where the boundaries of the churches were. "Thousands of members are only nominal Christians, wearing the old uniform simply because they do not wish to be charged with desertion." The church was a kind of social institution, a club with a creed instead of bylaws, "and the creed is never defended unless attacked by an outsider."

Daniel Dorchester summarized the attempts by the Ingersolls to defeat the churches. "Within the past thirty years they have rallied and assailed Christianity again without and within; but this time they have been unable, even temporarily, to check the progress of the Churches." The Dorchesterian rhetoric was triumphal: "Our banners have uninterruptedly advanced, even more than in any previous period in the history of Christianity." If the evangelical church was losing its hold on the intellect of the age, Dorchester (writing in 1881) wondered how and wherein. "When was it equally identified with the best, the most vigorous, and the most learned culture?" And Dorchester also had the positive answer to negativists like Ingersoll who argued that church growth had meant decorous worldliness, and embrace of and capitualation to the spirit of the times. As one who saw the move from a Protestant empire to a nation shaped by Protestant experience, the Methodist turned matters around: it was often declared that "the contrast between the Church and the world is less perceptible than formerly, and therefore the Church has degenerated." Not at all. "Christianity has largely transformed Christendom—morally, intellectually, and socially—and, therefore, it cannot look as bright on the new background as on the old. Her very success has dimmed the relief. Christianity has 'softened and shaded the world to her own likeness.'"

This was an age of progress and success, of boasting and excess in the Protestant churches, and church leaders did what they could to leave monuments celebrating their achievements. Church buildings are the most obvious evidence. Worship remained the central Christian activity in most of the churches, and people attended for christening and burial, for marriage and other rites of passage, but most of all for weekly sustenance. In their styles of building, as in so many other ways of adapting to a time of change, "they looked backward" and perpetuated styles of building from past ages. The Gothic Revival which had marked "High Church" American Episcopalianism in a movement dating from around 1840 swept beyond that church into denominations which made much less of their medieval heritage, church bodies whose forms of worship had little in common with the sacramental system and beliefs which had occasioned the Gothic. The Gothic style was splendid, it was expensive, it evoked religious values in the midst of a materialistic world—and it was approved.

Americans were not trained to allow art for art's sake, even in the churches, and in the later decades of the century the revival of Gothic was itself therefore seen as a part of a moral and spiritual renewal in the nation. Henry Van Brunt, an architect and critic, writing in *The Atlantic Monthly* in 1886 "On the Present Condition and Prospects of the Architecture," was disappointed at the slow development of the architectural revival. But he reckoned that the revival "of medieval art, had its basis in an awakened conscience" and was "the only instance in history of a moral revolution in art." Yet in England, where the revival had first occurred, little had come of the awakening and revolution; in America "we are left in a condition of freedom which is fatal to art while we are ignorant, but capable of great developments when we are educated."

While wealthy patrons, the "robber barons" of the day, paid for expensive churches and seminary buildings, the middle classes also organized in great crusades to leave behind monumental edifices, few of them of lasting architectural value—although occasional examples like Henry Hobson Richardson's Trinity Church in Boston prefigured the new age of architecture.

Churchgoing America was also family-centered America, and in the midst of the changes brought by immigrant intrusion into the cities, many saw that religion might help produce family bonds and a set of manners still associated with the word Victorian. Much has been made of the prudery of an age which called cocks "roosters" or "hen's husbands" and which spoke of the "limb" of a table, and covered such legs because they might inspire voluptuous thoughts about women's legs. The churches did contribute to this prudery and did engage in crusades against nudity, even in art galleries. It was a time of crusading against free expression which violated the meager canons of taste: Anthony Comstock, the sniffing censor, was in his prime, and so successful was he that he willed the word Comstockery to the American vocabulary as a symbol for petty outrage. When it was pointed out that a leading Shakespearean actor and actress were married, this brought a new moral stamp to their courting scenes, which would otherwise have been disapproved by churchgoers. Under the surface there was also a typically Victorian curiosity about sex and an underground culture devoted to pornography. "Female Pills" and medicines or devices designed to increase sexual potency were widely advertised in the public press. Henry Ward Beecher could survive a highly publicized adultery case with the wife of one of his most prominent members. Divorce was beginning to find public acceptability, although it must be said that the churches generally resisted laxity in marital affairs.

The churches were much involved in marital legislation; even those which generally forbade meddling in politics politicked for laws in this realm with a position later summarized by the Rock River Methodist Conference in 1912: "The safeguarding of the home is the chief business of the state." As science took on the questions of preventing conception and of birth control, the Protestant churches at first almost unanimously opposed these purported tamperings with the law of nature, because of their implied threat to procreation and family structure.

The church and the family were to be the two great conservative institutions, used to support and bolster each other. The National Council of

Congregational Churches formed a committee to deal with the decline of family worship, arguing that "the home is more directly under the control of a right church influence than is any other social group. The church, more than any other institution, still holds public semblance at least, to recognition of the family, in its family pews and in its personal ministry." Any breach between family pew and family life would be fatal to church and family. Support for the conventional family was widely advertised as a means of supporting the role of women, but the Protestant churches by and large did not assent to the feminist and women's rights movements and were explicit in their rejection of women in the pulpit. Feminist Elizabeth Stanton summarized the spirit of an age when she reported on an event in Presbyterianism in Philadelphia around 1880: "Some one suggested that the position of woman in the church should be considered, that some new dignity and honor might be accorded her." But "the proposition was received with derision and treated with as much contempt as if it has been proposed to make elders and deacons of monkeys." Churchgoing was often seen to be a predominantly female preoccupation, but church leadership still meant very much the survival of a man's world at the turn of the century.

These were years of continuing preoccupation with foreign missions, but domestic or home missions, neglected when first the glamor of overseas work displaced the ordeal of ministering to American Indians, began to come back into fashion. This recovery occurred in part because of the growth of immigrant populations in the cities and because by 1890 the American frontier had been used up and still the task of churching the nation was not complete.

The Lutherans and other Continental immigrant-based denominations did not, by and large, adopt revivalism as a technique. But their leaders soon learned that the people who got off the boats from Germany and Scandinavia did not automatically sign up for church membership. They had to be won. Elaborate schemes for winning the immigrants were undertaken. Often their agents ran into the Anglo-Protestant home missionaries, particularly the ubiquitous Methodists. Lutherans never tired of telling stories like the one about a Methodist "spiritual vulture" who conducted a communion service for immigrants in Michigan and boasted, "Look here at all the money the dumb Germans have given me for the little bread and wine I gave them!" The Methodists were "wolves and hucksters" who "plied their wares of false doctrine." But this was conventional Protestant rhetoric and referred only to minor levels of conflict. For the most part, Lutheran and Reformed home missions were carried off more in independence from than in opposition to the efforts of the previously established churches.

If ever the frontier dominated the thought of church extension representatives, these were the years. Josiah Strong's *Our Country* was only the best selling of the books which stood in the lineage of Lyman Beecher's *Plea for the West* to agitate for the churching of the nation. The Homestead Act, passed in 1862, encouraged the settling of the West and, because of problems of distance and isolation, called forth a whole new generation of church-planting and circuit-riding activity in the Great Plains. When gold, silver, lead, and other metals were discovered throughout the West, a period of frenzied and hectic missionary work was undertaken among people too hurried to have their minds on things above. But if much of the mining activity left only a legacy of ghost towns, it also produced permanent centers like San Francisco and attracted permanent church settlements at such places.

To meet the new needs, a whole new set of church extension societies was organized after the Civil War. Significantly, most of these followed denominational lines. The old network of nondenominational and lay-based societies could not be resurrected in an age of denominational "efficiency" and clerical professionalism. So the Methodists organized in 1864, the Congregationalists in 1865, and many others followed in the 1870s. Sometimes the more astute leaders worked with political and industrial forces, particularly railroad elites, to plot a course for churches wherever new populations were developing. Some boasted of having churches on the scene "at the next railroad stop" before permanent populations arrived. Nothing was left to chance in an age when efficiency had virtually become an ideology.

Congregationalism, which had moved successfully from New England across Ohio, Indiana, and Illinois, was less effective in the South or in the further West. The movement of Episcopalianism was also quiet and undramatic. No one could outdo the Methodists, whose Church Extension Society agent, Chaplain C. C. McCabe, boasted to Ingersoll that the Methodists were not dying out, as Ingersoll had claimed, but were building one church, and soon would be building two churches a day. The Baptists were less successful in the West than in the South, but they were energetic, as were the Presbyterians. None of these groups were successful at directing the main energies of their supporting people back to the neglected Indian missions, even though President U. S. Grant's Indian policy made it easy for denominations to have their way among these deprived people. Denominational competition at times and churchly apathy at others led to further neglect of Indians. The rootlessness of the life of tribes that were constantly being displaced worked hardships on them as well as on Protestants who tried to work among them. The Methodists were most strenuous in their efforts. By the time of the First World War over one third of the American Indians were denominated Christian, many of them Catholic.

Few activities inside the separate churches drew more attention than the support of foreign missions. The story of these missions themselves properly belongs, by the end of the century, in the context of American expansion. But the rhetoric of appeal to the home front was part of the complex which held the congregations together. Sermons which remain from the period show that ministers could assume some knowledge of the missionary endeavors of the denominations. The people were asked to identify with their overseas agents, to raise money for them, to rejoice with them in their victories over paganism. New lay and student movements were rising in support of a dream that would see the evangelization of the world "in this generation." By this was meant not that all people in the world would turn Christian, but that all would be exposed to the Gospel. At the same time, these nonclerical agents of world mission were coming back with stories of the beginnings of frustration to their mission because of a resurgence of other religions in missionized areas. Even more, they lost because of foreigners' bewilderment over or disgust with Protestant divisions. The first impulses toward the twentieth-century church unity movements came out of such reports and reactions.

For all their internal troubles, their growing divisions about the mission of the church, their schism over theology, their embrace of the world, the Protestant churches were enjoying successes by the standards they most enjoyed, and the sun shone through stained glass on millions who were buoyant and optimistic about the future.

VI · FROM EMPIRE TO EXPERIENCE

19 · The Two-Party System

A Division Within Protestantism

Josiah Strong, who was capable of spotting perils wherever he turned, was also alert to conflicts within Protestantism. Near the end of his career he looked back on decades of struggle within American Christianity and came up with a surprising view of the way two parties camped on the tradition. Writing in 1913 he noted that "there are two types of Christianity, the old and the older. The one is traditional, familiar, and dominant. The other, though as old as the Gospel of Christ, is so rare that it is suspected of being new, or is overlooked altogether."

In those few lines he pointed to a deep division with Protestantism, one which has haunted it and given it vitality. Strong was discerning as he noted that divisions were "not to be distinguished by any of the old lines of doctrinal or denominational cleavage. Their difference is one of spirit, aim, point of view, comprehensiveness. The one is individualistic; the other is social."

Many of Strong's readers would have agreed on all of his points but one. One Protestant party had become individualistic, while the other was social. The lines of division did not follow the base lines of denominationalism. Individualistic Protestantism was obviously familiar and dominant. Many Americans identified it as classic and normative. It belonged to their world just as farms and villages did and produced many of the myths and symbols that were easily recognized by masses of people in the nation. Social Christianity was rarer, and was suspected of being new.

Disagreement came over Strong's claim that what Americans regarded as traditional was actually of brief lineage, while what was often "suspected of being new" went back to the Gospel of Christ. The people he was implicitly attacking argued that they, indeed, represented and re-presented the original Gospel, while the rarer social Christians were heretics, innovators, and deviants.

The division into two parties to which Strong could refer in his lines about two types of Christianity was one of the fateful events of American Protestant history. The fact that Protestants were not able to patch their empire on racial or sectional lines after the war and Reconstruction determined much of the shape of the later Protestant experience. Many of the better-known Protestant leaders helped their faith and their church lose identity by blending them into the general culture through their complacent acceptance of a decorous worldliness; this created problems that were not easily overcome. The rise of the industrial city with its physical and psychic threats and its hordes of immigrants, who were surrounding and overwhelming urban Protestants, brought a disturbing new milieu to people of the old faith. But nothing did more to complicate the mission and ministry of all Protestants than the new internal divisions which came to light around the turn of the new century, to remain through subsequent decades.

Reference to this event brings up a set of topics that also complicates the lives of historians. So often they can refer to discrete events in the past, like the formation of the Federal Council of Churches of Christ in America on December 2, 1908, and set them into a chronological scheme. With not much more difficulty they can deal with a complex of events that have been styled through a symbol, as when they speak of "the Second Great Awakening," or "the social gospel." But to speak of the development of a two-party system in Protestantism is to refer to processes, ideas, covert and subvert actions, expressions that grow out of unwitting, unconscious, and surprisingly revelatory signals. Only over a long period of time did men like Josiah Strong find it possible to chronicle the phenomena. Even though the development raises problems for churches, it cannot be avoided, for without an understanding of the division, later Protestantism in America is incomprehensible.

Foreign visitors come to the United States and expect to find that denominations which have given shape to Protestantism will also serve to define its parties. Matters are not so easy as that. They may come across an Episcopalian and a Congregationalist. Their European textbooks, drawn from the doctrinal statements of these people's church bodies, will lead them to anticipate that what really separates these is that one believes in apostolic succession of bishops while the other stresses congregational order, or that one has a "catholic" view of the Lord's Supper and that the other has a "free-church" view. The visitor may not have been misled about the nominal differences. But he or she will soon find that the two have more in common with each other on almost every other topic than either may have with another Episcopalian or another Congregationalist. The former may stand on one side of a fundamental division with Protestantism and the latter two may be on the other.

One party, which may be called "private" Protestantism, seized that name "evangelical" which had characterized all Protestants early in the nineteenth century. It accented individual salvation out of the world, personal moral life congruent with the ideals of the saved, and fulfillment or its absence in the rewards or punishments in another world in a life to come. The second informal group, which can be called "public" Protestantism, was public insofar as it was more exposed to the social order and the social destinies of people. Whereas the word "evangelical" somehow came to be a part of the description of the former group, the word "social" almost always worked its way into designations of the latter. They pursued a social Christianity, the social gospel, social service, social realism, and the like.

Whereas the former took over and cherished revivalism and similar techniques for stimulating conversions and reaffirmation of faith, the latter party gradually lost faith in revivalism and worked instead with techniques and processes which strove for some transformation of the world. Without necessarily losing faith in another world and a destiny there, this "public" group supplemented or complemented that faith with a parallel accent on what a pioneer in the party, Washington Gladden, called "The Kingdom of Heaven on Earth." The Kingdom of God came to be a more frequently used symbol of fulfillment than heaven.

While discussion of the complex process by which these two parties came to light imposes the form of a topical essay on the historian, it is profitable at least to begin with a kind of chronological track, to place certain guideposts along the way.

In 1857–1858, during a financial panic, there occurred the last revival of religion which was demonstrably linked to the interpretation of temporal events. Lay people gathered in noon prayer meetings across the nation in a largely spontaneous revival of self-examination and scrutiny. What have we done wrong to displease God and to cause God to punish us with this setback? In many respects this revival was leaderless—no Jonathan Edwards or Timothy Dwight or Charles G. Finney emerged to serve as its catalyst. The outpouring of judgments and prophecies, of diagnostic and therapeutic statements, provided a starting point for the story.

The revival of 1857–1858 showed that those who advocated revivalism, soul-saving, and rescue out of the world were the same people who wanted to devote virtually equal energies to the reform of the society. While a certain contentment with the approved social contract still lingered with them, they were mostly postmillennial in their outlook. That is, they believed that the coming reign of Christ would occur after the earth and society had been partially transformed by the efforts of humans. This gave them a motive and basis for a more radical view of the way "the powers that be" that ran society affected the lives of people.

After the Civil War, there was a surprising rebirth of premillennialism, which seemed to be more pessimistic and fatalistic about the world. Historians have more difficulty agreeing about the reasons for the trend than noting its presence. The shattering effects of the war, the trauma of strikes and financial panics in the 1870s and 1880s, the formation of an urban world with its apparently intractable problems—perhaps all these together led many people of good will to give up on the idea of preparing for the Kingdom or transforming the world. In any case, under the inspired guidance of the second half-century's major urban revivalist, Dwight L. Moody, and a score of lesser people, premillennialism was revived. With it came a certain passivity about the social order. Since people could do little to improve the world, they would do best to get their own souls saved and to wait as holy men and women for Christ's Coming, at which time a new order would begin.

Moody was not a systematic theologian and he was not a precise thinker. He was a person of broad sympathies who enjoyed depriving the dogmatists of their definitions, by blurring distinctions and by absorbing the shock of warring parties into his own expansive personality. For that reason, many of those who continued to call for the transformation of society either did not see or did not care about the premillennial note in Moody, and they endorsed him. Meanwhile, people of more pessimistic and apocalyptic tastes, concerned with how their destiny would come out in heaven or hell, similarly were enthused about him. During the controversies about evolution, biblical criticism, and science, Moody was unmistakably on the traditionalists' side of things, but he was not the kind of man who would be eager to push people of slightly different views off the platform or out of his choirs. An examination of the endorsements of Moody in the late 1870s shows that two decades after the lay revival, the old coalition between individual and social evangelists still held. For all the doctrinal and denominational differences that were up for controversial discussion, the basic shape of Protestant unity had not been torn.

That shape was being tested, however, and old coalitions began to fall apart in the last two decades of the century. Friendships were strained. Protestants often spent more time fighting each other than they did fighting Catholics, Jews, and infidels. The celebrity preachers, while politically safe, began to put theological tests to the older evangelicalism. They gave lip service, at least, to the idea that Christianity was to transform the social order—as we saw in Beecher's injunctions to preach on every side of political issues. True, many of them found little to transform in the basically good Protestant culture around them. But the transforming motif came to be much stronger while the converting attempt remained in the revivalists' hands.

The rise of a new theology which was progressivistic and optimistic, even when it avoided explicit involvement in social issues, further strained the old unity. The better-known social gospel that was articulated by Washington Gladden, George Herron, Richard Ely, and Walter Rauschenbusch, among others, during the quarter-century before the First World War imposed an even greater strain on the conciliators who tried to keep Protestantism from becoming a house divided. These were people impatient with waiting for the millennium. They were innovative so far as theology was concerned, informed by European theological and secular social thought, and most of all distressed over the human damage they saw in the new industrial order. Certainly, they argued, the prophets and Jesus would not have faced such miseries and exploitation with repeated calls for personal conversion out of the world, without also lauding new Good Samaritans who would face present need, and good social thinkers who would tell how to do that in a world of interrelationships and interdependence of people in cities! Not a little of their expression was directed in reaction against the soul-saving revivalists who paid scant attention to the public order, but concentrated only on private vices and private virtues.

The heirs of Dwight L. Moody, almost all of them more inflexible and intransigent than he, were also reacting to the people who picked up social reform themes from earlier evangelicalism. People like A. C. Dixon, Reuben Torrey, and a score of reasonably well-known revivalists, began to use the social Christians as a foil. Soon traditionalists devoted more scorn to these than they did to non-Protestants. The evangelistic types began to organize Bible conferences and leadership training sessions and summer institutes to serve for study and for rallying around the individualistic motifs of the earlier revivalism. In their willingness to separate the person of sin-sick soul from community and to prepare him or her for heaven, they also tended to abandon the social notes still seen in revivalism around 1857 and 1858.

Each new public trauma—the panic of 1873, the railroad strike of 1877, the Pullman strike and Haymarket Square disaster still later—led the socially oriented Protestants further into the public sphere, to ask the nation to change the circumstances that brought about the troubles. The same threats worked the opposite effect among the evangelistic camp. They withdrew progressively from involvement and ran for cover to the advocates of the world as it was. They confined their social message to calls for order and law and their ethical appeals to calls for repentance from private vice and change to personal holiness.

One half-century after the lay revival, leaders of major Protestant groups gathered in Philadelphia late in 1908 to form the Federal Council of Churches. This new interchurch agency, the most important ecumenical organization of its time, found that the second, or "public," party was largely in command. The Social Creed of the Churches, written by social liberals like Harry F. Ward, tended to unite their concerns. Few of them repudiated evangelism or denied the importance of soul-saving, but almost all wanted these set in the context of transforming society and removing social ills. While the Federal Council was ready with a Commission on the Church and Social Service, not until 1912 were the evangelistic advocates in the component denominations able to balance this with their representative interest, a Commission on Evangelism. This latter commission was understaffed, low-budgeted, afflicted with low morale, and rejected (along with the rest of the Federal Council) by the conservatives, many of whom were forming a harder-core fundamentalist party within evangelicalism.

The Commission on the Church and Social Service in 1916 was still trying to hold things together. "In addition to the unquestioned historic mission and work of Christianity with the individual," one of its statements argued "that the scope of the gospel and the program of the churches must include the creation on earth of a Christian civilization, organized upon the ethical teachings and controlled by the spirit of Jesus Christ." By that time most alert Protestants had rejected this both/and spirit in favor of an either/or mood.

Before the First World War, a number of tussles between the parties served to illuminate the growing controversy. A. C. Dixon spotted Josiah Strong as a turncoat from the evangelistic and individualistic position and attacked him in print. But in 1912 the best-known evangelist after Dwight L. Moody, the flamboyant exballplayer Billy Sunday, took on the most noted social gospel advocate in the parish ministry, Washington Gladden. The setting of their encounter was Columbus, Ohio, where Gladden had piled up a record of achievement in a socially oriented ministry over three decades. But when Sunday came to town to carry on one of his proevangelistic and apparently "antisocial" revivals, Gladden quietly opposed him. And after the revival, Gladden was more outspoken over the meager returns he saw garnered from Sunday's raucous efforts. But Gladden was attacked by the vast majority of Columbus's ministers of all Protestant denominations. They rose to the defense of Sunday's approach and clearly identified with the conversionism of the revivalist. This action, like so many others, bore out the assessment of Strong that what the Dixons and the Sundays stood for was considered "traditional, familiar, and dominant" and that the Strong—Gladden party represented something "so rare that it is suspected of being new." Yet despite what Strong had said, it was no longer in danger of being overlooked altogether."

The conflict within Protestantism was evident on many fronts. Some of the evangelical partisans worried over the secular bent of the YMCA, as it turned progressively toward social service. In the seminaries, new departments designed for concentration on social problems and Christian social ethics were formed, to the consternation of individualistic conservatives. Doctrinal debates, while by no means always on the social theme, did contribute to the widening divisions.

This bare review from 1857 to 1916 demonstrates something of the high points of the controversy. At the root of the change was the fact that the old explanations of the human record were no longer satisfactory to many. It was difficult to interpret the bewildering world of industrial and urban life. Even many people congenial to Dwight L. Moody found his explanation of social wrongs and his prescriptions for righting them to be partial. Moody's definition of his mission struck them as inadequate: "I look upon this world as a wrecked vessel. God has given me a lifeboat and said to me, 'Moody, save all you can.'" What was more, his critics (like Josiah Strong's social party) could demonstrate that the Moodyites were, indeed, the innovators. They were the newcomers, the deviationists or heretics in evangelicalism. Jonathan Edwards did *not* look upon the world as a wrecked vessel from which people could be rescued, but as the site of the millennium, the locale for the Kingdom.

Criticism also arose when it became clear that, for all the revivalists' efforts to include the urban poor in their outreach, they had little effect on these. Much of the vision of social Christianity was born of experiences with urbanites whose world could not easily be penetrated by the people who offered salvation in heaven in Jesus Christ. Walter Rauschenbusch, the most notable of the social gospel thinkers, came from a long line of pietistic Lutherans and Baptists, and never deserted their typical concerns about each person's soul. But his experiences in New York's "Hell's Kitchen" with recent immigrants and population elements that lay beyond the soul-savers' outreach, led him to be interested in a Christianity that addressed itself to all their needs.

When Chicago's Haymarket Riot in May 1886 brought to focus public apprehensions about anarchy, socialism, and lawlessness among immigrant and workers' groups, Dwight L. Moody stayed with his individualistic message. "Either these people are to be evangelized or the leaven of communism and infidelity will assume such enormous proportions that it will break out in a reign of terror such as this country has never known." Such appeals brought funds from conservative middle-class elements who would give evangelism another try, even as it solidified middle-class sentiment against workers. To people of Rauschenbusch's outlook, either the people were to be evangelized and their needs were to be met and their rights faced, or the Kingdom of God would not come.

The social gospel leaders and other social Christian advocates did not abandon the old reform causes of the first half-century. They still opposed intemperance, profanity, prostitution, and other vices. But they rejected the individualists' preoccupation with these personally controllable faults to the exclusion of an address to the societal faults over which the single individual had little control. While the evangelists came eventually to put most of their efforts at social reform into the Prohibitionist cause, they tended to do it in a kind of punitive spirit against the vicious drinker. The socially oriented Christians, on the other hand, treated drinking more frequently as a social problem. It was the result, in part, of bad conditions among many classes of people; it was the refuge of the hopeless, the extravagance of the ignorant, the folly of those trapped by circumstance. While the individualists still "meddled" in the public realm, their activities were usually in the interests of limiting gambling or retaining Sunday "blue laws." To the "public Protestants," who were more frequently at home in the field of legislative issues, gambling and violation of the Protestant Sabbath were minor vices compared to those of being a slum landlord, an opponent of industrial workers, or keeper of sweatshops.

The spokespersons for the transformation-minded party were gathered at various intellectual centers and were often more sophisticated than the evangelists. So they did not lack gifted articulators who could spell out exactly what was meant in that old prophetic program that was being recovered as if it were rare and new. The University of Chicago's Shailer Mathews described social Christianity as the application of "the teaching of Jesus and the total message of the Christian salvation to society, the economic life, and social institutions;" he then added, "as well as to individuals." But these sophisticated expressions usually grew out of the experience of people with recall of the failures of their own religious upbringing. Thus Rauschenbusch recalled, "When I had begun to apply my previous religious ideas to the conditions I found, I discovered that they didn't fit." After a trip to Europe he outlined his faith in the Kingdom that would transform the world.

While the teachings of Jesus all center around the conception of the Kingdom of God, it came to Rauschenbusch "as a new revelation." "The perspective of life shifted into a new alignment." Rauschenbusch felt "a new security in my social impulses. The spiritual authority of Jesus Christ would have been sufficient to offset the weight of all the doctors, and I now knew that I had history on my side." But the social gospel leader also was saved thereby. He found this new conception of Christian purpose to be strangely satisfying. "It responded to all the old and all the new elements of my religious life. The saving of the lost, the teaching of the young, the pastoral care of the poor and frail," all elements in older evangelicalism, were fused with "the quickening of starved intellects, the study of the Bible, church union, political reform, the reorganization of the industrial system, international peace—it was all covered by the one aim of the Reign of God on earth." Once again the world was being affirmed in Christ's name. But this time, there would be no decorous worldliness, no acceptance of the status quo. With rage and passion, social Christians would use the Kingdom motifs to bring about change in the world.

From both sides, people tried to bridge the growing gaps in their own careers. Social Christian leaders like Gladden, Rauschenbusch, or George Herron were never willing to admit that they gave up the accent on the individual. But their opponents, perhaps with some justice, saw that they were neglecting evangelism. Certainly, they left most of the revivalistic techniques behind.

At the same time, a few people like Benjamin Fay Mills tried to stand in the camps of both the Moodys and the Rauschenbusches. Like George Herron, he approached social Christianity with evangelistic fervor and evangelists' techniques. In Columbus, Ohio, with the backing of Washington Gladden, he had a moderate success at combining the efforts. But soon other revivalists criticized him for degrading the Gospel by his attacks on church policies and by accenting social ethics too much. Mills was disenchanted with the reception he got from other revivalists and finally moved over to Unitarianism, leaving behind both the Protestant parties. After Mills, almost no one tried to follow the joint vocations of evangelist and agent of social change. Division of labor and hostility set in. At the Columbian Exposition at Chicago in 1893, people had to choose whether to participate in conferences on social Christianity or to join a competitive revival on the part of Dwight Moody. The twentieth century has not seen a new personal bridging of the two realms.

The social gospel Christians, in the spirit of Josiah Strong, contended that theirs was the older tradition. For once, at least, nontraditionalists like American Protestants found themselves arguing on whose side the fathers of the Church had been. The public Protestants could claim the prophets of the Hebrew scriptures and Jesus of the synoptic gospels. But while they accented Jesus' teachings and ethical injunctions, the revivalists claimed another aspect of the tradition, the Pauline accents on Jesus' atonement as a substitution for the human as sinner under the wrath of God.

While the social critics were able to point out that for a millennium and a half Christians would not have conceived of the possibility of divorcing the personal from the social in Christendom, they also could claim the prophetic note from the medieval sectarians and the left wing of the Reformation, and church historians did just that. They also reached back to the Puritan tradition to show that no areas of human life were to fall outside the range of the message of God and the purposes of the church, by showing how in John Calvin's world as well as in England and New England, when reformed Christians had the opportunity, they put together covenanted communities of organic character. There political and economic details were the concern of the Christian community. Personal redemption grew out of this context.

The social Christians also affirmed the reformist principles of their evangelical forebears. But they deviated at one point of innovation in the years of the evangelical empire. During the years of its formation, a new individualism had crept into the Protestant community. The evangelistic party kept on endorsing it. Personal manners, personal vices and virtues—these were in the path of salvation. The task of addressing these could not wait for the millennium or heaven. But the general body politic was to be approached only by individual Christians who had been regenerated, and not by the church as the People of God. To a Rauschenbusch, as one of his book titles made clear, the task instead was "Christianizing the Social Order."

The program of "private Protestantism" was more appealing to middle-class America, for it has tended more often to approve the given social order. And since most of the supporters of the white churches have come from such classes and tended to profit from identifying with the world as it is, disturbers of the peace like Rauschenbusch, Gladden, Herron, and other social Christians, have remained a minority.

Subsequent Protestantism has still seen that the Moodys and the Sundays draw the crowds while the Rauschenbusches work from academic centers or through influence upon the influential few.

Defenders of the approved social contract never came to respond with massive favor to the agents of social change in the name of Christianity, people who no longer looked on the nation as being a safe and self-assured Protestant nation. They listened with distaste to "meddlers" like George Herron who used words of personal liturgy for an act of public and social confession: "Christ is disappointed in this nation. We have done those material and political things we ought not to have done, and left undone the social and righteous things we ought to have done." In such a world, the optimistic social Christians always were confident that they had a gospel and a plan. But now they stood apart from their Protestant colleagues who said "I" and not "we" about faults, and restricted their effort to the "spiritual" realm.

20 · From Providence to Progress

A New Theology

"Providence" had been the term by which American Protestants had characteristically referred to the divine impetus behind their history. The colonists were convinced that it was Providence that had reserved the North American continent for discovery after the Reformation of the sixteenth century, even as they had no doubts but that the Reformation itself was the result of Divine Providence. Providence had guided the destiny of people on their errand into the wilderness, in their life as residents of a city set upon a hill, as people who had won their freedom and kept the faith.

When the world view itself changed at the time of the Enlightenment, and when even church people spoke in new terms about "the reasonableness of Christianity" and nature's laws, Protestants could unite with the national founders, many of them near deist, in perpetuating the use of the term Providence. The public pronouncements of many presidents from George Washington through Abraham Lincoln were studded with the term, and even more "enlightened" statesmen than Washington, men like Franklin and Jefferson, found ways of using the term Providence to describe the force that was giving impulse to the shaping of the republic and the destinies of its people. Meanwhile, the trustees of the Protestant empire referred to providential support of their mission and destiny with almost monotonous regularity.

While the term "Providence" was thus so deeply stamped in the culture that it has not been wholly eradicated even today and references to it have become habitual, during the final decades of the nineteenth century and into the twentieth, thoughtful people were replacing it and speaking of "Progress." For the Protestant leaders, this Progress was tied to some sort of idea of deity. To the emerging modernists, that deity could be either an impersonal force or some new transvaluation of the referred-to Being called Father by Jesus. To the moderates and the orthodox, Progress was the name for the way a personal God was pulling the nation. Providence allowed for a static view of history, with an accent, for some, on predestining power. Progress implied a dynamic view of history, full of development and change.

To the American of the turn-of-the-century years, progress was a demonstrable fact. The Amercian empire was extending itself to have domain over inferior peoples. The landscape was being transformed by railroads and machines which helped people subdue distance and reform the created world. But where progress was not always demonstrable, where in Walter Rauschenbusch's terms one or another area of life (unlike the family or education) had not yet been "Christianized," one could still affirm a belief in the unseen and the invisible. In short, a kind of metaphysic of Progress was coming to dominate.

The grand new scheme to which the change was related had to do with the Darwinian theory of evolution, articulated after earlier and more vague statements by Charles Darwin in England in 1859. It came to many Americans through the sociological laws propagated by the popular visitor to America, Herbert Spencer. The appropriation of Darwinian themes into Protestant schemes was the Anglo-American intellectual issue somewhat comparable to the wrestling with the "god-killers" in France and Germany in the nineteenth century. Thoughtful Christians were experiencing what might be called a crisis of historical consciousness in the nineteenth century. For faith, this meant that the uniqueness of Christ and the Bible was called into question by a world view in which flux and change seemed to relativize everything. Catholics like Johann Adam Möhler in Germany and John Henry Newman in England stressed that dogma was not static but that it developed dynamically in the course of history; with this teaching they inaugurated a trend that was to be cut off when Catholic Modernism was later condemned. Protestants on the Continent often related to Hegel and his views of development. In England and America the natural-science models of Darwin and his followers were attractive.

In other words, after about 1860, American Protestants began to undergo an extensive assault on their old world view and an impressive change to a new one. By a world view I mean a partly unconscious and partly consciously acquired way of looking at a universe of meaning, of appropriating the background to cause and effect, stability and change, that lies behind a specific historical order. Thus the Copernican world view meant that eventually most reflective people completely reoriented their thought about the location of the world in the universe and humanity in the world. The Hegelian or Darwinian world views meant that as people looked out at their worlds, they found some principle of development, evolution, or change operative. Even the conservative Christians who resisted theological Darwinism for its unproved assumptions and its implied or sometimes direct attack on the Bible and certain Christian doctrines, somehow appropriated elements of the Darwinian world view into their understanding of economic doctrine and social purpose.

Wrestling with evolution, development, and more specifically Progress, then, became the high intellectual drama for Protestants in much of the second century of their life in the United States. Across the lines of the two-party system which was developing, most individualists accidentally developed "Social Darwinist" views, although not necessarily under that name. On the socially oriented and more liberal side, many felt free to be explicit in their endorsement of a metaphysics of progress, and their efforts deserve scrutiny, for they set out to bring what they called a new theology to Protestantism. It was a theology well designed to help Protestant intellectuals make the move from serving a Protestant empire, based on an exclusive and particular revelation and covenant, to serving an America in which Protestants were the shaping and experiencing agents among others.

The new theology was intended to be an inclusive and universal Christianization of the world view, a philosophy that could be accepted by all or that would provide synthesis and meaning to all who bothered with it. In the words of one of the founders of the school, Theodore Munger (in 1883), the new theology justified itself by the belief that it could minister to faith, and "by a conviction that the total thought of an age ought to have the greatest possible unity, or in plainer phrase, that its creed ought not to antagonize its knowledge." To Munger, the old Protestant world view was leading people to an internal schism, in which their heart was to go one way while their eyes and mind were called to go another. Warfare between "kingdoms of faith and of natural law," according to Munger, "cannot, from the nature of things, have a basis in reality." The older Protestantism, he and his cohorts felt, was coming to support such an antagonism.

An assault on the old could not be carried on without the development of still another new antagonism within Protestantism. In general, the affirmers of the new theology were on the side of public Protestantism, with its social base, although by no means were all of them interested in social and political questions nor were they all considered to be progressives in the ways that their cousins and allies in the social gospel movement were. Yet they were lumped with these allies by the orthodox, who rejected the new theology and the social gospel together as a single modernism which had been designed to destroy the old faith, on which America had built its republic and on which the Protestant churches had thrived.

Formal theology has been the property of a rather small intellectual elite in the churches. European-style academic theology had few followers in America before the 1930s, and not even the majority of the preachers themselves would have read the works of men like Theodore Munger in their prime. With the exception of names like Edwards, Bushnell, Rauschenbusch, and Niebuhr in four different eras, few theologians' names have been widely recognized in the society including in ecclesiastical culture.

Despite the sequestering of specialized theology, however, now and then such theology was exposed to view and if one was to understand the transformations, looking at the time of the new theology is illuminating. Theologians ministered to the larger community of believers by serving as interpreters. They related the old faith to the new world view, using revelation or philosphy or some other means as the integrator. In doing so, when they were successful, they either reached more deeply into realities that others dealt with superficially, or they were ahead of their times—in both cases, acting somehow as much like artists as they did like scientists.

The general public took signals from preachers like Henry Ward Beecher or Phillips Brooks. It would not often have recognized the names of professional theologians like George Harris or William Newton Clarke. These theologians, operating from those gray and drafty corners of Protestantism called seminaries, were relatively obscure figures compared to the celebrity clerics. They may not have been public figures as the social gospel's leaders sometimes became. They certainly had no direct impact the way Moody, Sunday, and other mass evangelists did. But through their writings and teachings they influenced influential people, they taught thousands of preachers, they brought together ideas which could serve to unite and divide, to rally and disperse, to comfort and to frighten people.

What was distinctive about the heirs of Bushnell, the Mungers, and their colleagues was that they chose to call their efforts a *new* theology. In the public imagery, the theologian was somehow supposed to be the defender of the antique, the suspicious scrutinizer of others' orthodoxy, the grudging and reluctant adapter to inevitable change who must still look at the old books and make things come out right. The progress-minded new theologians chose the opposite role. By remaining Christian and Protestant they showed that they wanted to create the new out of a tradition, and they regularly scored the orthodox for perverting the tradition. But their commitment to a metaphysic of progress told them that the best was still ahead, and that proclamation of the Kingdom of God or celebration of the purposes of God committed them to the now and the new, or to the future and the not-yet, when all would be better.

The new theologians were not utterly original in their intention. The late colonial Arminians who had turned Unitarian early in the nineteenth century, along with Universalists, the Hicksite branch of the Quakers, or the Christian Connexion, all knew that they were innovating and made no secret of their repudiation of much of the evangelical past. In all such cases, new denominations eventuated. But the new theologians and the Protestant ideologues of progress grew up within the mainline evangelical churches. They stood in the developing tradition of New England theology. They remained in the Protestant churches, neither seeking to form new sects nor being willing to be put out of their denominations. Almost none of them were. Heresy trials were few and far between, rarely successful, and usually productive of such bewildering consequences that they did not initiate sequences of heresy hunts. The Protestant churches learned to live with these new voices, to make room for coexistence between theological parties. Whereas at midcentury, John Nevin could observe that all the Protestants were arguing that each alone was the faithful reproducer of the Bible, the new theologians were arguing that they alone were able to accommodate the new findings of science and philosophy and the new world view to the Protestant tradition.

Locating the new theology in the mainline of American Protestant thought is one way of saying that not every branch of Protestantism or section of the nation was equally involved. The churches of Continental background, notably the large Lutheran group, were almost totally untouched by modernism. While the Lutherans fought incessantly across the lines of their crazy-quilt ecclesiastical patterns, non-Lutherans would have found these differences to be minor, based usually on debates about how to interpret sixteenth-century German confessional documents. Southern Christians, we have already seen, were lapsing into a doctrinal intransigence and developing a strong aversion to anything but biblicism and a kind of primitive defense of the first Christian generation. While the Southern Baptists were capable of producing two celebrated heresy trials and thus, by implication, two celebrated heretics—Crawford H. Toy and W. H. Whitsitt—only Toy had been committed to Darwinian ideas and higher biblical criticism. The fact that such a highly admired and revered teacher could be purged was evidence of the way the largest southern group was prepared to hold the line.

The orthodox citadels such as Princeton Seminary joined the Continentals and the Lutherans in eschewing adaptations to the Darwinian and progressive views. Like the Lutherans, they repristinated seventeenth-century thought, the Protestant version of Catholic scholastic dogmatics. Princeton turned out giants like William H. Green, Charles Hodge, Archibald Alexander Hodge, and Benjamin Warfield, stalwarts all. These people produced massive works on dogmatic and systematic theology, explained away apparent contradictions in the Bible, and tried to adhere to the doctrinal schemes devised in the seventeenth century.

To these large clusters should also be added the black Protestant denominations, which were hardly free to develop an independent intellectual life and thus found themselves almost automatically committed to the more static doctrinal views.

Continentals plus Southerners plus intransigents-by-choice plus blacks equals a clear majority of American Protestants, especially if one adds to this the numbers of people in mainline or oldline denominations who were apathetic or resistant to the new progressivism. Yet the new theologians made history by the way they chose to innovate, to adapt, and to shape. Science dominated in the progressivist program, as Theodore Munger made clear when in 1888 he set down the gains from science which Protestantism had received. These gains included a new sense of reverence, a new respect for the laws of nature including those of cause and effect, a freedom from enslaving superstition, a quest for morality based on natural law, and liberation from automatic defense of traditional beliefs. Neither Munger nor his colleagues were as ready to note the ways in which they often uncritically accepted the new scientific view, which also had its myths and superstitions, and which also was dated and quickly came to be regarded as partly obsolete.

"In the beginning was Bushnell. . . ." So go most of the histories of the new theology, thanks in part to Munger who called himself a new theologian but announced himself to be the heir of Bushnell. Horace Bushnell, whose main work was accomplished before the Civil War, had tried to transform orthodoxy and to remain in the conventional pastoral ministry. The early dates for the newer theology, in the career of Bushnell, demonstrate the fact that explicit reference to Darwin was not needed by people who developed developmental views in Protestantism. These were, so to speak, in the air. For Bushnell, they meant that one tried to deprive conversion of its radical breach-making character and to criticize emotional revivalists in the interest of *Christian Nurture,* as his book title put it. In this view, he accented the quiet unfolding of faith and knowledge in the Christian.

Bushnell's view committed him to a progressive vision of the universe wherein God could also be found in nature, so he tried to blur the line between nature and super-nature. Concentrating on the doctrine of human nature, he did what he could to soften the old Calvinist views of original sin, predestination, election, and other teachings which, he felt, might rob people of their sense of responsibility for participating in God's act of creating and saving a world. While Bushnell appeared on the scene too early to have to cope with the full force of biblical higher criticism, formal Darwinism, and progressivist social thought, he did anticipate all of these and made easier the confrontation with them on the part of his heirs. His accents on the loving one, Jesus; on a benevolent God; on the human who was at least potentially good; on God's immanence in the developing creation, made it possible to think of him as a church father of his century.

Munger did not want to exaggerate Bushnell's influence, "to compare Bushnell with the great doctors of theology before him," but he could not resist saying that "he had what they had not,—a unifying law of thought that delivered him out of the antinomies into which they led the church while seeking to deliver it from existing ones." Then Munger turned lavish: Bushnell had been a theologian as Copernicus was an astronomer.

"He changed the point of view, but pointed the way toward substantial unity in theological thought."

Thought of this type went into some eclipse for decades following Bushnell's prime, although a popular version of one side of it was picked up, often without acknowledgment or a direct sense of debt, by the celebrity preachers who minimized the shock of revelation, maximized the doctrine of human goodness, and affirmed the world as it was and as it was coming to be.

The new theology that was to do for the Protestant experience in America what the old had done for the evangelical empire—to interpret the command of Christ, as Mark Hopkins had put it—dates from the late 1880s and the 1890s and clusters around names like Munger, Newman Smyth of New Haven, George A. Gordon of Boston, George Harris, an innovator at Andover Seminary, William Newton Clarke at Colgate, and finally William Adams Brown at Union Seminary. Their book titles reveal something of their spirit and principles: Munger's *The Freedom of Faith* and *The Appeal to Life;* Smyth's *Constructive Natural Theology* and *Through Science to Faith;* Gordon's *Progressive Religious Thought in America, Immortality and the New Theodicy,* and *The New Epoch for Faith;* Lyman Abbott's *The Evolution of Christianity;* Harris' *Moral Evolution,* and Brown's article, "The Old Theology and the New." They were all obsessed by newness and progress.

The transcendent God was now to be seen immanent in history, revealed in the most impressive way in Jesus of Nazareth. Theologians were not always clear whether Jesus was to be qualitatively or quantitatively set apart from other people, though they treated the human Jesus with highest respect and in tones that suggested their roots in pietist Protestantism. Experience and consciousness were now to be authorities as high as were the scripture. Jesus' activity for humans—as in the witness of the German disciples of Albrecht Ritschl—had not particularly been designed to substitute for others through his death, but to serve as an example for others through his life and sacrifice. The human was full of potential, as cocreator with God and participant in progress. Smyth found, despite empirical setbacks to the contrary, "unmistakable evidence of progress" in humanity showing forth life in history. The universe, said Gordon, exerts pressure against inhumanity.

Through it all, Progress dominated where once Providence had chartered and guided action. While faith in progress was to be shattered, or at least complicated, by World War I—Walter Rauschenbusch's later work is most eloquent evidence of the "deep depression" of spirit that came with it—almost up to that time the modernizers could be optimistic. "The largest and hardest part of the work of Christianizing the social order has been done," and Americans needed only "to complete the task of redemption," Rauschenbusch wrote in 1912. "This thing is destiny. God wills it." And then, in Bushnellian cadences, "What is morally necessary, must be possible. Else where is God?"

George Harris had indicated his faith in progress by noting that "by distant contrast, the moderns are better than the ancients. The retrospect which sobers also animates ... Optimism is more than a hope for the future." It was based, as it were, on a law of history. Abbot was less profound than Rauschenbusch when the war came to terminate an era: "The human race falls down occasionally, bruises itself, and weeps some bitter tears; but picks itself up and goes on walking, and persistently in the right direction." Gordon: "The historic movement is slowly but surely away from the brute." William Jewett Tucker in an autobiographical note in 1919 put it best: "The desire and struggle for progress became the unifying purpose of the generation."

The progressivist liberals were concerned, however, to accent not only the *new* but also the *theology*. They did not want to be thought of as mere evolutionists but as people who could synthesize Protestant and developmental thought. They carried over perhaps more than they knew of the older evangelicalism, and all but a few of them have later been capable of being dubbed "Christocentric evangelical liberals." For these reasons they stand in the tradition of transformative Protestantism.

The first mark of separation between them and their secular counterparts was in their assertion of the primacy of the spiritual world. For Munger, the new theology "asserts the reality of the spiritual as above the material, of force that is other than that lodged in matter, or truth realized in another way than by induction from material facts." It makes these assertions on scientific grounds and as inductions from phenomena." Abbott went further: "I reverently and heartily accept the axiom of theology that a personal God is the foundation of all life."

No mere Darwinian would have surveyed the record of all human history and singled out Jesus from the distant past. Yet to the new theologians, he stood above others in the historical process. He was author of progress because of the incarnation, which introduced into history a new principle of justice and love. Rauschenbusch knew that the consciousness of God "is weak, occasional, and suppressed. The more Jesus Christ becomes dominant in us, the more does the light and life of God shine readily in us, and create a religious personality which we did not have. Life is lived under a new synthesis." To Clarke, Christ comes "to infuse spirituality" into the being of humans. At Chicago, George B. Foster and Shailer Mathews also accented a Christ-centered faith, and Mathews in 1909 asked for a theology that was evangelical in that it "utilizes methodically the gospel as given by biblical theology." He asked for "the evangelic picture of a genuinely historical Jesus, the concrete expression of the supremacy of the spiritual life." Even if these people had difficulties with the literalists, they also found reason to evaluate the Bible above other books. They advocated the general moral course prescribed by bourgeois Protestantism in their day.

Given these evangelical backgrounds, they felt that they could move forward with ease. Clarke thought that "there is no ground whatever for foes to hope or friends to fear that Christianity must retire if the evolutionary idea gains entrance." The more reckless Minot Judson Savage even went so far as to say that "the underlying principles of Christianity, and the underlying principles of humanity, as it moves on toward perfection, are perfectly identical."

This kind of law of identity was sufficiently widespread in the new theology to create a problem for Protestantism. What happens to protest? With the exception of a few prophets of new theology, like Walter Rauschenbusch with his social gospel, the basic tendency of creation, the world, and especially America was apparently a proper one. In Abbott's sphere, where a World War could be described as only a stumbling and bruising event, following which humanity would walk as it persistently did in the right direction, radical views of evil were compromised. It was difficult for the new theologians to separate themselves from their tribe and their nation, to gain criticial distance. In some ways, theirs was but a more sophisticated version of the decorous worldiness of their popular preaching contemporaries.

A harmonizing, adaptive, accommodative theology, the new school was better at affirming than negating, at baptizing than exorcising. In a world of social evils, men like Shailer Mathews could counsel moderation: "In the long run, public opinion can be affected by modifying the sympathy and idealism of individuals." Protestants could help "allay discontent" and "forestall radicalism" in a time of social upheaval. "Let reforms come; make reforms come; but let everything be done decently and in order," wrote Mathews in a time when antireform forces were violent about suppressing even mild forms of discontent and agents of change. At times, new theologians even sided with the old individualists. Mathews was again a good example: "Reforms are for church members, not for churches." He was critical of socialism, even if it was a daughter of the church. By placing themselves in the evolutionary flux without making clear why Christ and the Bible were also to be seen apart from it, they found it difficult to find a normative viewpoint on the basis of which to judge the culture. They could speak only in general terms about what belonged and what did not belong to the general law of progress.

Those who look back on the turn of the century as the period in which American racialism was being stamped deeper and American imperialism was at its peak find that the new theologians and those of kindred spirit had created what might be called a "Protestantism without Protest." The environment was revelatory and redemptive; through it God would speak. How could they take a negative view of what went on in it? The agents of

God happened to be white Anglo-Saxon Americans who had funds to invest in the world, guns with which to subjugate the Spaniards, and a spiritual superiority which gave them license to determine the destinies of others.

Expansionism was seen by the progress-oriented to be one more part of the fulfillment of the plan of God, a new kind of semisecular missionary work in which American Protestants should participate.

John Fiske, a philosopher at the left edge of new theology, and Josiah Strong, a church leader at the social gospel's right, united in their defense of Anglo-Saxonism as God's highest human revelation to date. While Fiske wanted Anglo-Saxon manifest destiny eventually to embrace all people, Strong wanted it to be asserted at the expense of others. "Can any one doubt that the result of this competition of races will be the 'survival of the fittest?'" This competition would call the Protestant Christian world to move down upon Mexico, Central and South America, the islands, Africa, and beyond. The inferior races could only cry, "Prepare ye the way of the Lord!" In 1900 Strong wrote *Expansion under New World Conditions* to criticize antiimperialists. While he may have had limited impact outside the churches, he was typical of those who asserted ideas of Providence-turned-Progress to line Protestants up behind imperialist and expansionist ventures.

When Strong wrote, "We are the chosen people ..." who "can no longer *drift* with safety to our destiny. We are shut up to a perilous alternative," he called for Anglo-Saxon Christianization of the world. If he and the liberal missionaries sounded more racist than others, they at least found ready hearing among the Protestant thinkers who were convinced that the general movement of Progress equals God. And if white American Protestants were to be in the vanguard of that trend and movement, they had found no motive and had lost the motif on the basis of which they could have engaged in protest.

21 · Protestants for Protest

Progressives, Reformers, the Social Gospel

"Reforms are for church members, not for churches." Perhaps on this point and on no other could the old evangelical conservatives have agreed with representatives for the new theology such as Shailer Mathews. The older evangelicals were probably more passionate in their attacks on individual vices and in their attemps to reform manners than were the newer theologians, but most of them could have agreed with each other that wrongs would best be corrected by converting, in the former case, or transforming, in the latter, the individuals who make up society. Between these two were the partly fish, partly fowl popular preachers who would have agreed with both—as they tried to please everybody—in their accent on minor vices, even as they christened the business world as it was and pronounced benedictions on the doings of the great industrialists.

Out of the two-party split which we have seen developing through the decades up to 1908, by which time the schism was becoming formalized, there grew some parties which were ready to use their social point of view to undertake basic criticism and to engage in fundamental protest against at least selected elements of the society at large. Numerically few, yet well-placed and often eloquent, they introduced novelties into American Protestantism and produced effects which were to remain long after these factions, among them the social gospel, had passed their prime.

The times were ripe for protest, criticism, and reform. As had happened before in the United States, when the churches took on their decorous worldliness, identification with the American Way of Life as it was, and support for manifest destiny, prophets arose around and outside of the churches. The best-known examples of this came with the reformers of the 1820s through the 1840s and, during the war, with Abraham Lincoln in his partial judgment on self-assured chosenness and his opposition to the identification of the will of God with human parties and military forces.

The financial panics had revealed that not all was well with the economic system. Too many suffered abject poverty because of it. The great labor strikes near the end of the century betokened the end of the age

197

when the churches could side with mangement alone. Manipulation of the stock markets on the part of magnates plunged thousands out of work or meant the loss of the investments of other thousands. Great trusts were growing, threatening monopolies and the manipulation of prices. People were becoming aware of the inhumane living conditions of immigrants in the cities and blacks in the South or in their new northern homes. The old evangelical patterns of charity and benevolence now seemed almost to contribute to the problems rather than solve them. They created the impression that by dealing with the victims of the economic order one was dealing with the issue rather than distracting attention from needed change.

In such a world, the development or reformist and critical forces partly independent of or even in reaction against the Protestant churches, is understandable. Seldom in American history have such competing forces bid for attention than at the beginning of the century. If there had been "Protestantism without Protest," there was also "Protest without Protestantism."

In its most radical form, this tendency showed up in isolated but highly publicized movements of anarchism. All the churches united to oppose these, especially after they were accused of being responsible for the Haymarket Riot in Chicago in 1886 or when they surfaced in the assassin of President McKinley in 1901. While participating in the new legislation which prohibited anarchists from entering the country, a few early social gospel leaders took the occasion to remind Protestants that they were helping create the social conditions in which anarchy thrived.

Only slightly less radical, in Protestant eyes, were the Marxists, who made small headway in the circles of American labor. A few disciples of Karl Marx made their way to America, but the labor movement was generally not responsive to them. The conditions productive of a restless proletariat were not present in American cities. There was too much mobility. Too many workers had just come from Europe. They were too satisfied with American conditions, however bad, in contrast to what they had known, to provide recruiting ground for labor radicals. And the failure of Catholicism to engage in condemnation of moderate labor unions took some of the anticlerical impetus out of the movement. While Walter Rauschenbusch and other Protestant social critics read Marx and occasionally cited him, they were careful to make clear that they were not Marxian. Some of them used Marx only to cause Protestants to ask how they were creating a vacuum which Communists were filling.

Socialism was another quasireligious alternative to Protestantism in the reform movements and knew some more success than anarchism or Marxism. It was at least successful in establishing a movement and a party and came to power in some cities, like Milwaukee. But it was ordinarily a tempered form of socialism and some church people even joined the party, thus moderating its blanket criticism of the churches for their defenses of private property. The social Christians welcomed the criticisms that came from socialism, but their own theology caused them to introduce many features uncongenial to ordinary socialism. Their plea to "socialize Christianty" and to "Christianize socialism" met with rebuffs from both sides.

Utopianism came to another form of "Protest without Protestantism" and enjoyed a vogue around the turn of the century, particularly because of the popularity of books like Edward Bellamy's *Looking Backward: 2000–1887.* Bellamy's best-selling novel attacked private enterprise as being wasteful and causing poverty, and eventually inspired numbers of people toward cooperatives. The Populist Party incarnated some of these utopian ideas, and Bellamy offered a semirespectable ally for religious leaders, thus reopening the old utopian tradition in Protestantism. Works like Charles M. Sheldon's *In His Steps: What Would Jesus Do?* indicated something of the hunger Protestants had for utopian pictures of a better world, especially if these were presented as Sheldon did, in an economically moderate context.

Another inspiration for Protestant criticism came from the semiutopian single tax scheme of Henry George, who came from a pietistic background and whose moral appeals were expressed with religious fervor. An advocate of economic equality, he pioneered with *Progress and Poverty* in 1879. George wanted a single tax on land which would eliminate speculation on land and give people equal ability to trade on the nation's resources. A somewhat naïve book, it stimulated reform and inspired many young social gospel leaders.

In the nonurban areas, populism came to be an agency of reform in the vacuum the churches left. It took the form of a party in 1889 to represent the interests of farmers in debt and grew into a comprehensive social philosophy. The fact that the conservative Christian politician William Jennings Bryan was able to make political common cause with the Populists in 1896 shows the degree of common involvement between Protestants and Populists on some issues. Progressivism, an enormously complicated movement, prevailed for the quarter-century before World War I as the most far-reaching and acceptable reform program. It tried to comprehend the changes as America moved from rural to urban life and as the churches abdicated their role as centers of reform. The progressives were "protestant" in their attacks on the alliances of wealth and politics and in their agitation for antitrust legislation, laws which would protect consumers, and economic reforms. Like populism, progressivism was a sufficiently respectable movement to attract Protestants, although some leaders like Jane Addams were critical of the churches as being exploiting, conservative forces.

A list such as this could be extended almost indefinitely. The muckrakers in journalism found the churches among the most vulnerable of institutions, and Ray Stannard Baker's attacks on New York churches for their wealth and ownership of slums were widely heralded. The Wobblies, or Industrial Workers of the World, made up a labor party in 1905 which because of its socialist-anarchist commitments frightened off most Protestants. The Settlement House movement, under Florence Kelly, Jane Addams, and others, filled the gap left by the old evangelical humanitarian agencies as the Protestants left the inner city. Many of the leaders of these institutions had been brought up in Protestantism and had had their consciences formed in its moral pattern, only to turn against the churches for their selfishness and apathy in the face of the urban poor.

The secularization of higher education, occurring at this time, included elements who saw themselves as reformist over against the churches. Before the 1880s, virtually all higher education in America was in the hands of the Protestant churches. Small colleges remained the ideal. Many of these had been formed to produce ministers, teachers, and revivalists. Secular subjects were introduced largely to complete the spiritual education of students. These colleges became and long remained citadels for evangelical nurture and centers of resistance to the new intellectual currents.

In the 1880s and thereafter, however, one after another of these schools segregated their religion departments, sometimes into graduate schools of divinity. Their presidents and eventually their boards of trustees were no longer dominated by ministers. Compulsory chapel was dropped. The percentage of courses dealing with business and science grew. Religious tests for professors were gradually removed. Where modern universities came into existence, European seminar methods introduced new means of pursuit of knowledge, and the old evangelical idea of the advanced nursery disappeared. Those at state-supported universities like those at Ann Arbor, Michigan, soon learned that there was no way they could relate positively to the churches. Land-grant colleges contributed to the force of numbers of students in the secular schools that overwhelmed the religious schools. The new secular centers of higher eduction in the age of people like John Dewey became agencies for reform of education and other sectors of life, often in opposition to the antiintellectualism or repressiveness of many Protestant churches.

During these years, in short, America saw the rebirth of social criticism, but this time it was largely outside the churches. The evangelicals, who had built moral fervor into the American ethos, were preoccupied with building and running churches and sending missionaries. They found too few motives or resources to deal with the perplexing problems of the cities, and many had developed ideologies appropriate to village America and resistant to change in complex city life. Yet many of these new secular reforms which took up the slack traded on the evangelically formed conscience, now turned against evangelicalism. Something of the Protestant principle of protest had moved out of the churches and into these circles. They fused some of the thought of the Enlightenment with Protestantism and new social critical philosophies. Jane Addams spoke of her time as one with "a certain renaissance of Christianity, a movement toward its early humanitarian aspects." She meant to imply a judgment on the death of humanitarianism in contemporary institutional religion.

In some forms, reformist groups had to oppose the churches in the name of their own professed ideals. A good example is the women's suffrage movement. Suffragette leaders felt that they had been enslaved as blacks had been, with justifications based on a literal view of scripture. To free themselves, they found it worthwhile to publicize views of the higher criticism of the Bible; this only served to make them seem doubly dangerous to Protestants, even as it motivated them to enlarge their attacks on the churches. Elizabeth Cady Stanton went out of her way to denounce the churches, arguing in 1893 that "the most powerful influences against woman's emancipation can be traced to religious superstitions." If subjugation of women was seen not to be based on the divine mandate, men would not be able to sustain a religious base to their oppression. Wiser heads like Susan B. Anthony knew better than to take on the male clergy on their own ground: she wrote (in 1895), "*No*—I don't want my name on that Bible Committee—*You* fight that battle—and leave me to fight the secular—the political fellows." When Stanton's Bible Committee produced *The Woman's Bible,* the clergy responded, "It is the work of women and the devil." In time-honored fashion, Stanton claimed pure religion for her cause. The devil had been too busy attending synods, general assemblies, and conferences to study the languages and higher criticism. Her committee, she averred, had demonstrated greater reverence "for the great Spirit of All Good than does the Church."

As years passed and the criticisms of the Bible and the churches were moderated, women's suffrage became a more respectable idea, and Protestant women were more free to take part. Ironically, women's suffrage finally came first in the wide-open West, in part as a way of fighting off immigrant influences by assuring enough "Puritan" votes. As University of Colorado President (emeritus) James H. Baker said in 1927, "Puritan standards have become the public standards of America, and you will find more of New England in Colorado Springs, Boulder, or Greeley than in most towns of Massachusetts." The suffrage success came in part over against Roman Catholics, eastern political leaders, and the foreign born. The Protestants in their own way had won another round, temporarily— even though they had to accept ideas which only decades earlier their predecessors had contended were against the scriptural view of women.

If most reform went on apart from Protestant auspices, thus demonstrating the degree of secularization that had gone on under the surface of churchgoing America, along with the general moral abdication of churches in the public realm, this did not mean that there was no Protestant protest, criticism, or basic social reform. One movement in particular reproduced ancient Christian patterns of involvement with the whole order of society. This was the social gospel under the leadership of Walter Rauschenbusch, one man, at least, who freed himself from the simple progressivism of the new theologians. The social gospel remains one of the best known and most easily defined of American Protestant movements, and Rauschenbusch is often ranked with the three or four major leaders in American Protestant history.

The social gospel took root out of the postmillennial side of earlier American revivalism, after it had been submerged for several decades after the Civil War. To this were added some influences of the new theology, particularly its evolutionary progressivism and other outside influences. Walter Rauschenbusch himself studied briefly in Germany and was influenced by the Ritschlians in their proclamation of the Kingdom of God as a world-transforming reality. The social gospel leaders read their Edward Bellamy and Henry George; from a great distance and with proper caution, they read the socialists and sometimes Karl Marx. They were shaped in part by personal reaction to the America they saw dwelling in Hell's Kitchen in New York (Rauschenbusch) or in laboring sections of Columbus, Ohio (Washington Gladden).

The social gospel movement was an outgrowth of the older American evangelicalism. Like the new theology, it had few roots in the American South, although in the twentieth century the South was to see some Protestant involvement with reform causes. Lutheranism produced only one or two names that appear in histories of the social gospel. The theological reactionaries in general, like the Princetonians, resisted the movement for theological, political, and ecclesiastical reasons. It remained a minority voice in the denominations that were heirs of the "colonial big three," the Congregationalists, the Episcopalians, and the Presbyterians, and the frontier "big three," the Methodists, the Baptists, and to a lesser extent, the Disciples of Christ.

The social gospel leaders were in some rare instances parish clerics like Gladden. More often they were seminary professors, editors, authors, gadflies, heads of brotherhoods and similar movements. While they concentrated on changing industrial America and championing workers in a Protestant world where labor organization still was often described as "against the law of God," it must be said that they did not, for the most part, become well known to laborers or slum dwellers. Theirs was in part a movement of argument and agitation.

What the movement at its most clarified points set out to do was quite radical. It wanted to tear up the approved social contract which early nineteenth-century—evangelicalism had helped write and which its latter-day leaders were convincing America was normative, timeless Christianity. The social gospel thinkers wanted the church to meddle in politics. They were successful at showing that individualistic Protestants were not successful at staying aloof from politics. They noted that these were constantly taking stands on political issues of their own choices: gambling, Sunday laws, tax-exemption for religious institutions, and the like. They further noted that the votes of culture-affirming Protestants were constantly being counted on the side of the status quo. They were engaged in making commitments, even as they pretended not to be. The social gospel leaders decided to counter this weight which supported laissez-faire conditions by favoring moderate cooperation and socializing in society. If the new theology was not merely evolutionistic, so the social gospel was not merely socialistic, and the secular socialists would have questioned whether it was socialistic at all.

The social gospel was the first movement which demonstrated that Protestant thought was coming to terms with the way power was organized in urban America. As such, it had to work against the stream of the Protestant majority, which was retaining the rural ethos or adapting the small business (person-to-person) sense of ethics from the preindustrial city. Yet the social gospel advocates definitely remained in the evangelical tradition. It has often been pointed out that their methods were often evangelistic. They did not want a social involvement at the expense of historic American evangelical concerns with individuals, souls, and morality. They resorted to the prophets, to Jesus, to the Bible, and most of all to the Kingdom of God motif.

As years passed, social gospel proponents like Rauschenbusch came to see that their theology had been too optimistic and too progressivistic. Rauschenbusch came to concentrate more and more on "social sins," the sins which seemed to be built into the structures of society itself.

These protesting Protestants were selective about the areas of protest. Thus Josiah Strong is usually listed with the social gospel thinkers and was a fairly consistent advocate of social gospel policies early in the twentieth century. But he was ill-equipped to deal with some of America's most profound problems. By almost any definition, he was an Anglo-Saxon racist, with a paternalistic and condescending view of nonwhites, particularly of American blacks. In fact, the race problem (perhaps because the social critics were largely in the North, before the big black migrations) was a curious blind spot in the social gospel movement. On the surface of things, most advocates said some of the right things about doing good to all people, and they certainly evidenced compassion in their dealing with blacks. But rarely were there expressions of racial equality or of a sense that blacks might share equally with whites in bringing in the Kingdom of God. Similarly, Strong and other social gospel leaders expressed some sense that American Protestants had won credentials to have dominion over other parts of the world. Many social gospel thinkers had a blind spot for imperialism.

Christianization of society became the way these "transformationists" spoke of the changes the Kingdom of God would bring.

The attempt to produce a new social contract in America, one which would fuse the best of the old with emergent world views in the face of new needs, could not but be controversial. Most Protestants did not think that the church was in the world to change society, but to save souls. Gladden, Herron, Rauschenbusch, Ely, and their compatriots found that a wall of complacency greeted many of their efforts in the churches while reformist forces around the churches were responsible for much of the kind of change Christians had wanted to bring.

As he met resistance, Rauschenbusch revealed the ways in which he qualified the optimism which later generations sometimes associated with his name. "History laughs at the optimistic illusion that 'nothing can stand in the way of human progress.' It would be safer to assert that progress is always for a time only, and then succumbs to the inevitable decay." This word from 1907 anticipated more morose expression in his summation, *Theology for the Social Gospel,* ten years later. Nor was Rauschenbusch ready to say that better distribution of goods would remove the crisis of values. With poverty gone, other temptations would be present and there would be "universal pride and wantonness."

But if Rauschenbusch was rather conventionally evangelical in his defense of spiritual values and his pleas for regenerate and converted people, he was furious about the individualism which had served to wall off churches from human need. He had seen the attractions of secular social forces and warned that "if our theology is silent on social salvation, we compel college men and women, workingmen, and theological students, to choose between an unsocial system of theology and an irreligious system of social salvation." He was sure they would choose the latter, and if people would "keep Christian doctrine unchanged" they would "ensure its abandonment." The evangelists were producing skin-deep changes; the Kingdom of God called for more.

One can see how put off most secular socialists or reformers would have been by a thinker as religiously intoxicated as Rauschenbusch. His obsession was the Kingdom of God and his model was St. Paul's metaphor of the church as the body of Christ, "the highest philosophy of human society." Capitalism destroyed this organismic character. It "tempts, defeats, drains, and degrades, and leaves men stunted, cowed, and shamed in their manhood." It was in urban industry that we "encounter the great collective inhumanities that shame our Christian feeling, such as child labor and the bloody total of industrial accidents." It produced "a mammonistic organization with which Christianity can never be content." Its spirit was "antagonistic to the spirit of Christianity." It was "a spirit of hardness and cruelty that neutralizes the Christian spirit of love; a spirit that sets material goods above spiritual possessions."

Rauschenbusch's social analysis and prescription were not as profound as was his theological inquiry, and he and his colleagues were never able to carry their protest into a full program of redress. Now and then they would see minor successes. Often they could make common cause with other reformist forces. Repeatedly they would see that minor social legislation sapped the energies of people organized for total social reform. Yet the Social Creed of the Methodist Churches and the Constitution of the Federal Council of Churches in 1908 showed that they were having some ecclesiastical successes. Even if they were not successful at changing all of society, they had begun to get the Protestant churches to think about new involvements. The attempt of Rauschenbusch in his final book to rewrite Christian systematic theology from a social point of view was a high point in the transformation of American theology. More than almost any of his peers, Rauschenbusch tempered his theology with reference to the doctrine of original sin. He proved himself to be thoroughly Protestant when he turned his criticism against his own side: "One cause of distrust of the social gospel is that its exponents often fail to show an adequate appreciation of the power and guilt of sin." And he constantly feared that disappointed social Christians would drift off from the churches, into "a disembodied spirit of Christianity" which would lack power.

After World War I the social Christianity was partly quieted for a decade and a half, to revive in the age of Reinhold Niebuhr. It had picked up as many enemies as had the new theology. In the public realm, it could count on even more antagonism than could the theological movement. Theology seemed to be a bookish affair that concerned people in sanctuaries. But social reactionaries in the churches could always find allies and financing to oppose the social gospel, for it challenged existing concepts of property, wealth, and investment.

The social Christians were theologically vulnerable, as innovators often are. In the hands of almost anyone but Rauschenbusch, the tragic dimensions of human existence were neglected in favor of the pervasive progressivism of the era.

The enemies of the social gospel have tried to show that it was a hasty and superficial reaction to the wrongs of the industrial age and not a legitimate transformation of Puritan Protestantism from the colonial era. True, both dealt with a whole covenanted and organismic society. But the former had done so in the context of orthodoxy while the latter was so heretical that any social good that might have been implied in it was compromised or negated.

To the reactionaries, the immanentism of the social gospel was most threatening. Rauschenbusch's word that "the old idea that God dwells on high and is distant from our human life" was the natural basis for auto-cratic and arbitrary ideas of a remote deity. "On the other hand the reli-gious belief that He is immanent in humanity is the natural basis for the democratic ideas about Him." These words may have been the final devel-opment of Puritan logic, to the point where the "chained God" of which Perry Miller spoke was finally confined. The God of the American covenant and the evangelical empire had to be a God who was not wholly mysteri-ous. Ministers and elders, reading the codes, had to be able to find author-itative interpretations of God's will for the community. But the social gos-pel carried this too far for those who stressed God's transcendence.

When Harry F. Ward was to look back two decades later on the Social Creed of the Churches of 1908, he provided the text which political con-servatives in the churches needed to put the last nail into the social gos-pel's coffin. Ward asked readers to engage in a "revealing exercise to put in parallel columns the social creed of the churches; the earlier programs of organized labor; the populists and the socialists; the later platforms of the progressive party and the statement of ideals adopted by members of the national conference of social work." The authors of the Social Creed, "under the impulse of a long religious tradition" paralleled the thinking of writers of these other platforms, yet without borrowing. "A common movement in American life was coming to expression, that organized reli-gion should take both direction from it and put it into an older sanction and power as an instance of how God is revealed in human life." The alli-ance between protesting Protestants and protesters outside Protestantism was offensive to intransigents. But these soon found themselves with another battle on their hands.

22 · Conflicting Experiences

Controversies Through the Twenties

In 1927 the French author Andre Siegfried, in a book significantly titled *America Comes of Age,* made an observation which would have been less surprising in 1827. Protestantism is America's "only national religion and to ignore that fact is to view the country from a false angle."

Protestantism did help form America's national religion in a most significant way. Statistically it predominated over Catholicism, although Catholicism was larger than even the largest of Protestant denominations. Judaism was numerically relatively insignificant, and other non-Christian faiths were also shared by only a small percentage of the people. Protestantism was the national religion by the fact of its longer lineage, having the field largely to itself in the colonies and the United States from the early seventeenth century to the midnineteenth century.

Protestantism had provided the nation with the symbolism and mythology that shaped folklore as well as the sophisticated literature of novelists and poets. Its architecture highlighted the landscape; its hymnody, from the lips of blacks and whites alike, was the folk song of a majority of the people. What was often called the Protestant ethic had left its stamp on public institutions, the business and industrial creeds, and the ways people raised their families and styled personal life. Non-Protestant symbolism was arcane and exotic to all but those who adhered to minority creeds, while Protestant mythology and ethos were recognizable beyond the churches.

The great difference between 1827 and 1927 lay in the fact that the old "sameness," singleness, and homogeneity, so longed for, demanded, and patrolled by the trustees of the Protestant empire before the Civil War was gone in the twentieth century. And the most divisive forces had come not from without but from within.

From the 1880s to World War I the mainline Protestants saw much of their intellectual leadership adopt various versions of the new theology, and much of their reformist passion shaped into a new social gospel. Biblical criticism, evolutionary thought, and modern secular philosophy were absorbed into the liberal Protestant patterns of progressivist thought. But there was backlash, and the reactionaries were capable of organizing in

207

new, if defensive, ways to regroup and try to retake the leadership in thought, action, and political power in the denominations.

The intransigents' efforts were seen in opposition to the new theology and the social gospel. They were exerted in the form of highly successful urban mass evangelistic efforts from Moody to Billy Sunday. The conservatives stayed outside of the Federal Council of Churches in 1908, or fought for position in it. But not until the 1920s did enough of them coalesce in a party to challenge the progressives. When they did, a series of conflicts ensued which drew national attention, from non-Protestants and non-Christians alike. This public notice was ever after to leave Americans with the awareness that while their national religion was Protestant, the Protestants were too divided to provide clear leadership.

Through the years of the First World War and the following decade, two issues could still unite a wide spectrum of Protestants in a common experience: anti-Catholicism and Prohibition. Anti-Catholicism was an emphasis left over from the days when Protestants had endeavored to build an empire which would keep the hated papists out.

The revival of the Ku Klux Klan in the 1920s included an anti-Catholic note, which attracted only the extreme reactionaries in southern and midwestern white Protestantism. But moderates throughout the nation were no less disturbed than Klansmen about the threat that America would go Catholic by immigration. Eastern Orthodox Christians also experienced a dramatic gain in percentage of growth but their beginning figure was so small that this hardly upset the balance. Jewish immigration also increased in percentage growth, but remained comparatively small. In 1906 these faiths were represented by 129,606 and 101,475 people, respectively, while in 1958 they had 2,545,318 and 5,500,000. But Catholicism had the allegiance of 40 percent of America's church members in 1906 and 36 percent in 1958. Protestants had 60 percent in 1906 and 56 percent in 1958. Despite this fact, people of "Catholic-Orthodox-Jewish" population were still seen to be intruders, and Protestants across a wide range of attitudes favored restricted immigration.

The fact that the new immigrants congregated in the perilous cities, where Protestants were least at home, added to mystery and fear. That they were assuming political power in virtually every urban center served to complicate matters, even though archaic laws gave rural (i.e., Protestant) areas disproportionate state and federal voting power. By 1920 it had become clear that the immigrants were not easily to be melted into the American pot. The old quasi-Protestant idea of empire asserted itself in support of legislation which would impose quota laws to protect native-born workers from being swarmed over by cheap immigrant labor. In 1924 the Johnson-Reed Act was passed, and it virtually cut off new immigration. During these years books like Madison Grant's pseudoscientific *The Passing of the Great Race* (1916) achieved wide readership with its claim that after 1860 the Aryan Euro-American had been blighted by mixture with inferiors. Literacy tests had not been enough to keep the inferiors out. A well-meaning Protestant minister-missionary, Sidney L. Gulick, in order to help overcome discrimination against Orientals, advocated a formula which would limit all new immigration on the basis of a percentage of each ethnic group already in the United States. But the Immigration Act of 1924 admitted a smaller percentage than he had advocated, and instead of using 1910 as the base year, it lapsed back to 1890. By a savage irony, this meant that Gulick's friends, the Japanese and the Chinese, were ruled out entirely on this basis. By 1929 the policy was in full effect, and it proved to be discriminatory in character. The great age of immigration was ending.

With only a small number of Catholics and Jews entering, the Protestants should have felt free to relax, but the millions of newcomers already on the scene were asserting themselves. In 1924 there seemed to be a chance that an Irish Catholic might become a Presidential nominee, and in 1928 New York Governor Alfred E. Smith, a Catholic, was nominated. While the role of Protestantism in his defeat is still hotly debated—1928 seems to have been a bad year for a Democrat no matter what—the public representatives of conservative and liberal Protestantism alike made clear their opposition to him because of his Catholicism and his support for repeal of Prohibition.

Prohibition was the other uniting Protestant cause. Thus the liberal periodical, *The Christian Century,* under Charles Clayton Morrison, although it opposed Hoover on the Kellogg Peace Pact, on Latin American policies, on civil liberties, and on labor, and although it regarded Smith as the superior candidate, joined forces with extreme reactionaries in politics and religion to oppose Smith because of his support of the repeal of Prohibition and because of his Catholicism.

Not all Protestants had always been against drinking of alcohol. The Anglicans were mild on the temperance issue, and the Lutherans, who enjoy their beer, were so opposed to the Anglo-Protestant efforts to prohibit brewing it that they found their prejudices against political meddling simply confirmed. Long before, John Wesley had not always opposed liquor and, in moderation, alcoholic beverages were commonplace until the nineteenth century in most Protestant circles. Some of the antiliquor agitation grew out of social concern. The rise of urbanism and the industrial society made drinking a new kind of social problem. Protestantism often opposed it as part of a positive reform program in support of widows, orphans, and good stewardship.

As years passed, however, the Prohibition cause came to take on more and more of the individualistic note at the hands of the evangelical parties. It was a vice which could be controlled. The old support of the victim was beginning to be transformed to a vindictive spirit against the person who was seen to enjoy drinking. What is more, addiction to alcohol caused people to lose the self-discipline required of those who would save souls, spread holiness, and transform society. The social gospel thinkers differed hardly at all on this point, even though they could rarely otherwise agree with individualists on public issues. Prohibition's historian, D. Leigh Colvin, looked back on successes in 1926 and observed that "Prohibition would establish the social conditions of morality under which men are more likely to be moral than when living under an environment which is conducive to immorality and wrong-doing." Although individualistic Protestants were constantly criticizing liberal efforts to remake the world through law, they were eager to do so themselves on this issue, and Colvin defended them, quoting Gladstone: it was "the duty of government to make it easy to do right and difficult to do wrong."

The two Protestant parties began their attack not simply by excoriating the drinker but by trying to interrupt liquor traffic, by attacking the saloon. Yet they were not to know legislative success on a national scale until 1919, with passage of the Volstead Act and the Eighteenth Amendment to the Constitution. The Protestants knew their greatest imperial victory in the Congress and legislatures 100 years after their empire was in its prime. Why were they finally successful?

The answer lies in part in the nativist reaction to urbanism and immigrant populations, where the problem of drinking was seen to be most acute and in whose hands it was regarded as most repulsive. Thirty years later Virginius Dabney could look back on the way rural Protestant political power was able to rise up for this last stand by recalling that "when the movement for nation-wide Prohibition was approaching its climax in 1917, the political center of gravity of the country was not in New York or Chicago or San Francisco but in Junction City and Smith's Store and Brown's Hollow." The parts of the country that favored temperance legislation were rising up against those that did not. Advocates spoke in military terms, as if this interarea battle was a new Civil War. "The vices of the cities," wrote the Anti-Saloon League's chief editor in 1913, "have been the undoing of past empires and civilizations." "In our large cities the controlling vote is that of the dangerous classes, who are readily dominated by the saloon. City government is 'boss government,' and the boss rules by the grace of the grog shop," argued the Presbyterian Committee on Temperance just before the turn of the century.

After the turn of the century, urban evangelists like J. Wilbur Chapman, Billy Sunday, and Reuben Torrey began preaching "booze sermons" and added troops to the same cause that progressives and social gospel partisans were summoning. Old traditions separating civil from religious realms could easily be forgotten for this crusade, as they could not be for racial or economic justice. The Federal Council of the Churches of Christ was not attacked for support of Prohibition as it was for peace policies. By the time the Volstead Act was passed, both Protestant parties had united and helped legislate, by an average of 4 percent majorities, a policy which had to be repealed in 1933 because of the new problems it caused. The crusade had been accompanied by some of the last imperial talk to be regarded as plausible in Protestant America. The Reverend Sam Small is often remembered for his speech at the 1917 Convention of the Anti-Saloon League in Washington. Prohibition would mean that Protestants could "see this America of ours, victorious and Christianized, become not only the savior but the model and the monitor of the reconstructed civilization of the world in the future." Lyman Beecher or Dwight Moody could have said that—but so could Walter Rauschenbusch.

Small invoked the flag, Washington, Lincoln, Lee, and Wilson to envision the capitol overshadowing the fountainhead of the liberties of humanity so that no king and no crown, no throne and no slave, would miss the signal; there would be a "reconstructed, civilized Christianized world—a new world of which the United States of America will be the leader, through which God will say 'Well done' to all nations that live in Holiness before Him and do justice, everyone with his neighbor!" Instead of God's "Well done" and justice for all, the Prohibitionists got speakeasies, Al Capone, and finally repeal. They thereby lost the last issue which would unite them.

For the rest, the decade of the 1920s found Protestants fighting each other more than they fought immigrants and Catholics, drunks and unbelievers. The best-known and most prolonged of the controversies is remembered as that between fundamentalism and modernism, and a study of subsequent Protestantism is incomprehensible without some recognition of the fundamentalist contribution to the American national religion.

Today the word "fundamentalist" is often casually applied to people who are intransigent about change, advocates of resistance to modernity anywhere in the world. More properly, it should be applied to a loosely organized cluster of allies that could unite for certain causes in America. They made up a movement early in the century and under other names, including "neoevangelical," they have endured. But they shaped up into a specific party for the fundamentalist controversy of the 1920s.

Not by any means simply "classic Christian or Protestant Orthodoxy," fundamentalism chose a specific new set of fundamentals, put them together in a novel way, and argued for them on grounds that would have been bewildering to anyone before the late nineteenth century. Its partisans were as modern as the modernists, if one wishes to date the beginning of their coalescence and the choice of issues or ways of stating them. They represented a specific transformation of the evangelicalism whose name they chose to monopolize for themselves.

Fundamentalism picked up and exaggerated certain old evangelical themes. But it was born in reaction to modernity. Fearful lest acceptance of Darwinism would mean denial of God and the separate origins of the human race or the authority of the scripture, fundamentalists restricted their acceptance of Darwinism to the social-economic realms, in support of laissez-faire individualism and competition on "survival of the fittest" lines. They rejected out of hand the beginnings of liberal acceptance of the imported higher criticism of the Bible because it might undercut the divine authority of the scriptures—even though fundamentalists were themselves by no means safeguarded in their own hold on truth. They differed with each other, despite their assent to a verbally inerrant and infallible Bible. They had a strange attraction for a substantial view of truth and a devotion to the blood of the atonement and the physical details of the virginity of the mother of Jesus.

They never even agreed on exactly what made up the fundamentals, differing in their acceptance of five or nine or fourteen of them, depending on who was counting—and often not bothering to count. The sacraments, basic to Catholic-Anglican-Orthodox-Lutheran Christianity, were dismissed from the doctrinal tests imposed by the fundamentalists. They wanted to test people on issues like the physical resurrection, the Virgin Birth, the Second Coming of Christ, all in literal terms. Since the modern views of the physical universe and of time did not make acceptance of these versions of Christian teaching easy, the fundamentalists soon found that applying them as tests seemed to make the fence around Protestantism higher, the gate narrower, and the scandals or traps at the entrance more obvious; the principle of exclusion became simple.

Drawing its name from the pamphlets paid for by two wealthy Californians and stimulated after 1910 by evangelists Amzi C. Dixon and Reuben A. Torrey, *The Fundamentals* were distributed by the millions. They served to help rally several groups who held only partly related interests. Among these were some of the Holiness groups which after the Civil War had tried to revitalize a Methodism which they saw going to seed, and some Pentecostal groups which had sprung up to give moderns a new and exciting experience of the Holy Spirit, after 1900.

Much more important than these were the premillennialists, the party rescued from obscurity by Dwight L. Moody and his heirs after William Miller of the Adventists had missed his calculations about Christ's Second Coming in 1843. Why Moody made so much of premillennialism, the belief that Christ would come for a thousand-year reign, has never been made completely clear, but its acceptance on the part of millions had to do with a pessimistic reaction to the urban-industrial-scientific world, that world which postmillennialists, those who thought the world would be transformed in preparation for Christ's return (whether as a literal or symbolic event) regarded so optimistically.

Premillennialism was in the air in Britain and America, borrowing in part from German biblical sources who saw that Christ's reign would bring about a fulfillment of promises denied in ordinary history. In England the Plymouth Brethren under John Nelson Darby had fashioned "dispensationalism," which divided history into a sequence of ages in which God dealt with humans in a different way each time. The Darbyite witness was accepted far beyond the circle of his gatherings of Brethren. Beginning in 1878 prophetic conferences were held in the United States, and with the publication of the dispensationalist Scofield Reference Bible in 1909 the premillennialists had an authoritative commentary to help unite them.

Premillennialism served to keep some groups at a distance. The midwestern Lutherans—busy adopting the English language around that time because of pressures caused by the First World War—were in a shopping mood. They automatically rejected modernism, as one side of the liberal movement was coming to be called. Yet they could not assent to literal premillennial or dispensational views and sat at the sidelines during the conflict. But some other conservatives who rejected premillennial views were attracted to a different contributing agent to fundamentalism. This was the ongoing scholastic Protestant thought of Princeton Seminary and other citadels which provided intellectual fiber for the movement. The few major scholars of fundamentalism in its prime—people like J. Gresham Machen, who was easily a scholarly match for the modernists—represented this part of the element.

Such a coalition of people who agreed on some all-purpose test-doctrines but disagreed on other fundamentals, people of many different theological positions and personality types, always suffered from internal division and lack of purpose. They did best when united by a common despised object, such as the famed preacher Harry Emerson Fosdick of New York with his inflaming sermon, "Shall the Fundamentalists Win?" Although Fosdick had hoped to rally moderates and cool the issue, he succeeded chiefly in helping conservatives organize under the fundamentalist banner. He knew that "the Fundamentalist controversy [threatened] to divide the American churches, as though already they were not sufficiently split and riven," and wanted to counter it. "All Fundamentalists are conservatives, but not all conservatives are Fundamentalists," he observed quite properly. He argued that they had a right to their opinions but not the right to exclusive use of the name Christian. He closed by calling for a new clear insight into Christianity and a tolerant live-and-let-live spirit.

That spirit was to be denied the Protestantism of the mid-1920s, however desperately it was needed. The fundamentalists genuinely believed that coexistence meant denial of the faith, but many of them also mixed their sincerity with an ill-mannered reaction to other people's innovation and piled on to this a whole set of hostile reactions to changes in the world. So intense was their rage that they became almost stereotypically rude types—a fact acknowledged by their heirs who have taken every pain to leave this part of the legacy behind. Even a Lutheran cheerleader was put off by this. Carl J. Södergren wrote in 1925: "The intolerance and persecution evinced by the modern Pseudo-Fundamentalists, inhibits their usefulness. Sane men and women are becoming impatient with those who are so ready to consign to the flames those who do not agree with them in every particular." He finally had to part company with the "fuddlementalists" who evidenced "the vociferation of mere opinion, if not indeed the wrath of wounded egotism."

If the fundamentalists were not simply to be equated with classic orthodoxy, neither were their antagonists, the modernists, simply classic Christian liberals. They were shaped by specific modern experiences, most notably the modern scientific-evolutionary world views. They relied on a rather easy theism, were at home with a metaphysics of progress, implied an old white Protestant view of destiny, and wanted Christianity to be adaptive to modernity and involved with public issues. An anti-Fosdick could have said, "All Modernists are liberals, but not all liberals are Modernists," although none did, for one strategy of fundamentalists was to cluster as many people together in the opponents' camp as possible to serve as a foil for their own causes.

The battle had to be fought in the denominations. The Baptists were most torn, producing as they did some of the strongest personalities on both sides. John Roach Straton, William B. Riley, and T. T. Shields held the Baptist banners, arguing at the conventions from 1925 through 1927 against modernist takeovers of theological schools and missionary boards. The Methodists were a bit less involved with the controversy in their conventions, although the denomination was torn by contenders on both sides. The Disciples of Christ had their troubles. But the only other denomination whose drama matched that of the Baptists was the Presbyterian church, with the Princeton stalwarts doing battle against much more moderate liberals than many denominations had to contend with. One reason for this was that Presbyterianism had more rigid and more rigidly enforced doctrinal standards than did the more loosely organized Baptist and Disciples churches, which never did quite learn how to crack the whip or to impose the doctrinal standards.

Significantly, the fundamentalists lost in their efforts to gain control of any of the denominations. They set up parallel institutions to compete with some of those they felt had been taken over. Thus a Northern Baptist Seminary was built to fill the vacuum left by the liberalization of the Baptist Unversity of Chicago Divinity School. Only Princeton among the major contended-for seminaries stayed conservative, and even it did not long please Machen and the fundamentalists, who were to pull out and form new small schools and denominations because they despaired of purifying the host body.

The World's Christian Fundamentalist Association was formed to represent their positions. In 1923 it planned a southern invasion, where it found congenial response because southerners had long before chosen to resist the intrusions of modernity into their world views. Northern urban fundamentalism therefore fit well into their approach to life and doctrine. The swaggering J. Frank Norris of Texas was one of the few southerners among the remembered fundamentalist leaders. The South's religious individualism, conservatism, and biblicism made it a natural home for some aspects of fundamentalism after the main controversy.

Most of the Bible colleges or small seminaries started by the fundamentalists dwindled into insignificance or never took on significance. With few exceptions, they were derided for anti-intellectualism and satirized for the extreme rudeness expressed by their apologists. Fundamentalism was to live on in the 1930s and later through more respectable "National Association of Evangelical" type organizations which were devoted, as an official history put it, to *Cooperation without Compromise*. But the uncompromising character of fundamentalist true believers led to repeated schism in their groups, and the moderates prevailed statistically in later decades.

The modernists may have succeeded in retaining some kinds of power in the denominations, but they can hardly be described as having won, either. They had passed their peak of influence long before fundamentalism gave them new publicity. World War I had shattered the optimism that had given many of them impetus. The distractions of the 1920s led people away from the social causes devoted to the call for the Kingdom of God, and Christian liberals seemed to be irrelevant. The more extreme modernists were discredited by their own modes of fighting in the denominations. The scientific world view on which they had based much of their theology was undergoing new revision and causing them inner uncertainty. Early in the 1930s a new theological mood came on the scene, and very few on the Protestants' left wanted to be tabbed modernist any longer.

In some senses, all Protestants lost. Their attempt to make a graceful move from the days of their monopoly to the time when they would share the American experience was subjected to every kind of indignity by the infighting that tore the denominations. Social causes were neglected. Lutherans and others ready to find ecumenical company were befuddled by "fuddlementalists," and they rejected moderation because they saw the modernists pushing people away from the center. The national religion of which Siegfried could still properly speak in 1927 was not in the hands of people who could plausibly gain intellectual or moral leadership in a cynical decade.

One final irrelevancy remained, the Scopes trial. The best-remembered Protestant event of the decade, it pitted two notables, William Jennings Bryan and Clarence Darrow, in a legal battle and a national show at Dayton, Tennessee, in 1925. They fought over Tennessee's antievolution laws and the rights of a public school teacher, John T. Scopes, to teach evolution in spite of them. The fundamentalists and the jury thought that Bryan won; everybody else thought Darrow had made a fool out of old-line, antievolutionary Protestantism. The contest occurred fifty years late. It was hardly representative of the main Protestant parties, of serious people trying to make their way in faithfulness to historic traditions and modern inquiry. But it was a good show, it did attract attention, and it did help convince millions of Americans that Protestantism had abdicated its right to any kind of leadership by its internal divisions. Its attempt to speak to a nation was compromised because it had become concerned with the parties on both sides of these divisions. Recovery would be difficult and slow.

VII · THE EXPERIENCE TRANSLATED, TRANSFORMED

23 · Two Styles of Complacency

Southern and Urban Ways of Life

The fundamentalist-modernist controversy dominates the memory of people who think back to the 1920s in American religion. While it did bring to focus a longstanding conflict in Protestantism, it did not by any means represent all the concerns of the churches. As Harry Emerson Fosdick had reminded his hearers, not all conservatives were fundamentalists. Most of them might have identified with the fundamentalists, but were not directly involved in their battles. And not all liberals were modernists; some liberals had other things to do beside take on other parties in denominational warfare over the fate of seminaries, publications, and mission boards.

Two of these relatively innocent bystanders were represented by the South, the most conservative and most Protestant section of the country, where fundamentalists after their defeats were to find a natural home, and the urban social Christians, who were trying to keep Protestantism's conscience alive after the decline of the social gospel and in a new decade of complacence.

We will discuss the South first. While the northern urbanites never liked to be reminded of it, the southern states still housed the strongest concentration of Protestants and did most to perpetuate some aspects of the earlier Protestant vision of American empire. The exodus of northern industries seeking cheaper labor in southern small cities had begun, but the addition of newcomers was not yet large enough by the 1920s to include significant numbers of Roman Catholics.

Statistically, then, the Protestants stood out. In 1926, for example, 61.4 percent of southeasterners were church members at a time when only 54.3 percent of Americans at large were. Three fourths of these were Baptists and Methodists, the Baptists having grown by 34.6 percent in two decades, faster than any other large church in the United States. The churches grew faster in the cities than did the cities themselves—urbanization by itself, then, did not mean a decline of Protestantism.

Henry Louis Mencken, who chronicled the follies of William Jennings Bryan at the Scopes trial, summarized the ways in which southern church leaders exercised their dominion: "No bolder attempt to set up a theocracy was ever made in this world, and none ever had behind it a more implacable fanaticism." Mencken was never able to speak about southern religion without indulging in his own implacably fanatic kind of exaggeration. But that a theocracy was still in mind was evident. Edwin Mims, in *The Advancing South* in 1926, condensed the theocratic or imperial language into a couple of lines: "The hope of the world is America, the hope of America is evangelical religion of the most orthodox type, the hope of the American church is the Southern Evangelical churches." The racial myth on which this language had been borne was also very much alive. Bishop Warren A. Candler of the Methodist Church, brother of the Coca-Cola magnate and representative for official religion, was more emphatically racist than social gospel northerners like Josiah Strong had been early in the century: Anglo-Saxons were God's agents to bring true religion to all the world.

In order to advance southern religion, Candler had to attack Strong for not going far enough. The northern expansionist was too tied to liberalism, and "a languid liberalism bears no fruit." The two agreed on perils: Candler also spoke of "the peril of immigration; Mormonism, Christian Science," and other heresies; the great "menace of Romanism"; "the fires of socialism"; "intemperance"; "modern materialism," and added to Strong's list a number of attacks on Protestantism in the North. "The hope of mankind is in the keeping of the Anglo-Saxon nations, led by the United States; and evangelical Christianity, with Methodism in the forefront, is the hope of these nations." Revivalism alone would stand off the "perilous conflict of the irritable industrialism of the days that were to come." If the movement of Providence over the Anglo-Saxon nations was not to terminate, "they must continue to be lifted and strengthened by greater and greater revivals of religion till their mission is fulfilled."

The reform of society would follow individualistic lines; not one to tamper with the approved social order off which he and his brother lived, the good bishop had a policy. Through revivals, convert the rich; they and their fellow converts "will be turned to their needy brothers" to meet their spiritual wants and, to a lesser extent, their physical needs. "The next great awakening will be a revival of religion—not a political reform nor a philanthropic scheme of social amelioration."

The racism that lay at the root of Candler's point of view raised certain problems. Were there enough Anglo-Saxons to go around for the revivalistic conversion of the world? Hardly, if one used narrow definitions. But in the South, where one could use blacks as a measure of racial difference, one could also be more generous in defining Anglo-Saxonism. For Candler, Anglo-Saxons were "not only the people directly descended from the Angles and the Saxons, but those who, by collateral descent or by political association with them, have been conformed to their type and identified with their destiny." Candler, by the way, in rejecting Moody's premillennialism but adopting all the rest of Moody's approach, was able to help form a new prorevivalist coalition and thus to help write a twentieth-century charter for revivalism, one which retained a southern stamp even when it operated in northern cities.

Candler did not represent all of southern religion any more than Strong spoke for all the North. But he did give eloquent support to widely accepted symbols. He could trade on the semiliterate ethos of many rural southerners, people who held hostile views of the world outside their own. To the northern liberal the rural, poor, southern white's religion was the soft underbelly of the South, Protestantism's own soft underbelly. To the southern revivalist, that same kind of religion was the firmest part of the strong backbone of American piety.

To understand religion in the South, one must put aside the temptation to reduce everything to an elaboration of the black-white theme, however much it dominates many issues. The poor whites of the South, gleaning what they could from leached soil, or left in the hollows and on the ridges of unproductive mountain country, lived in abject poverty and in their own kind of slavery. Mining interests stripped the hillsides and left them as ugly monuments to greed, often after having had settlers sign away their interests to these hills for a few dollars. More neglected than the urban poor, these hill-country and backwater people were often not reached by even the most primitive educational and welfare forces. In their isolation, some sat in sullen despair. Those who looked for solace found it in otherworldly religion. It did not provide a base for people who wanted to engage in theological innovation or to adapt Protestantism to an industrial age.

In Edmund deS. Brunner's survey of seventy southern counties, published in 1923, the extent of deprivation and illiteracy was made known. Only one fifth of the ministers were full-time professionals, and 38 percent of them served at least four congregations. About 70 percent of the min-isters had been to neither college nor seminary, and only one in ten had been to both college and seminary. They were as poor as their people. One seventh of them earned less than $500 per year and 50 percent earned less than $1,250 each year. A premium was placed on religious illiteracy. Candler feared that people who studied theology would turn modernist. Congressman Hal Kimberly reduced his literacy program to a simple scheme: "Read the Bible. It teaches you how to act. Read the hymnbook. It contains the finest poetry ever written. Read the almanac. It shows you how to figure out what the weather will be. There isn't another book that is necessary for anyone to read."

Equally overlooked was the degree of secularization that was going on in the urban South. Under the veneer of churchgoing, there was more and more accommodation to the world—an accommodation that could be overlooked by the antinorthern revivalists when they looked at northern modernism, but which they unwittingly documented whenever they called for local revivals in their own section. Now and then an urban observer, without sociological data but with journalistic instinct for what was going on, would blurt out ugly truths about the Anglo-Protestant empire. In 1928 a Mongomery, Alabama, editor wrote about "We South-erners" for *Scribner's* national audience: "We are not half so religious, anyway, as reported. Our pulpit to-day is very much less of a furnace and more of a sun-parlor than ever before. Unquestionably the big dogs of the Christian church in the South tend more and more to expound ethics and ignore miracles."

To the outside world, of course, the miracles could not be ignored. The South was fighting the battle of evolution against timid proevolutionary northern forces which now and then helped influence educational policy in the South. Southern church leaders were fighting off the deleterious effects of German biblical criticism, as these were now and then proferred to the South. To say that the fundamentalist-modernist controversy did not preoccupy southerners is not to say that they would have had difficulty choosing sides, but that modernism was so rare it represented no local party and, housed largely in the North, served as one more focus for sec-tionalism inside Protestant denominationalism.

The South did have some notable centers of higher education, and not a few of these were equipped to turn out literate ministers. But these were under constant scrutiny by antievolutionist, anti-biblical-critical forces. The fate of the distinguished Dr. Crawford Howell Toy at Louisville's Southern Baptist Seminary was typical. As early as 1879 he had to resign under pressure because of a mild adoption of newer views, and the pattern was thereby set. Southern Methodist stalwarts had to give up in their battle to hold Vanderbilt University as early as 1914, and they abandoned it, in their imagery, to the northern sphere of influence. They beat a retreat to

Candler's Emory in Atlanta, Duke University in North Carolina, and Southern Methodist University in Texas.

None of these were to stay pure, however; since almost any new Methodist institution of higher learning found alien theories presented almost at once, not a few Methodists moved into ever deeper reaction against theological education of any kind. Even the Baptists were having trouble, as at Wake Forest, where William Louis Poteat was introducing students to the scientific world view and helping them harmonize it with the Bible. Poteat's lectures in 1925, "Can a Man Be a Christian To-day?" were a manifesto for open Christian learning by a man too revered to be undone. The devotion to Christ was unmistakable: "He has the words of eternal life. . . . No matter how wideranging and deep-running your culture, it can never get beyond them. Nor will they suffer discredit in the widening horizon of modern science." But Poteat advocated Christian-scientific synthesis, and some Baptists tried to oust him. The Wake Forest alumni came to his defense, indicating that not everywhere in the South were honest Christian inquirers to be expelled. People like Poteat, however, led the conservatives to go more and more into the camp of the northern fundamentalists.

Fundamentalist controversy in the denominations was past its peak before it found its echoes in the South, and after the Scopes trial, new issues came to light. Taste for antievolution laws began to decline after about 1928. When southern fundamentalists saw that they were only drawing attention to a cause that was dying elsewhere, bringing scorn down upon the South and upon Protestantism, this only confirmed their hostile views of an alien culture. While the mainline Baptists and Methodists turned to more moderate positions in the 1930s, the intransigents found otherworldly solace in more colorful Holiness sects.

The South was still able, however, to present a largely unbroken line of support for the individualistic views of salvation held by northern revivalists against the social gospel innovators. In Josiah Strong's terms, the southerners for the most part held to "traditional, familiar, and dominant" Christianity in its individualism over against Strong's other, social, version which was "as old as the gospel of Christ." The accent remained on "getting saved," on becoming converted, on pietist subjectivity, with the evangelist remaining the characteristic type of cleric and the morality preached restricted to the problems of the vices of individuals. Worship remained simple. A tragic sense of earthly life understandably prevailed in all but the affluent areas, and even there the symbolism from the areas of poverty was made acceptable. "Eternal life" was the most popular theme of sermons.

In the words of George W. Truett to the Southern Baptist Convention, the "great itch abroad in the land demanding 'reform'" had to be resisted so that personal redemption in Christ would alone be accented. Early in the century, whenever reform had been broached, it was presented as an entirely individual matter for isolated redeemed Christians. Church leaders tried to live up to the dictum of the Southern Methodist bishops in 1894, "Our Church is strictly a religious and in no wise a political body." They concentrated attacks, as evangelicals had a century earlier, on theater and dancing, drinking and profanity, prostitition, Sabbath breaking, gambling, and the playing of cards. Prohibition had no difficulty finding advocates in the South, which became one of the sections that used the temperance issue as a way of judging other areas of the country.

When a more social note entered the rhetoric, it was related to the conventional issues. The Southern Baptists in 1908 sounded like the Federal Council: "Every wrong, public and private, political and social, retards the consummation of the commission of our King." Christians were not "primarily to increase the census of heaven, but to make down here a righteous society in which Christ's will shall be done, his kingdom come." But a Rauschenbusch would have been hard pressed to find allies for his whole program after such declarations: the Baptists took all this to mean that politicans were to be more allied with antisaloon forces.

Southern Methodists pioneered in beginning to bring change in this picture. They advocated child labor laws, the right of "employees and employers alike to organize," and other fairly progressive programs. Baptists were coming to speak more moderately for social reform, and in 1914 the southern Presbyterians had gone on record in mildly progressive terms.

These early stirrings were quieted by the 1920s, when the progressive causes were less voguish in the political culture and as southerners preoccupied themselves with doctrinal conservatism. The disappointments over the aftermath of World War I and the moral decline as a result of Prohibition worked to help southerners lapse back into otherworldly individualism. The prorevivalists had their new day. The Southern Baptist Convention's progressivism of 1910 and 1915 was replaced in 1921 by a resolution showing that it was "fully demonstrated in the times in which we live that nothing but the power of the gospel in regeneration of individual men in large numbers can ever make the world safe for the highest happiness and real peace." In this climate, Bishop Candler could reassert himself. When northern Methodists tried to rebuild ties, he decried their Trojan horse. "The Churches of the South must save the cause of evangelical Christianity in the United States or it will be lost." "Sociological porous plasters" would not "draw out of human hearts the virus of sin." Southerners were being asked to choose again between otherworldly redemption and social transformation. There was to be either/or, not both/and. Mild prolabor statements by southern church conventions were denounced ("rank Socialism and Bolshevism") by industrialists, and Protestant leaders found it convenient to remain silent. Not until the time of the Great Depression in the 1930s was the social note to be picked up with courage again. Only then were professors, editors, and a few preachers free to take up the program of transforming social forms in the Christian cause. And even then their causes were restricted more to elites than to the mass of people. Among these, the preaching of otherworldiness alone remained a constant.

If the 1920s saw the southern churches in vigorous reaction to the mild progressivism that had arisen before the World War, the northern urban church leaders, who had advocated a more radical reformist policy, saw at least mild setback. The decade after 1919 did not see much extension of the postmillennialist or liberal attempts to relate the Gospel to all the spheres of life, including the political and economic. There were numerous reasons for the setbacks.

First, the schism within Protestantism meant that votes were not present for the controversial side of the causes of the day. When the social reformers wanted to be victorious, they had to choose issues that appealed to the laissez-faire individualists and otherworldly-gospel advocates. Only Prohibition filled this bill, and much of the energy of the 1920s went to support of temperance forces in a time of violations of the Volstead Act. Energies diverted to Prohibition were directed away from other social concerns.

Second, much of the energy that would normally have gone into service of the world had to be directed to the survival of parties in the churches. The 1920s was a decade of introversion and self-interest as people chose sides in the fundamentalist-modernist, evolutionist-antievolutionist battles. The attempt of progressives to hold power centers in denominations kept them from working together to draw attention to issues like poverty, hunger, racial deprivation, and labor.

Still another factor in the vacuum of the 1920s was the complacency of the age. One might compare it to the moment around 1877 when Protestantism had presented America with that "massive, almost unbroken front in its defense of the social status quo." While Protestantism now had more resources for effecting change in the culture, advocates of the status quo were also having their day. The nation was tired of trying to make the world safe for democracy or of attempting to Christianize the social order or effect an age of reform. Prosperity and ease were themes of the day. Not all the prophets were silent, but they had little momentum going for them.

In this new age of complacency, Protestantism was further immobilized by the fact of its tie to the middle class in America. From one point of view, this tie pointed to the success Protestants had in helping shape that class, in forming an ethic which helped bring prosperity to many. But it did prevent the reformist elements from leading the powers in the congregations toward seeing the needs of others. One telltale trace of this identification showed up in thousands of editorials in the church press. It was assumed, by defenders and attackers of management alike, that management was in the church and labor was out of it. Conservatives defended the managerial ethos as an expression of "our" Protestant ethic, while reformers constantly had to advocate some concern for "them," the urban workers.

The automatic identification of Protestantism with the middle-class way of life points to still another reality. The acceptance of social Christianity had never been widespread or more than skin deep. With the South and much of northern Protestantism permanently and deeply committed to revivalist individualism, only the few—however articulate they may have been—had been won to a deep involvement with the idea that Christianity should get out of its private corner, where it had reposed for one century, and get back into all the areas of life where it had been at home for many centuries.

A number of events around 1919 served to illustrate the setbacks to reformist causes. First among these was the defeat in the Senate of Woodrow Wilson's peace policies. While prewar pacifism in the clergy had been displaced by a crusading prowar spirit, after the war propeace forces regrouped in support of the League of Nations. But America was lapsing back into isolation and into delusions based upon military victory. Defeat of Wilsonian ideals led to disillusionment with international idealism. Through the 1920s some social Christians like Charles Clayton Morrison, in his defense of the Kellogg Pact of 1928, tried to keep Protestantism from accepting the national mood. And the Protestant churches on the official level did not forget the League and the peace causes between 1919 and 1928. They kept up a steady stream of propeace pronouncements through the denominations and the Federal Council, and organizations like the Church Peace Union and the World Alliance for International Friendship through the Churches knew some successes. When the Pact of Paris was signed, Morrison's *The Christian Century* exulted. "Today international war was banished from civilization." A score of other papers sang variations on his praise. While later critics have scorned the churches for their optimism, the churches did try to keep alive the propeace note when the political order was largely turning from it. The peace cause by itself, post-Wilson, was not enough to cause reformist forces to draw popular support.

More controversial because more immediate was support of labor after the steel strike of 1919 and a more localized textile strike at Lawrence, Massachusetts, three years later. Some churches, trying to keep alive the progressive spirit, began through their leadership to criticize management. But management responded massively, and many Protestants quickly lost taste for support. It was easy for management to tar any critics with the brush of bolshevism or socialism, for the "Red Scare" following the Russian Revolution could be used to unite Americans against reform causes. Few Americans in the labor movement overtly supported Communism, and the numbers of church leaders who advocated Russian-style approaches were so small as to be negligible. Yet the one exception was enough to prove to management the danger of flirting with labor organization. And there were Communist-led strikes; how could churches separate good strikes from bad ones?

When the president of the Brotherhood of Locomotive Engineers was asked "what labor thinks of the church" he responded "that labor does not think very much of the church, because the church does not think very much of labor." Historian Robert Moats Miller believed that both propositions were well founded. Yet he also observed that some of the best studies of churchly indifference to labor were written by ministers, so some must have been concerned to reverse the ancient antilabor course. They must have been few. Liston Pope found that ministers did not lack social consciousness, for they did not hesitate to denounce syphilis, pool halls, low-flying airplanes, slot machines, and Hollywood marriages. But virtually no preachers in the county under Pope's study "have made clear and definitive statements concerning child labor, the mill village system, wages and hours, or other social questions. . . ."

Another study, by Arthur Edwin Shelton, concentrated on southern communities and found similar indifference, matched by the fact that companies supported the churches and company officials dominated congregations. When Protestant churches said that they chose to be silent on labor issues, they were by no means silent—they were speaking for their side, which was ordinarily that of management.

The Interchurch World Movement, despite this background, took heroic steps to get out of the pattern in its *Report on the Steel Strike of 1919*. It served to divide the churches into prolabor and a much larger promanagement camp. Management's reply, written by Marshall Olds', argued that steelworkers liked to work long hours because they were foreigners who knew they would idle their time away when off duty. Olds' became the majority position, and the churchly support of labor through the 1920s rarely was free to go beyond mild denominational resolutions. Heroic attempts were made, after 1920, to regather prolabor forces in Protestantism, but the strikes of 1919 had turned too many followers away. Not until the Depression era were leaders to find many to go along with them in more firm support of labor.

The rising issue of race relations was another on which the churches' record in the 1920s was compromised. The lonely prophets were not able to rally widespread Protestant opposition to immigration-exclusion laws. Anti-Semitism was common, also in some of the church press. But the front on which Protestants found it most difficult to take courageous stands against the drift of their culture was on white-black relations. A race riot at Chicago in 1919 led to 38 deaths and 537 injuries. Washington had a smaller riot in the same summer. Returning black soldiers found it impossible to be accepted in their home society and some were lynched in their military uniforms. The Ku Klux Klan came into a period of revival. Racial fears were stimulated, prejudices reawakened. The Protestant churches, widely regarded to be the most segregated institutions in the nation, were in little position to gain moral authority to correct abuses. The southern white churches presented a united front for segregation, and northern white Protestants had largely bought the southern Reconstructionist church policies, even though their racial ideologies may have been somewhat more moderated and refined.

During the decade, charities were stepped up and some advocates of black rights in white circles began to be heard, even as a new generation of black leaders presented their case. Men like William E. B. DuBois were to put the matter on the Christian conscience. Writing in 1931, he said, "The church, as a whole, insists on a divine mission and guidance and the indisputable possession of truth. Is there anything in the record of the church in America in regard to the Negro to prove this?" The answer: "There is not." If what the churches in the 1920s had done was called "divine," "this is an attack on the conception of God more blasphemous than any which the church has always been so ready and eager to punish."

The Y.M.C.A. was pioneering, as was the new Federal Council of Churches' Department of Race Relations. But these had small budgets and little support for their causes. Denominations did little. The northern Protestants found it easier to blast the Klan for lynching than to face their own racism and segregation. But the miracle of the decade lay in the fact that any kind of interracial movement could be initiated, as America's was a racially tense climate.

Disillusionment over peace policies, reaction to strikes, fear of race riots, the death of social gospel leaders, concentration on Prohibition and anti-Catholicism, distraction over fundamentalism-modernism, an era of complacency—all these served to make the voices of prophets in the 1920s sound lonely and muffled. The northern churches, like the southern, were closely identified with the defense of the given order on the part of their clienteles. If their policies, in retrospect, look less blatantly racist and reactionary, less anti-intellectual and antimodern, they still did not represent a forward movement as they had two decades earlier or during the Depression of the 1930s one decade later. Despite the presence of prophets, particulary in interdenominational publications and in a few bureaus, the churches had once again verged on acceptance of a decorous worldliness. André Siegfried, the observer of Protestant national religion, looked at the mainline and liberal church leadership and wrote in 1927: "The worldliness of this Protestantism and its pretensions to be a national religion reserved for the privileged few have antagonized many of its followers as well as its adversaries. They feel that something is lacking, almost the spirit of religion itself. . . ."

24 · The Church Against the World

The Recovery of Protest and Realism

In 1919 an advocate of social reform, Herbert C. Willett, announced that "the program of the Interchurch World Movement includes nothing less than the complete evangelization of all life." While the I.W.M. was among the more ambitious Protestant forces for a brief moment it was no more successful at evangelizing all of life than John R. Mott's missionary forces two decades earlier had been at "evangelizing the world in this generation." In fact, the program for evangelizing all of life knew many setbacks in the 1920s, when it was easier to segregate soul-saving from the rest of life and to concentrate on it.

The Great Depression of the 1930s found some Protestant church leaders once again working to return to the concept of evangelizing all of life, of trying to bring Christianity's moral claims to domains other than personal redemption. The needs were obvious. The financial crashes of 1929 and the early 1930s had brought new insecurities to the complacent. While they were not as ready as the financiers of 1857 had been to ask the theological question, "What did we do wrong, to cause God to punish us so?" more of them were ready at least to see that they were in trouble.

If the complacent had become anxious, the hungry had become desperate. People who had never known poverty were reduced to joining bread lines and awaiting handouts with the people who had long been poor. Since many of these newcomers to the welfare ranks had done nothing to deserve their fate—they had not been idle or indolent, had not lacked daring to invest or will to work—they put the lie forever to the unquestioned Protestant assumption voiced by Henry Ward Beecher in the 1880s that poverty was always the result of one's vices. They now had to seek new answers to new questions about their circumstances, even as the new presidential administration under Franklin D. Roosevelt worked to try new policies to bring about social change.

The Great Depression was to dominate religious thought until the beginning of World War II. Protestant ministers who had long prided themselves on their ability to avoid comment on current affairs found that their people hungered for address to their actual situation. The panic of 1929 was the worst in national history and it reached into every aspect of life. Crises in mining, farming, and textile industries; overspeculation and unsupervised stock market manipulation; the decline of real estate booms in Florida and elsewhere; bank failures—these touched the daily life of all Americans at a time when as high as sixteen or seventeen million people were unemployed. Such physical circumstances could no longer be overlooked by cautious Protestant clerics, even though they differed vastly in their diagnoses and therapy.

The decade of despair brought some recovery of reform and a discovery of realism into Protestant thought and action. Children of social gospel leaders, appropriating more than they knew from the progressivism of their parents, did what they could to disclaim their heritage and to cast social thought against a different theological background. The social gospel progressivists, relying on a metaphysic of progress, announced the coming Kingdom of God with the confidence that orders of society could easily be criticized. They could appropriate the better tendencies of the world, which was already half-Christianized. With the exception of Rauschenbusch, few of them had to indulge in deep probings about the nature of sin and the demonic, about the intractable character of human nature and the ways in which human history failed to turn into utopia.

The Church Against the World, the title of a book by layman Francis P. Miller and theologians H. Richard Niebuhr and Wilhelm Pauck, set the tone for the recovery. Standing in a kind of Calvinist tradition, Miller and Niebuhr could not content themselves with expressing regret about a fallen world. They were committed to seeing it rescued and transformed. But they saw how penetrated it was by forces over which good people had little control. Not for them was the old decorous worldliness with which Protestantism's popular preachers could christen the culture, nor the new worldliness spotted by André Siegfried in 1927, when he saw that the spirit of true religion was lacking in Protestantism.

In two sentences Miller wrote the epitaph for the old white Anglo-Saxon Protestant empire and its dreams of taking over the world: "The plain fact is that the domestication of the Protestant community in the United States within the framework of the national culture has progressed as far as in any western land. The degradation of the American Protestant church is as complete as the degradation of any other national Protestant church." Niebuhr in his introduction noted that the world has always been against the church, but "there have been times when the world has been partially converted" and church and world lived at peace. Not now. "The church is imperiled not only by an external worldliness but by one that has established itself within the Christian camp." The church had made retreats and then compromised with the enemy "in thought, in organization, and in discipline."

With typical Niebuhrian charity to the past, the author of the introduction did not fault the "earlier, individualistic time" when "evangelical Christians raised the question of their salvation one by one." But now "we are more aware of the threat against our collective selves than against our separate souls." What must we do to be saved? Then he raised the point that had no place in the century and a half of Anglo-Saxon self-assuredness. The church "knows the ways of God too well not to understand that he can and will raise up another people to carry out the mission entrusted to it if the Christian community fail him."

It would be tempting to let H. Richard Niebuhr write this whole chapter, for his words posed the issues of the 1930s so well. The problem the church presents, humanists thought, "is that of a conservative organization which has not kept abreast of the times, which has remained medieval while the world was growing modern, dogmatic while civilization was becoming scientific; which is individualistic in a collectivist period and theological in a time of humanism." But these views of the cultured despisers were beside the point. Niebuhr was less interested in one more adjustment to the world than he was to separate from it in order to serve in it. "The crisis of the church from this point of view is not the crisis of the church in the world, but of the world in the church." The church had adjusted too much rather than too little to the world in which it lived. Not a changing world but an unchanging God was judging it. Niebuhr asked for a return to scriptures and the prophetic note.

In this little book, written in 1935, the outline of the social realist recovery in the Protestant churches was stated as succinctly as anywhere. The modernists were angered because it dismissed them as obsolete and irrelevant. The fundamentalists accepted its attack on modernism but rejected its criticism of the individualist approach. The cultured despisers saw in its support of the dynamism within the Christian tradition a retrogression to a dead orthodoxy. And its advocates found themselves accused of being neo-orthodox, a term some of them accepted. This meant to some that they were too pessimistic, too obsessed with original sin and with a view of the demonic in social structures to serve as levers to lift an America in depression.

On the face of things, there were good reasons to worry about the latter charges. Historian Robert Handy, with rather compelling documentation, has styled the period one of "religious depression," to match the Great Depression. These were hardly years to launch a movement of recovery from within the churches. Leaders were dispirited as they saw their Protestant culture disintegrate under their eyes. Progressives were disappointed that their programs had failed and reactionaries were confused because the Second Coming of Christ had failed to occur despite the presence of all the signs associated with his return. The programs of the churches had bogged down. Handy quoted Dartmouth professor William Kelley Wright's statement of 1933: "Today we are passing through a period of religious depression not less severe than the concomitant moral and economic depression."

There were fewer missionaries in the field from the mainline churches. Young men and women were not being recruited for foreign fields, and as a Laymen's Inquiry (titled *Rethinking Missions,* directed by Harvard philosopher William Ernest Hocking in 1933) revealed, notable Protestants no longer kept their old soul-saving motivations for mission. They were less sure of their manifest destiny to bring the whole world under Protestant Anglo-Saxon imperial domain. They were beginning to take positive views of the world's high religions, which had been downgraded by fund raising missionaries of the past. Their failure of nerve about missions had led to a decline in missionary giving.

For that matter, financial support of religion had actually declined on the home front. Presbyterian Charles Steltzle showed that the prosperity of the 1920s had not benefited church giving. Per capita gifts for charities had fallen from 1921s $5.57 per person per year to 1929, when the church member gave only $3.43. The church giver was not in a position to do better in most of the ensuing decade. While there was no dramatic downturn in church membership, a statistic that meant rather little when the church embraced the world, church attendance was down. Fewer services were being held. Sunday school attendance in proportion to the population decreased. Ministers were afflicted with low morale.

The numbers of cultured despisers rose. The American university of the 1930s found it housed an elite generation which sometimes held rather romantic views of Stalinism, and these pro-Communists took over from Marxism the belief that religion was the opiate of the people. Editors and lawyers like H. L. Mencken and Clarence Darrow were joined by a generation of novelists like Sinclair Lewis and Ernest Hemingway who saw no positive place for the churches. The academic-intellectual style wavered between mere agnosticism on one hand and satiric or vitriolic rejection on the other. Fundamentalists, revivalists, peddlers of religion, and mountebanks were on the scene to provide these despisers with raw material for their attacks. Not until late in the decade were the beginnings of a "return to religion" noted and the first trickle of celebrated intellectual conversions noticed (many of them to Roman Catholicism).

H. Richard Niebuhr's brother, Reinhold, announced in 1927 that "a psychology of defeat, of which both fundamentalism and modernism are symptoms, has gripped the forces of religion." His voice was one which helped raise Protestant leadership beyond that defeatism, even though he was typed more than most as a pessimist. In *The Church Against the World,*

German-born Wilhelm Pauck had looked over the desolate American scene and concluded: "Perhaps the time is not far distant when a prophet will arise among us who, fully imbued with the mood and spirit of our era, will speak to us in the name of the living God with such power and authority that all who long for salvation will be compelled to listen." In Reinhold Niebuhr, many Protestants began to feel they had found such a prophet. A magnificent preacher, a tireless journalist and advocate of causes, a well-known teacher, a gifted theologian, he towered over the 1930s, and two or three decades later was still being regarded by secular leaders as the only religious figure to have played a formative role in their thought.

Niebuhr's whole accent, growing out of a "church against the world" position, was devoted to Christian realism. He derided the old Protestant American dreams of empire, but wanted to take the raw materials of the Protestant experience in America and apply them to the urgent needs of the people of his time. Never content with addressing only the material problems or working on political institutions, he was persistently concerned with questions of value. His Gifford Lectures, *The Nature and Destiny of Man,* showed the scope of his concern for cosmic and ultimate questions. But in "the Niebuhrian decade," he more than any other was responsible for reawakening the note of protest against churchly pretensions, of reform of societal institutions. He represented a turning point as had Edwards, Bushnell, and Rauschenbusch before him. He was the only one of these who did not share a kind of postmillennial chauvinist view of the American Protestant empire.

Niebuhr, of course, was not alone. His brother's influence came to be virtually equally respected in circles where Christian social ethics was debated. European refugees like Paul Tillich were eventually able to infuse American Protestant thought with both some European religious socialist ideas and the stark and dramatic notes of existentialist thought. Within the liberal denominational tradition there were celebrated conversions, like that of Edwin Lewis at Drew Seminary, a man of great influence in his denomination. Drew's maverick was also a church-against-the-world figure and an antiimperialist in ecclesiology: "We borrowed our criteria of evaluation," he wrote in 1934, "from the world around us—a world gone mad in its worship of mere size. And we were guilty of the incredible folly of supposing that 'Christ's church was of this world,' to be judged by the world's standards, to be modeled on the world's ways, to walk in the world's procession, and to keep step to the crashing discord of its brazen shams."

To all these voices must be added that of European theology, which had greater influence now than ever before. In many generations, American Protestants were isolated from the rest of Atlantic culture. In the nineteenth century, German theology was feared, because under Hegelian influence it often seemed to produce a kind of atheism inside and around the churches. Late in the nineteenth century Walter Rauschenbusch did some study under the pro-Kingdom of God Ritschlians, and the American theological community, modeling itself somewhat after German university seminars, also picked up some German liberal theology.

Not until the 1930s, however, was a massive force of European theology present. The giant responsible for the turn in Europe from progressive optimism and liberalism to a tone of church-against-the-world crisis was Karl Barth, a Swiss pastor-professor. Barth surveyed the wreckage to the humanist venture caused by World War I and the collapse of liberal values. In a commentary on St. Paul's *Epistle to the Romans* in 1917–1918 he returned to biblical notes about God's distance from humanity and humanity's need of rescue. It was a major event in American Protestantism when in 1933 Douglas Horton translated Karl Barth's *The Word of God and the Word of Man,* just as it was when Walter Marshall Horton, formerly a liberal, wrote his own *Realistic Theology.*

In 1932 Walter Lowrie, a Kierkegaard translator, issued a call, *Our Concern with the Theology of Crisis.* Tillich's *The Religious Situation* appeared in the same year. Reinhold Niebuhr's manifesto was *Moral Man and Immoral Society* and Lewis's was *Christian Manifesto.* Within two years, near the end of Handy's "religious depression of 1925–35," there had been a theological about-face, chronicled in 1939 in *The Christian Century* series, "How My Mind Has Changed." Fundamentalists were gleeful: the change only proved that liberals were fickle. The leftover modernists sulked: this only proved that the younger generation had lapsed into despair. To the secular outsider, all this was confusing. Why did the conservatives not pick up Barth and the Niebuhrs, for they were so biblical, so sin-preoccupied, so full of the language of redemption, so useless for social change? What did liberals ever see in this theological realism?

See something they did, however. It would be beside the point to try to argue that neo-orthodoxy ever sounded from the majority of American pulpits or that the theology of crisis swept away the last notes of optimism. Crowds came to hear Niebuhr preach in a decade that lacked notable evangelistic preachers. But just as many continued to hear or buy the books of less reconstructed liberals like Harry Emerson Fosdick, and Christian social realism probably never was comprehended by masses outside Protestant intellectual centers. Yet these ideas about changing the world on a new (or *very* old) set of terms were filled with consequence for the churches and for the society.

Looking out over the social ills that caused the Depression and that afflicted America during it, the Niebuhrians isolated the problem of the worker more than any other. They were influenced just enough by their reading of Marx to see matters in class terms more than their predecessors had. But no less than Rauschenbusch did they isolate the industrial order as being, in Rauschenbusch's terms, the "least Christianized" of realms or, in their own, the one least tractable in the face of change.

The passions which later Protestantism was to bring to the racial question and which earlier evangelicals had brought to personal vices and reforms of them, the social realists directed to the problem of labor. From a later vantage, after labor had joined the affluent society, made its point, served as a locale for backlash against blacks, and established its own elites, it was difficult for many people to look back on the struggles during the Depression in the context of their original setting.

For all the insecurity involved in striking in a time of unemployment, these workers did strike. When strikebreakers appeared on the scene many church leaders reacted against violence, rejected the strikers, and sided with management in a time of labor oversupply. To side with organized labor in such a time was an act of courage or folly that a few major Christian social leaders chose to make.

Union membership dropped to three million and less by 1933. President Franklin D. Roosevelt and certain elements in the Congress promoted legislation protecting labor, and membership grew to eight million by 1939. At the peak, in 1937, over 4,700 strikes involved two million workers. While unions exercised strong discipline, management was even more fierce—so much so that fashionable preachers like Fosdick, George Buttrick, Ralph Sockman, and others were moved to ask Congress to investigate mining conditions in 1933. When they themselves visited the mines they came back with greater prolabor passion. At scene after scene the clergy began to commit themselves, no matter what the expense to their reputation, or however much they came to be regarded as traitors to their class.

A turn came when the "sit-down" strike became a technique in the automobile industry. Niebuhr defended that tactic, but he was in a small minority. Most of the vocal clergy favored striking but not by such techniques, and spoke up more for arbitration and peace. Never during the 1930s did labor and Protestantism come to an easy peace. Prolabor efforts were rarely acknowledged by union leadership, while antilabor expressions by ecclesiastics were given wide publicity. Yet by the end of the decade and the beginning of the Second World War, dialogue had begun, understanding was present, and Protestantism was no longer regarded *a priori* as the enemy of labor.

The course of Protestantism in race relations was at least as problem-filled, at least as slow to change. The South could not bring itself even to consider change. Fifteen out of sixteen Protestant blacks among America's eight million blacks were in black denominations and were almost entirely out of churchly contact with whites. The other half million blacks were in largely white denominations, but not one in a hundred of these were in integrated congregations. It has been estimated that about eight thousand out of eight million blacks were in integrated congregations around 1939.

The Southern Baptist stance was symbolized by the action of Dr. William J. McGlothlin in 1932; the then president of the Southern Baptist Convention said that as "the representative of four million Southern Baptists" he could not violate taboo and attend a banquet in Rochester, New York, because of the presence of one black. Southern Methodism was not able to settle century-old problems of division with its northern counterpart largely because of the race question. True, there was some fear of northern "Modernism, Liberalism, etc. and doubt" but this was usually combined with integrationist fears. Thus Georgia's exgovernor John M. Slaton feared that after merger "no more will we hear preached from [the] pulpit Christ and Him crucified but a conglomeration of political, sociological and interracial questions." The solution was to support a Central Jurisdiction, in which blacks were separated, on the argument that they would prefer to run their own show.

However bleak the southern picture, later apologists for the North rarely pointed to any glories on the scene in the cities of the North, to which blacks were migrating *en masse* in the Depression years. In the urban slums where they were forced to congregate, churches played a major part in the organization of life, but these were almost always churches without a white presence, as whites fled changing neighborhoods. Charity of a rather meager sort was designed to bridge the gap between Christian community and the actual situation of hostility. The path-breaking in the North was done by theological professors and editors of independent journals like *The Christian Century* and *World Tomorrow.* Significantly, these were people most protected from immediate reprisal by "the person in the pew," who could more easily control the preacher and have their minister conform to local prejudice. Niebuhrian Christian realism was better at employing the racial picture to point to the depth of human sin than it was to motivate Protestant churches to go "against the world" on this cause. Later Christian black representatives have found almost nothing in the record of pre-World War II white Protestantism to use as a sign of a tradition of creative race relations.

The issue which brought the Niebuhrians into most direct conflict with their sometime-partners in liberal Protestantism was pacifism. Here Niebuhr parted with *The Christian Century,* which had so often hosted and fêted him and with which he had been earlier associated. The magazine's editor, Charles Clayton Morrison, continued to live in the world of the Kellogg Peace Pact of 1928, even during the years of the rise of Fascism in Italy and National Socialism in Germany. Not that he underestimated their threat, but rather he believed that Christians could not casually be nonviolent one year and proviolence the next. He also believed, as did other near-pacifists, that Christians and Americans had not begun to exhaust peacemaking means in international affairs.

Through the years, however, the rise to power of Hitler was proving to be too loud an argument, and the peace forces—regrouped from pre-World War I (pacifists in American Protestantism seem to live long!) and recovering from the 1920s—were put on the defensive. Niebuhr's realism and anti-idealism made him more ready to accept violence and what Morrison eventually had to call "the tragic necessity of war." Throughout the 1930s Niebuhr gave evidence of being influenced by Marxist advocacy of violence in the class struggle, and as early as 1933 he was writing on the limits of arbitration. "In the hour of crisis both [factions] will probably use the same weapons. For the weapons of physical combat are finally available." His vision of the violence which ruling parties have built into their rule was deeper than Morrison's, but he worried less than Morrison did over how to square this vision with Christ's mandates against the use of violence, a matter which Niebuhr tried to solve by restricting Christ's terms to interpersonal relations and by seeing them as inapplicable in the social realm, which had no room for perfectionism.

Not that Niebuhr savored international conflict. "War," he had written in 1928, "is morally so impotent and so perilous" because it aggravates rather than solves issues and because it destroys the innocent. But in 1939 he had to leave all traces of this pacifism behind. "Unwillingness to run some risk of war in the present moment," he wrote during Mussolini's war against Ethiopia, "means certain war in the future." By 1939, "certain war" was on the scene. In the face of the Nazi terror, the liberal pacifists found themselves taking on a policy of isolation that they found uncongenial in other aspects of international affairs. Niebuhr fought off both the "holy war" which came easy to the old-line Protestants and the new isolationists. When the United States was involved after Pearl Harbor, few continued to hold to the pacifist position.

The struggles between Charles Clayton Morrison and Reinhold Niebuhr, involving significant ranks behind each, belonged very much to the mainline tradition of American Protestantism. However much their mutual enemies dismissed them both as some kind of socialists disguising their villainies with Christian symbols, they wrestled over central Protestant themes, including the role played by Jesus Christ in history. For the post-modernists, Jesus remained the peaceseeking exemplar of God's love, the one who best demonstrated the family of man under god's fatherhood. For the neo-orthodox, there was resort to some classic doctrines of Christology, a readiness to re-explore the ways in which God had spoken definitively in Christ.

Both groups agonized over the role of the church. Neither considered for a moment that the church should not strain itself in involvement with the world, but the Niebuhrians were less idealistic. After it had taken its measure of distance in the church-against-the-world stance, the church should be free to plunge back and seek to serve. For the liberals who resisted Barth or Niebuhr and their cohorts, the church would ever be more ready to be at home with congenial humanism. In Morrison's magazine, for example, liberal theist Henry Nelson Wieman of the University of Chicago had determined to claim John Dewey, the philosopher who wrote *A Common Faith,* as a coreligionist—an embrace Dewey resisted. To the neo-orthodox, such attenuation of Christian distinctives in theology was to be rejected. It represented a new, if more sophisticated, sellout of Christianity to the world and underestimated the depth of the demonic in the social process.

In the middle of the decade, Paul Tillich wrote an autobiographical sketch, *On the Boundary,* in which he tried to come to terms with two parts of his personal heritage. In the course of his struggle to define himself, he pointed to aspects of his thought held in common with much European theology, which did not easily relate to what we have been calling Protestant postmillennialism, or transformationism. He saw that a realistic view of life "includes a consciousness of the corruption of existence," something which Rauschenbusch held in a modified form but the modernists tended to let slip. To this Tillich added "a repudiation of every kind of social Utopia." To the degree that he was able to sell this position to his contemporaries, Tillich helped them separate from the social gospel on a distinctive point. The social realists could no longer speak of "Christianizing the social order," in such a view.

Finally, in this context, Tillich spoke of "an awareness of the irrational and demonic nature of existence." That nature revealed itself in the conflicts of the Depression and prewar decade, and came with such power that glib preachers and the genteel theologians found themselves on the defensive. A new note of realism had come into the Protestant experience, one that had been neglected since colonial times and picked up rarely, as in the case of Abraham Lincoln in his ministry to an "almost chosen people."

25 · Any Number Can Play

The Rise of Ecumenism and Pluralism

The Protestant churches in the nineteenth century are usually pictured as having a centrifugal momentum. By their missionary activity, every move they made seemed to spin them out from a spiritual center through a competitive principle to divisions all over the world. In the twentieth century, their momentum has been centripetal: they noted the limits of their competition and division, experienced frustration in mission around the world, and began to draw back together in the ecumenical, or Christian unity, movement.

To the critics of nationalism and colonialism, the centrifugal movement was an expression of Anglo-Saxon and even of American empire. To the partisans of mission, it was an enlargement of witness to the power of the Kingdom of God and a fulfillment of Christ's command to go into all the world. To the cynical outsider, or the antiecumenical Christian, the ecumenical movement represents a great retreat, a failure of nerve, the kind of compromise people make when they no longer have much to profess, when their faiths are vague and meaningless.

The missionary movement of the nineteenth century and the ecumenical movement of the twentieth, however, had common roots. Both were, in their origins, expressions of northwest European and Anglo-American desires to reduce the world in the name of Christ to the faith and the culture of the superior West. Missions would convert and transform people; they would save souls, spread holiness, bring education and healing, help develop cultures. Unitive movements would be the agent for missions and the follow-up to them.

Nothing better illustrates the twentieth-century Protestant movement from the dreams of empire to the willingness to share the American experience, than does the change in the mission-unitive movements.

Contrary to the rewritten history of some twentieth-century mythology that rejects the nineteenth century as being a time only of division, the missionary and benevolence movements had their unitive sides. The evangelical "errand of mercy" that brought together British agencies and

237

American institutions in the first three decades of the nineteenth century was often a lay-based, interchurch or nondenominational pioneering effort. Leaders did not devote themselves much to the discussion of theology. Many of them lacked theological training. Most of them would have been so self-assured about their healing and saving purposes that they would have said theological differences were secondary. All of them assumed enough theological unity to help get their program adopted. The Americans who took part were confident that their churches shared a common vision of Christ and his saving work and that they could fuse this with Anglo-Saxon culture and bring their superior product to inferior people.

When the self-assertive denominations began to complicate this picture, people of good will had to work at evangelical unity. In 1846 an Evangelical Alliance, Anglo-American with contacts in Germany, France, Switzerland, and elsewhere, was formed. It received a new impetus in the 1870s. But the beginnings of theological divisions within the evangelical churches led to neglect of this organization, and once again missionary activity around the world became competitive, unregulated by Christian desires to cooperate, to present a single Christ to a divided world.

When near the end of the century lay groups, student organizations, and missionary agencies again worked to change the competitive assumption, they brought a mildly liberal but durably Anglo-Saxon imperial concept to their work. They had not yet begun to doubt their cultural superiority or the advantages of their faith over that of the world religions. But they had become self-critical about competing with other Christian churches.

In 1908 the formation of the Federal Council of the Churches of Christ in America occurred on a generally liberal basis, with a social creed critical of the laissez-faire individualism that marked the older Protestant evangelicalism by that time. Because of the social creed, the implied secondary status given missionary and evangelistic work, and the vaguely defined theological basis, most conservative denominations stayed out and many traditionalist members of participating denominations criticized the Council from within.

Two years later, at Edinburgh, Scotland, an international conference on missions was held. While delegates there were also self-critical about their own divisions, many western conferees did continue to breathe the spirit of Anglo-Saxon imperial mission to the world. American denominations participated in this conference and its follow-ups on missions. Meanwhile international conferences on Life and Work and Faith and Order were held in the 1920s and 1930s. Out of these international gatherings came the World Council of Churches, formed in Amsterdam in 1948. The rather dormant Federal Council was altered and renewed in the National Council of the Churches of Christ in the United States in 1950.

Between 1908—1910 and 1948—1950, landmark dates in the Christian unity movement, most expressions of Protestant unity were neglectful of the Eastern Orthodox one third of the Christian world. Americans were often heedless because the Orthodox were such a minority presence in the United States and because the Orthodox seemed so aloof, so alien. Enemies of ecumenism on the theological right were put off by nothing so much as the inclusion of the Orthodox in the National Council. Carl McIntire, professional agitator for fundamentalism of the extreme sort at ecumenical meetings, spoke of banners, crossbearers, and candles. He said these meant that the pompous Orthodox were like the "papal pageantry in the Vatican at St. Peter's." But after 1948 and 1950 it was clear that Christian unity was to include also the Orthodox. Never again was ecumenism to mean simply Protestant housecleaning.

More radical and more painful were the steps taken to bring about some measure of entente with Roman Catholicism. Without question, much advocacy of Protestant ecumenism—as in the arguments of Charles Clayton Morrison of *The Christian Century*—had an anti-Catholic bias. Progressive Protestants feared Catholic traditions as these bore upon American tendencies in "the separating of church and state." Catholic subjection to papal authority violated Protestant lore about "the right of private judgment of the Scriptures." Many Catholic practices were as offensive to the ecumenical liberals as to the fundamentalists.

When the World Council of Churches made efforts to welcome Roman Catholics, the liberal ecumenists at first resisted, fearing that such efforts would, among other things, retard movements for Protestant ingathering and reunion. When during the 1950s conferences were held to bring about some concord between American Catholics and others on matters of church and state, these liberals grew even more strident, more fearful that the Protestant heritage would be bartered away.

To the fundamentalists, the doctrinal and liturgical lineage of Catholicism remained problematic and could be used to stigmatize the ecumenical movement. James DeForest Murch, official historian of the National Association of Evangelicals, a group against the National Council, and World Council, in a work called *The Growing Super-Church,* said that these ecumenical organizations had "all the Babylonian admixture of truth and error found in the Church of Rome, universal in scope, and eventually leading up in the Romish abomination itself."

The "Romish abomination" was to change after the accession of Pope John in 1958 and with his subsequent call for an ecumenical council, which came to be known as the Second Vatican Council. It met in Rome in the autumns of 1962 through 1965. Protestant observers, Americans among them, were invited and consulted throughout. It was clear that they welcomed these signs of Catholic openness just as they perceived dramatic changes in Catholicism, changes which made conversation profitable and some concord a hopeful possibility. The divisions between the two Protestant parties became clearer than ever before. Spokesmen for the organization called Protestants and Other Americans United for the Separation of Church and State, then a liberal-conservative anti-Catholic coalition group, were almost frantic in their charges that ecumenical liberals had sold out to Rome, having been seduced by an unchanging Catholic church, a church which had simply learned a new approach to public relations—a church eager to convert Protestants through the new means.

By the time of the Vatican Council, then, the mainstream Protestant ecumenical movement was no longer designed on anti-Catholic lines. If ever Protestant unity had been conceived as a means to bring Protestants to the situation of a kind of monolithic authority, as it had been believed that Catholicism was monolithic, that conception no longer endured. The enemies of the movement were correct in their observation: ecumenism meant a great blow, if not the death blow, to the old dreams of Protestant empire in the world. Discussions with Orthodoxy and Catholicism not only slowed down Protestant unitive moves. They also guaranteed that any long-range Christian future would be catholic and reformed in outlook—something that the nineteenth-century leaders had not had in mind.

Enemies of ecumenism like Murch, C. Marcellus Kik, and Stanley Lowell now began to focus more attention on the "selling-out" Protestants than on their old enemy, Catholicism. They charged that the Protestants had been beguiled by dreams of a superchurch in which doctrinal matters would be secondary and neglected, or in which doctrinal basis would simply be papal and Roman. These critics pointed out that the churches in the ecumenical movement had been less successful at keeping missionary fires alive than were fundamentalists, Holiness groups, "faith missions," and other forces that stood apart from the Christian unity moves. They were less careful in their diagnoses of reasons for change in mainline Protestant missionary understanding than they were at pointing out the statistics of decline in missionary support.

A further charge across the two-party lines in Protestantism was that ecumenism had, by deserting the Anglo-Saxon dream of Christian empire, simply accommodated itself to the secular world on the world's terms. Critics were quick to point out that the National and World Councils devoted themselves regularly to worldly topics like race, poverty, war, hunger, and revolution, and that these organizations were very much open to influence by nonchurched leaders from the secular world.

After stating their theological and sociopolitical or economic disagreements with Protestantism's ecumenical involvements, the critics characteristically moved on by pleading for support of paraecumenical organizations. Thereby they demonstrated that the old denominational assumption was living on borrowed time and was not believed in so passionately as before. Denominations had as much life as earlier, but the theological rationale was disappearing. So the conservatives in 1943 organized the National Association of Evangelicals and the more extreme fundamentalists later formed an International Council of Christian Churches. Both of these, in addition to serving the purposes of uniting the voices of conservative church bodies, spent much of their time criticizing what they saw to be the betrayals of Protestantism in the Protestant-Orthodox-Catholic ecumenical movement.

The criticisms included not only theological positions but also socioethical ones. Because the World Council of Churches included the Russian Orthodox and other churches from the Eastern European orbit, they were able to suggest that American Protestants would be tainted by exposure to Communism. At Amsterdam the report on economics was qualified to ward off such criticism by the phrase: "The Christian Church should reject the ideologies of both communism and laissez-faire capitalism, and should seek to draw men away from the false assumption that these are the only alternatives. Each has made promises it could not redeem." Such efforts at seeking to separate Christianity from laissez-faire capitalism only added to the criticism on the part of reactionary Americans who saw the two to be dependent upon each other. When the World Council or the National Council spoke favorably of the United Nations, the latter-day premillenarians would be critical. Thus V. Raymond Edman, president of Wheaton College in Illinois, countered such efforts to bring "world government" by saying "it will come to pass when the World Sovereign Himself, The Lord Jesus Christ, returns to the world, as He promised."

The National Association of Evangelicals, while it included many such premillennialists, revealed that it was not simply awaiting the Second Coming. It continued to include people who stood in a tradition which saw Protestant America as the site for the coming Kingdom, and supported policies of nationalistic character. More extreme was the appearance in 1946 of the Christian Amendment Movement. This movement was a second round for the old National Reform Organization which had proposed a Christian amendment to the Constitution in 1894 and 1910. During the early efforts, Robert Ingersoll reminded Protestants of their difficulties to "put God into the Constitution because there was no agreement on the Divinity which was to have the honor. Would it be the Deity of the Catholics, the Calvinists or the Puritans?"

The amendment, as favored by the Protestant conservatives, would have read, "This nation devoutly recognizes the authority and law of Jesus Christ, Saviour and Ruler of nations, through whom are bestowed the blessings of Almighty God." While unsuccessful in their repeated attempts to have the amendment passed, the conservatives have continued to resist neutral definitions of the American charter.

When the Supreme Court of the United States in two decisions, *Engel v. Vitale* in 1962 and *Abington School District v. Schempp* in 1963, qualified or eliminated prayer and devotional Bible reading from the public schools and similar places, the battle lines within Protestantism were exposed. Subsequent hearings before the Committee on the Judiciary of the House of Representatives in the spring of 1964 produced hundreds of pages of testimony from church leaders. This testimony dealt with the subject of a proposed constitutional amendment which would allow for such school prayer. In general, the conservatives-fundamentalists were in support of such an amendment and of school prayer. In effect, they were keeping alive a theocratic concept of American institutions, even though they were the ones who were most critical of any intrusions on the "line of separation of church and state."

Meanwhile, again with exceptions, the proecumenical Protestants, often speaking through leaders of denominations or interchurch agencies, were critical of the proposed amendment and enthusiastic about the court decision. They were reaching back to a different aspect of American origins: the nonreligious character of the United States Constitution. They believed with the court that the government should express a "wholesome neutrality" in the matter of bringing official religion into public institutions, arguing that secularity has as many rights as religion and that there is no such thing as a neutral expression of religion. Many of these were somewhat less wary of governmental programs which crossed the line of separation between church and state.

Throughout the religious revival of the 1950s, the neoevangelicals favored the fusion between religion and politics. They supported the phrase "under God" inserted into the Pledge of Allegiance to the flag in 1954 during a time of crusades against "atheistic communism." They were for the printing of "In God We Trust" on stamps in 1954 and as a national slogan in 1956. The ecumenists tended to oppose these programs and slogans for the most part, feeling that they violated the rights of nonbelievers and were part of a false and prideful attempt to parade what Senator Joseph McCarthy of Wisconsin contended for, features which would "be of great spiritual and psychological value to our country" over against its atheistic enemies.

During the 1950s and 1960s, then, a tendency had become manifest in both Protestant parties. The traditionalists were more and more identified with the American Way of Life, the defense of laissez-faire capitalism, and the crusade against Communism. They tended to equate elements in each of these with the mission of Christ to the world. In the presence of Orthodox, Jewish, Catholic, liberal Protestant, and secular forces, they wanted America to go back to its point of origins in Protestant republicanism and supply motifs which the founders had neglected to include or which they had excluded. But these were motifs that had been contended for by the old evangelical empire-builders who had tried to recover in national manners what they had had to give away in laws and charters.

The ecumenical moderates, meanwhile, were trying to extricate the Protestant churches from their identification with the American Way of Life, a single economic pattern, and a crusading spirit. They reached back to the other element in the American constitutional tradition and supported a pluralism whose ground rules were that "any number can play," whether believers in the God of Protestants or another God or twenty Gods or no God. They were trying to break away from the provincialism or chauvinism of their predecessors who had equated the Kingdom of God with the evangelical empire.

In other respects as well, the old white Anglo-Saxon Protestant identification with the Kingdom of God was called into question by Protestant ecumenists. The United Church of Christ, born at Cleveland in 1957, was the joining of two churches that had merged earlier. One was a Congregational-Christian alliance from 1929; the other was a combination of the Evangelical and Reformed Church, dating from 1934. These were groups that had been on the American scene from the beginning of the seventeenth and the eighteenth centuries, respectively. Yet when the two alliances came together in 1957, for the first time the old "Anglo-" versus "Continental" divide had been crossed. The Evangelical and Reformed were of largely German provenance, while the Congregational-Christians were of old-line Anglo-Saxon lineage.

When the Congregationalists had talked merger in 1929, a footdragger was reported to have said, "I've been a Congregationalist all my life, and no one's going to make a Christian of me now." When the new merger was being prepared for 1957, not a few Congregationalists were put off by the fact that the cultural company they would now keep would be with churches that had once had German in their official titles. And not a few Evangelical and Reformed midwesterners were concerned about the cultural problems of dealing with the New England way and the eastern urban mentality of these churches. For some Congregationalists, these cultural (and certain polity) differences seemed so great that they never went along with the merger.

If the Anglo-Saxon mythology finally was transformed by a church merger after only 350 years, the white exclusivism in ecumenical and denominational patterns also began to break up after a similar period of years. The Protestant denominations of white predominance began to favor integration however timidly in the 1950s.

Still another ecumenical trend was revealed in a movement that might one day be more dramatic than an expanding United Church of Christ. This was the Consultation on Church Union (C.O.C.U.), advocated by Presbyterian Eugene Carson Blake in a sermon in San Francisco in 1960. The United Presbyterian, Methodist, Episcopal, and United Church of Christ pioneers in this consultation might well have sounded like an old gathering of the early national elites. But they were soon joined not only by the Disciples of Christ and the Evangelical United Brethren churches but also by the African Methodist Episcopal church.

The Consultation on Church Union could eventually produce an American denominational cluster of over twenty million members. The inclusion of a large black denomination, with the prospect of the presence of still others, an inclusion that met with absolutely no controversy, was another mark of the end of white imagery in Protestant ecumenism. The Consultation came so late in national history that many in the younger generation of church leaders paid little attention to it—they had come to take both Protestant-Catholic and even "secular ecumenism" (alliance on many causes with nonchurch forces) so much for granted that intra-Protestant ecumenism seemed less than thrilling.

Few black militants would have taken the representation of the African Methodist Episcopal Church in the Consultation as a major sign of racial change or promise. All this was beside the point in the black revolution. But as a symbol, viewed in the light of white Protestant history, it was another sign of the end of the old empire and the greeting of a new kind of experience. What was most remarkable about the C.O.C.U. records was the general absence of recognition that one of its constituents was black— a silence more significant than trumpeting would be, given the centuries of separation that preceded it.

The white Anglo-Saxon Protestant empire was being transformed by majority Protestantism's exposures to and alliances with nonwhite Christians abroad and at home, with blacks in local congregations and national conferences and councils, with Orthodox and Roman Catholics at every level. Still another evidence that Protestants were ready to be experiencing agents in the American nation and not merely the dominant wielder of symbols was the change in Protestant-Jewish relations by midcentury.

Too few Jews had been on the scene in early America to create Protestant anti-Semitic response on any large scale. Yet many of the early charters and constitutions included trinitarian clauses which ruled out Jews from full legal status in communities. In the early nineteenth century, Jews were usually lumped with socialists, atheists, Unitarians, and Mormons as "unevangelical bodies." The great influx of Jews between the 1880s and the First World War created a new situation, and anti-Semitism began to rise in Protestant America. Jews responded by developing numbers of defense organizations or agencies to relate themselves to other American groups. Among these was the Anti-Defamation League of the B'nai B'rith.

As Jews more and more left the ghetto and became exposed to Protestants and other Christians, it became clear that inclusive institutions would have to be established to contribute to interfaith relations. Most prominent among these was the National Conference of Christians and Jews, which worked in hundreds of communities to promote tolerance, good will, brotherhood, and common activities. Studies of Protestantism by sociologists Rodney Stark and Charles Y. Glock in 1966 showed a connection between *Christian Beliefs and Anti-Semitism.* While some of the Glock-Stark assumptions were widely questioned, there seemed to be no doubt that the more conservative Protestant groups still carried over much theological anti-Semitism (the "Christ-killer" charge), while members of more urban and liberal denominations more frequently expressed kinds of anti-Semitism based on personal exposure people in the rural conservative groups lacked.

Bernhard E. Olson's *Faith and Prejudice* in 1963 had studied Protestant Sunday school literature and also proved that the more conservative works carried persistent anti-Semitic references based on theological interpretations.

At the same time, a number of surveys, including an extensive Gallup Poll in 1965, documented a visible decline in Protestant-Jewish prejudices. At the very least, these polls showed that anti-Semitism was no longer fashionable, that it created a sense of bad conscience. The German extermination of Jews had built much sympathy; the suburban move had exposed Jews to Protestants; a proliferation of conferences modified the theological arguments; an era of "dialogue" had been born. Many American Jews felt that American Protestants were too much opposed to the birth of Israel in 1948 and too unenthusiastic about the results of the Six-Day War in 1967, and new tensions developed. But few Protestants were able or willing to see that their political views on the Middle East were in any way to reflect on their understanding of American Judaism or Judaism as a religion, and the failure of the two groups to communicate better with each other threatened the future of dialogue. It did not in any way, however, jeopardize the slowly-gained Protestant understanding that Jews were full partners in the American republic, an equal constitutive element in its institutions.

The acceptance or recognition of Jews was the point at which definitions of Americanism formally moved beyond Protestant-Christian interpretations. Protestants were now more ready to accept the influence of Zen Buddhism and other eastern religions. At the same time, moderate Protestants were making clear that they were open to what some called a "fourth American faith," secular humanism—the quasireligion of the unchurched and "unbelieving."

The Center for the Study of Democratic Institutions stimulated studies of the nature of American pluralism and gave definition and publicity to these studies through a major public conference at New York in 1958. John Cogley's edition of papers from that conference under the title *Religion in America* showed the extent of acceptance of the definitions of pluralism and dialogue. Pluralism meant that no religion was to have a monopoly or a privileged position and none should be a basis for second-class status for others. Dialogue meant that people could have exposure to each other across the lines of differing faiths without attempting to convert in every encounter, without being a threat, and with the hope that new understanding would result. The goal would be a richer coparticipation in "the city of man," the republic, or the human family.

When Will Herberg published *Protestant-Catholic-Jew* in 1955 he chronicled the maturation of the pluralist interpretation of American life. Not only the old evangelicals had resisted such a trend, even though their grandchildren were most persistent in criticizing the de-Protestantizing of American official life and public manners. The turn-of-the-century social gospel leaders also had sought a Protestant interpretation of the Constitution and national institutions and ethos. As late as 1951 the editors of *The Christian Century* could grumble about the pluralist trend and warn about the future with an editorial "Pluralism—A National Menace."

A few years later these editors and their colleagues in Protestant leadership had come to accept the pluralist definition. Herberg's book showed that for decades America had not been simply a Protestant empire, nor did most Americans find it necessary to blend into a melting pot stirred by Protestants. They had instinctively and persistently related themselves to the American scene through three melting pots, through Judaism, Catholicism, or Protestantism—and now some were even finding it possible to do so on secular interpretations.

Catholic Father John Courtney Murray contributed by showing how each group could and did interpret the First Amendment to the Constitution through their own theological tradition. Murray suggested that most Protestants had imposed an interpretation which other full-fledged and rights-possessing Americans could not share. He himself did not find it easy to define life along pluralist lines. Pluralism seemed to be against the will of God, but was written into the cards of history. Some Protestants were learning this slowly and accepting it grudgingly. But the majority had relinquished their imperial vision and welcomed both ecumenical and pluralist experiences in an America which some had come to call post-Protestant.

26 · Everything Can Become Almost Anything Else

The Revival and the Revolution

In her study of a world unsure of authority, Hannah Arendt describes a sense of loss of the world's groundwork, a world which shifts, changes, and transforms itself "with ever-increasing rapidity from one shape into another, as though we were living and struggling with a Protean universe where everything at any moment can become almost anything else." Worldly permanence and reliability were gone, she argued in *Between Past and Future*. She might as well have been speaking of Protestant religious life in America and, indeed, she did include religion in the field of lost authority and sudden change.

In the 1950s American Protestants participated in a general revival of interest in religion. In the 1960s they were part of what was called a revolution in religion. Energies devoted to building up one day were directed to tearing down the next. Devotion to religious institutions in one decade became massive assault on religious institutionalism in the next. People who said "Never!" in one decade became agents of change in the next. Analysts vacillated in their interpretations of American life as being religious, or secular, and religious again. The same culture could produce contradictory signs which were interpreted in a wildly disparate fashion "at any moment."

An understanding of Protestantism after two centuries of national life begins with a recovery of the sense of renewal and revival that marked the decade and more after World War II. While many Protestant energies were going into ecumenical endeavor, interfaith relations, and the attempt to come to terms with pluralism, others were devoted to restoring Protestant institutions. One way to do this was to fill them with people, to house them well, to have them regularly supported, and to seek their good name. After the American religious depression of the 1930s and the preoccupations of World War II, it became clear that by 1950 many Americans were in a settling-down mood. They needed a means of justifying their complacencies, soothing their anxieties, pronouncing benedictions on their way of life,

247

and organizing the reality around them. Millions turned to religion, and Protestantism profited from the return to religion.

All the old tendencies of Protestantism came to the surface again, but by far the best known and in its own way most curious was the celebrity status extended one mass evangelist, Billy Graham. A study of his career suggests some of the directions Protestantism was taking. Not for almost half a century, since the prime of Billy Sunday, had Americans all come to know and recognize one outstanding evangelist. Not for almost a century, since Dwight L. Moody, had they turned for an interpretation of history to a premillennialist. Graham was one, explicitly and overtly, if not with full consistency. His not always sympathetic biographer, William G. McLoughlin, Jr., at the height of the Graham crusades in 1960, gathered some of Graham's premillennial expressions. Premillennialism, it will be recalled, is a pessimistic view of human history. It was well expressed in Moody's statement, "I look upon this world as a wrecked vessel. God has given me a lifeboat and said to me, 'Moody, save all you can.'" Graham spoke in similar terms.

Premillennialism, a view that would have been heretical to colonial and early national period evangelicals, says in effect that the churches cannot do much about the nagging issues of their day. The only substantial change in history will occur with the Second Coming of Christ, after which apocalyptic change a millennium, or thousand-year reign of peace and justice, will come about. Most premillennialists used the signs of their own time to interpret the imminence of the millennium. Graham was no exception, and in his prime Communism and Russia abroad and immorality at home provided the basic metaphors and illustrations.

In McLoughlin's little treasure, Graham is heard as follows: "I sincerely believe, if I can study the Scriptures aright and read current events and keep up with my current reading, that we are living in the latter days. I sincerely believe that the coming of the Lord draweth nigh." Ever after William Miller in 1843, premillennialists had been wary of predicting the day. But in 1950 Graham indulged in the temptation. "I believe the judgment hand of God is about to fall upon you tonight. . . . We may have another year, maybe two years . . . [then] . . . I believe it's all going to be over. . . . I said in Los Angeles one year ago that we had five years. People laughed; some sneered. I'd like to revise that statement and say that we may have two years. Two years and it's all going to be over."

The Middle East, to a biblical literalist, had to be the beginning of the scene. "The Bible teaches us that history began in the Middle East . . . and the Bible teaches us that it will end in the Middle East." Russia was both the great enemy of the Kingdom and the agent of apocalypse. And America was to hold the fort until the Second Coming. Here Graham picked up the mainline evangelical note: "I believe that America is truly the last bulwark of Christian civilization," he said in 1952. In spite of "corruption, crime, and moral decay," which he chronicled in detail, "we were created for a spiritual mission among the nations." But "until this nation humbles itself and prays and . . . receives Christ as Savior, there is no hope for preserving the American way of life." In classic revivalist tones he reminded that if one was converted, "when you make your decision, it is America through you making its decision."

In *World Aflame,* Graham persisted in explicit premillennial talk. One would have expected the American public to have to wrestle with the problem of the mythological context of his Second Coming, with the many mistaken predictions of its timing, the embarrassments to social planners, the pessimism about the political and reformist orders. None of these problems came to the surface. By 1950, mass evangelism was so domesticated and its only well-known advocate so much accepted for his sincere approach and his contribution to spirituality that his incredibly particular and specific Protestant point of view did not offend many.

The only offended people were a few social action oriented Protestant theologians like Reinhold Niebuhr and the editors of *Christianity and Crisis.* The public regularly listed the evangelist among the ten most admired figures in the country. Catholic bishops, after a decade of half-hearted warnings to the faithful about attending his rallies, threw in the towel and often came to Graham's support. Pious Jews found him acceptable, and secular Jews, editors, columnists, celebrity interviewers, "secular figures" on television, producers of comic shows and movie magazines, editors of *The Reader's Digest* and golf magazines, and presidents of both national political parties found him a thoroughly comfortable and congenial symbol of America's Way of Life.

Graham himself, in a world where "everything at any moment can become almost anything else," often contributed to the confusion by making his image acceptable. He could also speak in optimistic terms despite his contradictory speculations that the world was hopeless and "has reached the end of its tether," and that even if all Americans would be converted it would not affect "the solution of [the] concrete problem" of Soviet aggression. Yet, while premillennialists were supposed to wait for Christ's coming to bring peace and racial justice—as Graham said in *World Aflame*—yet, paradoxically, they were to "maintain strong military power for defense at any cost," as Graham said in Washington in 1952. At various times Graham advocated offensive action with military force in both Europe and Asia. These efforts were to be taken on the basis of the optimistic view that helping God along was necessary.

The acceptance of Billy Graham demonstrated how theologically inclusive and ethically disengaged the revival of the 1950s had become. The churches in that decade were not notable for their devotion to the cause of racial justice. The Supreme Court had to take the initiative on that front in 1954 and the Protestant churches were everywhere regarded as latecomers. The issues of world population, hunger, poverty, and disease were minor emphases in a decade of sermons devoted to Billy Graham's *Peace with God,* Rabbi Joshua Loth Liebman's *Peace of Mind,* Bishop Fulton Sheen's *Peace of Soul,* or Graham's fellow Protestant and other best-known symbol of the revival, Norman Vincent Peale's *Power of Positive Thinking.* All advocated a kind of escape from the world, even as they implied that serene souls would help transform it. Graham's pessimism was easily overlooked in his alliance with these optimists. What gave him internal power was that his self-confessed secret may have been important to his fellow neoevangelicals, but was conveniently overlooked by the culture which made him a celebrity.

The postmillennial party which tried to relate to the Kingdom of God by seeking to transform the situations of people in the world, was in recess during the revival. Many intellectuals and sophisticates pursued the private goals which positive thinkers advocated through more complicated existentialism blended with European theology. Theology began to acquire bestselling status. Yet reformers and radicals did not come back into their own during the Eisenhower era, but had to await their turn in the 1960s, when President John F. Kennedy, Pope John XXIII, and Martin Luther King served as a troika for inspiration.

Everywhere the indicators that America was enjoying a return to a generalized religion were recognized. As standards for church membership went down, membership rose and Protestantism benefited from its climb. In 1920, 43 percent of the populace were on the rolls; in 1930, 47 percent; in 1940 this had grown only to 49 percent, but in 1950, 57 percent were members, and by 1956 this had grown to 62 percent. Eventually the crest was reached at 63 percent or 64 percent, and almost 50 percent of the American people claimed to have attended church in any given week.

The Gallup polls in the 1950s indicated the degree of interest in morality and religion, and the Ben Gaffin survey for *Catholic Digest* revealed that Protestants in 1952 favored historic doctrines or symbols of faith. One billion dollars was spent annually on church building. Motion pictures made heroes of people like Senate Chaplain Peter Marshall.

This generalized religion adapted the Protestant doctrine of God and marketed the deity as a convenient and benign figure, a "man upstairs." The formulator of the new faith on the highest level was the newly converted Presbyterian, President Dwight Eisenhower, who picked up the old theocratic and imperial language. God supported the American crusade. "America is the mightiest power which God has yet seen fit to put upon his footstool." "America is great because she is good." And in the midst of new material affluence, "Happily our people have always reserved their first allegiance to the kingdom of the spirit." Protestant distinctiveness was disappearing, and Professor Arthur Mann could note that to nationalists

"American Catholicism, American Protestantism, and American Judaism appear like parallel shoots on a common stock."

Now it was the liberal Protestants who had occasion to grumble as they saw the neoevangelicals being swallowed up in a new theology of identification with the world as it was. Reinhold Niebuhr wrote in 1955: "Our religiosity seems to have as little to do with the Christian faith as the religiosity of the Athenians. The 'unknown God' . . . in America seems to be faith itself."

The revival was self-defeating, and produced a surfeit. People tried *Positive Thinking* and still Russia would not go away. The Second Coming did not occur, although the Graham rallies came to be racially integrated. Suddenly after 1957 or 1958, and certainly by 1960, a dramatic cultural shift had occurred.

People were reacting to organization men and suburbia and peace of mind. The Russians had lofted Sputnik and the Space Age placed a new premium on mass higher education. Words like "third world" and "Sputnik" and "cybernetics" came into common currency. The movement for racial integration was sweeping the churches, and the American conscience began to be awakened. In southeast Asia a war in Vietnam was increasingly involving American material, technical aid, and was eventually to see a commitment of American soldiers. Latin America verged on revolution, and Cuba went Communist. A different religious impulse and a different religious interpretation became necessary. What resulted was sometimes described as a revolution in religion.

A symbol for the shift: in the 1950s metropolitan newspaper editors enlarged the religion page in Saturday newspapers. They gave more space to announcements of sermons and parish fashion shows, cornerstone-layings and smorgasbords. In the 1960s, they reduced these pages and placed religion back on the front page. Protestantism shared in this relocation of religion. The old explanations no longer seemed to explain, and the old forms no longer seemed to sustain. Young people often lost curiosity about denominations, parishes, Sunday schools, foreign missions, and even the ecumenical movement. They were obsessed with themes of race and peace, university life, "soul," and spiritual values.

As so often was the case, the change was made under transformed theological symbolism, and professional theologians took up their task this time with vigor. At the base of their interpretation was an updated version of postmillennial thought. Few used the biblical symbol of the millennium, but many returned to the talk about the Kingdom of God. In the most successful and style-setting book to come out of Protestantism, Professor Harvey Cox spoke of *The Secular City,* the modern metropolis or technopolis as the workshop of God, the milieu for his church and his avant-garde people.

The new writings of Cox, England's Bishop John Robinson (whose *Honest to God* was also an American bestseller) and a number of other new theologians breathed a spirit of optimism. The Second Vatican Council under Pope John was an endorsement of church unity strivings, and Protestants would never again be so lonely in their attempts to build the Kingdom. Through a score of books with the word "secular" in the title, a number of theologians spoke again of the potential in the world around them. They embraced the empirical method, celebrated the pragmatic style, and urged people not to be too concerned with otherworldliness or metaphysics. The new model Protestant was to be a cool, problem-solving, social activist who celebrated life in the world and was not too concerned about sanctuaries or the "noise of solemn assemblies."

The secular theology seemed to be producing a new style of theologian. No longer given to private and technical vocabularies, the theologian picked up current cultural terms and issues and was briefly rewarded with bestseller status. No longer isolated in ivory tower seminaries or aloof from the day's concerns, the theologian was invited to join the "jet set," to appear in popular magazines and on television. No longer seen as the custodian of the Christian antique shop, the person who was chartered to check up on other people's heresies, the new style theologian, was expected to be in the vanguard, the innovator, the radical reinterpreter. When it was pointed out that such a person stood in a utopian, optimistic, and progressivistic tradition, this did not ordinarily disturb the Protestant thinker. It was not even an insult to him or her to be labeled as an adherent of the social gospel, although an older sibling would probably have shied away from such a label. The severe existentialism of the neoorthodox generation was to be set aside by its heirs.

Just as suddenly as the new progressivism appeared, it was threatened by cultural change and subjected to corrections and revisions from within. At the turning point, in late 1965 and early 1966, a number of Protestant thinkers tried to work out a complete transformation of the most cherished symbols and spoke of "the death of God." It was widely surmised that they had probably diagnosed the issues properly. People today were regarding metaphysics the way they regarded alchemy. They found it difficult to see how God made a difference in human affairs. Sensitive people were reacting to the cheap usage of the term "God" in the years of the religious revival. The theater of the absurd was portraying a universe in which the old questions about the doctrine of God did not even come up. Yet Jesus was a figure who could impart meaning and freedom to life, so one could become a "Christian atheist."

While the diagnosis may have been correct, the name given not the disease but the cure—the celebration of "the death of God"—was rejected. The theological community found the metaphor largely unsatisfying. But more devastating was a change in the culture itself. In 1965, after Protestant participation in prointegration marches at Washington, D.C., and Selma, Alabama, and after some civil rights legislation, the community of Watts in Los Angeles burned in a riot. The dream of racial integration, having been widely accepted but hardly acted upon, was repudiated by articulate young blacks. The Black Power movement swept the churches. As black militants became increasingly assertive in the churches, many Protestant thinkers who had once advocated integration of races now followed the mood and urged separation, so long as blacks wanted it—often claiming that that was what God had in mind all along.

The peace movement was often frustrated after President Lyndon B. Johnson committed land troops to Vietnam, and the war there was seen to be morally and militarily pointless and plotless. After 1965 Protestant leadership was in the front rank of opposition to the war and to the military draft, several years before the majority of the American people indicated their distaste for the war to inquiring pollsters. And many Protestants who began resisting the war on nonviolent bases now turned to the support of violence in the racial revolution and in the "third world"—and sometimes against universities or "the military-industrial complex" at home. Once again, everything could turn into something else very suddenly.

What was consistent in the mainline Protestant leadership's response to the issues after the religious revival was this: they would not retreat into self-serving institutionalism. They were committed to seeing the churches, with what power remained among them, as agents of change in the world. The conservatives who resisted the mainline regularly accused them of having chosen to meddle in politics. The World Council of Churches held a study conference at Geneva, Switzerland, in the summer of 1966 and subsequently at Detroit, in a localized version. Reaction to these conferences, filled as they were with representatives and advocates of "third world revolution," included anger and backlash. The result was a growing gulf between the pulpit and the pew.

"Between pulpit and pew." That was the conventional way of pointing to the tension, although it would be more accurate to say that a certain kind of clergy-lay coalition teamed up against another kind of clergy-lay team. Once again, the century-old developing schism in Protestantism's parties was being widened. To the radicals, conservatism was not as neutral as it claimed to be. To claim to be neutral meant that one's votes were being counted on the side of the status quo: in support of the Vietnamese War, slum housing, school segregation despite laws to the contrary, and of American support of rightist regimes in Latin America. To the conservatives, radicals were compromising the Gospel by tying it to questionable public causes and losing the confidence of people by their frequent changes.

What was occurring was still another variation on the ever-changing attempt of American Protestants to come to terms with their environment.

The church's early adjustments to modernity's charter, an innovation which conservatives made appear ancient, was being torn up. That charter had decreed that the churches would be favored so long as they endorsed the approved American way of life and stayed with private affairs. Public Protestantism wanted to return to a pattern of many more centuries' standing, in which the people of God concerned themselves with all the areas of life, no matter what the risk. This attempt placed its leadership in a situation of unpopularity with "the powers that be" and in tension with much of their own clienteles.

To the observer of Protestant history it must often have seemed as if one half of Protestantism had more in common with certain "outsiders" than it did with the other half of Protestantism. The neoevangelicals were closer to secular Social Darwinists on almost all their attitudes to the world than they were to the social gospel leaders, who seemed to be closer to the socialists. The evangelical critics of the social involvement of the church in the 1960s often seemed to be closer to the American Medical Association, the National Association of Manufacturers, and sometimes to the White Citizens' Councils than they were to other Protestants like ecumenist Eugene Carson Blake or Harvey Cox. In many senses the schism was that deep.

Yet Protestantism somehow cohered. Through all the travails of change, the trend was toward more interdenominational unity, not less; there were few substantial schisms. The schisms in denominations were few and late. Few new seminaries were started to fight the vast majority of existing ones, almost all of whom were committed to change. Conservative journals like *Christianity Today* could be started to give a voice to neoevangelicalism, but these efforts of conservatives did not seem to pull people away from moderate denominations. In each denomination "concerned laity" rose to support a tie between Christianity and latter-day laissez-faire stances. They did challenge that leadership which was more moderate on such issues.

The Protestant community, then, remained strong even when most of its members could no longer speak in imperial terms. Born in a secular age (in the time of the "Enlightenment"), Protestant America seemed to have resources for living again with secularity. Born suspicious of religious institutions, Protestants somehow seemed to weather the worst of anti-institutionalism. Despite revolutionary changes in institutions, there were few immediate drastic declines as a result of backlash or weariness, and membership, attendance, building, giving, and the seeking of churchly vocations seemed to be relatively stable in the 1960s, although, as we shall see, scholars were soon forced to speculate on the consequences of the changes that occurred in that decade.

Whatever would happen in the future, scholars immediately foresaw that at least two factors would be present for some time to come. They are a Protestant deposit in the culture and a two-party approach to that deposit.

In his study *Thought and Change,* British philosopher Ernest Gellner compared western Judaic-Christian societies to Marxism in Russian society. He pictured that the religion or philosophy with which a society interprets itself at a time of fundamental change will tend to remain as a constituent element for some time to come. Since industrialization has been the most inclusive event of modern times, accompanied as it was by political revolution, the societies who experienced political-industrial revolution will revert repeatedly and even constantly to the set of ideas that helped carry them "over the hump of transition."

The world changes, however. America cannot crawl back into the thought world of the Enlightenment or of the Protestantism that fused with it to help produce the national ethos. Instead, it is constantly reshaping the images and ideas of that historic moment of fusion. In Gellner's picture, Jewish-Christian religious phenomena are part of our landscape just as glacial moraine is a semipermanent part of the landscape where a glacier has been. The Protestant deposit may not be the working, living faith of later Americans. Citizens may devote and, indeed, they have devoted themselves to variations on this faith, including belief in nationalism, the self-made man, the work ethic, success, or sex—or a combination of all of these. But they found it difficult to do so without some reference to the original symbols. In the American case, these included words derived from Protestantism, Puritanism, and evangelicalism.

In a complex society, certain people are recognized as the translators or transformers of symbols. In American religion, the presidents of the United States, poets and prophets, evangelists and theologians, preachers and pamphleteers have played that role from time to time. It was their task to assure the nation that the moves it was making were in line with the original covenants, covenants which made the old social contracts possible. At the same time, they served as jeremiahs or judges whenever it seemed that the people moved too far beyond the confines of the covenant. They called people back.

After 200 years, America seemed in some respects to have moved irretrievably beyond the thought world of its earlier Protestantism, and in many ways it had. From time to time restless and gifted sectors of the population—including the young, blacks, intellectuals, rebels, and poets—try to go elsewhere for their spiritual interpretation of life. Most notably, such ventures in the 1960s led people to the world of eastern religions, to the *I Ching* and yoga and Zen. Just as rapidly these ventures could be deserted in a faddist world where "everything at any moment can become almost anything else." But however creative these moves, they seemed to demand greater heroism and energy than any one was prepared to invest or a greater societal upheaval than could then be foreseen to expect eastern modes to replace western Protestant impulses. In Gellner's terms, the translated and transformed set of symbols, often robbed of their original meanings, provided a kind of "civil" or "folk" religion which canceled out the messages of the particular faiths. So it has been with generalized Protestantism in America.

Resort to the old covenants in American Protestantism gradually came to be in the hands of two clusters of interpreters. Both groups could with some reason claim elements of the old covenant, for the original charters were themselves ambiguous. Jonathan Edwards stood at the head of the postmillennial tradition: "The latter-day glory, is probably to begin in America." The millennium was attainable here; in the *History of the Work of Redemption* he saw that the thousand years of good would come *before* the Judgment. Dwight L. Moody picked up the loose strands of premillennial theory and reversed the process. The Edwardseans, with countless variations, have been the more optimistic transformers of society, without neglecting the individual. The Moodyites have been the more pessimistic, concentrating on rescuing the individual and then turning him loose, if he will, to help save other persons in the society.

The transformers have usually been out of step with the powers that be, defining themselves as innovators, inconveniencers, agents of change. Their rhetoric made them sound more happy with the world as being God's workshop, his secular city, the scene of his kingdom. But their programs were upsetting to people who had put the world together a certain way. The rescuers have usually been adopted by representatives of the approved world, supported by manufacturers and fêted by presidents. Their language made them sound more discontented with the world as being beyond God's power—until he ushers in a new age with Christ's Second Coming. They may have seemed strident about the signs of the times and angry about the vices of individuals. But their postponements of reform were comforting to people who would stay in control short of a millennium, in which many of them only half believed.

So long as the American republic contains people who will be responsive to both sets of symbols, it is probable that there will be two kinds of Protestantism. Neither has been successful at displacing the other, and perhaps neither ever shall be. Both of them have too much tradition going for them. In each generation, both have been blessed with ingenious and dedicated people who could translate their symbols one more time.

These two kinds of Protestantism were to struggle with each other during a power shift that few foresaw when the "postsixties" generation began to take shape. That struggle and shift provided much of the drama for years to come.

27 · Can You Go Home Again?

Power Shifts and Protestant Prospects

On December 16, 1971, Yale historian Sydney E. Ahlstrom dotted the last *i* and crossed the last *t* on a most ambitious and successful book, *A Religious History of the American People.* As Ahlstrom traced larger history he found a thread in that Puritan Protestant legacy which took later form in the empire we have been observing. His last chapter on "The Turbulent Sixties" saw Ahlstrom losing the thread or, better, seeing America lose not only the thread but also much of the fabric.

His chapter on turbulence recounted the succession of tests and revolutions that were coming to the old, mainstream, male-dominated, white Protestant domain. Some of these resulted simply from the recognition that so many other peoples were also there: "Catholic, Orthodox, Lutheran, Jewish, infidel, red, yellow, and black," peoples held varying views of American meaning and destiny. Pluralism, in short, was running wild. No one could hold their old privileged place and set the terms for everyone.

A second test, Ahlstrom thought, came from within as well as from around the mainstream. A new kind of radical thought marked both theology and social concerns. The secular and "death of God" theologies, while few people expressed them, indicated how hard it was to retain the old ways for all. The staid ecumenical organizations were being rocked. New morality and new styles of life challenged old Puritan ways. "Religious antitraditionalism" was the main feature in all this. People doubted whether inherited institutions or meanings might still speak to the culture. Ahlstrom asked, "Why should a moral and intellectual revolution that was centuries in the making have been precipitated in the 1960s? . . . Why . . . did so many diverse processes drop their bomb load on the sixties?" He observed that "as the decade of the sixties yielded to the 1970s, dissensus was more visible than consensus."

After he had traversed almost five centuries of Protestant-centered religious history, Ahlstrom quoted Frank Kermode: "It is one of the great charms of books that they have to end." Ahlstrom's own charm had to be expressed "in a rather somber mood," he wrote, "for we have been considering a time of calamities." Attenuated "was the Puritan's firm conviction that America had a divine commission in the world. The nation's organized connections with the sources of its idealism and hope were withered." At the very least, the Puritan epoch was ending. The last thing Ahlstrom, to say nothing of the lesser historians and social analysts in his trail, would have predicted at the end of the 1960s was an imminent and impassioned revisiting of Puritan, Protestant, and mythic American pasts.

Readings of the signs of the times such as his were almost universal. Almost all of them were shortsighted. None of these foresaw that in less than a generation virtually all candidates for the United States presidency would be calling themselves "born again" or using other terms from the old-time religion. If their claims were not in the style of old and new evangelicalisms—as were those of Presidents Richard Nixon, Gerald Ford, Jimmy Carter, and Ronald Reagan—almost all candidates found it necessary or advisable to invoke moral visions from a more social kind of Protestantism with which they had grown up: one thinks of George McGovern, Walter Mondale, and unsuccessful contenders like Gary Hart or the black leader who in the 1984 presidential primaries fused personal piety and social involvement in the black tradition, Jesse Jackson.

The prophecies of chaos and uncertainty also did not take into account the ways in which, after the Vietnam War and the Watergate scandal, Americans would return to conservative forms of civil religion. A succession of presidents before and after the bicentennial in 1976 waved the flag that Ahlstrom and others had last seen desecrated in radical protest movements. By the time of Ronald Reagan's presidency in the 1980s, there were sounds from the White House of the old language of American righteousness over against its enemies, notably the Soviet "evil empire." The call for "traditional values" was widespread as, in reaction to turbulence and pluralism, many Americans invoked images of the simpler days: the little white church and the little red schoolhouse; prayers in the public school classroom; military victories of the kind now effected once again against Cuban troops on the island of Grenada in 1983; the claims that God was on the American side and that its people were especially virtuous. Such expressions of a revived imperial civil religion led to the legitimate question: was the Protestant empire, now enlarged to include some congenial non-Protestants, to be available for citizens again? If all that represented "home," in the terms of novelist Thomas Wolfe who wrote *You Can't Go Home Again,* was it possible that America was trying to "go home again"?

Such a route home, wherever that was, could not be easy to find or to follow. In pluralist America there were now confusing directions and signals, a bewildering set of paths, and any number of dead ends. Yet it is valid here to make an attempt to follow some of these paths, not in order to be able to predict a future but to make sense of the American past and present.

One sign that Americans could not simply go home again in the religious sphere was made evident when the black churches, which had been excluded in the years of the Protestant empire, were seen to be among the most vital of the surviving Protestant church clusters. No personality dominated these churches spiritually as had Martin Luther King, Jr., before 1968. King's Southern Christian Leadership Conference came upon hard times. Black religious causes did not always prosper. The radicalism of black theology, which employed the language of the oppressed against the dominant, was visible to the larger public chiefly through the efforts of a few thinkers like James M. Cone, Vincent Harding, and Preston Williams. While such scholars may have given authentic expression to black discontents, more evident to the public was the contentment of blacks with churches where "the old-time religion" was so vital. There was political power in the churches, to be sure. It was effectively wielded within the black orbit and often in the Democratic Party, most notably by a number of mayors and presidential candidate Jackson. They all made use of church energies. Yet theirs were now essentially mainstream expressions, through leadership of political parties in cities by representatives of people who were more eager to have their fair share in the existing American covenant than to tear up the old charters and replace these with radically new ones. They seemed close to some of the terms of the Protestant ethic and showed an at-homeness in America. Yet these black churches, because they were black and because they had not shared in the dominant ideology for two centuries, complicated life for those who would simply "go home again" and turn their backs on pluralism.

A second factor that worked for continuing change in a time when many wanted to repeal change was the rising sense of participation by women in mainstream and often evangelical Protestantism. In the latter camp there were not always clearcut justifications for feminism. Yet there were calls for biblically based women's rights, such as Letha Scanzoni's and Nancy Hardesty's 1975 book, *All We're Meant to Be*. Evangelists supported feminist caucuses, movements, and journals like *Daughters of Sarah*. Even where a conservative theology prevailed, which taught that women should be submissive to dominant males "as unto the Lord," a generation of articulate and gifted women who opposed feminism acquired power as authors, lecturers, and innovators. They presented strong role models to a new generation of women who would not always be content with the theology of submission.

It was in the churches of the mainstream, however, that the most significant changes occurred. Most of the plot of this book deals with churches whose majorities were women but whose major figures—circuit riders and theologians, social activists and bishops—were men. Women had been excluded from places of power. In recent decades, however, women were inspired to revisit biblical and historical sources to interpret their plight in their previously limited spheres. From these sources they found inspiration to move more aggressively toward fulfillment.

One facet of the change was the movement to ordain women. In the mainline seminaries, the numbers of women enrolled sometimes turned to be near majorities. By the late 1970s well over seventy Protestant denominations ordained women; in 1976 at Minneapolis the most bitter battle over ordination was fought in the Episcopal church, where traditionalists brought most resistance. Feminist biblical scholars in all churches linked with liturgical students in efforts to produce translations of the Bible and orders of worship which minimized, if they did not purge, male "sexist" language.

Such stirrings did not lead to complete or simple victories. More women, it turned out, were being ordained than could be placed in parishes. They complained that they often were assigned offices of secondary status, even by congregations where women were in the majority. Yet numbers of them did come to be heads of denominations, and they were highly visible agents in church conventions and task forces. Even arguments over their status showed how far churches had moved from the old male-dominance that characterized the years of empire.

If the black movements and Protestant feminism were signs of vitality and change in the mainstream, it must be said that for the most part the generation after the 1960s saw this mainstream, increasingly called the mainline, go into recession. In 1972 Dean Kelley of the National Council of Churches wrote an analytic and prescriptive work called *Why Conservative Churches Are Growing.* Kelley might as well have named this noteworthy and trend-setting book *Why Mainline Churches Are Declining.* The United Methodist Church lost two or three million members in two decades, while Episcopal, United Church of Christ, and Presbyterian churches, the colonial "old line," also experienced losses. The merging Lutheran groups at best held their own, while northern Baptists and Disciples of Christ also were anything but on the move. These denominations did not keep pace with their own earlier expansion rates or with national population growth.

Why? One could say a bit cynically that they were not sufficiently angry with anyone; they did not appeal to those who use religion for "over against" reasons—to be over against Satan or Antichrist, secular humanist or outsider, heretic or pagan. These mainstream churches had become friendly to Catholics, appreciative of Jewish faith and of world religions, at home in a secular culture. They favored low, figurative walls and weak boundaries. Thus they did not provide people with clear identities. Many of them lost the impulse to invite other people, to evangelize them. They suffered internal division and were therefore distracted from cherished causes. Many thought they suffered a bit because some members lost interest after their leaders participated in civil rights and peace movements, although this turned out to be an unsatisfying explanation. These churches were victims of demographic trends, being largely northern while the Sunbelt grew. They belonged to social classes where families were usually smaller.

This is not to say that these churches were not vital. The hospitality to the women's movement and the full seminaries suggest otherwise. If national staffs were cut to meet changes in financing, local congregations remained centers of loyalty. If mainline churches shunned celebrities and encouraged few people to move into the national spotlight as Martin Luther King, Jr., Episcopal Bishop James Pike, and theologian Harvey Cox had done in the 1960s, people in thousands of local congregations welcomed strong leadership on the part of their own pastors, teachers, and other church members. If there was now less social action in the form of public demonstrations and passage of social justice resolutions, there were compensatory local expressions. Local churches developed hospices and worked for better distribution of health care. Many welcomed "boat people," refugees from Southeast Asia, and took steps to improve care of the aged. They provided sanctuaries for Central American dissidents and participated in debates over nuclear armament. Most of all, spiritually, they tended to "go home again."

This going home meant a selective retrieval of elements of their traditions. They seemed henceforth less progressive ecumenically. They did not by any means turn antiecumenical, but they wanted uniting movements to allow for more expression of their own churches' diversities. There were widespread recoveries of meditative and devotional traditions. Churches in the 1970s used the language of the "spiritual pilgrimage" and "the journey." They gave more of a hearing than before to major figures of the past, for instance on the millenium anniversaries of Martin Luther (1983) and Huldreich Zwingli (1984), or also in 1984, the two-hundredth year of organized Methodism in America. They were not becoming traditionalist and nostalgic, but they showed less desire than before to repudiate their traditions, to live in the "now," to work for utopia.

One might compare their revised status to that of the Greeks, who had to yield space when the energetic and efficient Romans came to dominate. The Greeks thought of themselves as having the longer traditions, the more profound cultural achievements, and better ways of life. The Greeks lost energies to shape a new empire, however, and left the task to the aggressive, improvising, and, in their eyes, more superficial Romans. In America the old mainstream kept its congregations as strong as possible but did not try to build their symbolic walls thick again. They looked on at the bustling evangelists sometimes appreciatively, sometimes a bit enviously, often in bewilderment.

And who were these evangelicals? They went by many code names. Dean Kelley had called them "conservatives," but not all conservative churches grew and not all of the growers were truly conservative. Some were quite radical, ready to innovate. The group included evangelicals, fundamentalists, and pentecostalists, in often uneasy transdenominational alliances. The forces symbolized by Billy Graham in the 1950s, forces that seemed to be losing morale when Ahlstrom wrote his last sentences, came back to power. Now they were often more militant and "righteous" than Graham had been in his prime. He was now an elder who often seemed wary of the aggressive politicking of his successors.

These conservatives, if we should call them that, united in their desire to go home again to the America they thought they remembered. This was an America that rejected "secular humanism." For this claim, they had to minimize the heresies of the founders, whom the conservatives claimed for their cause, their cause being that America had been shaped by the Bible, and they wanted it to have a privileged place in national life. Thus Southern Baptists, heirs of people who had long been suspicious of government-sponsored or endorsed prayer, in national conventions in the mid-1980s, began to pass resolutions approving constitutional amendments that would support prayer in public schools. These parties were not always anti-Catholic, especially since they shared antiabortion views with Catholic leadership, after the Supreme Court in 1973 gave legal legitimacy to abortions at certain stages of pregnancy. Nor were they often anti-Jewish, especially since many of them had a vision of Jesus' Second Coming which was to be anticipated by a restored nation of Israel. But they were still militantly Protestant in their picture of righteousness.

What resulted was a sort of testing of the classic "two-party" situation described in these chapters. The realignment that could result would disrupt a century-old pattern; that would not be the first time Protestants revised their implicit charters in respect to society. Thus the best known of the New Christian Right leaders, evangelist Jerry Falwell, who used a television ministry in alliance with secular right-wing politicians to become a national figure in the 1980 and 1984 elections, boasted that he did a complete reversal of positions, and many followed him. In 1965 he was denouncing all involvements in politics by clergy. They were, he thought, compromising the Gospel, distracting people from soul-winning for Jesus, meddling where they did not belong. Less than twenty years later Falwell was openly declaring that he had been wrong in 1965. Now it was sinful for God's leaders in churches *not* to be involved. They had to support "traditional values" or they would lose America as a training ground for evangelists who would announce the last days.

Not in all respects did this mean that the old "private" Protestantism was turning "public." For one thing, great numbers of evangelicals, fundamentalists, and pentecostals told pollsters or found other voices to say that the aggressive leaders did not represent them. They might vote in patterns that matched those of the militants, but this was coincidental. They did not take signals from the New Christian Right. They still believed that the church should concentrate on soul-winning and care. Only 17 percent of citizens polled during the 1984 election welcomed clerical endorsement of candidates and what these endorsements represented. Many conservatives were in the huge majority that still wanted to keep a distance between religious leadership and politics. There were also articulate evangelicals in radical movements that produced magazines like *Sojourners* and *The Other Side*. They were most loud in rejecting the new alliances that they saw "between throne and altar."

This religious leadership was no longer private; it had clearly become political. Whether the new word for their location was properly "public" was another question. The public theology of the mainstream Protestants was in that part of the Christian tradition which saw God active also among people who did not acknowledge God as the source of this activity. Although secular-minded people, humanists, Jews even when not in the act of supporting Israel, people who did not invoke the Bible or the Judeo-Christian tradition might not be "saved," they *were* serving the purposes of God in civil society. The tendency of the New Christian Right was of a different sort. It repudiated the humanists and those of secular mind, rejected religious liberalism, and connected God with rather focused partisan views and specific candidates. Without using the term, they had a theocratic impulse and they wanted to give privilege to the Christian tradition in politics.

The civil religious expression and the new politics in the name of the "old-time religion" were not, of course, the only expressions of the impulse to "go home again." Through the whole generation there was a flowering of movements that made an appeal to the revivalist tradition. Their publishing and television empires grew. The successors of Billy Graham became the new religious celebrities. It became fashionable for television and cinema stars, beauty queens and professional athletes, successful people of commerce and politicians, to express publicly their faith and delight in the old-time religion. They feared modern secularists and immoralists and liberals who were charged with compromising or subverting. These flowerings took many forms. By 1971 observers were noticing that while the Age of Aquarius was ending, the hippies were dispersing, collegians were going straight, and the "cults" had begun to peak, there was a "Jesus Movement" among the trend-setting West Coast and southern youth. In 1972 a "Youth Expo" in Dallas attracted 80,000 young people. Rock music, which had earlier been seen as the beat of the devil, began to be linked with Jesus-words. While the extravagances of this primitive Jesus Movement soon lessened, youth movements in the revivalist-minded churches still prospered.

Pentecostalism, long despised as hillbilly, holy-rolling or redneck, changed styles. Leader David Wilkerson said that it "moved uptown." This exuberant form of piety, which centered in an expression of the Holy Spirit, especially glossolalia, or "speaking in tongues" that were not intelligible, found a new home in some churches within the Episcopalian, Lutheran, and other denominations. The great growth, however, came in Assemblies of God and formally Pentecostal churches, which gained significantly. Not always did the revivalist tradition's respectability pay off in church membership. Large percentages of the American people told the Gallup Poll organization that they had been "born again," but they were never to be found on church rolls. The percentage of Protestants attending church stayed about the same through all the recoveries.

Instead, being born again had become culturally fashionable. The old claim that such a conversion meant turning a back on the world was seldom heard, since the new revivalists often displayed expensive lifestyles on even more expensive television networks. This "electronic church" set out to convert, gather funds, entertain, and build morale. It was often more successful at all of these than were the churches. The bestselling books that came from evangelical and fundamentalist presses were not often works of theology or calls for sacrifice. They offered successful salespersonship techniques, schemes for time management and efficiency, advice for newly approved sexual techniques (inside the marital bond), and advice about cosmetics, bodily care, charm, or being *The Total Woman,* as best-selling author Marabel Morgan advised readers to be.

More serious leaders began to ask what had happened to the symbol of the suffering Jesus on the cross? What had come of conservative theology? A series of meetings—such as the Congress on Evangelism in 1969, "Key 73" in 1973, and the Lausanne Convention that took Americans to Switzerland in 1974—kept theologians like Baptist Carl Henry busy trying to give substance to the evangelical movement. Meanwhile the Chicago Declaration on Social Concerns in 1973, followed by a number of less celebrated conferences, gathered evangelicals with social justice interests who offered another voice as they scorned the New Christian Right's identification of God's way with American political conservatism.

It was clear that the whole spectrum of Protestant evangelicalisms was crowding the mainline and in some cases moving into a new center in Protestant life. When the Sunbelt grew twice as fast as the northern states and as its styles of old-time and new-time religion were projected by television, publishing, and politics, it came to be more familiar to many Protestants than the respectable but aging Episcopal, Presbyterian, or Methodist churches in their own towns. Some of the Sunbelt churches that had been turning more moderate, most notably the Southern Baptist Convention, later elected a series of successful urban pastors who worked to appoint leaders who would resist moderation in defense of biblical inerrancy and the imperial vision for America. Conservative forces such as the Good News movement made their more moderate case in the United Methodist church. Traditionalists took over the Lutheran Church–Missouri Synod. Intransigents emigrated in 1973, 260 congregations strong, from the Presbyterian church in the United States. A few left the Episcopal church when it ordained women and revised the cherished prayer book. Ecumenical organizations like the National Council of Churches and the Church of Christ Uniting lost some favor as conservatives attacked them.

What was going on? It was easy to see these movements as the use of modern devices to react against modernity itself. Everywhere in the world the trend was away from cosmopolitan and ecumenical thinking, away from supranational and universalizing thought, from images of "global village" and "spaceship earth." In their place the tribe prospered, if by tribe we mean the connection of race-ethnicity-religion-culture. What was going on in Iran in the late 1970s and elsewhere in the Islamic world, and what was motivating many African movements or religiously based conflict in the Asian subcontinent and Northern Ireland, was now occurring in milder forms in the United States.

The forces of modernity needed interpretation. People were confused by pluralism. They felt powerless in the face of homogenized ideologies. They wanted a religion that gave them a sense of authority: the Qur'an or the Bible says, and that settles it. There was to be no ambiguity. They wanted religion to give them an identity. They needed to know to whom to belong and who to trust and fear. They wanted religion to give them vital experiences. They did not want to be told only that once people felt the presence of God. They felt they deserved such expressions now. The movements that reached for "old-time religion" symbols and techniques and gave them modern dress were effective instruments against unwelcome features of modernity. Yet these movements allowed believers to select very worldly features of modern life that they had once been taught to reject.

Some scholars could not believe that pluralist America would move into a future where this tribal and traditional style would remain strong permanently. William G. McLoughlin, Jr., then the most notable historian of revivals and awakenings, tried to make sense of things in 1978 by seeing this renewed emphasis on the tradition as a necessary stage in cultural revitalization. Borrowing theories from anthropologist A. F. C. Wallace, he looked back on the 1960s as the time of "the period of individual stress," when people lost bearings. Later came the second stage, "the period of cultural distortion." People see that their problems are connected with institutional life, in this case schools, churches, courts, media.

After this stage, in this case during the 1970s and 1980s, there comes a third style: "There almost always arises a nativist or traditionalist movement within the culture." Those with rigid personalities or with much at stake in the older order then argue about the dangers to their ways. "First they call for a return to the 'old-time religion,' 'the ways of our fathers,' and 'respect for the flag','' and the like. Then they find scapegoats, outsiders. They look back to a golden time when the system worked for them. Wallace and McLoughlin also envisioned later stages which would offer new world views. They would appeal to the more flexible, often younger experimenters. Eventually these would help transform the culture. McLoughlin pictured the emergence in the 1990s of a political leadership that could combine gentler versions of the older evangelical tradition and an expansive civil religion.

Ahlstrom had said good-bye prematurely to the old ways and to the Puritan epoch. When they came back with a vengeance, McLoughlin saw it all as a stage or a phase. Both scholars may have known much to give credibility to their views, but one learns from them not to hazard too much of a prediction. At the very least it has become clear that the old symbols do not disappear easily.

All things being equal, short of a violent revolution, if American pluralism survives at all, it is more likely that the new Protestant aggressives will become a very large, very important subculture, sometimes in and sometimes out of favor with political leadership. From time to time their symbols will speak with special power and at other times they will seem to be part of a mere "faction," in James Madison's term, to be met then by counteraction by other factions and forces.

Black, mainline, and evangelical Protestantisms alike reveal the enduring power of symbols and inherited styles of life. One envisions their total disappearance at great hazard, just as only with shortsightedness is one likely to believe that they represent a true "going home again." "Home," whatever and wherever it was, offered sights, sounds, smells, styles, and substance that pilgrims in later, now bewildering, times could draw upon to assist them in their ceaseless search for meaning in life, for objects of loyalty, for something to which to belong. The righteous empire has made available some of these elements for millions. Ancestors, would they come home again from the past to look around, would not likely feel at home. Still, they at least would recognize many old elements in the new settings of late twentiety-century America. Surprisingly, they would also play a part in the indefinite American future.

NOTES

Access to numerous quotations from otherwise obscure primary materials was gained through a number of "secondary sources." I acknowledge my debt to the authors in whose works I found them. Many of their books, cited here, could serve "for further reading."

I. To amplify the introductory essay see the book on which it draws, Martin E. Marty, *Protestantism* (New York: Holt, Rinehart and Winston, 1972) because of its 100-page bibliographical essay. For the materials in subsequent chapters, see Robert F. Berkhofer, Jr., *Salvation and the Savage* (Lexington: University of Kentucky, 1965); Thomas F. Gossett, *Race: The History of an Idea in America* (Dallas: Southern Methodist University, 1963); William T. Hagan, *American Indians* (Chicago: University of Chicago, 1961); John R. Bodo, *The Protestant Clergy and Public Issues, 1812-1848* (Princeton: Princeton University Press, 1954)—used also in Sections II and IV; Ruth Miller Elson, *Guardians of Tradition* (Lincoln: University of Nebraska, 1964); Winthrop Jordan, *White Over Black* (Chapel Hill: University of North Carolina, 1968); Nicholas Halasz, *The Rattling Chains* (New York: David McKay, 1966); Charles S. Sydnor, *Slavery in Mississippi* (Baton Rouge: Louisiana State University, paperback edition, 1966); Richard C. Wade, *Slavery in the Cities* (New York: Oxford, 1964).

II. Loren P. Beth, *The American Theory of Church and State* (Gainesville: University of Florida, 1958); Ernest Lee Tuveson, *Redeemer Nation* (Chicago: University of Chicago, 1968); Charles I. Foster, *An Errand of Mercy* (Chapel Hill: University of North Carolina, 1960); James W. Silver, *Confederate Morale and Church Propaganda* (Tuscaloosa: The Confederate Publishing Company, 1957).

III. Walter Brownlow Posey, *Frontier Mission* (Lexington: University of Kentucky, 1966); William G. McLoughlin, Jr., *Modern Revivalism* (New York: Ronald, 1959)—also used in Section VII; Perry Miller, *The Life of the Mind in America* (New York: Harcourt, Brace and World, 1965); Charles C. Cole, *The Social Ideas of the Northern Evangelists* (New York: Columbia University Press, 1954)—used also in Section IV; Timothy L. Smith, *Revivalism and Social Reform* (New York: Abingdon, 1957; Ann Douglas, *The Feminization of American Culture* (New York: Knopf, 1977); R. Pierce Beaver, *All Loves Excelling* (Grand Rapids: Eerdmans, 1968); Nancy A. Hardesty, *Women Called to Witness* (Nashville, Abingdon, 1984); Aileen S. Kraditor, *The Ideas of the Woman Suffrage Movement, 1890-1930* (New York: Columbia University Press, 1965).

IV. Marvin Fisher, *Workshops in the Wilderness* (New York: Oxford, 1967); R. W. B. Lewis, *The American Adam* (Chicago: University of Chicago, 1955); Ray Allen Billington, *The Protestant Crusade 1800-1860* (New York: Macmillan, 1938).

V. Rufus B. Spain, *At Ease in Zion* (Nashville: Vanderbilt University, 1961); Forrest G. Wood, *Black Scare* (Berkeley: University of California, 1968); David M. Reimers, *White Protestantism and the Negro* (New York: Oxford, 1965); Sidney Fine, *Laissez-Faire and the General-Welfare State* (Ann Arbor: University of Michigan, 1956); Robert Green McCloskey, *American Conservatism in the Age of Enterprise 1865-1910* (Cambridge: Harvard University Press, 1951); Winthrop S. Hudson, *The Great Tradition of the American Churches* (New York: Harper and Brothers, 1953)—used also in Section VI; Aaron Ignatius Abell, *The Urban Impact on American Protestantism 1865-1900* (Cambridge: Harvard University Press, 1943); F. Dean Lueking, *Mission in the Making* (St. Louis: Concordia, 1964); Arthur W. Calhoun, *A Social History of the American Family*, Vol. III (New York: Barnes and Noble, 1960; first published in 1919).

VI. Jean Miller's unpublished doctoral dissertation at the University of Chicago provided both quotations and plot for the first chapter in this section. Lloyd J. Averill, *American Theology in the Liberal Tradition* (Philadelphia: Westminster, 1967); H. Shelton Smith, *Changing Conceptions of Original Sin* (New York: Scribner's 1955); Aileen S. Kraditor, *The Ideas of the Woman Suffrage Movement* (New York: Columbia University Press, 1965); Charles Howard Hopkins, *The Rise of the Social Gospel in American Protestantism* (New Haven: Yale University Press, 1940); James H. Timberlake, *Prohibition and the Progressive Movement 1900-1920* (Cambridge: Harvard University Press, 1963).

VII. Kenneth K. Bailey, *Southern White Protestantism in the Twentieth Century* (New York: Harper and Row, 1964); George Brown Tindall, *The Emergence of the New South 1913-1945* (Baton Rouge: Louisiana State University, 1967); Robert T. Handy, "The American Religious Depression, 1925-1935" in *Church History* (March 1960); Louis Gasper, *The Fundamentalist Movement* (The Hague: Mouton and Company, 1963); William G. McLoughlin, Jr., *Billy Graham: Revivalist in a Secular Age* (New York: Ronald, 1960); Dean M. Kelley, *Why Conservative Churches Are Growing* (New York: Harper and Row, 1972); Sydney E. Ahlstrom, *A Religious History of the American People* (New Haven: Yale University Press, 1972); William G. McLoughlin, Jr., *Revivals, Awakenings, and Reform* (Chicago: University of Chicago, 1978).

OTHER BOOKS BY
MARTIN E. MARTY

The New Shape of American Religion
A Short History of Christianity
The Improper Opinion
The Infidel
Baptism
The Hidden Discipline
Second Chance for American Protestants
Church Unity and Church Mission
Varieties of Unbelief
The Search for a Usable Future
The Modern Schism
Protestantism
You Are Promise
The Fire We Can Light
The Pro and Con Book of Religious America
A Nation of Behavers
Religion, Awakening and Revolution
The Lord's Supper
Friendship
By Way of Response
Health and Medicine in the Lutheran Tradition
The Public Church
A Cry of Absence
The Word
Being Good and Doing Good
Christianity in the New World
Christian Churches in the United States
Pilgrims in Their Own Land

INDEX

Aaron, Daniel, 120
Abbott, Lyman, Reverend, 159
  The Evolution of Christianity, 183
    progress and, 194
Abington School District v. *Schempp,*
    241
Abolitionism, 94, 123–124
  Grimkés and, 99
Adam, 78
Adams, John, 30, 110
Adams, Oscar Fay, 170
Addams, Jane, 199, 200, 201
Advancing South, The, 218
Adventists, 212
Advocate of Moral Reform, 92
Africa, slaves colonizing, 37, 94
African Methodist Episcopal Church,
    36, 146, 244
African Methodist Episcopal Zion
    Church, 33, 146
Agnosticism, 1930s and, 230
Agrarian model, city versus, 158–159
Ahlstrom, Sydney E., 262, 266
  *A Religious History of the American
    People,* 257–258
Albigenses, 8
Alcohol. *See* Prohibition
Alexander, Archibald, 79
All Loves Excelling, 98
All We're Meant to Be, 259
Allen, Ethan, 117
Allen, Richard, 33
Amana, 128
America Comes of Age, 207

American Anti-Slavery Society, 94
American Bible Society, 52
American Board of Commissioners for
    Foreign Missions, 16–17
American Colonization Society, 37
American Enlightenment. *See*
    Enlightenment
American Female Moral Reform
    Society, 90
American Home Missionary Society, 86
American Missionary Association, 141
American Protective Association, 160
American Revolution, 26, 28
American Sunday School Union, 75
American Tract Society, 56, 89, 91
American Transcendentalists, The, 120
Anabaptists, 11, 12
Anarchism, 198
Andover Seminary, 193
Anglican Church, 4
  in colonies, 12, 26
  Prohibition and, 209
  in the South, 69
Anglo-Saxons, 21–29
  Baptists and, 27–28
  Catholicism and, 28–29
  in colonies, 21–29
  Congregationalists and, 26–27
  dominance of, 22–24
  Episcopalians and, 26
  Lutherans and, 28
  missions and, 238
  North versus South and, 24–25, 219
  Presbyterians and, 26, 27

Anglo-Saxons (*cont.*)
  Providence and, 22
  Quakers and, 28
  Reformed Church and, 28
Anthony, Susan B., 105, 201
Anti-Catholicism, 131–132, 134, 208
Anti-Defamation League, of the B'nai
    B'rith, 244
Anti-Saloon League, 105, 210, 211
Anti-Semitism, 129, 162
  in 1920s, 225
  in 1950s and 1960s, 244–245
Anticlericalism, 47
Antimissionaries, 56
Apocalypse de Chiokoyhikoy, Chef des
    Iroquois, 20
Appeal in Four Articles, 36–37
Appeal to Life, The, 193
Architecture, Gothic Revival in, 172–
    173
Arendt, Hannah *(Between Past and
    Future),* 247
Arminianism, 54, 80–81
Arminius, Jacob, 80–81
Asbury, Francis, Bishop, 33, 64
Assemblies of God, 264
Association for the Relief of
        Respectable Aged Indigent
        Females, 90
Atlanta College, 141
Aurora, 128
Awful Disclosures of Maria Monk, 134

Bacon, Leonard, 22, 23, 27
Baird, Robert, 71, 79, 83, 91, 112, 150
Baker, Ray Stannard, 200
Baptist Church, 7, 27–28
  to America, 12
  growth of, 218
  in mid-1850s, 90
  modernism and, 214
  in new nation, 26
  in 1970s, 260
  progress and, 191
  Reconstruction and, 142, 150
  in revivalists, 61, 62
  sectional divisions after
        Reconstruction, 140
  slavery and, 32, 33, 124
  in South. *See* Southern Baptists
West and, 175

Baptist-Disciples of Christ, 62
Barbarism, the First Danger, 51, 133
Barnes, Albert, 82, 93, 133
Barth, Karl *(The Word of God and the
    Word of Man),* 232
Bear Rib, Chief, 14
Beaver, R. Pierce *(All Loves Excelling),*
    98
Beecher, Catherine, 100
Beecher, Edward, 51, 53, 88
Beecher, Henry Ward, 147, 149–150,
    151, 190
  on equality, 152
  on infidelity, 171
  poverty and, 227
  social gospel and, 158
Beecher, Lyman, 82, 100, 108, 127, 151
  Catholicism and, 160
  city and, 111
  denominations and, 90
  on evangelicalism, 54–55, 79
  on foreign missions, 56
  on ministers, 86
  Plea for the West, 48, 133, 175
  radicalism and, 93
  reform and, 88, 91–92
Behrends, A. J. F., Reverend, 152
Belcher, Joseph, 150
Bellamy, Edward
  Looking Backward: 2000–1887, 199
  social gospel and, 202
Bellamy, Joseph, 81
Benton, Thomas Hart, Senator, 15
Between Past and Future, 247
Bible
  blacks and, 37–38, 64
  as central, 5
  fundamentalism and, 212
  rich and, 150
  slavery and, 64, 142
  Southern adherence to, 64–65
  United States seal taken from, 30
  women and, 99, 104, 105–106,
    259
  see also New Testament; Old
    Testament
Bigelow, Jacob *(Elements of
    Technology),* 110
Bill for Establishing Religious
    Freedom, 46
Birth control, Protestant church and,
    173

Bishop Hill, 128
Bishops
 Anglicanism and, 10
 Protestantism and, 5
Black Hawk War, 15
Black Power movement, 253
Blacks
 Bible and, 37–38
 churches of, 145–146
 colleges for, 141
 in colonies, 41
 Consultation on Church Union and,
  244
 evangelicals and, 126–127
 excluded from theological
  interpretation, 79
 free northern churches for, 33–34
 freed, 138
 1960s and, 253
 1930s and, 233–234
 1920s and, 225–226
 power in churches of, 259
 as Presbyterians, 141
 progress and, 191
 Protestantism and, 32–34
 Reconstruction and, 142–146
 reform and, 198
 removal to Liberia, 37, 94
 revivalist-rural religion of, 63
 sexual fears towards, 15
 social gospel and, 203
 see also Slavery
Blake, Eugene Carson, 243
Blavatsky, Helene, Madam, 106
Book of Mormon, The, 14
Book of Wealth, The, 114
Booth, Catherine Mumford, 103
Booth, William, 164, 165
Born again, 264
Boudinot, Elias *(A Star in the West; or,
 A Humble Attempt to Discover
 the Long Lost Ten Tribes of
 Israel),* 14
Brace, Charles Loring *(The Dangerous
 Classes of New York),* 162
Bradford, William, Governor, 23–24
Brainerd, David, 16
Brewer, Justice, 47
Bridgeman, Howard, 98
British Oxford Movement, 80
Brooks, Phillips, 150, 156, 190
Brotherhood of Locomotive Engineers, 225

Brown, Antoinette, 103
Brown, William Adams ("The Old
 Theology and the New"), 193
Brownlow, Parson, 139
Brownson, Orestes, 120
Brunner, Edmund deS., 219–220
Brunson, Alfred *(Western Pioneer),*
 17–18
Brunt, Henry Van, 172–173
Bryan, William Jennings, 199, 215, 216
Bryce, Lord, 40
Buchanan, James, President, 71
Buddhism, 5
Bushnell, Horace, 52, 65
 Barbarism, the First Danger, 51, 133
 Christian Nurture, 192
 Munger and, 192–193
 poor and, 114
 progress and, 192
 theology of, 84–85
 Westward expansion and, 51
Business, clerical invocation regarding,
 151–154
Buttrick, George, 233
Byrd, William, 15

Calvin, John, 9, 78, 185
Calvinism
 antimission force and, 56
 Arminianism and, 81
 New Divinity and, 82
 Unitarianism and, 81
 Westward expansion and, 54
Camp meeting, in southern revivalism,
 62
Campbell, Alexander, 53, 70, 83, 118
Candler, Warren A., Bishop, 218–219,
 220, 222
Capitalism
 ecumenism and, 241
 Rauschenbusch and, 204
Carnegie, Andrew, 153, 155
Carroll, Charles *(The Negro A Beast),*
 144
Carter, Jimmy, President, 258
Cartwright, Peter, 53, 70–71, 72
Catholic Church, 5, 6, 169–170, 208
 American West and, 52
 in colonies, 28–29, 41
 ecumenism and, 239–240
 France and, 25

Catholic Church (*cont.*)
  Graham and, 249
  immigration and, 131–133, 134, 157,
      159–161, 208, 209
  in Middle Ages, 8–9
  Protestantism separate from, 4–5
  Providence and, 22
  Reconstruction and, 149
  in South, 61
  see also Anti-Catholicism; Popes
Catholic Digest, 250
Catholic Modernism, 188
Celebrity clerics, 149, 150–152, 180–
    181, 190, 193
Center for the Study of Democratic
    Institutions, 245
Century of Dishonor, A, 20
Channing, William Ellery, 81, 117
Chapman, J. Wilbur, 210
Chauncy, Charles, 80
Cherokees, 15–16, 17
Chevalier, Michel, 115
Chicago Declaration on Social
    Concerns, 264
Children's Aid Society, 162
Chosen people, Americans as, 48–50
  see also West
Christian Amendment Movement, 241
Christian Beliefs and Anti-Semitism,
    245
Christian Century, The, 209, 224, 234,
    239
  "How My Mind Has Changed," 232
  "Pluralism–A National Menace," 246
Christian Connexion, 127
Christian Fundamentalist Association,
    214–215
Christian Manifesto, 232
Christian Nurture, 192
Christian Science, 106, 149
Christianity and Crisis, 249
Christianity Today, 254
Church Against the World, The, 228–
    229, 230–231
Church buildings, Gothic Revival for,
    172–173
Church of Christ Uniting, 265
Church of England. *See* Anglican
    Church
Church Extension Society, 175
Church of Jesus Christ of Latter-Day
    Saints. *See* Mormon Church
Church Peace Union, 224

Church and state
  religious freedom and, 39–47
  separation of, 241–242
Churches of Christ, 83–84
Churchgoing, 7, 169–170
  1930s and, 230
Cities, 107–115, 170
  agrarian model versus, 158–159
  blacks to in 1930s, 234
  communitarian freethinkers and, 118
  complacency among social
      Christians in 1920s in, 217,
      222–226
  congregationalism and, 163
  denominations and, 163
  development of, 107–108
  drinking and, 209
  immigration in, 208
  industrialization and, 110–115
  institutional churches in, 165
  Moody and, 163–164
  poor of, 200
  Reconstruction and, 148, 157–166
  reform and, 198
  Salvation Army and, 164–165
  social gospel and, 203
  of South, 220
  spiritual problems of, 159, 162–163
  Sunday school and, 163
  unions and, 112
  Young Men's Christian Association
      and, 164
  see also Immigration; Middle class
Civil War, 58–66
  see also Reconstruction
Clarke, John, 28
Clarke, William Newton, 190, 193, 194,
    195
Class system, of Wesleyan revivalists,
    62
  see also Middle class; Poor; Upper
      class
Clergy
  celebrity, 149, 150–152, 180–181,
      190, 193
  city and, 112–115
  communitarian freethinkers and, 118
  number of, 72
  poor and, 152–154
  Reconstruction and, 149–151
  upper class and, 151–154
  on women as supporters, 97–98
  see also Ministers

Cobb, Sanford H., 40
Cobb, T. R. R., 65
Cogley, John, 245
Colgate College, 193
Colleges
　for blacks, 141
　fundamentalism and, 215
　industry and, 111
　land-grant, 200
　South and, 220–221
　Westward expansion and evangelical
　　values and, 55
Colton, Calvin, 51, 82, 89
Columbian Exposition, 185
Columbus, Christopher, 13
Colvin, D. Leigh, 210
Commission on the Church and Social
　Service, 182
Commission on Evangelism, 182
Common Faith, A, 236
Communism, 224–225
　ecumenism and, 241
　Graham and, 248
　1930s and, 230
Communitarian freethinking groups,
　118–119
*Compendium of the Tenth Census,
　1880,* 157
Competition
　churches and, 73, 113, 114, 115
　expansion and, 196
　fundamentalism, and 212
　missionaries and, 238
　Social Darwinism and, 154
　Sunday school and, 74
　two-party system and, 185
　see also Ecumenism
Complacency
　among social Christians in 1920s,
　　217, 222–226
　in South in 1920s, 217–222
Comstock, Anthony, 173
Concio ad Clerum, 82
Cone, James M., 259
Congregationalists, 70, 80
　Christian alliance, 243
　city and, 163
　in mid 1850s, 90
　in new nation, 26–27
　Reconstruction and, 141, 150
　Separatists, 27
　social gospel and, 202
　West and, 175

Congress on Evangelism, 264
Connecticut, 12, 43
Connecticut Missionary Society, 18
Connecticut Society for the
　Suppression of Vice and the
　Promotion of Good Morals, 90
Connectionalism, of Methodist
　revivalists, 62
Constantine, 39
Constitution
　Christian Amendment to, 241
　Eighteenth Amendment to, 210
　First Amendment to, 46, 246
　Native Americans and, 14
　religion and, 46
Constitution of the Federal Council of
　Churches, 205
Constructive Natural Theology, 193
Consultation on Church Union
　(C.O.C.U.), 243–244
Continental Congress, Native
　Americans and, 20
Conversion, revivalists and, 62
Conwell, Russell, 152
　Acres of Diamonds, 150
Cooper, Thomas, 60
Copernican world view, 188
Cotton gin, 34
Covenant idea, in theology, 78
Cox, Harvey, 261
　The Secular City, 251
Cranmer, Thomas, 11
Cultural superiority, of Protestants and
　westward expansion, 51–52
Cultured despisers, 230
Cumberland Presbyterian Colored
　Church, 146
*Curse; or, the Position in the World's
　History Occupied by the Race of
　Ham, The,* 143
Custodianship, Protestantism and, 5

Dabney, Virginius, 210
Dana, Charles A., 165
Dangerous Classes of New York, The,
　162
Darby, John Nelson, 213
Darbyite witness, 213
Darrow, Clarence, 215, 216, 230
Darwin, Charles, 149
　progress and, 188, 189, 191,
　　192
　Scopes trial and, 215–216

Darwinism
  fundamentalism and, 212
  social, 154–155, 164, 189
Daughters of Sarah, 259
Dawson, John L., 143
De facto establishment of church, 41,
  47
de Tocqueville, Alexis, 87
Declaration of Independence, 46
Declaration of Rights, in Virginia
  Constitution, 46
Deism, 45
  in colonies, 42, 45, 46, 47
  militant, 117–118
  see also Enlightenment
Delaware, religious freedom in colony,
  43
Denominations
  city and, 163
  competition within, 56–57
  1850s and, 90
  evangelicals and, 41
  fundamentalists and, 214
  Gothic Revival architecture for,
    172
  integration in, 243–244
  invention of, 68, 69–71
  middle class and, 170
  Native Americans and, 175
  1950s and, 243–244
  1960s and, 254
  North-South issues dividing, 62–63,
    65
  number of, 3
  pentecostalism and, 264
  reform and, 87
  Sunday school and, 74
  West and, 175
  women and, 102, 106
Dewey, John, 200
  A Common Faith, 236
D'Holbach, 45
Diet of Speyer, 9
Diggers, 11
Disciples of Christ, 53, 61, 70
  modernism and, 214
  in 1970s, 260
  social gospel and, 202
  in South, 61
Disciples of Christ and Church of
    Christ, "Christian Connexion"
    in, 127

Disestablishment, 47
  Anglican church and, 69
  invention of forms and, 68
  societies and, 91
Dispensationalism, 213
Dissent
  in colonies, 40, 41, 42, 43, 44, 45–46
  movements on, 10–11
  see also Protest; Reform
Divine right, rule by, 39
Divorce, Protestant Church and, 173
Dixon, Anzi C., 181, 182, 212
Dorchester, Daniel, 170, 172
Drew Seminary, 231
DuBois, William E. B., 226
Duke University, 221
Dunkers, 11
Dunning, Williams A., 138
Dwight, Timothy, 50–51, 82, 108

Eastern Orthodoxy, 4–5, 5, 6
  ecumenism and, 238–239
  immigration and, 208
Eastern religions, 1960s and, 255–256
Ecumenism, 236–245
  Catholicism and, 239–240
  Consultation on Church Union and,
    243–244
  Eastern Orthodoxy and, 238–239
  enemies of, 240–241
  integration and, 243–244, 245–246
  Jews and, 244–245
  mission-unitive movements and,
    237–238
  1970s and, 261
  1960s and, 252
  pluralism and, 243
  politics and, 241–242
Eddy, Mary Baker, 106
Edman, V. Raymond, 241
Education. *See* Colleges; Parochial
    schools; Sunday school
Edwards, Jonathan, 16, 78, 183
  evangelicalism and westward
    expansion and, 50
  *The History of the Work of
    Redemption,* 77, 256
  1960s and, 256
Edwards, Jonathan, the Younger, 81
Edwards, Joseph, 89
Eighteenth Amendment, 210
Eisenhower, Dwight D., President, 250

Elements of Technology, 110
Eliot, John, 16
Elliott, William, 74
Ely, Ezra Stiles, 91, 204
Ely, Richard 181
Emancipation Proclamation, 138
Emerson, Ralph Waldo, 109, 119, 159
Emmons, Nathanael, 89
Emory University, 221
Empire, 76
  charter for, 39–47
  perfection of. *See* Reform
  two-nations theory for, 58–66
  see also Evangelicalism
England
  dissenting movements in, 11
  Reformation in, 10
  see also Anglican Church
Engel v. *Vitale,* 241
Enlightenment.
  Arminianism and, 81
  congregationalism and, 70
  Congregationalists and, 80
  church and, 49
  protesters against Protestantism
    based on, 116–118
  southern national religion opposing,
    59–60
  theology of, 78
Episcopal Church, 79
  establishment in America, 69
  in 1800s, 26, 90
  High Church, 79–80, 127
  in new nation, 26
  in 1970s, 260–262
  pentecostalism and, 264
  Reconstruction and, 139–140, 141,
    150
  social gospel and, 202
  South and, 61
  West and, 175
  women and, 260, 265
Episcopal High Churchmen, 79–80,
    127
Establishment, religion in colonies as
    the, 40, 43, 44, 45, 46
  de facto establishment, 41, 47
  nonestablishment, 41
  see also Disestablishment
European theology
  1930s and, 231–232
  revival of 1950s and, 250

Tillich and, 236
Evangelical Alliance, 71, 171, 238
Evangelicalism, 9, 69, 183
  achievement of, 55–56
  cities and, 110–112
  Graham and, 248–250
  individualistic Protestantism and,
    179
  middle classes and, 110
  1980s and, 262, 263
  North and South division and, 57
  Prohibition and, 184
  Protestant-style religious groups as
    challenge to, 127–128, *see also*
    Immigration
  protests against, 116–125
  religion and government and, 46
  religious thought of, 76–85
  slaves and, 33
  social gospel and, 202, 203
  two-nations theory for the Protestant
    empire and, 58–66
  ultra-orthodox among, 127
  United Church of Christ and, 243
  Westward expansion and, 48, 49, 50,
    51, 52, 53, 54–55
  see also Forms; Reform; Social
    Christianity
Evarts, Jeremiah, 15–16
Everett, Edward, 24
Evolution
  progress and, 188–189
  Scopes trial and, 215–216
  see also Darwinism
Evolution, 193
Evolution of Christianity, The, 193
Existentialism, 231
*Expansion under New World
    Conditions,* 196
Expansionism
  Native Americans and, 14
  progress and, 196
  see also West

Faith and Prejudice, 245
Fallen Timbers, battle of, 15, 49
Falwell, Jerry, 262
Federal Council of the Church of
    Christ in America, 181–182,
    208, 210, 224, 238
Federal idea, in theology, 78

Federalists, Enlightenment and, 60
Female Moral Reform Society, 92
Feminism. *See* Women
Field, Stephen J., 155
Fifth Monarchy Men, 11
Finley, James B., 56
Finney, Charles Grandison, 82, 92, 102–103, 110, 111, 114
First Amendment, 46, 246
First Great Awakening, 78
First Plenary Council, 132
Fisk College, 141
Fiske, John, 196
Flag, religion and, 46–47
Flint, Timothy, 19
Ford, Gerald, President, 258
Foreign missionaries, 18, 74, 100–102, 174, 175–176
Formal theology, 189–190
Forms, 67–75
    cities and, 109–115
    industrialization and, 110–115
    see also Denominations; Parish; Sunday school
Forty-eighters, 130
Fosdick, Harry Emerson, 213, 217, 232, 233
Foster, George B., 194
Fox sisters, 106
Franklin, Benjamin, 30, 42, 110, 116
Free African Society, 33
Free expression, Protestant church and, 173
Freedom of Faith, The, 193
French Catholics, 11
French Protestants, 25
Friends, in mid-1850s, 90
    see also Quakers
Fundamentalism
    Catholicism and, 239
    Eastern orthodoxy and, 239
    modernism versus, 211–216
    1930s reform movement and, 229, 232
    South and, 221
Fundamentals, The, 212

Gaffon, Ben, 250
Gage, William, Reverend, 98
Gale, George W., 110
Garrison, William Lloyd, 37, 94, 124

Gellner, Ernest *(Thought and Change),* 255–256
General Convention, Episcopalian, 140
George, Henry
    Progress and Poverty, 199
    social gospel and, 202
German theology, 232
Germans
    Anglo-Saxon view of, 25
    as immigrants, 129–131, 157
Gibbons, Cardinal, 160, 161
Gladden, Washington, 179, 181, 182, 185, 186, 202, 204
Glock, Charles Y. *(Christian Beliefs and Anti-Semitism),* 245
Gordon, George A.
    The New Epoch for Faith, 193
    progress and, 194
    Progressive Religious Thought in America, Immortality and the New Theodicy, 193
Gospel of Wealth, The, 155
Gothic Revival, in church architecture, 172–173
Good News movement, 265
Graham, Billy, 248–250, 251, 262
    Peace with God, 250
    World Aflame, 249
Grant, Madison *(The Passing of the Great Race),* 208–209
Great Awakening, 26, 27, 42, 44
    First, 78
    see also Second Great Awakening
Great Depression, 227, 228
Green, William H., 191
Gregg, William, 111
Griesinger, Karl, 114
Grimké, Angelina and Sarah, 99
Growing Super-Church, The, 239
Grund, Francis, 113
Gulick, Sidney L., 209

Hall, Gordon, 18
Ham, racism and, 143–144, 145
Hampden-Sydney students, revivalism and, 61
Hampton College, 141
Handy, Robert, 229–230, 232
Hardesty, Nancy *(All We're Meant to Be),* 259
Harding, Vincent, 259

Harris, George, 190
  Moral Evolution, 193
  progress and, 194
Harrison, J.B., 156
Harrison, William Henry, Governor, 15
Hart, Gary, 258
Hawthorne, Nathaniel, 121, 122
  The Scarlet Letter, 119
Hayes, Rutherford, President, 20
Haymarket Riot, 183, 198
Haystack group, 54
Hebrew scriptures. *See* Old Testament
Hedge, Frederic, 79
Hegel, Georg, 188
Hemingway, Ernest, 230
Henry, Carl, 264
Henry, Patrick, 44, 46
Henry VIII, King, 10
Herberg, Will *(Protestant-Catholic-Jew),* 246
Heretics. *See* Unevangelicals
Herron, George, 185, 186, 204
Herz, Henri, 113
Hicksites, 127
Higginson, Francis, 22
High Church, 79
Higher education, secularization of, 200
  see also Colleges
Hirsch, Maurice de, Baron, 162
History, to Protestants, 4
History of the Work of Redemption, The, 77, 256
Histrionic theology, 82–83
Hitler, Adolf, 235
Hobart, John Henry, Bishop, 69, 79–80, 127
Hobsbawm, Eric J., 153
Hocking, William Ernest, 230
Hodge, Archibald Alexander, 191
Hodge, Charles, 50, 51, 79, 191
Hogan, Bishop, 160
Holiness groups, 212
Holmes, Oliver Wendell, 120–121
Holy Communion, 7
Home Missionary, 49, 51, 52, 123–124
Homestead Act, 175
Honest to God, 252
Hopedale, 128
Hopkins, John, 78
Hopkins, Mark, 76, 85, 193
Hopkins, Samuel, 82

Horton, Walter Marshall *(Realistic Theology),* 232
"How My Mind Has Changed," 232
Huguenots. *See* French Protestants
Hume, David, 45
Hunt, Thomas P., Reverend *(Book of Wealth),* 114

I Ching, 225
Immigration, 129–134
  Catholics, 159–161, 208, 209
  denominations and, 174
  1800s and, 23
  Eastern Orthodox and, 208
  Germans, 129–131, 157
  Irish, 157, 161
  Jews, 129, 159–160, 161–162, 208, 209
  Protestants against, 208–209
  reform and, 198
  1700s and, 23
  urban industry and, 112
Immigration Act of 1924, 209
Imperialism
  missionaries and, 238
  social gospel and, 204
  see also Expansionism
In His Steps: What Would Jesus Do?, 199
Indian Removal Bill, 15
Indians. *See* Native Americans
Individualism
  church supporting, 115
  clergy and, 112
  ecumenism criticizing, 238
  fundamentalism and, 212
  in late nineteenth century, 169
  Rauschenbusch on, 204
Individualistic Christianity, South and, 221
Individualistic Protestantism, 177–178, 179–181, 185, 186
  Prohibition and, 210, 211
  social gospel and, 203
Industrial Workers of the World, 200
Industrialization
  city and, 110–115
  clergy and, 151–154
  invention of forms and, 68
  North/South division and, 63
  Rauschenbusch and, 204–205
  Reconstruction and, 158

Infidels, Westward expansion and, 53
Ingersoll, Robert G., 170–172, 241
Institutional churches, 165
Intemperance, moralists and, 92–93
  see also Prohibition
Interchurch World Movement, 225, 227
Intermarriage, with Native Americans,
  15
International Council of Christian
    Churches, 241
Irish, immigration and, 157, 161
Iroquois, 20
Islam, 5
Isolation, after World War I, 224

Jackson, Andrew, President, 15, 89
Jackson, Helen Hunt *(A Century of
    Dishonor)*, 20
Jackson, Jesse, 258, 259
James, Henry, 122
Jamestown, 26
Jefferson, Thomas, 30, 42, 59, 60, 116
  agrarian realm and, 107
  Bill for Establishing Religious
    Freedom of, 46
  blacks and, 36, 37
  cities and, 111
  *The Life and Morals of Jesus of
    Nazareth,* 45
  religion in Virginia and, 44–46
Jehovah's Witnesses, 71
Jesuits, 89, 133, 134
Jesus Christ, 4, 5, 6
  Arminianism and, 81
  death of, 6
  interpreting command of as
    religious thought of
    evangelicalism. *See*
    Evangelicalism
  Niebuhr versus Morrison on, 235
  progress and, 194–195
  social Christianity and, 184–185
Jesus Movement, 263, 264
Jew-clauses, in state constitutions, 47
Jews, 5
  in colonies, 41
  ecumenism and, 244–245
  Graham and, 249
  immigration and, 129, 159–160, 161–
    162, 208, 209
  Inquisition, 8
  Protestantism distinct from, 4

John XXIII, Pope, 239, 250, 252
Johnson, Lyndon B., President, 253
Johnson-Reed Act, 208
Jones, Absalom, 33
Jones, Hugh, 32
Jones, J., Reverend, 65
Joseph, Chief, 19
Judeo-Christian religion, 4
  in U.S. seal, 46
Judson, Adoniram, 53–54

Kelley, Dean, 262
  *Why Conservative Churches Are
    Growing,* 260
Kelley, Florence, 200
Kennedy, John F., President, 250
Kermode, Frank, 257–258
"Key 73," 264
Kik, C. Marcellus, 240
Kimberly, Hal, 220
King, Martin Luther, Jr., 250, 259, 261
Kingdom of God
  ecumenism and, 243
  1960s and, 251
  social Christianity and, 184–185
  social gospel and, 202, 203, 204, 228
Kingsbury, Cyrus, 18
Kneeland, Abner, 118
Know-Nothing party, 133, 134, 160
Knowles, James D., Reverend, 57
Knox, John, 10
Ku Klux Klan, 142, 160
  anti-Catholicism and, 208
  Judaism and, 129
  in 1920s, 223, 226

Labor
  Catholicism and, 161
  clergy and, 112
  communitarian freethinkers
    supporting, 118
  Reconstruction and, 148
  social realism in 1930s and, 233
  see also Strikes; Unions
Laboring Classes, The, 123
Laissez-faire, 84
  church supporting, 113, 114
  ecumenism and, 238, 241
  fundamentalism and, 212
  social gospel and, 203
Latter-Day Saints. *See* Mormon Church

Lausanne Convention, 264
Lawrence, William, Bishop, 152
Laymen *(Rethinking Missions)*, 230
League of Nations, 224
Leaves of Grass, 119
Lee, Ann, Mother, 106, 129
Lee, Jason, 17
Leland, John, 46
Levellers, 11
Lewis, Edwin, 231
   Christian Manifesto, 232
Lewis, Sinclair, 230
Lexington, Kentucky, 60
Liberal Kentucky, 60
Liberator, 37
Liberia, blacks to, 37, 94
Liebman, Joshua Loth, Rabbi *(Peace of Mind),* 250
Life and Morals of Jesus of Nazareth, The, 45
Life and Work and Faith and Order, international conferences on, 232
Lincoln, Abraham, 65–66, 124, 236
Literature, Transcendentalists and, 119–123
Looking Backward: 2000–1887, 199
Louisiana Purchase, 49
Lowell, James Russell, 89
Lowell, Stanley, 240
Lowrie, Walter *(Our Concern with the Theology of Crisis),* 232
Luther, Martin, 9, 78, 261
Lutheran Church, 4
   to America, 9–10
   in 1850s, 90
   Germans and, 130
   immigrants joining, 174
   in middle colonies, 28
   in 1970s, 260
   pentecostalism and, 264
   premillennialism and, 213
   progress and, 191
   Prohibition and, 209
   social causes and, 215
   social gospel and, 202
   Reconstruction and, 139–140, 141
   theology of, 80
Lutheran Church-Missouri Synod, 265

McCabe, C. C., Chaplain, 175
McCarthy, Joseph, Senator, 242

McCloskey, Robert Green, 155
McCoy, Isaac, 16
McGlothlin, William, Jr., 234
McGovern, George, 258
McGready, James, 61
McLoughlin, William G., Jr., 248, 265, 266
Machen, J. Gresham, 213, 214
Macomber, Eleanor, 101–102
Madison, James, President, 59, 116
   church/state relationship and, 40, 41–42
   orthodox Protestantism and, 42
   religion in Virginia and, 44, 45, 46
Madison, James, Bishop, 61
Magdalen societies, 92
Mandeville, Henry, Reverend, 56
Manifest destiny, 1930s and, 230
   see also Expansionism
Mann, Arthur, 250–251
Marriage
   intermarriage with Native Americans, 15
   legislation on, 173
Marryat, Captain, 90
Marshall, John, Chief Justice, 16
Martineau, Harriet, 63, 73, 97
Marx, Karl, 198
Marxism, 198
   social gospel and, 202
Maryland, religion in colonial, 12
Mason, George, 46
Massachusetts, religion in colonial, 12, 43–44
Massachusetts Bay, as colony, 12
Mather, Cotton, 13, 24, 31
Mathews, Shailer, 184, 194, 195
May, Henry F., 147
Mead, Sidney, 82
Melville, Herman, 48, 121, 122
   Moby Dick, 119
Memorial and Remonstrance, 46
Mencken, Henry Louis, 218, 230
Mennonites, 11
Mercersberg "Puseyites", 127
Metaphysics, 1960s and, 252
Methodist Church, 70, 103
   in 1800s, 90, 170
   growth of, 218
   Holiness groups and, 212
   immigrants joining, 174
   modernism and, 214
   Native Americans and, 175

Methodist Church (*cont.*)
  in new nation, 26
  Northern, 222
  Reconstruction and, 139, 140, 141,
    142, 150
  reunion of, 140
  as revivalists, 61, 62
  slaves and, 33
  Southern, 61, 222
    colleges and, 141, 220–221
    1930s and, 234
  West and, 175
Methodist Discipline of 1784, 73
Methodist Episcopal Church, 123–124
Middle Ages, Catholicism in, 8–9
Middle class
  churchgoing among in late
    nineteenth century, 170
  communitarian freethinkers and, 118
  individualistic Protestantism and,
    186
  Protestantism and, 223–224
  social Christianity and, 183
Middle colonies
  Presbyterians in, 27
  un-English churches in, 28
Middle East, Graham and, 248
Milburn, William H., Reverend, 19
Miller, Francis P. (*The Church Against
    the World*), 228–229
Miller, Perry, 79, 206
  The American Transcendentalists,
    120
Miller, Robert Moats, 225
Miller, William, 106, 212, 248
Millerites, 129
Mills, Benjamin Fay, 185
Mills, Samuel, 54
Mims, Edwin (*The Advancing South*),
    218
Ministers
  Beecher on, 86
  of South, 220
  status of, 72–73
  see also Clergy
Mission
  evangelical concept of, 76
  reform and, 87
Missionaries, 11
  foreign, 18, 74, 100–102, 174, 175–
    176
  Native Americans and, 13, 16–18,
    101, 175

1930s and, 230
slaves and, 31, 32, 34
unitive movement for, 237–238
West and, 50, 53–54
women and, 55, 100–102
Moby Dick, 119
Modernism
  fundamentalism versus, 211–216
  1930s and, 229, 232
  South and, 220
  see also Progress
Möhler, Johann Adam, 188
Mondale, Walter, 258
Moody, Dwight L., 186
  Candler and, 219
  evangelism and, 149, 163, 208
  1960s and, 256
  premillennialism and, 180, 212
  revivalism and, 185
  social wrongs and, 183
"Moral Argument Against Calvinism,
    The," 81
Moral Law of Accumulation, The, 114
Moral Man and Immoral Society, 232
Morality
  church and, 173
  industrialization and, 111
  reform and, 92–93
Moravians, slavery and, 31
Morgan, Marabel (*The Total Woman*),
    264
Mormon Church, 71, 128, 129
  Reconstruction and, 141, 149
  women and, 104
Morrison, Charles Clayton, 209, 239
  Niebuhr versus, 234–236
  The Christian Century, 224
Morse, Jedediah, 14, 15, 18, 19, 24, 25
Morse, Samuel, F. B., 52, 133
Moses, United States seal and, 30
Mott, John R., 227
Muckrakers, 199–200
Munger, Theodore, 189, 192–193, 194
  The Appeal to Life, 193
  The Freedom of Faith, 193
Murch, James De Forest (*The Growing
    Super-Church*), 239
Murray, John Courtney, 246
Murray, W. H. H., 155

National Association of Evangelicals,
    215, 239, 240, 241

National Conference of Christians and Jews, 244–245
National Council of the Churches of Christ, 238, 239, 240, 241, 260, 265
National Council of Congregational Churches, 173–174
National Reform Organization, 241
Native Americans, 13–20
   in colonies, 41
   extermination of, 19
   missionaries to, 13, 16–18, 101, 175
   origins of, 13–14
   removal-reservation plan for, 14–16
   Westward expansion and, 52
Nativism, 160
Nativist Party, 134
Nature and Destiny of Man, The, 231
Negro A Beast, The, 144
Negroes. *See* Blacks
Nevin, John Williamson, 77, 191
New Amsterdam, Reformed in, 9
New Christian Right, 262–263, 264
New Divinity, 81–82
New England
   Arminianism and, 54, 80–81
   Congregationalists in, 26–27, 80
   Presbyterians in, 27
New Epoch for Faith, The, 193
New Hampshire, religion in colony, 43
New Jersey, religious freedom in colony, 43
New School, Presbyterians and, 82, 140
New Testament, 4
   slavery and, 64
   women's role in, 99, 100
   see also Bible
New theology, 192, 207
   opposition to, 208
   progress as, 187–196
   social gospel and, 202
New York, as colony, 12, 43
New York Evangelist, 87, 90
Newell, Harriet Atwood, 101
Newman, John Henry, 188
Newspapers, religion covered in 1950s and 1960s in, 251
Niebuhr, H. Richard, 228, 229, 230, 231
   The Church Against the World, 228–229
Niebuhr, Reinhold, 205, 232
   Graham and, 249
   Moral Man and Immoral Society, 232

Morrison versus, 234–236
The Nature and Destiny of Man, 231
   pacifism and, 234–235
   revival of 1950s and, 251
Nixon, Richard, President, 258
Noble, David W., 84
Nonestablishment of church, in America, 41
Nonevangelicals. *See* Unevangelicals
Norris, J. Frank, 215
North
   blacks to cities of in 1930s, 234
   complacency among social Christians in 1920s in, 217, 222–226
   national religion in South distinct from, 58–66
   South conflicting with after Reconstruction, 138–142
North Carolina, religion in colony, 43
Northern Baptist Seminary, 214
Northern Missionary Society of the State of New York, 17
Northwest Ordinance of 1787, 49
Noyes, John Humphrey, 128
Nudity, Protestant church and, 173

Oberlin College, 102–103
Ohio, religion in, 44
Old School, Presbyterians and, 82, 140
Old Testament, 64
"Old Theology and the New, The," 193
Olds, Marshall, 225
Olson, Bernhard E. *(Faith and Prejudice),* 245
On the Boundary, 236
Oneida, 128
Ordination of women, 102–104, 174, 260, 265
Orientals, immigration of, 209
Orthodox. *See* Eastern Orthodoxy
Other Side, The, 263
Our Concern with the Theology of Crisis, 232
Our Country, 157–158, 174–175
Owen, Robert, 53, 93, 112, 118

Pacific Garden Mission, 165
Pacifism. *See* Peace cause
Paine, Thomas, 117

Paine College, 141
Palmer, Benjamin M., 58
Palmer, Elihu, 117
Palmer, Phoebe, 103
Parish
  cities and, 109–110, 163
  invention of, 68, 71–74
Parker, Daniel, 72
Parker, Theodore, 119
  A Sermon on Merchants, 122–123
Parochial schools, 75
Passing of the Great Race, The, 208–
  209
Pauck, Wilhelm *(The Church Against
  the World),* 228–229, 230–231
Paul
  Rauschenbusch and, 204
  social Christianity and, 185
  women's role and, 99, 105–106
Peace cause
  Niebuhr and, 234–235
  1960s and, 253
  reform support and, 224
Peace with God, 250
Peace of Mind, 250
Peace of Soul, 250
Peale, Norman Vincent *(Power of
  Positive Thinking),* 250, 251
Penitent Females Society, 90
Penn, William, 12, 28
Pennington, J. W. C., 38
Pennsylvania
  as colony, 12, 43
  Quakers in, 28
Pentecostalism, 262, 263, 264
Perfectionist movement, 103
Personal religion, Sunday school and,
  167–168
Philadelphia Society for the
  Encouragement of Faithful
  Domestics, 90
Philosophy, new theology and, 191
Pietism, 49
Pike, James, Bishop, 261
Pius IX, Pope, 132
Plan of Union, evangelicalism and, 55
Plea for the West, A, 48, 133, 175
Plumer, William S., 88, 93
Pluralism, 244–245, 257
  ecumenical moderates and, 243
  in modern times, 258
  1970s and, 265, 266
"Pluralism—A National Menace," 246

Plymouth Brethren, 213
Plymouth colony, 12
Politics, New Christian Right and, 262–
  263
Polk, Leonidas K., Bishop, 64
Poor
  church despising, 112–115
  financial panics and, 197
  institutional churches and, 165
  1930s and, 227–228
  reformed, 93–94
  settlement houses of, 200
  social Christianity and, 183
  Social Darwinism and, 154–155
  Sunday school and, 74
  whites of South and, 219–220
Pope, Liston, 225
Popes, 5, 7, 9
  Henry VIII and, 10
  John XXIII, 239, 250, 252
Populism, 199
Postmillennialism
  individualistic Protestantism and,
    179–180
  after 1919, 223
  revival of 1950s and, 250
  social gospel and, 202
Poteat, William Louis, 221
Poverty. *See* Poor
Power of Positive Thinking, 250, 251
Preachers. *See* Clergy; Ministers
Predestination, New Divinity and, 82
Prejudice. *See* Blacks; Racism
Premillennialism
  fundamentalism and, 212–213
  Graham and, 248–250
Presbyterian Church, 70, 79
  blacks and, 141
  modernism and, 214
  in new nation, 26, 27
  1950s and, 250–251
  1970s and, 260
  Reconstruction and, 140, 141, 150
  in Scotland, 10
  social gospel and, 202
  in South, 61, 141, 222
  West and, 175
  women and, 174
Presbyterian Committee on
  Temperance, 210
Preston, John, 78
Primitivists, as Antimission forces,
  56

Princeton Seminary, 191
  modernism and, 214
  premillennialism and, 213
  Presbyterians at, 79
  social gospel and, 202
Private Protestantism. *See*
    Individualistic Protestantism
Progress, 187–196
  see also New theology
*Progressive Religious Thought in
    America, Immortality and the
    New Theodicy,* 193
Progressivism, 199, 228
  South and, 222–223
  see also Social gospel
Prohibition, 208, 223
  evangelists and, 184
  Protestants united for, 209–211
  South and, 222
  social Christianity and, 184
  women and, 105
  see also Anti-Catholicism
Propeace forces. *See* Peace cause
Property, clergy and, 112, 113
Prosser, Gabriel, 35
Prosser, Thomas, 35
Prostitution, reform of, 92
Protest
  in late nineteenth century, 170–172
  progress and, 195
  see also Reform; Social gospel
Protestant-Catholic-Jew, 246
Protestant ethic, 207, 223–224
Protestant Jesuitism, 89
Protestant Vindicator, The, 134
Protestants and Other Americans
    United for the Separation of
    Church and State, 240
Protesters of Protestantism. *See*
    Evangelicalism
Providence, 22, 187
  see also Progress
Public Protestantism. *See* Social
    Christianity
Puritanism, 11, 12
  latter-day, 88
  1960s and, 258
  West and, 52

Quakers, 7, 11, 12, 28, 43
  Hicksite faction, 127
  ordination of women among, 102
  slavery and, 31

*Quarterly Register of the American
    Education Society,* 90
Qur'an, 5

Racism
  Candler and, 219
  in 1920s, 225–226
  Reconstruction and, 143–146
  see also Anti-Semitism; Blacks;
    Immigration; Ku Klux Klan
Radicals. *See* Reform
Raikes, Robert, 74
Rainsford, W. S., 165
Rappites, 128
Rationalism, church and, 49
Rauschenbusch, Walter, 186
  feminism and, 104
  Kingdom of God and, 184, 185, 232–
    233
  Marx and, 198
  progress and, 188, 193–194, 195
  social gospel and, 181, 183, 201–206,
    228
  Theology for the Social Gospel, 204
  Tillich and, 236
Read, Hollis, 52
Reagan, Ronald, President, 258
Realism. *See* Social realism
Realistic Theology, 232
Reconstruction, 137–148
  problems resulting from
    black/white conflict, 142–146
    North/South conflict, 138–142
Red Jacket, Chief, 20
Reform, 86–95, 197–206
  anarchism, 198
  concerns of, 89
  leaders of, 88–89, 91–92
  Marxism, 198
  moral problems, 92–93
  Muckrakers, 199–200
  in 1930s, 227–236
  poor and, 93–94
  populism, 199
  Progressivism, 199
  Puritans (latter-day), 88
  single tax scheme, 199
  slavery and, 94–95
  social gospel, 197, 201–206
  socialism, 198–199
  societies, 90–91
  utopianism, 199

Reform (*cont.*)
  women and, 94, 98, 99, 201
  see also Complacency
Reformation, in England, 10
Reformed Church
  immigrants joining, 174
  in mid 1850s, 90
  in middle colonies, 28
  theology of, 80
  United Church of Christ and, 243
Reformed faith, 4
Religion in America, 245
Religious freedom
  bases and roots for, 39–47
  in colonies, 39–40
Religious History of the American People, A, 257–258
Religious Situation, The, 232
Report on the Steel Strike of 1919, 225
Republicanism, evangelicals and, 116–118
Rethinking Missions, 230
Revivalism
  cities and, 110, 163–164
  in colonies, 42
  early nineteenth century, 17
  Great Awakening and, 44
  individualistic Protestantism and, 179–180
  in 1950s, 247–251
  in South, 61–63
  theology of. *See* Evangelicalism
  waves of, 126
Revolution, in 1960s, 247, 251–256, 257–258
Rhode Island
  Baptists in, 28
  religious freedom in colony, 43
Rice, Luther, 100
Rich. *See* Upper class
Richardson, Henry Hobson, 173
Riddle, David, Reverend, 78
Riley, William B., 214
Ripley, George, 121
Ritschl, Albrecht, 193, 202, 232
Robinson, John, Bishop (*Honest to God*), 252
Robinson, Solon, 34
Rock music, Jesus-words in, 263–264
Roman Catholic Church. *See* Catholic Church
Roosevelt, Franklin, D., President, 227, 233

Roosevelt, Theodore, President, 19, 145
Ruralism, in southern religion, 63

Sabbath, moralists and, 92
St. Augustine, 39
Saint Bartholomew's Church, 165
St. George's church, 165
Salvation
  revivalism and, 61–62
  women and, 103
Salvation Army, 7, 164–165
Savage, Minot Judson, 195
Savonarola, Girolamo, 9
Saxons. *See* Anglo-Saxons
Scanzoni, Letha (*All We're Meant to Be*), 259
Scarlet Letter, The, 119
Schaff, Philip, 23, 24, 28, 71
Schmucker, Samuel S., 80, 130
Scholastics, 127
Schools, prayer in, 241–242
  see also Education
Science
  industry and, 111–112
  Modernism and, 214, 215
  new theology and, 191, 192
  racism and, 145
  Social Darwinism and, 154–155
Scofield Reference Bible, 213
Scopes trial, 215–216, 221
Scotch-Irish, 25, 27
Scotland, Presbyterianism in, 10
Scudder, Vida, 104
Seabury, Samuel, 69
Second Coming of Christ, 230, 248, 249
Second Great Awakening, 17, 20, 77
  eastern phase of, 82
  reform and, 89
  revivalism and, 61
Second Plenary Council, 161
Second Reader, 114
Second Vatican Council, 239–240, 252
Secular City, The, 251
Secularization, in urban South, 220
Seminaries
  celebrity clerics versus, 190
  fundamentalism and, 215
  1960s and, 254
  social Christianity and, 182–183
  women enrolled in, 260

Seminole Wars, 15
Seneca Falls (New York), feminism
    and, 103, 104
Senecas, 20
Separatists, 11, 12, 27
Sermon on Merchants, A, 122–123
Settlement houses, 165, 200
Seventh-Day Adventism, 106
Sexuality, Protestant Church and, 173
Shakers, 90, 106, 129
Shaw, Anna Howard, Reverend, 106
Sheen, Fulton, Bishop *(Peace of Soul),*
    250
Sheldon, Charles M. *(In His Steps:*
    What Would Jesus Do?), 199
Shelton, Arthur Edwin, 225
Shields, T. T., 214
Siegfried, André, 215, 226, 228
    America Comes of Age, 207
Simons, Menno, 11
Sioux, 15, 16
"Sit-down" strike, 233
Slaton, John M., 234
Slavery, 99, 103
    baptism and, 32
    communitarian freethinkers and, 118
    evangelicals and, 94–95
    literacy and, 34
    missions for, 31, 32, 34
    onset, 31
    paternalistic Protestantism and, 34–
        35
    reform and, 89
    religious justification of, 38, 63–64,
        142
    slave revolts and, 35–37
    see also Abolitionism; Blacks
Small, Sam, Reverend, 211
Smith, Alfred E., 209
Smith, Joseph, 71, 128
Smith, Newman, 193
    Constructive National Theology, 193
    Through Science to Faith, 193
Smith, Samuel Stanhope, 37
Social Christianity, 177–178, 179, 181–
    186
    complacency among, 1920s, 217,
        222–226
    progress and, 189
    Rauschenbusch and, 181, 183, 201–
        206, 228
    setback to, 224
    socialism and, 199

Social Creed of the Methodist
    Churches, 182, 205, 206
Social Darwinism, 154–155, 164, 189
Social gospel, 168, 183, 197, 201–206,
    207, 228
    opposition to, 208
    Prohibition and, 210
    reform and, 95
    see also Progressivism; Social
        Christianity
Social Protestantism, Prohibition and,
    210, 211
Social realism, 231–233
    Niebuhr and, 231–233
    pacifism and, 234–235
    Tillich and, 236
Socialism, 198–199
    Mathews and, 195
    social gospel and, 202
Society for the Propagation of the
    Gospel, 31, 101
Sockman, Ralph, 233
Södergren, Carl J., 214
Sojourners, 263
South, 63
    Anglican Church in, 26, 69
    colleges in, 220–221
    complacency in, 1920s in, 217–222
    fundamentalism and, 215
    national religion distinct from
        North, 58–66
    North conflicting with after
        Reconstruction, 138–142
    poor whites in, 219–220
    religion in 1920s in, 218–222
    revivalism in, 61–63
    see also Slavery; Southern Baptists
South Carolina, religion in colony, 43
Southern Baptist Convention, 221, 222,
    234, 265
Southern Baptist Seminary, 220
Southern Baptists, 141, 221–222
    colleges and, 221
    militant Protestantism of, 262
    in 1960s, 260–262
    in 1930s, 234
    see also Baptists
Southern Christian Leadership
    Conference, 259
Southern Christians, progress and, 191
Southern Methodist University, 221
Spaulding, Henry H., 17
Spelman College, 141

Spencer, Herbert, 188
Spiritualism, 106
Spotted Tail, Chief, 16
Spring, Gardiner, 114
Stalinism, 230
Stanton, Elizabeth Cady, 105, 174, 201
Star in the West: or, A Humble Attempt
    to Discover the Long Lost Ten
    Tribes of Israel, A, 14
Stark, Rodney *(Christian Beliefs and*
    Anti-Semitism), 245
Steltzle, Charles, 230
Stiles, Ezra, 26, 27
Stockton, Betsey, 102
Stone, Lucy, 103
Stowe, Harriet Beecher, 100
Straton, John Roach, 214
Strong, Josiah, 221
    Catholicism and, 160
    Expansion under New World
        Conditions, 196
    Jews and, 162
    Our Country, 157–158, 174–175
    progress and, 196
    social gospel and, 185, 203
    South and, 221
    on two-party system, 177–178, 182
Suffrage, 104–105
Strikes
    Reconstruction and, 148
    reform and, 197–198
    social realism in 1930s and, 233
    support for, 224–225
    see also Labor
Sumner, William Graham, 155
Sunbelt, 264–265
Sunday, Billy, 182, 186, 210, 248
Sunday school
    city and, 163
    1830s and, 230
    as facet of personal religion, 167–
        168
    invention of, 68, 74–75
    women teaching, 100
Sunday School Union, 75
Supernatural rationalism, Arminianism
    and, 81
Supreme Court, prayer in public
        schools and, 241
Survival of the fittest
    city and, 164
    expansion and, 196
    fundamentalism and, 212
    Social Darwinism and, 154–155

Swedenborgianism, 90, 122
Syllabus of Errors, 160
Symbols
    Candler and, 219
    celebrity clerics and, 150–152
    city industrialization needing those
        of continuity, 107–115
    1960s and, 251, 255–256
    transcendental era and, 119
    translators or transformers of, 255–
        256

Tappan, Arthur and Lewis, 93
Tarbox, Increase N. *(The Curse; or,*
    The Position in the World's
    History Occupied by the Race of
    Ham), 143–144
Tax, single tax schemes and, 199
Taylor, Nathaniel William, 82
Television, born again and, 264
Temperance, moralists and, 92–93
    see also Prohibition
Temperance Society, 92
Theologians
    celebrity clerics versus, 190
    of 1960s, 252
Theology
    formal, 189–190
    German, 231–232
    Niebuhr versus Morrison on, 235–
        236
    progress as new, 187–196
    of Rauschenbusch, 204–205
    as religious thought of Evangelicals.
        See Evangelism
    secular, 252
    see also European theology
Theology for the Social Gospel, 204
Theosophy, 106
Thoreau, Henry David, 109, 159
    Walden, 119
    A Week on the Concord and the
        Merrimack, 119
Thornwell, J. H., 64
Thought and Change, 255–256
Through Science to Faith, 193
Tillich, Paul, 231
    On the Boundary, 236
    The Religious Situation, 232
Torrey, Reuben A., 181, 210, 212
Total Woman, The, 264
Toulmin, Harry, 60
Toy, Crawford Howell, 191, 220

Transcendentalists, 79, 109, 119–123, 128
Transformation minded party. *See* Social Christianity
Transylvania University, 60
Trinity, 5, 6
Trinity Church, 173
Trollope, Frances, 88, 98
Truett, George W., 221
Tucker, Dean Josiah, 50
Tucker, William Jewett, 194
Turks, 9
Turner, Frederick Jackson, 148
Turner, Henry M., 146
Turner, Nat, 36
Two-party system, 177–186
  in 1980s, 262–263

Unevangelicals, 79, 108, 127
Union Seminary, 193
Unions, 112
  Catholicism and, 161
  communitarian freethinkers supporting, 118
  Jews and, 162
  social realism in 1930s and, 233
  see also Labor; Strikes
Unitarian Church, 60, 70, 79, 81
  Enlightenment and, 117
  in mid-1850s, 90
  Mills and, 185
  ordination of women among, 102
  transcendentalist movement and, 119
  women and, 94
United Church of Christ, 243
  in 1970s, 260
United Methodist Church, 260
  Good News movement and, 265
United Nations, 241
United States seal, Judeo-Christian tradition in, 46
Unity movement. *See* Ecumenism
Universalists, 127
  in mid-1850s, 90
Universities. *See* Colleges
University of Chicago Divinity School, 214
Unonius, Gustav, 113
Upper class
  church buildings sponsored by, 173
  clergy and, 112–115, 151–154

after Reconstruction, 149
  Social Darwinism and, 154–155
Urban evangelists. *See* Chapman, J. Wilbur; Sunday, Billy; Torrey, Reuben
Urbanism, invention of forms and, 68
  see also Cities
Utah, woman suffrage in, 104
Utopianism, 199

Vanderbilt University, 220
Vatican Council of 1869–1870, 161
Vermont, religion in colony, 43
Vesey, Denmark, 35–36
Vietnam War, 253, 258
Virginia, religion in, 44–46
  Anglicans to, 12
  religious freethinking of demise of established church in, 61
  opposition to, 59–60
Volstead Act, 210, 211, 223
Voltaire, 45
Voluntaryism, in colonies, 40, 42, 44

Wainwright, Jonathan Mayhew, Reverend, 113
Waldensians, 8
Walker, David *(Appeal in Four Articles),* 36–37
Wallace, A. F. C., 265, 266
Walther, Carl F. W., 80
Wanamaker, John, 93
War Between the States. *See* Civil War
War of 1812, Native Americans and, 14
War of Independence, Native Americans and, 14
Ward, Harry F., 182, 206
Ware, Henry, 81
Warfield, Benjamin, 191
Warren, William F., 171
Washington, Booker T., 145
Washington, George, 59
  religion in Virginia and, 44, 45
Washington College, revivalism and, 61
Watergate, 258
Wayland, Francis, 86, 93, 94
  The Moral Law of Accumulation, 114
Wealth. *See* Upper class
Webster, Daniel, 42, 47

*Week on the Concord and the
    Merrimack, A,* 119
Weld, Theodore, 94, 99, 110
Wesley, John, 68, 108, 209
Wesleyans, 54, 62, 68, 82, 83, 152
West
    antimissionaries and, 56
    Arminianism and, 54
    Catholics and, 52
    Christianity in, 4–5
    church extension societies in, 175
    colleges and, 55
    cultural superiority of Protestants
        and, 51–52
    evangelicalism and, 48, 49, 50, 51,
        52, 53, 54–56
    expansion to, 48–57, 133–134, 148
    infidels and, 53
    missionaries and, 50, 53–54
    women's suffrage and, 201
Western Pioneer, 17–18
Westminster Confession, Finney on, 83
Wheaton College, 241
White, Ellen Gould, 129
White, William, 33, 69
Whitman, Marcus, 17
Whitman, Walt, 122
    Leaves of Grass, 119
Whitsitt, W. H., 191
Wieman, Henry Nelson, 236
Wigglesworth, Michael, 13–14
Wilkerson, David, 264
Willett, Herbert C., 227
Williams, Eleazar, 17
Williams, Preston, 259
Williams, Roger, 28, 40
    civil authorities and, 43
    Native Americans and, 16
Williams, William R., 51
Williamson, Hugh, Dr., 38
Willson, Marcius *(Second Reader),* 114
Wilson, Woodrow, President, 224
Wise, Henry A., 134
Wobblies, 200
Wolfe, Thomas *(You Can't Go Home
    Again),* 258
Woman's Bible, 105, 201
Woman's Christian Temperance Union,
    105
Women, 97–106
    Bible criticized by, 105–106

biblical, 105–106
    clergy on, 97–98
    denominations founded by, 106
    foreign missionary activity by, 100–
        102
    ordination of, 102–104, 174, 260, 265
    Prohibition and, 105
    Protestant churches and, 174, 259–
        260
    Reconstruction and, 148–149
    reform and, 94
    suffrage, 104–105, 201
    as Sunday school teachers, 74, 100
    suppression of, 99–100
Word of God and the Word of Man,
    232
World Aflame, 249
World Alliance for International
    Friendship, 224
World Council of Churches, 238, 239,
    240, 241
World and National Councils of
    Churches, 5
World Tomorrow, 234
Wright, Frances (Fanny), 93, 112, 118
Wright, William Kelley, 230
Wyandottes, 17
Wyclif, John, 9

Y.M.C.A. *See* Young Men's Christian
    Association
Yahweh, 5
Yoga, 255
You Can't Go Home Again, 258
Young Men's Christian Association
    (Y.M.C.A.)
    blacks in 1920s and, 226
    city and, 164
    New Orleans branch of, 58
    reform and, 95
    social Christianity and, 182–183
Young Men's Hebrew Association, 162
Youth Expo, 263

Zen, 255
Zoar, 128
Zwingli, Huldreich, 9, 261